Sanctuary

Sanctuary

How an Inner-city Church Spilled onto a Sidewalk

Christa Kuljian

First published by Jacana Media (Pty) Ltd in 2013

10 Orange Street
Sunnyside
Auckland Park 2092
South Africa
+2711 628 3200
www.jacana.co.za

ISBN 978-1-4314-0475-9

Cover design by publicide
Cover image Paul Jeffrey
Set in Sabon 11/16pt
Printed by Ultra Litho (Pty) Ltd Johannesburg
Job no. 001884

See a complete list of Jacana titles at www.jacana.co.za

To my daughters Nadia and Mila

whose maternal great-great-grandmother
left Armenia and Turkey for Syria,
whose great-grandmother left Syria for Cuba, then the US,
and whose mother left the US for South Africa –

whose paternal great-great-grandfather left Madeira,
and others on their paternal side left India,
St Helena, Holland, Kimberley and the Eastern Cape,
to arrive in Johannesburg, the city of migrants,
the city of their birth

Contents

Acknowledgements

OVER THE PAST SEVERAL YEARS, I have learned that although writing is a solitary endeavour, writing a book requires the involvement and support of many people – publishers, editors, colleagues, the people you've interviewed and written about, friends and family.

Without the support of all the people I interviewed and talked to and learned from, this book would have gone nowhere. You are too many to mention individually by name here, but all of you who are listed in the Interviews, References and Notes section, I am grateful for your time and for the help you gave me in trying to understand some aspect of the many, often complex, issues and stories covered in this book. I need to make special mention of Reverend Peter Storey, Reverend Mvume Dandala and Reverend Paul Verryn. The three of you played a particularly important role at Central Methodist Mission and I thank you for the time you spent with me, in interviews and follow up emails, to review your years at Central Methodist. Also, without the support of Cleo Buthelezi, Freedom Chivima, Reason Machengere, Reymond Mapakata, Ambrose Mapiravana, Priscilla Manyere, Wellington Mukwamba and Takudzwanashe Chikoro, I would not have made it through. You helped me again and again to make sense of things.

There were a large number of people, many of whom were residents of Central Methodist, who welcomed me, spoke to me about their lives, encouraged me with this book, or just hung out with me in the foyer. Please know that I greatly valued your support and wish you well in the future. I also appreciate the staff at Central Methodist for putting up with my hanging around the building, the office and the waiting room: Mafika Dlamini, Bafana Radebe, Ella Mjandana, Lungi Xonti, Justice Khanyile, Bongani Kumwenda and Nontle Mlamla. For anyone else not mentioned here who assisted me along the way, I appreciate your support.

Penny Foley helped me to embark on this project. She listened to me patiently for close to two years as I expressed an interest in writing about Central Methodist and then helped me make that first visit to the church. Little did she know that it would mean three more years of meetings and questions and phone calls from me on a regular basis. Thank you for your assistance, your perspective and your knowledge at every turn. Elina Henkela and Reason Beremauro were both writing their PhDs about Central Methodist Mission when I first arrived on the scene and I greatly appreciated their support and guidance as well.

This book would not have been written had it not been for the support of the Ruth First Committee at Wits Journalism. Without the Ruth First Fellowship, I would not have set aside the resources and time to pursue my idea of writing about Central Methodist Mission. It was a great honour to deliver the Ruth First Lecture in August 2010, which further propelled the project forward. Thank you to each member of the committee, including Anton Harber, Shireen Hassim, Liza Key, Jackie Cock, and particularly to my fantastic supervisor and editor, Indra de Lanerolle. Thank you to Naadira Munshi for research assistance in gathering newspaper articles about Central Methodist in preparation for the lecture.

It turns out that Bridget Impey and Maggie Davey of Jacana Media were sitting in the audience the night of my Ruth First Lecture. A few months later, Maggie asked me if I had ever thought about expanding the lecture into a book. My answer was "Yes. Yes. Yes!"

If it wasn't for Khosi Xaba, I would have thrown up my hands long ago. In the early days, when I was reaching for an editor, or a supervisor, or a crutch, she reminded me that I just needed to keep writing! Thank you to Khosi for reading the first version of the manuscript when it didn't even have an ending. She helped me to keep going. I am grateful to Khosi and Erica Emdon and Gerald Kraak from my writing group for telling me that they liked the draft chapters they were seeing and that I should keep writing.

Ivan Vladislavic provided invaluable assistance to me with an early reading of the manuscript, which pointed out important flaws and offered wise guidance so that I could improve the book in countless ways.

Another group of external readers read through the entire manuscript and gave me useful feedback and for this I am enormously grateful: Karen Hurt, Safiya Mangera, Indra de Lanerolle, Penny Plowman, Roger Jardine, Elinor Sisulu and Ishmael Mkhabela. Thank you to Professor Ian Kennedy for your reading of the chapter on Central Hall.

There is another very long list of people – those who are mentioned and quoted in the book – who read certain sections and chapters to help me check facts and make sure I quoted them accurately. Your input and feedback was critical.

ANFASA (the Association of Non-Fiction and Academic Authors of South Africa) awarded me with an author's grant in 2011. Kundayi Masanzu's enthusiasm and support for this book project helped me believe that it was a good idea. Debora Matthews and Elizabeth Marima of the South African History Archive helped me as well, as did Meryl Federl, the librarian at the Legal Resources Centre.

Siven Maslamoney, David Goldblatt, Alon Skuy, Sam Wolson, Lesley Lawson and Paul Jeffrey helped me with photographs. They were all very generous. Special thanks to Ruth Muller who helped me with researching photos and visual material for the book.

Thank you to Russell Clarke of Jacana Media who supported me before there was a manuscript and was always excited by the project. I'm thankful to Bridget Impey, Maggie Davey, Kerrie Barlow and Megan Southey for taking over in the wake of Russell's departure and guiding me through the final production.

This book would not have reached its full potential if I did not have the good fortune to work with Alison Lowry as my editor. As I like to say, Penguin's loss was my gain. The first time I ever saw Alison Lowry in person, by coincidence, was at Central Methodist Church. I think her assignment was meant to be. Thank you Alison for your professionalism, deep engagement and shared passion for the subject of this book. I remember telling Alison stories and she would respond. "You have to put that in!" I also want to thank Alison for her patience as I sent what felt like thousands of emailed corrections and additions over the final weeks.

Thank you to all my friends who remained my friends over the three years that I worked on this project. I missed many invitations and didn't see many of you as often as I would have liked.

Lastly, I am grateful to my family – Bob Kuljian, Jewel Kuljian, Sarah Kuljian, Anne Jardine and the extended Jardine family for supporting me through this process. My husband Roger Jardine was a fan of this project from beginning to end, even if it meant many Friday night refugee meetings and many Saturdays spent writing. Roger and Nadia and Mila, thank you for listening to me talk incessantly about the book. Writing a book has been a dream of mine since I was a child and you helped me achieve my dream.

PART ONE

Prologue

14 May 2008

A CHANCE REMARK BY A police officer – "Zulus are attacking all the foreigners" – overheard by one man, was all it took. By 9pm over a thousand men had assembled on Pritchard Street outside the Central Methodist Church in downtown Johannesburg. It was a cool evening with a breeze. The men wore jackets and jerseys and stamped their feet against the cold. In their hands they grasped their weapons tightly. The weapons were unconventional, hastily gathered. Mostly they consisted of wooden planks that had been forcefully pulled off the pews of the chapel inside the church, and metal bars that had been wrenched from stairway railings. Desperation and fear, and the memory of another terrifying time just a few months before, had prompted these men to act, and they had pulled the church apart in an effort to find some makeshift tools with which to defend themselves. Some held the odd brick in their hands, or the leg of a stool, but they stood ready and waiting, shoulder to shoulder.

They had left the women and children in their sleeping places inside the church and gathered in the street because word had come to them that a crowd of angry men was on its way to attack them, burn down the church, and kill all the foreign nationals inside.

Some of these foreign nationals, standing armed in the street, had left their home countries in extreme circumstances and they came from many different parts of Africa – the Democratic Republic of Congo, Malawi and Burundi, amongst others. But most of the men were from Zimbabwe. Most of them had fled the deteriorating economic and political situation that was the reality there under Robert Mugabe's rule. They didn't want to be in Johannesburg. They didn't want to be living in a church. They would far rather have been at home. But here they were, in South Africa, now facing a new threat, the threat of an angry mob, and they were not going to go down without a fight.

Bishop Paul Verryn, who had led the Central Methodist Church since 1997, was often in the building after midnight, catering to the many men and women who arrived at his door seeking a place to stay. But on this night in May 2008 he was not there. An important Methodist Synod meeting was under way and he had been obliged to attend, so he had not been on hand to see the crowd of armed residents forming outside his church. Someone had thought to call him, however, and warn him there was trouble brewing. Immediately, he left his meeting and got to the corner of Pritchard and Smal streets at about 10pm. It was a clear night. The moon was three-quarters full. As he approached the church there was enough light for him to see a large body of restless, fearful men, talking together in groups, holding implements in their hands that he could not at first identify. What he could tell, though, was that these men were ready to defend themselves, their families and their home.

Holding back for a minute, the Bishop saw someone he knew. "There could be a bloodbath tonight," he said. "I need to get everyone back inside." Then Verryn walked amongst the men, yelling as loudly as he could. "Come inside! I want you all to come inside! I want to speak to you!"

Paul Verryn was acutely aware that for the past three days everyone in the church had been on edge. That week South Africa had been rocked by the worst wave of violence it had experienced since the end of apartheid in 1994. This time the violence had a different name: xenophobia. The violence had begun in Alexandra township, no more than ten kilometres from Central Methodist, and had spread to many other townships and informal settlements. It had also moved right into the city centre and had displaced people from their homes to seek refuge at two local police stations. The aggressors were local South Africans, their targets foreign nationals. The thousands of residents of Central Methodist Church knew that it was just a matter of time before the aggressors came for them.

Word spread on the street that the Bishop was calling for everyone to move inside. Gradually, reluctantly, the men followed him into the building and into the sanctuary, the large main room of worship in the church. Verryn stood in the pulpit and looked out across the restless crowd. He saw their anger. He saw their fear. Then, slowly and calmly, he spoke.

"Do you think that you would have any chance, with your sticks? Do you think that your sticks would defend you against guns? We don't want to start a war. You must bring all of your weapons up to the front and drop them here."

Silence. Verryn waited. No one moved.

Then two men came forward and dropped their metal poles in front of the pulpit. The gathering shifted uneasily and a low murmuring went around the room. Verryn saw their hesitation, but he continued to stand in front of them, waiting, not speaking. Then another man walked forward and dropped his wooden stick. Slowly, a motley pile of weaponry began to form. As each man came forward, the pile grew higher and higher. It took more than 20 minutes for everyone to give up their weapons of defence, but they did. Miraculously, Verryn had defused a volatile situation that night. The battle never happened. The bloodbath was averted. Central Methodist settled back into an uneasy sleep.

One

Friday Night Refugee Meeting

On a chilly April evening in 2010 the entrance to the five-storey Central Methodist Church building in downtown Johannesburg was crowded with people buying supper. Outside the entrance, women sat behind low tables, selling chicken and spinach, *pap* and gravy, sweets, oranges, snacks and coffee. Their stalls were pressed against a palisade fence that ran parallel to the front wall of the church, creating a corridor lit only by streetlights some distance away, a long narrow space that was filled with people jostling past each other in the hustle-bustle atmosphere of a busy street market. I walked slowly along the corridor, easing my way past the stalls, until I reached the front door. The door opened onto a large foyer that itself resembled an indoor food market at a train station. The smell of *vetkoek* and oil, food waste, damp and sweat hung heavily in the air. My destination was the third floor but with two divergent flights of stairs in front of me, I wasn't sure which way to go. Noticing my hesitation, a security guard assigned a young man to escort me.

I had called Bishop Paul Verryn to say that I wanted to learn more about this church, which had offered accommodation to the homeless for several years and which had attracted a great deal of negative attention in the media over that time. The building was viewed by many as only an eyesore and a problem, but for migrants into the city from elsewhere in South Africa and many other countries on the continent, and especially for people from

Zimbabwe, it had become a refuge, a haven and a home. I had told Verryn that I was hoping to write a long article about the church and that I had heard about its Friday night refugee meetings that were held there every week. My request was to attend as an observer and the Bishop had agreed. I was to meet him in his office on the third floor.

The young man and I threaded our way through the scores of people sitting on the set of stairs to the right. We walked past men, women and children standing in groups on the dimly lit first floor. Instead of pushing open a door, my guide stepped casually through its frame where I imagined a central glass panel used to be. I followed gingerly. We entered a stairwell and then climbed in near darkness up several more flights of stairs until we finally arrived at Verryn's office. I was a little out of breath and wondered whether I would find my way out again. As I sat on a sunken couch in the waiting room, a small grey mouse scuttled by. There were several other people waiting as well but, to my slight discomfort, I was led into the office ahead of them.

Verryn's office had the look and feel of a storage room. There were piles of boxes everywhere, a coffee table whose surface was completely obscured by books and papers and, on the floor leaning against the far wall, a large painting of a biblical scene which I thought I recognised as a Rembrandt reproduction. To the left was a desk and on the right a sitting area with a faded grey couch and two matching chairs. Bishop Verryn came forward to shake my hand. "We get a lot of journalists and researchers here," he said. "The Friday night meeting is an opportunity for visitors to introduce themselves to the community. It's important for you to tell them about your plans."

Verryn was in his late fifties, of medium height, with greying hair, glasses and a beard. He looked as if he could be a guitar-playing folksinger from California. He had in fact been suspended three months earlier by the Methodist Church of Southern Africa, but given his presence at his office at 7pm on a Friday night, one wouldn't have guessed.

Verryn's welcoming manner and calm serenity belied another truth about him. It would be fair to say that for those people who were adults during the height of apartheid in South Africa, Paul Verryn was a household name. His past encompassed much about the political struggle against apartheid. His name evoked memories of the trauma and violence of the late 1980s, and especially of the horrific tragedy of Stompie Seipei, a young man to whom Verryn had once offered shelter. Verryn's name would be forever intertwined with the names of Stompie Seipei and Winnie Mandela.

But that was over 20 years before my first meeting with him and Verryn had been through a lot since then. Offering refuge and shelter to people in need continued to be one of his defining qualities, and his arrival at the helm of Central Methodist Church in 1997 ushered in an era of providing not only political refuge, but also physical shelter and accommodation to the homeless and the destitute. From many countries on the continent, including South Africa itself, people would find their way to the church. It was those who were fleeing from political and economic ruin in Zimbabwe, especially, who came and found a place that would take them in.

Paul Verryn's name had flashed again in the newspapers in May 2008 when the "xenophobic" violence had hit South Africa and it was all over the media, which was when Central Methodist caught my own attention for the first time. Like many others, I was astonished to discover that the church had been providing refuge and accommodation for years already and that there were over a thousand people living in the building in 2008. The church and Bishop Verryn had become greatly controversial as a result. All this made me wonder. How had over a thousand people come to live in a church? What role had Bishop Verryn played in their finding accommodation there? What were the circumstances under which each foreign resident had come to Johannesburg, and what were their hopes for the future?

Still it took me two years before I finally got my act together, in April 2010, and I visited the church for the first time. Now that I had finally got here, I had no idea what lay ahead of me in my efforts to find the answers to my questions.

"Okay, let's go," Paul Verryn said after we had shaken hands, and "I'll be back" to the people still waiting patiently to see him.

I had a picture in my mind that we were probably heading to a small conference room elsewhere in the church where I would be required to introduce myself to a handful of people who were involved with Central Methodist and tell them about my writing plans. I was in for a rude awakening. I followed the Bishop down to the first floor where he led me into the main room of worship in the church, which I later learned was known as the sanctuary, and that's where he left me. At a glance I reckoned there were already about 500 people sitting in the pews.

Verryn strode to the front where he sat down at a wooden table on the dais in front of the pulpit. There was a large gold cross on the wall behind him. He was joined by a petite woman wearing a silk shirt and highly polished boots. She held a notebook in her hands, her arms resting on the edge of the table. This, I would soon discover, was Elizabeth Cheza, a resident at the church since 2006. In time I would get to know Elizabeth and understand the difficult circumstances that, as with so many others, had precipitated her journey south from Zimbabwe to South Africa.

Between the main floor and the gallery above, I guessed the room could seat over a thousand people. As I stood uncertainly, I watched several men in threadbare clothing walking in carrying flattened cardboard boxes under their arms, while women and children sat close together towards the front and a group of boisterous toddlers played near the pulpit. I noticed that the green carpet was frayed, that many of the seats in the pews were broken and the lighting was poor. A set of stained glass windows on one wall let in a small amount of light from the street.

I took a seat on the aisle. One person coughed, then another. Then there was a cacophony of coughing. Someone handed me a copy of the minutes from last week's meeting. Minutes? I hadn't expected minutes. Actually, I hadn't expected this at all. It was starting to sink in that this was the refugee meeting itself, the Friday night meeting to which every single one of the thousand current residents was invited and that I would be introducing myself to a crowd, not to a select few. I looked around nervously. The meeting was about to begin.

One at a time, over 20 men and women came forward and gave presentations about various ongoing projects at the church. These included a pre-school, adult education, computer training, sewing, book club, and drama. I was surprised that so much activity was under way among the church's residents and began quickly to realise how little I knew.

Then Paul Verryn motioned me to come forward. I walked up the steps onto the dais and paused. Hundreds of expectant faces gazed back at me. I took a deep breath and introduced myself.

"I would like to spend time at the church to learn from your experiences," I said. "I would like to try to write about all that has happened here over the past few years. I'm not a journalist, so I won't be writing just one news article. I'd like to write something longer." Without a microphone, I had to work hard to project my voice out to the huge group of people listening to me, many of whom, to my relief, were now looking up with interest. "You can tell from my accent," I continued, "that I'm from the States, but I've lived in South Africa for more than twenty years and I've worked with many NGOs." I took another breath. "Now I have started writing stories."

After Verryn closed the meeting with a prayer, I thought we might at least have a short follow-up conversation, but he disappeared out of a side door and I did not see him again. I was, however, pleasantly surprised when several people came over to talk to me. My first refugee meeting had introduced me to a whole new community of people, many of whose extraordinary stories I would learn over the coming months. My long article was going to get a lot longer.

On my second Friday night meeting I went straight to the sanctuary on the first floor. This time I didn't have to introduce myself to the gathering, but I continued to meet new people. Before the meeting started I bumped into Elizabeth Cheza. "Oh, you've come back," she said in an energetic voice. "How is it going?" She told me that in addition to taking the Friday night minutes, she also worked as the secretary at the Albert Street School. This school, now educating some 500 children, had been started by Central Methodist in July 2008 and drew some of its learners and most of its staff from residents and former residents at the church. I also met Freedom Chivima, another Zimbabwean and a plumber by profession. Freedom was a former resident and he boasted a brown belt in karate. He came back to the church every week night to hold karate classes.

This evening sanitation was a key topic. A tall, lanky resident named Ambrose Mapiravana, who was also head of security, stood up, walked to the front of the sanctuary and addressed the audience sternly. "I am not very happy with the rate at which we are destroying our toilets," he announced. "Maybe the blame is on the security for being lenient with you. We need to sustain life in this building."

Verryn clearly agreed with him. "I've spoken more about toilets and plumbing in this church than I have about Jesus," he said. Then, pounding the table with his fist, he said: "I don't understand how people go to the toilet and get angry with the toilet. Who puts oil and *pap* or *sadza* in the sink? I'm not prepared to tolerate this vandalism any more. From now on, we are going to have security in the toilets. You'll close the door and security will listen to what you're doing in there. I got this idea from the Rosebank Mall."

Verryn proceeded to pace slowly back and forth along the platform. "Let me review what Médecins Sans Frontières has told you. In order to prevent cholera, there are five 'Fs' we have to remember. Food. Fluids. Fingers. Faeces. Flies." He stopped and looked at the crowd. "Are you with me?" He waited for nods of approval and then started pacing again. "We must applaud MSF. They have been handling the plumbing in the building since September last year. But now they will no longer be overseeing the toilets so it will be the community that is responsible. Today we did a walkabout with MSF and the drains and the toilet between the third and fourth floors are blocked. We paid a R49 000 water bill yesterday and we didn't get one cent from the City of Joburg."

I was impressed by how many organisations worked with and visited the church on a regular basis. Besides Médecins Sans Frontières, which ran a clinic on the ground floor, there were the Solidarity Peace Trust and the Centre for the Study of Violence and Reconciliation, both of which had a regular place on the agenda, using these meetings as their opportunity to communicate with the residents. Some Friday night meetings included cultural presentations as well – a skit from the drama group, a poetry reading, or a karate demonstration.

But tonight Verryn wasn't finished with the bad news. Someone, a resident of the church, he said, had stolen money from the blind community. He had given an office in the building to The Blind Association, out of which they conducted their business. Consisting predominantly of blind people from Zimbabwe, they had been raising money to hire a bus so that those blind people begging on the street corners of Johannesburg could go back to Zimbabwe if they chose to do so. With difficulty they had raised R24 800 and now the cash had disappeared. "It's disgraceful that anyone from this building did this," Verryn said. "But the blind community is not as blind as you think they are. They are not stupid." He then reported that the thief had been identified and arrested, but that the money was still missing. I wondered who could have done such a callous thing.

As before, the Bishop ended the meeting with a prayer at about 9:30pm and, as before, he left out of the side door and I did not see him again. The next thing I knew, the meeting had morphed into a dance performance on stage, complete with sound system and a flashing disco light.

I exited out of a side door myself and found that I was in a dark passage, having to step around people's belongings and over their heads as they readied themselves for bed. Residents were laying their mats and blankets on the floor outside the sanctuary and very soon there was no place to walk. Those flattened cardboard boxes I had seen so many of the men carrying into the meetings, I realised, served as people's beds. I would also learn that there were designated rooms for women and children and for married couples. The landings and stairs had now become bedrooms, with clothes hanging over the railings, and I saw a church transforming into an informal settlement as I watched.

Over the following months I attended as many meetings as I could, gradually getting to know the routines and the issues and meeting more residents and hearing about their lives. Each meeting would begin with Bishop Verryn reporting on any media coverage the building had received during the past week, as well as sharing a list of visitors who had been to the church. The many different activities that the church and its residents were engaged with were regularly reported on – adult education, the Albert Street School, the crèche in the basement called For the Love of Children, or FLOC, which had been started way back in 1978, computer training, sewing, hotel and catering training, book club, dance and drama, soccer and karate. Each week there were presentations relating to the ongoing projects and the platform was used to discuss any particular issues that might have arisen during the week – commonly, security in the building, job opportunities, and the challenge of the toilets. After each presentation Verryn would ask for questions.

The Friday night refugee meetings had started formally in early 2006 when the number of people living in the church had increased to over 300. Regular meetings were an effort to create some order amidst the growing chaos and to provide greater social cohesion. At that time, the church instituted eight rules for residents. No smoking. No drinking. No fighting. No stealing. No sex in the building unless you were in the married couples' accommodation. Keep yourself and your area clean and attend a service every night at 7pm. Lastly, the church required that all residents be involved in at least one educational activity. Many people were struggling to find jobs during the week, so the Friday night meetings were also a social gathering when they would head down to the foyer to compare notes, talk to one another or buy something to eat.

At each meeting there would be new things for me to absorb. For example, I learned that since the computer classes had started in 2007, 1 035 people had finished the course, passed an exam and received a certificate.

On one Friday night in May, with the 2010 Soccer World Cup in July around the corner and the world's attention becoming more and more focused on South Africa as host nation, security was the hot topic (as was often the case). Ambrose Mapiravana expressed concern about people being arrested in a general drive to "clean up" the city. "Police are back on the street arresting people," he warned. "You should be inside the building early so the police don't find you outside at night." There were plans for an anti-xenophobia soccer match, in the hope that this would promote goodwill in the face of concerns that xenophobic violence could return. Memories of 2008 were still strong among those residents who had been in the church at the time, and even those who had not been there could relate to the stories.

On another Friday evening, after the report from the book club suggested that no one was taking out books, Verryn stood up and spoke about libraries and the importance of a reading culture, registering his disappointment that people weren't reading. "You have a beautiful opportunity," he said. "You must think it's better to blow bubbles than to read. Do you hear me? Blowing bubbles. One of the rules of this building is that you must be involved in at least one educational activity. We are going to enforce this rule. Is that OK?" The crowd clapped and cheered. "Good," said Verryn, and sat down.

A man who was on the staff at Médecins Sans Frontières and who often made announcements on a Friday night was Evans Kuntonda. A former resident, he seemed to be well liked. He still did a lot for the community, from delivering babies in the building to helping create a database of residents. One evening I watched him keeping a careful eye on several toddlers who were playing on the three wide steps up from the pews as he took his turn at the dais. He kept looking over to them with concern, anxious they might fall, as he announced that the clinic would close at 3pm the following Friday because its staff would be attending a workshop relating to xenophobia. "Also," he added, his eyes flickering to the children, "those who have been tested for their CD4 count, please come and collect your results." I was interested to meet Evans and learn about his experiences.

Reason Machengere was from the Solidarity Peace Trust. He was another regular at the church, not as a resident, but someone who worked with the community in many ways. Dressed in a wool blazer and silhouetted against the stained glass windows, tonight he had a few things to say. "On average," he told the audience, "four hundred people are being fed here on Monday, Wednesday and Friday. We have disbursed the monthly foodstuff to Home Based Care and to FLOC." Home Based Care was the facility in the building for the very ill. Referring to his notes, Reason went on. "We are saddened by the events surrounding blind people who are being harassed and tortured by South African Police Service (SAPS) and the City of Johannesburg in their purported attempt to clean up the city. As SPT, we challenge those who are stampeding the poor for the sake of the World Cup." Next he announced a meeting regarding the constitution-making process in Zimbabwe, urging people to attend and to contribute. Lastly, Reason asked people to visit an exhibition that was currently being held at the Albert Street School. "It showcases the lives of refugees and children living at Central Methodist, their journey and their aspirations," he said.

As I allowed Reason's words to sink in, I realised that I was only just beginning to get a sense of all that was happening at Central Methodist and how much I still had to learn. I could feel how I was being drawn more and more deeply into the fabric of this place and the evolution of life at the church. I was setting off on a journey of my own.

For that, I needed a guide.

Bishop Paul Verryn once told me that of his 37 years in the ministry, the last five years at Central Methodist had been the toughest and the most rewarding – tough because of the difficulties of housing so many people, rewarding in his ministering to them. Describing an inner-city church, he said, "You can either put razor wire around the church or you can open the doors."

Verryn maintained an open door policy at Central Methodist, so no one was ever turned away. For several years his office had issued laminated registration cards for residents but this came to an end in late 2008 when the numbers simply became overwhelming. For the most part Verryn didn't have regrets about having used the building for purposes for which it wasn't originally intended, with perhaps one exception. "The church used to have an amazing organ," he told me. "A few years ago, it was pulled apart and sold for scrap. That's like using a Rembrandt painting to wipe the floor." I had seen a few of the remaining organ pipes. They were in two plastic buckets on the floor in his office.

Built in 1965, the church had many modern facilities, including two full apartments and many meeting rooms. Even after a few visits, I still felt disorientated, so Verryn asked Ambrose Mapiravana to give me a tour. A walking tour was important, he advised, not only because it would give me a sense of some of the activities under way at Central Methodist, but also because without a guide it would be hard to navigate the "geography" of the building with its many nooks and crannies.

Ambrose and I started at the top, on the small fifth floor. From there we could access a balcony that overlooked the roof of the sanctuary. I could also see how the church was nestled between the Johannesburg Sun Hotel to the north and the Pitje Chambers building to the east. Walking down the stairs to the fourth floor, I observed exposed plumbing pipes in the corners of the walls of the stairwell, while next to the stairs was an elevator shaft, the elevator itself long since defunct. On the fourth floor there was one full apartment, which included a lounge, a kitchen, two bedrooms and a bathroom. While the apartment had housed church staff in the past, it has been used for Home Based Care since 2002, which provided ill residents of the church with round the clock support, similar to a hospice. Although Ambrose couldn't tell me actual numbers, he said that over the years many people had taken their last breath in these rooms.

There was another large open room on this floor with windows that looked out onto Pritchard Street. "This room used to be where the children slept," said Ambrose, "but now they stay at the Community Centre in Soweto. We use it as a dorm room for the younger guys in their twenties who are working and studying. During the day we use it as a classroom." Filing cabinets and bookcases served as cupboards for clothes and belongings. Mattresses were stacked against the wall. We stuck our heads into a small room at the back to find men and women working at three sewing machines there, piles of fabric on the floor around them. Shirts and pants hung on hangers from nails in the wall.

Ambrose and I chatted as we went. He had trained as a carpenter in Zimbabwe and also worked as a welder before economic hardship in early 2008 had forced him to travel to South Africa to look for work. Although he didn't have any formal security training, he admitted, he had led the security team at Central Methodist since August 2008. The team comprised about 20 men and women who worked shifts and covered different floors, making sure that people obeyed the rules – although they often broke them. Ambrose told me that he had a good working relationship with the station commander at Johannesburg Central Police Station. "He knows me by name," he said.

When we got to the second floor, we passed the gallery of the sanctuary. In the past it had been kept clear, but Ambrose told me that women had started sleeping there at night and that it was also now being used for secondary school classrooms during the day. This had led to some conflict between the older women, who had to get up every morning and clear the space, and the students who claimed that the area wasn't clean enough when they got there for class.

In front of the imposing wooden doors that provided access to the gallery, there was a large, wide passageway or foyer that looked out over Pritchard Street. This high-ceilinged space was where people, mostly men, slept on the floor at night but it was used for other activities during the day, such as dancing lessons.

On either side of the entrance to the gallery there were two small rooms. I later learned they used to be called "cry rooms", where mothers would take their babies when they were crying during services. They had windows looking over the sanctuary, and speakers, too, so that the mothers could see what was going on and follow the service. But the purpose of these rooms had changed years ago.

Now one "cry room" was where Elizabeth Cheza lived and slept. The other was where Leothere Nininahazwe taught French and ran the Urban Institute, a programme to support newcomers to the city as they found their feet. I had not yet come across Leothere and I hoped I might get an opportunity to talk to him. I wondered what his story was and how he had come to the church. In fact it would take quite a long time and many visits to Central before I would hear Leothere's story first hand and discover the long and circuitous route he had travelled to arrive at Central Methodist. I would also discover that he was among the very earliest residents there. His story was a powerful one, of courage and determination.

Ambrose told me that the norm was for everyone living in the church to clear their area and leave the premises early in the morning to try and find work, and not to return until the end of the day. There were some people who stayed behind, however. On the day of our tour, quite a few people, I noticed, were standing around outside the cry rooms, talking in groups, looking out of the windows onto Pritchard Street, while others sat on the floor.

Next we went to the "boardroom". At least that's what Ambrose called it. When we walked in, it didn't look like a boardroom to me, although there was one large table with a few chairs around it. The wall to the right was lined with computers. I counted ten. Ambrose told me they had been donated by Anglo American and that the boardroom doubled as a computer training room. At the back of the room I spotted two mattresses on the floor. The boardroom tripled as a bedroom, it seemed. Ambrose confirmed this. "I sleep here," he said.

I realised that we had come down a different stairway from the one we had gone up earlier in the day and I was grateful for my guide. I already had a sense of how easy it would be to get lost in the building. Now it was beginning to feel like a labyrinth.

Because of the high ceilings of the sanctuary and the gallery in the centre of the building, there were mezzanine levels between the first and second, and the second and third floors. Various rooms and storage areas existed on the mezzanine levels at every turn. The "first floor lounge" conjured up images of couches, coffee tables and a TV, which was probably the way it had been set up in the 1980s. Today, however, the room bore no resemblance to that image. It had been partitioned repeatedly with blankets and sheets, as had a storage room on the same floor, creating a honeycomb of spaces in which couples lived and slept. It was hardly a private space. Everyone in those rooms could hear what anyone else was doing.

Back down on the ground floor, Ambrose told me that many people slept on the stairs, on the first floor in front of the sanctuary, and on the floor of the foyer, too. He himself had slept on the stairs for three months when he first arrived at Central. It was difficult to monitor the front door in the evenings he said and men often showed up drunk, wanting access to the building in the middle of the night.

The JB Webb chapel, named after a past Superintendent Minister at Central Methodist, was also on the ground floor. The chapel had brown wooden pews and could hold about 150 people. While the main 10am Sunday service was always held in the sanctuary, the smaller 8am service and the 9:30am French service were held in the chapel. At no point during the past few years had any of these services stopped, even when the building was overflowing with residents.

On the other side of the foyer, Ambrose pointed out the Solidarity Peace Trust's storeroom. This was where SPT housed people who were recovering from traumatic situations or political violence, people who needed greater privacy than another room in the church might provide. Next to the SPT storeroom was the Roberts Room. It had a kitchen, where SPT cooked meals for residents. It was also used for workshops and it was where Freedom Chivima taught karate.

Ambrose took me to two sections of the basement, accessible by two different sets of stairs. The first set of stairs led down to the crèche, FLOC. This was a huge room, with cubbyholes for the kids' shoes and coats and large areas for reading and playing and nap time. This was where the People Centre used to be, a restaurant that Central Methodist had run in the 1980s. In a large adjacent hall, the church used to hold meetings of up to 500 people.

The second set of stairs led down to another mezzanine floor with multiple rooms. One of them, Minor Hall, was filled with piles of clothing, suitcases, cardboard boxes, and plastic carrier bags. The many mattresses on the floor shared space with small stoves, plastic buckets and crawling babies. "This is the main women's sleeping area," said Ambrose. It was crowded and very hot, with no ventilation.

Ambrose told me that during the xenophobic violence that had gripped South Africa in May 2008 there were over 3 000 people living in the church. "You couldn't move up or down the stairs without stepping on someone," he said. "It was difficult for security in those days. Traumatised, stressed people are always the first to overreact. There were lots of fights, lots of domestic violence. Now it's quiet. The numbers are below a thousand, I'd say."

I tried to imagine it. The building as it was right now appeared to be brimming with people and poverty and resilience. Three thousand inhabitants seemed impossible.

I looked down the passage, made narrower by several mattresses on the floor and a few people sitting on them, listening to a radio and chatting. At the end of the passage was a door with an Emergency Exit sign on it. I didn't want to think about what might happen if there was a fire in the building, especially at night.

By the end of the day I was worn out, and I thought I had seen all there was to see. I didn't know that I had missed the vestry, an area behind the sanctuary, as well as another area that led from the vestry up into the air-conditioning ducts. I learned later that the space around the air-conditioning ducts was the base of one Godfrey Charamba, the man who the Bishop had said was involved with stealing from The Blind Association. We had also missed another area called "Soweto", which was down in the basement and where a gang of South Africans was purported to live. Perhaps, as Ambrose was head of security, these two places might not have housed his best friends and he'd deliberately left them out of our tour.

Two

A Clear Voice to Take on the Powers

When Bishop Peter Storey of the Methodist Church recommended Reverend Paul Verryn to become the Superintendent Minister at Central Methodist in 1997, he thought that Verryn would be an appropriate choice because he had "a very clear voice that was not afraid to raise the issues, to take on the powers". These proved to be prophetic words, with perhaps an even broader scope than Storey envisaged.

Paul Verryn was born in 1952 in Pretoria, the younger brother by sixteen years to his sister. His father, a staunch supporter of Jan Smuts, who had fought in the Second World War, and went on to work as an electrician in Johannesburg, left the family when Verryn was four years old. Although his mother struggled financially, working her way up through the ranks of the Permanent Building Society from teller to manager, she believed in the value of education and saved to send Paul to a private Methodist school, St Stithian's College to the north of Johannesburg. Her own education had stopped at Standard 6 because her father hadn't believed that girls needed to be educated.

Verryn hadn't always given the impression of a firebrand, however. At school, he was quiet and obedient and never in trouble. His first conscientising was at a very young age. The family's helper, Julia Nkadimeng, would share stories with him of how apartheid affected her family, especially the humiliation of the pass laws. When Paul was seven, she predicted that by the time he was sixteen he would treat her just like all the other whites did. She took a bet with him that he would forget what she had taught him, and he vowed never to do so.

The voice "to take on the powers" that Bishop Storey had heard in Verryn first reverberated during his period of compulsory military service at the age of seventeen and he began to get into a great deal of trouble. He rebelled with every fibre against the army, questioning authority at every turn and refusing to comply with orders. His family thought he was a disgrace. His mother believed that compliance was the better way and although he understood that she had had to be compliant in order to survive, this was never going to be his own route when it came to the things he believed in.

After the army came university, a Bachelor of Arts degree from the University of South Africa, and straight after that, the ministry. It was 1973 and Verryn was 21 years old. His first assignment, a move from Pretoria to the industrial town of Uitenhage in the Eastern Cape, was a massive change and it brought him into contact with the poverty and neglect that existed in South Africa's rural areas. In those early years, he established himself as an excellent listener and counsellor. He worked as a minister in Uitenhage, Butterworth and Grahamstown, and completed a Bachelor of Divinity degree at Rhodes University in 1977. It was his five years as a minister at St John's Methodist Church in downtown Port Elizabeth from 1979 to 1983, however, that had the greatest impact on him politically. It was during this time that he joined Lifeline, a counselling organisation, and became active in the Detainees' Parents Support Committee, which supported people who had been detained for political reasons under apartheid. He was elected chairman of the Committee. For Verryn there was no better way of conscientising himself. Having to take responsibility for an organisation and all that went with it politicised Verryn. It wasn't that he was unpoliticised before, but he had certainly not been at the coal face. His faith and his calling meant that he had to confront apartheid. "What would Jesus have done?" was a question that often helped to guide his actions.

As a result of his growing engagement with the politics of apartheid and the townships of Port Elizabeth, Verryn began to shelter people in his apartment when they were on the run from the security police. Saki Macozoma was one of the activists at the time to whom he opened his home.

After five years in Port Elizabeth, in 1984 Verryn was posted to Roodepoort, west of Johannesburg. Peter Storey had just become Bishop of the Central District and had oversight of all the churches in the District, including Verryn's. Verryn's congregation, called Princess, was a small one, and in a mining suburb. It was in that same year that Bishop Desmond Tutu won his Nobel Peace Prize, that the United Democratic Front celebrated its first anniversary, and that the protests against the tricameral parliamentary system peaked. Uprisings took place in the Vaal Triangle, an area outside Johannesburg, resulting in violent responses from the security police, who harassed those suspected of being involved in instigating them.

One day Verryn came home from a Detainees' Parents Support Committee meeting and as soon as he walked in the front door, he smelled cigarette smoke. He walked quietly down the passage and looked left into his study, where he could see that some of his files had been moved. The lounge was on his right but before he could look into the room or react, the men who had been waiting for him there quickly overpowered him. They held him hostage in his home for eighteen hours, eventually forcing him to sign a cash cheque for R15 000 before they left.

For Verryn, the break-in was a turning point. He decided he no longer wanted to stay alone in the house, and from then on he began to offer refuge to larger numbers of political activists. Thabo Mosiane, now in the leadership of North West province, was one who sought sanctuary there, as did Edgar Pieterse, now Director of the African Centre for Cities at the University of Cape Town. Pieterse fled the Cape Town security police in 1986 and stayed at Verryn's house for a couple of weeks. "There was always food available," he recalled gratefully.

Verryn's political activities didn't sit well with his conservative white congregation in Princess. A photograph in which he could be seen standing alongside Reverend Mvume Dandala in front of the Communist flag at a funeral for the Cradock Four, appeared on the front page of the *Sunday Times* in July 1985. In late 1986 he again appeared on the front page of the Sunday paper, having the day before ministered at another funeral, this time for 24 black youths who had been killed by the South African Police.

Paul Verryn was attracting attention, not only at home, but internationally as well, and the media were hungry for political stories. The *Philadelphia Inquirer* carried a report. "At Mr Verryn's all-white, all Afrikaner church, some members of the congregation were incensed. They grumbled about their 'terrorist' and 'communist' minister." Verryn may have lost some of his congregation as a result, but he was committed to his faith and his religious activism. The *Inquirer* said, "Verryn believes he is obliged to confront injustice – and in South Africa, he says, that means confronting the government… As a minister, he attends to the personal crises – suicides, divorces, alcoholism – of the conservative Afrikaners who are members of his congregation. As an activist, he counsels blacks who are detained under the government's state of emergency."

Verryn went on to tell the *Inquirer* that not only had black people suffered severely under apartheid, but also that whites had suffered what he called "psychic numbing". Whites were able to rationalise apartheid, he said, because they refused to examine it. "The system has provided them with prosperity and security. It has dehumanised blacks… because only then can their exploitation be tolerated." In the same article he said that his own family was "racist, but not irredeemably so. They are not entirely comfortable with apartheid but they condone it by not questioning it." He told the paper: "Whites here have black maids raise their children, but they don't even know their last names. They don't know their maids' own children are being detained and beaten and scarred for life. I sometimes think if they saw their 'girl' lying bleeding in the street, they'd walk right past her. They wouldn't even see her." During this time Verryn was also interviewed for a BBC documentary, *Suffer the Children*, calling attention to the large numbers of children in detention in South Africa and how they were also beaten and tortured.

In addition to his political activism, Verryn was legendary for something else entirely – his notorious lateness for meetings. One day, while still at Princess Methodist, Verryn was so late for a meeting that his Superintendent Minister took note and phoned him about it. "We are going to have to talk about this," he said. "Meet me at my office tomorrow at 9am." Verryn was terribly late for that meeting as well, late for a meeting to talk about being late. There was going to be no easy remedy for this failing.

It was Bishop Storey who asked Verryn to move to Soweto in December 1987. Storey saw this cross-cultural appointment as a pioneering move, and chose Verryn because he was already deeply involved with people in the township. His counselling, particularly with ex-detainees and torture victims, was ongoing. Verryn moved into the Methodist manse in Orlando West and began to serve the Methodist congregations, or societies as they are called in the Methodist Church, in Orlando West, Soweto. His work as a pastor was demanding, caring for individuals in the township in turbulent times. "There was a pastoral intensity that characterised his ministry," Storey said of him some years later, and he was not wrong. Verryn continued at that pace for another nine years in Soweto before he took up his post at Central Methodist in 1997. He would continue to live in Soweto and commute every day to his office at the church.

Ten years later, in 2008, Verryn's belief in not turning anyone away who came to his door asking for refuge was as steadfast as ever, but this time it was the church in downtown Johannesburg they came to. By then Central Methodist was housing literally thousands of people and, while its doors remained open, the building was seriously straining at the seams.

It was after 11pm on Wednesday, 30 January 2008. As usual, Bishop Verryn was in his office on the third floor, meeting with new arrivals to the church. William Kandowe, who taught computer classes, and another man were busy working in the office as well, making laminated registration cards for new residents. They all heard sirens, but police sirens at night on Pritchard Street in Johannesburg weren't unusual so although the sound registered, it caused no alarm.

Most people in the building had settled down to sleep by then. Like cars bumper to bumper on a highway, people lay head to toe and next to each other on flattened pieces of cardboard, most of them covered with grey blankets, in the space outside the sanctuary on the first and second floors. Hundreds of others were sleeping on the floors of the Roberts Room and Minor Hall. The JB Webb chapel was crammed with people under the pews. Inside the main entrance of the church on the ground floor, the foyer was another sea of grey blankets, with the occasional person lying on his side, knees bent to his chest, without any covering at all. Everywhere one looked in the five-storey building, there were sleeping bodies, even on the stairs. Over 1 300 people were sleeping inside that night, with close to 500 more outside the church on the pavement.

Freedom Chivima was asleep behind the vestry in a cupboard that he had turned into his bed, first spraying inside it with Doom to make sure to rid it of any insects. He had arrived at the church earlier that month. Born in Zimbabwe in 1980 – the year of his country's independence – he had come to Johannesburg on his own, looking for work as a plumber, leaving behind his parents, five sisters, his wife and daughter. Freedom was strong from his years of karate training, but he was not a very tall or heavy man, so he could contort himself into a small space. He reckoned that the cupboard was the cosiest place in the building. He was sleeping especially peacefully that night because a few days earlier he had been thrilled to land a plumbing job at another building in the city.

Back up on the third floor the persistent sirens started to penetrate Verryn's consciousness. Then he heard sounds of commotion coming from downstairs, and screaming. The Bishop's office did not have windows on the Pritchard Street side, so he went out into the waiting room to take a look outside. A queue of police vehicles, including police vans, cars and trucks called "gumba gumbas" were parked along Pritchard. A column of armed police were on duty. People were running in every direction.

Before he could do anything, Verryn's cellphone rang. It was Alpha Zhou, one of the residents in the church. He was calling from downstairs. "The police have broken into the building," he said urgently. "They broke down the front door."

Verryn went back into his office and made two phone calls, one to Mary Metcalfe and the other to Carleen Gerber. Metcalfe, a close friend of Verryn's, was the head of the Wits School of Education, and also a former minister in the Gauteng Legislature and a prominent member of the African National Congress. She in turn immediately phoned the national broadcaster, the SABC, and a local radio station, Talk Radio 702. Carleen Gerber, from the First Congregational Church in Old Lyme, Connecticut in the US, with whom Verryn had worked for 20 years, called Voice of America and the Associated Press. By midnight, not only were the police swarming around Central Methodist – the media were as well.

Verryn walked down the many flights of stairs to the ground floor. It was difficult to get down because of the general chaos and lots of people running up the stairs in their panic. On the way he found Alpha Zhou, whose mouth was bleeding. Zhou said to Verryn, "Let them kill us here. Then the world will see what they're doing to us."

Ambrose Mapiravana was sleeping on the fifth step up from the foyer on the ground floor. He woke up to people running over him down the stairs. Because there was such a loud noise, Ambrose thought that maybe the building was collapsing. "I couldn't do anything but roll down the stairs. I was forced outside with only my night shorts and a T-shirt. I was forced into a row of guys on Smal Street."

Once Verryn reached the foyer, he confronted the police. "What are you doing?" he demanded. "Why do you need to break down the door? Why are you assaulting these people? This is a church."

One policeman responded, saying, "You are a disgrace to the church for allowing these people to stay here", and he shoved the Bishop back towards the door.

By this time Freedom Chivima and everyone else who had been sleeping in the vestry had been forced up and out of the church building onto Smal Street. Most hadn't had a chance to gather anything together, not asylum papers nor any other documents. They were manhandled into queues on the pavement and then carted off in trucks to the police station. It was Freedom's first time in a police vehicle. "I was traumatised," he said. "I thought I was going to be deported. I was sitting there thinking, Now my job is gone."

A South African resident of the church, Cleo Buthelezi, was asleep in one of the small rooms on a mezzanine floor when the raid began. She and her Zimbabwean boyfriend, Taurai Gundumure, were woken by the commotion that was being made by police officers across the passage in Minor Hall, but they decided to stay where they were, Cleo hoping that her five-year-old son Mihlali would stay asleep. The first policemen who came into their room were not aggressive. They asked to see Cleo's papers and she showed them her ID book, which seemed to satisfy them. After they left a second crew came in and their attitude was quite different. They kicked in the door and took Taurai away when he couldn't produce any papers. Then for good measure they took the couple's DVD player as well. Cleo frantically waved her South African ID book at them. One of the policemen took it and slapped her across the face with it, saying, "I don't care what you are." While police dogs sniffed around her mealie meal and bottle of oil just inside the door, Cleo tried to comfort Mihlali. Still on the bed but now fully awake, he pushed his back into the corner as far as he could, his eyes wide with fear.

"They came in military style and turned the church upside down," said Bishop Verryn. "Doors were broken, windows shattered. They basically vandalised my church, acted despicably, kicking anything that moved, including pregnant women, children and disabled people. They didn't want to identify themselves. They didn't have a search warrant."

Reverend Kim Alexander, another minister at Central Methodist, who lived in the church manse in Greenside, woke to the sound of her cellphone ringing beside her bed. It was Tina de Rijke, Verryn's personal assistant.

"Central is being raided by the police," she said. Alexander peered at the clock. It was just after 1am. She tried to call the Bishop but couldn't get through, so instead she phoned her colleague, Minister Khanyisile Nduli, and they agreed to go together to the church. They drove in silence through the deserted Johannesburg streets, not knowing what to expect. As they approached the church, they saw the police trucks, about 20 of them, lining the road. They parked a little way along the street but before they could get out of the car, a policeman was at the window. "Who are you?" he demanded.

"We work here," Alexander said firmly, and she and Nduli got out of the car and began walking determinedly towards the church. She estimated that they saw around 50 officers that night. The streets around the building were strewn with papers and clothes and blankets. Men sat on their haunches in rows, their eyes filled with fear. The police were everywhere.

Later the police informed the media that they had been acting in the interest of safety and security and that they were "following complaints from residents and businesses around the area that the church harboured criminals". Putting the number of arrests at around 500, police captain Bheki Mavundla said, "The raid was part of a sustainable crime-combating operation that was legally authorised in order to eradicate criminal elements from problematic buildings and streets that include the Methodist church."

The two ministers picked their way through the mess, wondering how to help. They found Mary Metcalfe out on the street, also wandering through the debris, the detritus of people's lives left behind in the rush. One area on the street that clearly had been a living space for a family that night had caught her attention. There was a mattress with several blankets on it. Next to it were children's schoolbooks and other reading material. Looking at the meagre belongings, Metcalfe thought of a family that must have made an enormous effort to retain a centre of integrity and belonging out of just a few blankets and a pile of books. She bent down and picked one up. It was a small black address book, with sections for each letter of the alphabet. Flipping through the pages, Metcalfe marvelled that, despite what they must have been through, this family had somehow remained functional and shown great resilience and care. They still had networks of people, friends and family, recorded in this book. The image of that family stayed with her for a long time. "I have no idea what happened to them," she recalled years later, "whether they ever found their things or whether they were devastated by the events of that night."

Reverend Alexander found her way to Minor Hall, surprised to see so many women and children still there. All of them had been forced outside earlier by the police, but fortunately none of them had been found worthy of detention so had been allowed to return. Some were even trying to get back to sleep, while others were soothing their crying babies. One young woman was standing with a passport in her hands and Alexander asked her if she was OK. The woman's eyes filled with tears. "I need to get this passport to my brother," she said, "but I am afraid to leave this room."

"Come," said Alexander. "Let's go and try to find him."

A policeman stopped them as they passed through the church entrance. "Who are you?" he asked Alexander.

"We are looking for her brother," she said in a bold voice and, not waiting for his response, she linked the woman's arm in hers and they walked out onto the street. They passed rows of men squatting on their haunches out on the pavement, scanning faces as they walked. Near the set of traffic lights on the next block, miraculously, the woman saw her brother and she pushed his passport into his hands.

Monica Chiwetu was one of the many women sleeping in the Roberts Room that night, just off the foyer on the ground floor. Months earlier, her father had died in Zimbabwe and she had made her way to South Africa, hoping to find work and send money home to her family. When she first heard the noise and shouting she thought it was people fighting and she dozed off again. Suddenly, police officers burst into the room. "They put the lights on," said Monica. "They had big guns. 'Everybody out!' they said. 'Get out. Get out!' People were shivering. Babies were crying. We were trying to cover ourselves. A few of us tried to hide, leaving through the broken window at the back into the small courtyard behind the building, but they found us there and took us outside. It was crowded outside in the dark. People were lined up in rows along Smal Street. Police and police vans were everywhere." As a Zimbabwean, Monica was very frightened. "I had left my passport inside," she said, "so the police let me back inside to get it. When I got to the door of the Roberts Room there were two policemen standing there. There were about ten women still inside with their babies. I went inside and got my passport. The two policemen at the door asked to see it so I showed them. There was no visa in it." She held her breath. They looked at it and then, to her surprise, said, "'OK, go and sleep. Hide yourself. Don't go outside.'"

Outside the church, a film crew was trying to film people being loaded into the back of a police van. A policeman put his hand over the camera but the crew was not deterred and stepped further back to continue filming. Other members of the media were interviewing Bishop Verryn.

After 2am Mary Metcalfe was still there, still trying to move abandoned belongings inside the church, but there was just too much. On one of her last trips outside, she stopped and watched as about 30 homeless people began sifting through the remaining items on the street. They were weighed down by the dirty rags they were wearing and the bags of belongings on their backs. As she watched them, Metcalfe thought how those people were even more alienated than the ones who had just been carried away by the police. There was another layer of homeless people in this city that one never really saw, people who had lost all sense of community. Metcalfe tried to greet them, but they wouldn't make eye contact. It was then that she realised that it was vital to help people coming into the city to maintain their sense of connection, their sense of community, their sense of belonging before it was too late. For those homeless people who were scurrying to gather a blanket, a book or a few slices of bread off the street, it might be too late already. She watched them make their way through the remains of the raid, and then they were gone.

In the early hours of the morning Bishop Verryn gathered people into the sanctuary on the first floor and asked each of them to share their experiences of the night with the person next to them. Some people sang together. Others returned from the police station and joined the impromptu service. Verryn invited people to share with the whole group. He said that although the police had been looking for criminals in the building, "they themselves became the perpetrators of criminal action". One woman told the gathering that she was an illegal immigrant but she had gone up to a police officer and showed him her clinic card and told him that she was here because she was HIV positive and was getting treatment. He told her to go back to sleep.

Kim Alexander and Khanyisile Nduli finally left the building after 4am, but Alexander was back at the church by 10am the next day to attend a retreat for the Central District that had been scheduled for that morning. "I could hardly believe it," she said. The devastation from the previous night was nowhere to be seen. "Everything looked normal. A film crew was doing an interview with Paul."

It was the first time something like that had happened in the many years since Central Methodist had been housing the homeless, the vulnerable and the sick, Verryn said in the days after the raid. Not since the days of apartheid had he experienced anything like it, when he used to shelter ANC activists at his home and was frequently raided by security police. "In a sense," he said, "this was my nightmare come true. If this is a statement to the Church as an official body in this country, then we are at the dawn of a very profound problem in this nation." Verryn repeatedly stated that he could not understand the necessity for such violent entry, why they had needed to cause such damage. "We can fix windows and we can fix doors," he said, "but the most serious violation is of the people – that's the violation, that's the desecration, that's the blasphemy. People sometimes come here who have not eaten for three or four days. I have had grown men weeping in my office. These people are desperate."

The public response to the raid was immediate and vehement. The Treatment Action Campaign, a prominent non-governmental organisation focused on advocacy for those living with HIV and Aids, condemned the raid and called upon the Johannesburg Central Police Station commander to explain the police's actions. They wanted to know whether the raid had been authorised or called for by the Department of Home Affairs. They also demanded the immediate release of those who had been detained, and called on Home Affairs to deal humanely with refugees who were seeking proper documentation to enable them to stay in South Africa.

The Centre for the Study of Violence and Reconciliation and other NGOs also condemned the raid. As trauma counsellors who worked with many Zimbabwean torture survivors, they defended Central Methodist's policy of providing shelter.

Eddie Makue, General Secretary of the SA Council of Churches, said that for many years the church had welcomed Zimbabweans and others who had been displaced by political conflict and economic turmoil in their own countries. He was particularly upset because the action had been taken without any attempt to engage with the church, especially since the church and municipal officials had recently been exploring ways in which to co-operate and work with each other. "In the apartheid era," said Makue, "we often were able to hide people in the churches, because we knew that even the brutal apartheid police were reluctant to violate the sanctity of the church." Now, overnight, this had changed.

Bishop Ivan Abrahams, Presiding Bishop of the Methodist Church of Southern Africa, also lent his support and voice to the condemnation of the police raid. He publicly urged other churches to follow Central Methodist's example of what he referred to as "radical hospitality".

It took much of the day on Thursday 31 January for the police to book all of the detainees into the cells. Bianca Tolboom, a young, dynamic nurse from The Netherlands, who was head of the Médecins Sans Frontières clinic at Central Methodist at that time, was frustrated that they were having difficulty accessing the detainees, some of whom were suspected of having been physically injured by the police. The possibility of fractured ribs and possible lung contusions after receiving blows was high. Others were on HIV or TB treatment and needed a certain amount of food in order to take their medication. MSF had left medicines for some of the patients at the cells but the police officers had failed to give them the drugs even though they had promised to do so. In addition, the cells were overcrowded as they rarely had to hold hundreds of people at the same time. The police on duty didn't seem to know how to handle the situation either, so they were loud and aggressive, which left some of the detainees in a state of panic.

It wasn't only health workers who had trouble getting access to the detainees. Attorneys from the Legal Resources Centre had also been trying. Janet Love, the national director of the LRC, was worried that there had been delays in the detainees receiving legal help and that the police had physically mistreated some of them and had asked for bribes. She was also concerned by the vagueness of the charges which had now been brought against them – being "illegal" under Section 49 of the Immigration Act – and that the police and the prosecution in the case were poorly prepared. Love said that the police refused to give the LRC access and that it was only after she threatened an urgent application to the High Court that the police agreed to let them consult with the detainees.

In the days after the raid, about 141 people were released from Johannesburg Central Police Station because they were able to produce valid documents allowing them to be in South Africa. A further 380, despite their lack of documents, were also freed without charges. Freedom Chivima was released the morning after the raid because, he said, he had managed to convince a policewoman that he was from Botswana by speaking Setswana, his mother's home language. "I was lucky," he said. Ambrose Mapiravana was held for the weekend and then released.

First to be charged was one not so lucky group of fifteen men who were sent to the magistrate's court on Friday, 1 February, where they applied for bail. Presiding magistrate Du Pisani was not impressed with having to deal with them late on a Friday afternoon. She wanted to go home and be with her family and she said so. The prosecutor told her that the accused spoke "Zimbabwean" and the magistrate then asked each man in turn, in an aggressive manner, whether he spoke Shona or Ndebele. When the accused indicated that he spoke English, she ignored him and repeated the question, in some cases up to three times, with increasing volume and vigour. Despite objection by the LRC, the magistrate postponed their cases until the following Monday and sent the men back to the cells for the weekend.

On Monday the LRC brought a team back to court, this time with some of their big guns, including George Bizos SC and former Constitutional Court judge, Johann Kriegler, who was in the courtroom to observe. The police did not provide satisfactory evidence in court so the magistrate remanded the case until 12 February. And so, while over 500 of the detainees from Central Methodist had already been released and returned to the church, these fifteen men were stuck in the system because they had been sent to court to apply for bail and so a legal process was now under way.

On Tuesday, 5 February, Paul Verryn and the LRC met with Gauteng Community Safety and Security minister Firoz Cachalia, the station commander of the Johannesburg Central Police Station Simon Mpembe and the provincial police commissioner. As a result, the station commander agreed to meet with the leaders of the church to work out how to improve communication. Cachalia said afterwards that in order to be effective in fighting crime, "all our police officers have to uphold the Constitution and behave in a professional manner at all times." On the same day, flanked by representatives of MSF, the LRC, Lawyers for Human Rights, and the AIDS Law Project, Verryn gave a statement to the press, comparing the raid once again to "the worst days of the pass raids during the apartheid era".

The head of the Independent Complaints Directorate in Gauteng, Advocate Siphokazi Moleshe, announced that the conduct of the police officers who had taken part in the raid was to be investigated "in the interest of the public". As it turned out, the investigation never proceeded because, according to Advocate Moleshe, people at Central Methodist were not forthcoming when the Directorate sent its people to investigate, so they closed the file without completing a report on the events of that night.

The January 2008 raid and its outcome raised many unanswered questions, the first one being who had authorised it. Was it the Mayor of Johannesburg, the National Minister of Safety and Security, or had the commissioner of the Johannesburg Central Police Station acted alone? The commissioner's spokesperson seemed to be the only one willing to accept responsibility. As South Africa is party to international law which gives refugees the right to claim asylum, another unanswered question was why had the raid taken place when it was common knowledge that Central Methodist housed many asylum seekers? If the police were concerned, as they'd said, about criminals operating out of the church building, why did they not find evidence there of criminality? Why were none of the more than 500 people released by the police over the following days ever charged? If they had hoped to find guns and drugs in the building, where were they? Or could the police have been influenced by the xenophobic view that all foreign nationals commit crime in South Africa? Some residents of the church said that the police had told them that they didn't care if they had legal documents and that their "Mbeki papers" had expired the day Jacob Zuma had been elected president of the ANC in December 2007. The ANC leadership never formally endorsed the raid, nor did they condemn it. Perhaps it was the view that "undocumented foreigners" at Central Methodist were "illegal aliens" and should be arrested for the lack of proper documents, but was this reason enough to burst in in the dark of night, and use violence and treat each person like a criminal?

Nearly five years after the raid, in late 2012, I had the opportunity to talk to General Simon Mpembe, who was station commander at Johannesburg Central Police Station from 2006 through early 2009. I asked him to describe to me the circumstances around the church in 2007 and what had led the police to consider a raid in January 2008. "There were complaints from the church members," he said. "One of the challenges was robbers committing crimes and then hiding there. That was a safe haven for them. We got a report from Central Intelligence that there was an arms cache in the church, that there were firearms in there that were used for robberies. And business people had petitioned the local authority. You can't receive complaints and then do nothing about it."

I asked Mpembe why he had decided to conduct a raid at night with no warning. "That place is huge to search," he replied. "It is easy for things to be removed. I worked in Cape Town for twenty years. If you get information about firearms, you must conduct your raid when they are there. People who are dealing with firearms, they are not stupid." Since the police did not find any guns during the raid, I asked Mpembe if he had been disappointed. "That was fine," he said. "We made the criminals aware. We let them know that we are aware of what they are doing."

I asked Mpembe whether he had received an order of any kind to conduct the raid. "No," he said, "I gave the instruction. I'm the general. I'm the senior person."

I then asked Mpembe about the levels of force that were used in the church and at the police station. "This issue is like Marikana," he explained. "We were told it was excessive force. If you don't act, people complain. If you act, people complain. We are not appreciated."

General Mpembe claimed that the relationship between the church and the police, ironically, improved greatly after the raid. "We had a meeting with Bishop Verryn. We agreed that we must not raid the place with no warning. We agreed that if the people in the church saw something funny going on, they must phone me. Then there was a partnership. Previously, the church was not talking to us. There were only reports from individual church members. After the raid the partnership worked well. They would call us to say they suspect this… Can you please deal with this? There was a lot of interaction that solved a lot of problems. That was a bit more preventative. There was no need for further operations."

Despite General Mpembe's emphasis on fighting crime, hundreds of people who were arrested that night had nothing to do with guns. They were taken in because they did not have proper documentation from Home Affairs. Some commentators made the point that the process of providing documentation from Home Affairs was inefficient, and that the absence of refugee reception centres was part of the reason why it was so difficult for foreign nationals to get the proper documents. If Home Affairs offices were in working order, they claimed, it would drastically reduce the number of "undocumented foreigners" in South Africa, thereby freeing up the police to focus on real crime prevention. Ironically, at the time Home Affairs seemed to be giving more attention to deportation than to issuing documents. In 2007 South Africa deported over 300 000 people, 50 000 more than in 2006. It seems reasonable to ask what this resource-intensive process had achieved.

On 15 February, more than two weeks after the raid, the remaining group of fifteen men was still in police custody. The LRC sent an urgent application to Judge Roland Sutherland, who ordered their immediate release. He also ordered that the Magistrates Commission conduct an investigation into Magistrate du Pisani's conduct. Judge Sutherland apologised to each applicant for the manner in which he had been treated. They were human beings, he said, not just "pieces of paper". Reading the affidavits from the raid reminded him of "grotesque apartheid era abuses" of 20 years before.

While the many questions about the raid on Central Methodist continued to spark debate in South Africa, the flickers of xenophobia had already been smouldering for some time, and 2008 was the year when the flickers flared into a fire that the country would not be able to ignore.

Three

An Unexpected Thunderstorm

VIOLENCE AGAINST FOREIGN nationals was on the rise in early 2008. In February of that year hundreds of foreign nationals were evicted from their homes by xenophobic attacks in townships outside Pretoria. They sought refuge in temporary shelters set up in Laudium and Atteridgeville. Two men were burned to death in the same area when their shacks were set alight. The violence continued in March. A Mozambican businessman, Isaac Hlabathi, had one of his shops burned down and he was terrified. When asked by a journalist why he wanted to burn down Hlabathi's shop, one township resident answered, "He's a foreigner. He takes our jobs and rapes our women. He is bad like all foreigners and must leave South Africa."

Some organisations tried to warn the authorities about this growing problem and its causes. One report from a Paris-based human rights organisation observed that South Africa's migration policies focused on population control and were criminalising migration and fuelling xenophobia. It said that these policies were "rendering South Africa inhospitable for undocumented migrants through arrests, restricting access to jobs, services and temporary residence". The report also said that the police were confusing undocumented migrants and criminals.

On 26 March 2008 Bishop Paul Verryn appeared before the Portfolio Committee on Home Affairs at the National Assembly in Cape Town. These public hearings were reviewing the Refugees Amendment Bill and

Verryn had been asked to brief the Committee on the police raid that had taken place at Central Methodist in January. Verryn used the opportunity to express his concern that refugees and asylum seekers were being systematically criminalised. "I think this is part of the problem with the press," he explained, "but it is also certainly the attitude of the police service that the nexus of crime in South Africa lies in the refugees. They are treated like criminals."

The authorities, however, were disinclined to listen to these warnings. ANC Member of Parliament Mtikeni Sibande suggested that Verryn was in breach of South Africa's immigration laws by accommodating illegal immigrants in the church. Verryn was asked how he verified that people were genuine refugees or asylum seekers. Acknowledging that the system was open to abuse, Verryn responded: "We work on an open door policy. The church relies on the police to root out individuals who are ill disciplined or suspected of being involved in criminality." Home Affairs Committee chairperson Patrick Chauke said, "Whatever we do, Bishop, we must do it within the confines of the law. The issue of harbouring illegal immigrants is an offence and you can be charged." Unfortunately, the chairperson did not explore Home Affairs' responsibility for providing the growing numbers of immigrants with proper documentation.

The problem was further fuelled by the unstable political situation in Zimbabwe and increasing numbers of Zimbabweans fleeing to South Africa as a result. On 29 March 2008 Zimbabwe held a general election. For the first time in close to 30 years, Robert Mugabe's Zanu-PF party was defeated in the parliamentary elections. The results of the presidential elections were not as clear cut, however, and the Electoral Commission stalled for weeks before announcing them. During the several days when it appeared that Morgan Tsvangirai's opposition Movement for Democratic Change had in fact won the election, some Zimbabweans living at Central Methodist began making preparations to go home. Those hopes were short lived and time dragged on. As one church resident put his feelings about the election: "Mugabe's stolen it and no one's going to do anything about it."

There were increasing reports of election-related, state-sponsored violence flaring up in Zimbabwe and the pressure for a final announcement of results was building. When a Chinese ship was scheduled to offload its cargo of weapons in Durban harbour for onward delivery to Zimbabwe, trade unionists and church leaders successfully prevented its landing. Methodist Church Presiding Bishop Ivan Abrahams, who was also the chairperson of the South African Church Leaders' Forum, put out a statement at that time, warning that the situation in Zimbabwe was very dangerous and that levels of conflict were escalating. Introducing more weapons into an already violent situation would have had dire consequences.

South Africa's President Thabo Mbeki was criticised for maintaining there was "no crisis" in Zimbabwe. It seemed that Mbeki was not willing to criticise Mugabe in any way, even when he was clearly stalling in order to throw the election results. At a SADC summit in Lusaka on 13 April, SADC stated that there might be a need for a run-off election but they did not condemn the fact that Mugabe should have announced the results weeks before.

The security team at Central Methodist was already on anxious alert when xenophobic violence moved closer to home and broke out in Alexandra township on 11 May 2008. This was a day the country would not easily forget. It turned out to be the spark that started off weeks of violence throughout South Africa. Violence spread quickly to Diepsloot and the East Rand outside Johannesburg and then to Cape Town, Durban and the Eastern Cape. On 12 May *The Star* ran a front page story with the headline "Faces of Xenophobic Hate: Victims Tell of Night of Terror". The headline in the *Daily Sun* on 14 May was "War Against Aliens: Thousands Forced to Flee Alex".

Freedom Chivima was still living at Central Methodist in May, working his plumbing job during the day and security at the church at night. The police raid in January was still fresh in his mind but this time if they were attacked, he knew the men would not be in uniform. William Kandowe was also a member of the security team and he went a step further. "We are not going to fold our hands and wait," he said. "We have to prepare to defend ourselves if we are attacked." And so the men of Central Methodist put their makeshift army together and turned pieces of furniture ripped from inside the church into their weapons. And this was how Paul Verryn found them on the pavement of Pritchard Street on the night of 14 May, stamping their feet to keep warm, looking anxiously but defiantly down the road, straining their ears for sounds of danger.

Despite a potentially violent conflict averted when the Bishop persuaded the men to go back inside the church, the residents continued to feel threatened as the violence against foreigners spiraled. At the corner of Pritchard and Kruis streets, there was a construction site. "We took about a thousand bricks from there," admitted William Kandowe. "We put bricks on each floor so that people would have them for self-defence. The Bishop was very angry. 'No, no, no,' he said. 'This is a church. Return the bricks.'"

"We did return them," said Kandowe. "At least we returned more than half. Then we decided to make petrol bombs on the roof. We had over fifty."

Freedom Chivima said, "I don't know if the Bishop ever knew about those petrol bombs."

Years later, when I asked Verryn, he said that he did not, but that someone in the church had phoned the police who came and searched the building but they didn't find anything. Verryn told the security team that there would be no fighting back. "We don't want an eye for an eye," he said. "We'll end up with a blind world."

Security monitored Pritchard Street and Smal Street from the roof of the fourth floor, and from the fifth floor balcony. As the violence spread, Freedom Chivima was convinced there would be another raid, but this time the police in fact offered Central Methodist protection. "The police were patrolling every day," said Freedom. "One day the police weren't here. That day, these guys were coming down Jeppe Street. About fifty guys with sjamboks. Coming for us. But then the police came and the crowd dispersed."

Freedom's instincts were not wrong and there were other planned attacks on the church. "They already tried to attack us twice," one resident recalled. "On Sunday, a lot of Zulus came in kombis. They were dropped off by taxi drivers at four places. They were shouting '*Makwerekwere*!'"

There was an atmosphere of fear in the church during that time and the restlessness was palpable. At evening services the Bishop offered people the opportunity to talk about what was happening and this seemed to calm things down. Verryn also expressed concern for the country. "We must no longer ignore that communities are very disgruntled," he told them. "This is really the poor fighting the poor." He also felt that the situation was getting so serious the police could no longer control it.

Among those who sought refuge at Central Methodist in May 2008 were Alois Mutenanhene and his wife Leona. The couple and their daughter had fled to South Africa in 2007 after Alois was badly beaten in Zimbabwe because of his work with the MDC. Initially, they stayed at Central Methodist but they soon moved into rooms of their own in the George Goch hostel. The hostel had been built in 1961 to house male migrant workers on the mines but had been converted more recently into family units.

One evening in mid-May, at the peak of the violence, Alois and Leona were getting ready to go to sleep.

"It's so noisy," said Alois. "What's going on?"

"It must be kids playing," said Leona.

"But it's so loud. Is there a stadium around here?" Alois wondered.

There was a knock on the door. Alois opened it to find a five-year-old girl standing there. "My name is Lindiwe," she told him. "My grandmother sent me to say that they are beating the Shangaans."

"OK," said Alois, but the little girl didn't move. Well, I'm not Shangaan, I'm Shona, he thought to himself, not really understanding the concern.

Then the little girl said, "They are beating the foreigners, too."

Stunned at first, Alois's next thought was how he was going to run. He had Leona, who was newly pregnant, and their two-year-old baby daughter, who cried every night. He went next door to alert another Zimbabwean man who was living there, but the man had already left and Alois never saw him again.

"Let's just lock the door," was Leona's suggestion, hoping that the baby would be quiet.

Before Alois had a chance to reply, they heard a crowd of men coming down the passage. They kicked heavily at Alois's and Leona's door. Leona rocked the baby, her eyes on the door handle. The men were speaking isiZulu. Then they heard an older woman who lived two doors away tell the men, "Those people have already gone," and the men moved on. As they waited for the group to go, Alois looked out of the window and saw another, much larger crowd gathering outside. Men were singing and dancing, holding their sticks high. Alois thought, I will die here if I make a mistake.

Alois and Leona took their daughter and ran to the old woman down the passage. She helped them hide under her bed and then she sat down on it to wait. "I was shaking," remembered Alois. "I was shivering. I thought it was the last day for me." For some reason, the men outside had gone quiet and after a while the old woman went to check if they were still there. She said she thought they had gone so Alois crawled out from under the bed to see if he could find a way out. What he couldn't know was that yet another large group of men was on its way.

"I left my wife and my baby under the bed. I went back to our place and put on my trousers and a leather jacket. As I left the building, I could hear what they were saying. They were looking for *makwerekwere*. I found my own stick and I joined them. I joined them in their singing '*Buyela. Buyela. Hamba kwerekwere.*' Go home. Go home. Go home, foreigner. I moved about one kilometre with that group. Eventually, I escaped into the bush, in an area where trucks were dumping their containers.

"The drivers of the trucks were also Zulu but they were a bit helpful. I told them that I had to go back to save my wife in the hostel. 'We don't know how we can help,' they said. 'If we help you, those men might come and burn our trucks.' They did direct me which way to go, though, to avoid the different groups."

As Alois made his way back to the hostel he saw a police truck and approached it. He took a chance and told the officers his story. They took him to the hostel to fetch Leona and the baby and then wanted to take them to Germiston City Hall, which had been set up as a temporary shelter for those fleeing the violence, but Alois declined the offer. "I want to go where I trust people," he told them. The police dropped the family downtown close to Absa Bank, and from there they walked to Central Methodist. In parting, one of the policemen told Alois the Zulu word for "elbow" so that if they were stopped again, they could convince their accosters that they were Zulu.

"I trusted people as my friends at George Goch," Alois said later, "but they never warned me. They never helped me. It was that old lady who helped us. I never knew her. She wasn't my friend, but she helped me."

Alois and Leona weren't the only ones drawn to Central Methodist. Verryn estimated that at least an extra 300 people came to stay at the church during that weekend of violence alone.

In the midst of this national crisis, Bishop Verryn was running back and forth to Weltevreden Park on the West Rand to lead the Synod, the annual business meeting of the Central District of the Methodist Church. Despite the fear and desperation that was being covered day and night in the media, the growing violence barely affected the proceedings at the Synod, which was focused on the internal business of the Church. Penny Foley, who participated as a circuit steward, reflected that there was a very marked contrast between dealing with Church business and addressing the Church's mission under the circumstances. "It wasn't that people didn't care," she said, "just that the formality of how things work mitigated against people talking about the crisis."

The major agenda item at the Synod was the elections for Bishop of the District. Verryn had served four terms in this position, twelve years since 1997. The caucusing was intense. Verryn would need to receive more than 75 per cent of the vote in order to serve another term. Before the vote was announced, however, Verryn stood up, thanked the Church for the opportunity to serve, but indicated that he was not available for re-election.

While many people outside the Church assumed that Verryn lost his title as Bishop after his suspension in 2010, in reality he had already agreed in May 2008 to step down from the position, so he knew then that his term would come to an end in December 2009. "Twelve years was plenty," he told me a few years later.

During the Synod, Verryn continued to field calls on his cellphone from all over the world. Journalists wanted to find out what was happening at Central Methodist in the midst of the xenophobic violence. For several days the police parked in front of the church, right near the front door, and another patrol car parked near the red clock in front of the High Court. "Those officers were friendly," said William Kandowe, and the residents were grateful.

Still more and more people came to the church, seeking safety and some kindness and counselling. The MSF clinic there broadened its role and Bianca Tolboom and her colleague Tragedy Matsvaire offered their assistance to some of these displaced foreigners. They saw extreme anxiety and shock as a result of the levels of violence that had been used against them. Many people who had been living peacefully in the country for several years now felt rejection and hatred.

Eleven days after the violence began, about 200 clergy gathered at Central Methodist. They discussed their concerns about the violence and wondered particularly about the lack of response from government. "Where is the national leadership?" Sidwell Mokhutu, a priest from Pretoria, asked.

Almost two weeks after the first night of violence, neither President Mbeki nor Jacob Zuma, the new President of the ANC, had altered their diaries to visit any of the people displaced by the violence or the communities that had been profoundly affected. It was only on 25 May, Africa Day, that Mbeki finally addressed the nation. "Sadly," he said on radio and television, "here in South Africa, we mark Africa Day with our heads bowed. The shameful actions of a few have blemished the name of South Africa through criminal acts against our African brothers and sisters from other parts of the continent… Our television sets, newspapers and other media have brought us shocking images of violence against people from other countries who live in our country, including cold-blooded acts of murder, brutal assault, looting and destruction of property… Everything possible will be done to bring the perpetrators to justice. Last week, we approved the deployment of units of the South African National Defence Force… We have issued the necessary instructions to these forces and other law enforcement bodies to do everything necessary to stop and apprehend the killers and looters." The President went on to say, "I must restate that our government is firmly of the view that it would be wrong to isolate and segregate our foreign guests in special camps. Instead, we must build on the tradition of many decades of integrating our foreign guests within our communities."

Perhaps Mbeki had delayed his response because he was concerned that he would have to deflect criticism that his "quiet diplomacy" in Zimbabwe and his lack of action over the failed election in that country in March had led to a further influx of Zimbabweans into South Africa, which had contributed to the growing xenophobia. His speech did not once mention conditions in Zimbabwe, nor the increasing numbers of Zimbabweans crossing the border and fleeing south.

Asked at the Synod meeting how Central Methodist was coping with the constant flood of new arrivals, Verryn said that they had started to take a collection of R5 on Saturdays and were using the money to pay for nine cleaners and 20 security staff. Central Methodist had also been receiving donations because of all the press coverage. Many organisations, including Islamic Relief and Gift of the Givers, had given generously, and individuals arrived at the church almost daily with carloads of blankets, canned goods and clothes. Over the course of 2008 Central Methodist received unsolicited donations of about R1.2 million. They used the money to pay for utilities, security and cleaners, as well as to support medical care and funeral costs for people living at the church.

For all that, Verryn cautioned that the outpouring of generosity for the situation facing foreign nationals should not mask the fact that many South Africans were also facing desperate situations. "A 40 per cent unemployment rate is very high," he said, "and so we need to be very, very careful that things are distributed to everybody equally."

By the end of May the violence had subsided across the country but the cost had been high. Nationally, over 100 000 people had been displaced, 670 people had been injured and 62 people were dead. In Gauteng, 23 police stations around the province offered refuge to foreign nationals. Community halls and churches also offered shelter. In the broader scheme of world violence and tragedy, 62 deaths might be viewed as a modest number, yet the scope of the violence and displacement hit a nerve in the psyche of many South Africans. The image of one man from Mozambique, Ernesto Nhamuave, who was set alight and killed on the East Rand of Johannesburg, came to symbolise the violence. It came as a shock that despite fourteen years of democracy, all was not well in the "rainbow nation".

There were structural underpinnings to the flaring of anger and violence. Poverty and inequality had increased in South Africa since its first democratic elections in 1994 and internal and international patterns of migration had changed since the demise of apartheid and the end of influx control legislation. Violence against foreign nationals was not new. It had existed since the mid 1990s, but leadership in the South African government had done very little to discourage it. In fact, some statements from government to grassroots communities had even suggested that immigrants were a threat. The events of May 2008 should not have come as a great surprise, but they were a disgrace all the same and the absence of national leadership to address the xenophobia was abhorrent.

"Like an unexpected thunderstorm, the 'xenophobic' attacks swept across our country with unprecedented horror and unabated anger," said Bishop Paul Verryn at a Wits University seminar. "The warning signs were very much in place before the full onslaught happened. But somehow we were completely unprepared as a nation for the unleashing of such violence towards some of the most vulnerable people in our midst. The image of a pleading, burning Mozambican met by laughing onlookers is etched in our memories. Is this what we have come to?"

Despite the initial delay in government intervention, by the end of May the Gauteng provincial government had established a task team, led by Dorothy Qedani Mahlangu, a minister in the provincial cabinet responsible for the Department of Local Government, to identify locations for temporary shelters for the displaced foreigners. Mahlangu was quite powerful within the ANC, having helped to establish its structures in Gauteng in the 1990s after the movement was unbanned. She brought Russell McGregor onto her team. McGregor had been leading community development workers for the province, and his and Mahlangu's subsequent involvement with the temporary shelters in 2008 alerted them to the role that Central Methodist had already been playing for some years in providing accommodation for foreign nationals. Mahlangu thought the situation at the church was highly unusual.

During the violence many foreign nationals in downtown Johannesburg had initially sought shelter at the Jeppestown and Cleveland police stations to the east of the city. The province intended to relieve those two police stations by constructing a tent shelter on Vickers Road at the site of an old railway station and a nearby mine dump. The proposed site, however, was directly across the road from a group of hostels, most notably the George Goch hostel, which housed some foreign nationals and many South Africans.

A retired doctor named Tim Wilson, who was working with the Centre for the Study of Violence and Reconciliation and had been helping to co-ordinate humanitarian relief efforts since the xenophobic attacks, realised that this could present a problem and he called Paul Verryn. Verryn in turn called Jodi Kollapen, the chairperson of the South African Human Rights Commission and, with the assistance of the Legal Resources Centre, swiftly submitted an urgent application for an interim interdict preventing the residents of the police staions from being moved to the Vickers Road shelter. The court granted the interdict until government could show that adequate security arrangements were in place.

The thousands of people staying in police stations and shelters across the province had a long list of emergency needs, including clothing, medication for chronic illnesses, mattresses, blankets, primus stoves, cutlery, plates and cups, water supply, toilets, disposable nappies, hygiene requirements for women, bathing and washing soap, toothpaste and toothbrushes, baby food, baby bottles, toilet paper and food.

At this point, there were over 2 000 people sleeping in and around Central Methodist. Many non-governmental organisations provided support and came to the church almost daily with donations. One of these, a Jewish organisation called Habonim Dror, visited the church on 19 May and then compiled a report, calling on its members to donate supplies. "There are currently sixty babies sleeping at the church," the report stated. "The carers are doing a phenomenal job... The kids are in a clean, quiet room and were well tended, but Habonim should be willing to tend to them and give them attention as well... Bishop Verryn and his team need to be lauded for their Herculean efforts. The Jewish community needs to support the church's efforts to provide a safe, clean haven for the refugees."

Given the outpouring of support for the displaced foreign nationals, and given the high levels of poverty and unemployment amongst South Africans, the South African government was reluctant to appear to be favouring foreigners in terms of access to essential services. They did not want the camps, which provided the foreigners with accommodation, food and primary health care, to remain in place for long. By the middle of June over 5 600 people had moved into government established or supported shelters.

Dorothy Qedani Mahlangu, who was in charge of resettlement, wanted resettlement to happen as quickly as possible. Despite this, communication from Mahlangu and the Gauteng provincial government about how long the camps would remain open was not very clear. Initially, Mahlangu had estimated two months at maximum. Her view was that by the end of July there would be no more tents in Gauteng and that those foreign nationals who did not want to be reintegrated into local communities would be repatriated to their respective countries. When the end of July came, however, the camps' site managers were still in the dark as to whether they would remain open into August. In anticipation of a July closure, contracts for security and catering hadn't been renewed but a comprehensive reintegration plan was still not forthcoming from Mahlangu's task team. The Wits Law Clinic and the Consortium for Refugees and Migrants in South Africa (CoRMSA) took a decision to pursue a court order to keep the sites open until such a plan was in place.

According to Amnesty International, by mid-August the numbers of people in Gauteng shelters had declined from 5 600 to 4 340. The Gauteng government set a revised target to close the shelters by the end of August. A group of camp residents and CoRMSA brought an application to the Constitutional Court and an order was handed down on 21 August instructing the government "to engage meaningfully with all relevant stakeholders with a view to reintegrating the victims of xenophobic violence who are entitled to be in South Africa into local communities". The order said that the objective of the engagement would be "to secure the closure of the camps by no later than 30 September 2008".

On 27 August the SA Human Rights Commission and the parliamentary task team hosted a meeting to probe the attacks on non-nationals and discuss the site closures of all of the temporary camps and the reintegration of the displaced people. The meeting was attended by representatives of civil society as well. The minutes noted that "it was a matter of regret that [the Executive] government had not been able to attend and to hear how much support was available to support their work". It was curious that national government seemed to take such little interest in events that had national importance. While the Gauteng provincial government might have been responsible for the temporary camps, it was also having to deal with much broader issues, such as migration and housing, issues which were surely the responsibility of national government. In any event, government's voice was conspicuous by its absence.

Another meeting hosted by the Human Rights Commission in September revealed tensions among different levels of government, as well as within civil society. The minutes of that meeting stated that there was a need for joint leadership on the reintegration process, which required a commitment to finding solutions and exhibiting consensus. There was great concern that public communication projecting conflict could fuel antagonism and undermine reintegration.

Given the growing tension, at the end of that meeting Russell McGregor distanced himself from the record, indicating that he took instructions from two structures: a national committee chaired by the Minister of Safety and Security, Sicelo Shiceka, and a provincial committee chaired by the MEC for Local Government, Dorothy Qedani Mahlangu. He could not commit government to any agreements until he had consulted with his principals. Why government hadn't given this operation a higher priority was puzzling, and why one individual with relatively limited political influence had been left to co-ordinate things between national and provincial governments also seemed bizarre.

In early September Dorothy Qedani Mahlangu praised the country's humanitarian and charitable organisations, calling their efforts and generosity a "good South African response" at a time when "brand South Africa" had been damaged. But Minister Mahlangu remained concerned. While the generosity of all parties was to be acknowledged, she maintained, any excessive response from government could fuel further resentment towards foreigners. This was why she had wanted to see the temporary camps closed as quickly as possible.

Minister Mahlangu remained suspicious of Central Methodist and Paul Verryn. Two years later, I asked her about this. "I don't know how Paul Verryn got those people to settle there," she said. "Why did everyone pass all those other churches and go to Central Methodist? There's something funny there." She had hoped that the church could be closed down, at least in terms of its accommodation function, at the same time as the other temporary camps.

This diffence of opinion was not only about the role of government in a crisis, nor was it only about whether to focus government attention on the needs of foreign nationals or those of local citizens, but it was also a tension between two very different perceptions of the role of a church. Mahlangu, who was a practising Methodist, could not imagine a church being used for the same purpose as a refugee camp. Verryn couldn't imagine turning people away who were in need of emergency shelter.

Four

The Rise and Fall of Central Hall

PAUL VERRYN'S PERSPECTIVE WAS not shaped only by his personal experience. It was also shaped by the history of his church. Central Methodist had been in existence for more than a century and had a history of providing support and refuge to those who were vulnerable and in need. Verryn's initial decision to offer accommodation to the homeless had come more than a decade before the May 2008 xenophobic violence happened, and soon after he took over the leadership of Central Methodist in 1997. The background to that decision was built on a history of providing sanctuary in various ways which went back to the founding of the Central Methodist Church in 1886, the same year that Johannesburg was born. In fact it went even further back, to the idea that an inner-city church exists to serve the people of that city, back to the original concept of a Methodist Central Hall.

In the mid-19th century, in Sydney, Australia, a traditional Methodist church was dying. A young minister named WG Taylor, newly appointed, took one look at the congregation and said, "Inside this church is dead. Outside there are people. I'm going to go where the people are." He began to preach on the street corner outside. A short time later he purchased a vaudeville theatre. According to Reverend Peter Storey, who spent time in Sydney and later became the Superintendent Minister at Central Methodist

Church, Taylor turned the church into a place of worship for very ordinary, "unchurched" people, who didn't feel intimidated going into a vaudeville theatre the way they might have been stepping into a church. That was how, Storey said, "the very first Central Methodist Mission in the world was born. A church deliberately designed to be accessible and welcoming to poor people."

The movement spread from Australia to England, and in every major English city, including Manchester, Birmingham and Bristol, a Methodist Central Hall, not a Methodist church, could be found. These buildings were more like auditoriums than churches, built deliberately without any steps so that people could walk right in at street level. The Westminster Central Hall, across from Westminster Abbey in London, was opened in 1912. It could hold 5 000 people. During the Second World War it became the largest air raid shelter in England, housing hundreds of people every night for the duration of the war.

Half a world away, gold was discovered in the Transvaal and the seeds of Johannesburg and South Africa's only Central Hall were planted. Methodists were amongst the first diggers on the mining camp when Johannesburg was founded in 1886, so the Central Methodist Church of today can date its founding to that of the city itself. Methodist meetings, at first held in the miners' shanties, were possibly the first religious meetings to be held in Johannesburg.

The first minister of the Methodist Church, appointed from Pretoria in April 1887, served his congregants from an oxwagon for six months before he moved on to using temporary shelters. The congregation's first building, the Wesleyan Church Hall, was opened in 1889 and was designed after the great Central Halls of England rather than as a traditional church building. It was built at the corner of President and Kruis streets, only two blocks from the current site of Central Methodist Church.

In addition to the architecture, another aspect of the Methodist Central Halls that migrated from Australia to England to South Africa was their focus on social concerns. When typhoid broke out in Johannesburg in 1890, killing many residents, including 40 Methodists, the church responded by establishing the Deaconess Institute as "the caring arm of… Methodist Central Hall." The Deaconess Society, as it was later called, is one of the oldest welfare organisations in the city and still operates today. The Deaconesses were women who dedicated their time to serving the poor and their social work gave the Central Hall its reputation for service.

By the time the Deaconess Society was formed, the mining camp had grown into a bustling town with shops and hotels and a stock exchange. By 1892 it was linked by rail to Cape Town and by its tenth year, a population of 102 000 made Johannesburg the largest city in Africa south of the Sahara. It was not until 1910 that the Transvaal, Natal, the Orange Free State and the Cape Colony formed the Union of South Africa. However, many aspects of what would later become known as "apartheid" were already in place. Africans had to carry passes, couldn't ride on public transport, and were largely confined to specific areas of residence.

As a result of crowded conditions at the Wesleyan Church Hall, the foundation stone for a larger Central Hall was laid in April 1917 on the corner of Pritchard and Kruis streets. In November 1919 the congregation moved to the new site "just opposite the entrance to the Courthouse", as *The Star* reported, where it remained for close on 50 years. This made the church only one block away from the current building, meaning that Central Methodist has functioned in the same three-block radius for over 125 years.

Reverend Peter Storey described the Central Hall as "a massive auditorium", with nothing "churchy" about its exterior at all. "The miners used to come up from the diggings and come up the dirt roads of Johannesburg singing hymns. Because they were largely Cornishmen and Welshmen, people from mining districts in the UK, there was a strong Methodist presence amongst them. This was a working class church." It is likely that some of the members of the congregation took part in the 1922 white mineworkers' strike. Following the drop in the gold price, companies tried to cut their costs by decreasing wages and enabling black miners to take on roles as supervisors. The strike's slogan was "Workers of the world unite, and fight for a white South Africa".

Reverend William Meara, a loud Irishman and a powerful evangelist, arrived in Johannesburg in 1899 and he led the Central Hall from 1920 through 1934. Reverend Storey describes most Central Halls firstly as putting a strong emphasis on evangelism, and secondly, focusing on "the upliftment and care of the poor". A booklet published by the Johannesburg Central Hall under Meara in 1926, entitled *The Challenge of the City*, shows that again it was the Deaconess Society that brought the church's social concern into practice: "These Sisters are the ever-willing helpers of the poor, irrespective of class or creed… Many stories could be recorded of hope restored to despairing hearts and homes through the help they have been able to render. The biggest and most difficult problems of civilisation are found in the City, as are also the largest opportunity, as well as the greatest responsibilities… The Hall stands for aggressive Christianity along both religious and social lines… Here is to be found a clash of races and creeds and colour, that constitutes a supreme opportunity for the Church of Christ… The tragedy of the black man crying out in this disillusionment for elementary justice, the challenge of wealth and poverty, capital and labour, the salon and the slum."

Make no mistake, the Central Hall in the 1920s was serving a white English congregation, a reality that continued through the 1970s. However, its awareness of and engagement with social issues in the growing city were clear and continued through to the end of the Second World War.

Reverend Storey describes the evolution of Central Hall under Meara as "vigorous preaching and concern to reach people with the Gospel, followed by increased social work that led to an engagement with institutional injustices and power." Part of Reverend Storey's interest in this era is because Storey's was the seventh generation in his family to become a Methodist minister. His father, Clifford K Storey, was converted under William Meara's preaching, and in 1926 was the first person from the new Central Hall to become a candidate for the ministry.

During those years many African labourers lived in municipal compounds or hostels. Others lived in slum yards at the rear of factories, businesses and shops within the inner city. At the same time, affluent white suburbs were developing to the north. By the end of Meara's ministry in 1934 there were close to half a million people living in Johannesburg, with half of those being Africans who were largely employed by the mines or industry and as domestic servants. Most churches, including the Methodist Church, reflected this segregation.

Central Hall was a haven for white servicemen during the Second World War as people in uniform would have to move through Johannesburg in order to go "up North", which meant going to North Africa and on to Italy. It offered these servicemen canteens, clubs and general entertainment, demonstrating its continued commitment to hospitality.

Reverend Joe Webb was the next significant figure in Central Hall's history. He was appointed its Superintendent Minister in 1942 and he served for 22 years. He made Central Hall famous through his national radio broadcasts in the 1940s and '50s. Reverend Mvume Dandala, who succeeded Reverend Storey at Central Methodist in 1991, remembers listening to Webb on the radio as a child. "I was very young," he said. "I immediately associated Central Hall with great preachers." Webb had a speech defect, a stutter, and he had to work hard to correct it. He developed a conversational style of preaching to help him control it, and this worked very well on radio.

Webb embraced the Central Hall philosophy and maintained much of the concept, with its focus on serving the poor in an inner city, until after the Second World War, when he went to the United States and spent some time there. This was at a time, according to Peter Storey, when the First Methodist Churches "were in their absolute heyday", developing an image and philosophy that was moving in a different direction from the Central Hall concept, which, he said, never took root in the US. "There was never an engagement in the same way with the poor in the cities. The city churches tended to become middle class and fairly affluent. Joe Webb was completely taken in by this very different image of a downtown posh church, although perhaps posh is the wrong word." On his return to Johannesburg Webb turned the emphasis very much to one that echoed a First Methodist Church of the United States. The Deaconess Society continued to operate but in a much more limited way. Towards the end of his ministry Webb was no longer seen as a crusader for social issues, Storey said, but rather "as a bastion of conservative white attitudes".

It was also during this post-war period that Hillbrow and the Central Business District (CBD) of Johannesburg grew rapidly. Highrise apartment buildings and tall office blocks flew up, resulting in large numbers of white people flowing into the central shopping area downtown, just blocks from the Central Hall. The CBD became a popular place to work. It was during this period, in the late 1940s, that Reverend Webb began talking about moving from the Central Hall to another building, one that would better fit his new conception of the church and its role in the city.

Reverend Joe Webb's leadership was also shaped by events on the national stage. He led Central Hall from 1942 through to 1965 so he saw the National Party win the 1948 elections and usher in the legislating of apartheid. He had grown up in Potchefstroom, and Storey believed this had given him a deep appreciation of the Afrikaner people. He also believed that this background might have influenced Webb's unwillingness "to take them on face to face. I would say that the Webb years was the period when we ceased to be a Central Hall," Storey said, "and had not yet discovered what it meant to be a Central Methodist Mission. We were a Central Church."

Storey went on to characterise Webb's leadership as one of caution.

Webb insisted quiet diplomacy would be more effective than public denunciations of the Nationalist Party government, which frustrated some of the younger ministers in the Church, of whom Storey was one. Some even felt that Webb's own relationship with people in government was too close during this period of early Nationalist rule. The Methodist Church's public stance was therefore one of silence.

It was around this time that the decision was made to build something that looked a lot more like a church, and so the current Central Methodist Church, with its stained glass windows and thousand-seat sanctuary, opened its doors on the corner of Pritchard and Smal streets in 1965. Central Hall was demolished a year later.

Reverend Stanley Pitts took over as Superintendent Minister in the new church. He was a very formal, high church Methodist and during his term Central Methodist became a more stable, traditional church and it did very little in the way of outreach programmes for the city's poor. Central's congregation was ageing, too, and was far less reflective of the people who now lived and worked in the city. It was a far cry from the warm and welcoming place that the early miners, who had formed the congregation 90 years earlier, had seen grow and flourish around them.

When Reverend Stanley Pitts left Central Methodist, the congregation had no idea what was about to hit them. It was January 1976 and, in more ways than one, their lives were about to change.

Courtesy of Christa Kuljian

Freedom Chivima (second from the left in the back row) and his karate class on 22 July 2012. Elizabeth Cheza, Christa Kuljian and Shephard Zikuyumo are in the front row.

Meetings at Central Methodist / 2010

I often went to Central Methodist for scheduled meetings or interviews, but sometimes I went just to walk around outside, along the Smal Street Mall and Pritchard Street, to check out what was happening. I'd walk by shops like Just for Feet and Street Gear, Kiddies Flair and Mona Lisa Fashions, before turning the corner at the red clock. There were always people sitting on the low wall next to the clock and on the benches in front of the High Court and there was bound to be someone I recognised.

One day in June 2010, I spotted a young man named Divine sitting on one of the benches and I walked over to say hello to him. I had first met Divine when I happened to sit beside him at a Friday night refugee meeting and he had asked me if I had a job for him. I'd said no, but told him that I was working on writing an article about the church and he'd seemed interested. We hadn't talked much since then and I was curious to know his story.

Divine shifted up on his bench to make space for me and we sat together for a few minutes, watching people walk past us and into the entrance of the court. I asked him how old he was and he told me that he was 26. "I came to South Africa for a better life," he said. "My parents died when I was in grade six so I didn't finish school. My brain isn't good at school but I'm good at art." Then he asked if I would bring him some drawing paper and pencils. I said I'd see what I could do. I asked about his name. He told me that his mother had given him the name Divine and that his second name was Love. I couldn't believe it. I had met a homeless man living in a church whose name was Divine Love.

Divine told me that sometimes he would push a heavy trolley for a woman who was working at a market. She would pay him with a plate of food. "I heard the church is going to close the refugee centre at the end of the month," he said. "That will be bad for me." He looked at me. "Is it true?" he asked.

"I don't think so," I said. "I haven't heard that, but I don't know for sure."

I told Divine that I was going to walk towards Von Brandis Street and he asked if he could walk with me. "Sure," I said, but once we reached the corner, he changed his mind and turned back. "Don't forget to bring me something for my art," he called out.

A few minutes after Divine and I had parted, I met Esther Thomas1 for the first time. Esther was sitting on a piece of cardboard on the pavement, selling spools of cotton wool, packets of cockroach powder, earrings and sweets. She was a short, compact woman and had on a dark skirt and a head scarf. I stood and talked to her for a while, and then sat down beside her on the cardboard, something I would do regularly in the months to come. Weeks later, after we had gotten to know each other a bit more, she said to me, "You can write about me, but only if you change my name. If someone in Zim reads about me, I'll be in soup."

Esther had moved into Central Methodist Church in August 2009 where she slept on the floor outside the sanctuary every night. Born in 1970, she lived most of her adult life in Gweru, a large town north-west of Bulawayo on the road to Harare. She worked for many years importing goods from Botswana to sell in Zimbabwe but as the economy worsened, she was unable to continue because "no one was buying". She supported her three children, aged 17, 12 and 7, as well as the two children of her younger sister who had passed away. Her dream was to build a house, but "now there's no dream," she said. Things were so bad in Zimbabwe she was forced to travel to South Africa to look for some way to bring in an income.

"You need foreign currency to buy anything in Zimbabwe," she told me. "How do they expect us to get foreign currency? You have to leave. Now I buy clothes at the Salvation Army and send them home."

"What are your plans for the next few months?" I asked.

"You can only have plans if you have money," she said. "I have no money so I have no plans. When the police need money, they come to us." Alongside the SAPS, private security companies were employed to patrol the area, one of which was Top Ten Bravo. The name was emblazoned on the back of their guards' T-shirts. "These guys, they bribe us," Esther said. "They want to get paid."

---

1 not her real name

Across from Esther's spot was a man who had a pile of remote control handsets for sale set out on a blanket, and further down on the same side of the street, there was a man selling CDs. We watched two men walk by. They were wearing Top Ten Bravo T-shirts and they looked like body builders. They stopped in front of the man selling CDs and stood there for five to ten minutes, pushing him for R15. "If they don't get the money, they take your stock," Esther said. "You see that woman with the green jersey, green pants and the green high top boots? She is the notorious one. She is the supervisor. She teaches the others to bribe."

I hoped the security guards wouldn't come for Esther. She didn't have much to confiscate, but she relied on it for a small income to buy supper. Under the red clock, women were selling *vetkoek* out of large plastic tubs. Sometimes Esther would buy a late lunch there, she told me, when she was finished selling for the day. Sometimes she would wait until evening and buy a plate of *pap* in the foyer of the church instead.

Later that night, on the same day I saw Divine and met Esther, Bishop Verryn spoke to the Friday refugee meeting about hanging around on the street. "There is a part of me that agrees with the people in this area who are unhappy about everyone sitting on the street," he said, "especially if you are sitting there doing God knows what. Don't waste your life sitting on a court bench in the sun. You must be working and trying to educate yourself. This place is meant to be a stepping stone."

One person who had heeded the Bishop's words was Freedom Chivima. He had found himself a plumbing job, and had moved out of the church in 2009 when his wife, Lakidzani Ndlovu, and his four-year old daughter Tshepang came to join him in Johannesburg. He found accommodation in another building further down Pritchard Street but Tshepang continued to attend FLOC at Central Methodist and he continued to teach his karate classes there. Freedom said, "This is my family. I'm attached to the church. If I don't come here for a day or two, I don't feel good."

I arranged with Freedom to attend a karate class one day. He used to teach classes at 4pm to cater for most of his students who were at the Albert Street School. However, things had shifted and now he was offering classes at night and his students were mostly adults. We agreed I would attend a class one Wednesday after the evening service.

I had never taken a karate class in my life but I thought it would be a chance to meet some of the others in the class and more informally get to know some of the church residents. Elizabeth Cheza had taken classes before and she agreed to join me that evening. I was very relieved. At least I wouldn't be the only woman in the group. Including Freedom, Elizabeth and me, there were nine people in the class. Freedom himself and several others wore white karate outfits, some with a blue or an orange belt. The rest of us wore T-shirts and gym pants or jeans. No fancy facilities in the Roberts Room, but the basics were all we needed. Push-ups to begin with, then line up and kick and kick and kick. We counted in unison in Japanese, *"Ichi, ni, san, shi, go,"* as we punched the air with our fists and gripped the wooden parquet floor with our bare feet.

I got back onto more familiar ground when I had a short interview with Freedom at the end of class. I asked him to take me back to events at the church that had happened in 2008 and 2009. Afterwards Elizabeth and I made an arrangement to meet again at the church the next day. I was curious to learn about what had brought her to this place.

Five

Reverend Peter Storey and the Apartheid City

FOUR GREY-HAIRED WHITE MEN sat behind a table in an office boardroom preparing to interview their next candidate. They had been trying to find a successor to Reverend Stanley Pitts, who was leaving the Central Methodist Church in downtown Johannesburg. They had hoped to bring in Alex Boraine, but Boraine had decided to enter politics in 1974 and was no longer a candidate. They wanted to find someone dynamic, someone who could lead the premier pulpit of the Methodist Church in South Africa.

Into the room walked Peter Storey. In his early forties, he was tall and slender and had a strong presence about him. They knew Storey had been influenced by his father, a strong justice advocate in the Church. They knew that he had had an unusual history in the ministry since he had been ordained fourteen years before. His first appointment was with two small churches in Cape Town, in Camps Bay and Milnerton, with a post as a part-time chaplain on Robben Island. He had in fact been on the island when Nelson Mandela was brought there.

They knew that Storey had spent two years in Sydney, Australia under the tutelage of Reverend Alan Walker, who now led the dynamic and famous Central Methodist Mission there with its major focus on the needs of the city. They knew that Storey and others had invited Walker to South Africa in 1963 and that the visit had been controversial because of Walker's head-on confrontation with apartheid and his outspoken opposition to the racist "white Australia" policy and treatment of Aborigines.

As Storey sat down across from them they knew that he came back from Australia to work for five years in District Six, a multi-racial community in Cape Town that had been decimated by apartheid and the Group Areas Act. He had worked there as the forced removals were peaking. Storey once said, "Preaching to eight hundred people each Sunday, all of whom have a date in their calendar when their homes are going to be destroyed, that's tough." He also said, "I don't know how to thank God for those five years. It brought me into existential engagement with poverty and oppression. To the degree that a white person could, I was able to feel the pain."

For the past few years in Johannesburg, Storey had been based on the outskirts of the city, building the Civic Centre Methodist Church in Braamfontein, and during this period he had also founded the Methodist newspaper, *Dimension.*

The interview panel listened attentively to the conditions under which Storey told them he would consider a move down the hill from Braamfontein to central Johannesburg. "The first thing I will want to do," he said, "is integrate the congregation. If you're unhappy with that, you shouldn't invite me." There was more. "The second thing I will do," said Storey, "is turn the congregation around, away from itself to face the city. That will mean profound changes to what is important in the life of the church." He paused, and the panel indicated that he should continue. "The third thing I would do is use the pulpit as a platform for engaging the issues in our land today. You must know that will not always be comfortable."

There was silence as the four men allowed Storey's words to sink in. Then they told him they would get back to him within a week.

"I really take my hat off to those four old men because they had never heard anything like that in their lives," Storey told me 35 years later. "I think they knew that something had to happen because of the demographic changes in Johannesburg. They couldn't guarantee that people were going to continue driving into the city from the suburbs to hear the choir and the preacher. That arrangement was beginning to fray at the edges. They realised something needed to happen but I don't think they had heard it in such stark terms before. Anyway, they came back to me and said, Yes."

When Peter Storey arrived at Central Methodist in 1976 he inherited a very conservative congregation. Not many of its members had any memory of the Central Hall tradition that had held during the first half of the century, although a large number of them were ex-servicemen who had served in the Second World War, and their spouses and families. "Good folk," Storey described them, "folk who believed in fairness. Folk who'd never ever engaged the issue of race seriously. They were people who had the Jan Smuts political philosophy. They were largely very typical of the racial attitudes of English-speaking South Africans at the time."

As Storey put it, Central had become a suburban church in the wrong place. All its priorities were suburban and it had no engagement whatsoever with the needs of the city. Most of the people who worked or shopped in downtown Johannesburg came into the city on a Monday and left on a Friday. Central Methodist opened its doors on a Sunday, the only time when the city was empty. It was irrelevant to the city.

"Even the architecture was irrelevant to the city," Storey recalled. "The walls of Central were stone façades. When people walked past the building, they picked up their pace because there was nothing to look at, no shop windows, so they walked on until they got to a more interesting spot. The doors were solid wood – forbidding wooden doors."

In the 1970s central Johannesburg was changing and becoming more decentralised. By the time Reverend Storey arrived at Central city government offices had left the CBD for Braamfontein, and the South African Broadcasting Corporation had moved to Auckland Park to the west of the city. It was also the time of the rapid development of the suburban shopping mall. These malls sprang up one after another in the suburbs of Johannesburg to cater for white suburban customers, and some businesses were also beginning to move their head offices from downtown out to the suburbs as well.

Storey's challenge for the church was how best to engage the city in ways that would make it relevant and meaningful. His goal was for Central Methodist to become "a centre of togetherness, of community, in a lonely city. To become a centre of peace in a violent city. To become a centre of care in a callous city. To become a centre of justice in a very unjust city. These were the things that concerned us."

Storey was determined that the church would once again play the role it was meant to play. He had a steep road ahead.

He began his ministry with one minister and one assistant. "That was it," he said. Soon after he arrived at Central he hired the church's first black employee. Her name was Lindiwe Myeza and he appointed her as a community worker. Myeza had worked for sixteen years at the Christian Institute with Beyers Naude, the outspoken Afrikaner cleric and critic of apartheid. When the Insitute was banned, Myeza was worried that she would never get another job. "I was contaminated," she said. "My reference book has Beyers' signature. No one was going to employ me." Her colleague at the Institute, Reverend Brian Brown, was also left without employment. It was his suggestion that the two of them approach Storey at Central Methodist. "I'll wash the dishes," Brown said. "I'll scrub the floor," Myezi responded. As it happened Peter Storey employed them both.

As a community worker it was Lindi Myeza who started offering assistance to homeless people who arrived at the church in need of food and clothing. At the time, most destitute people in the city were white. "I'm sorry," said Ma Lindi Myeza, "but this is not right. I can't be dishing food and clothes to people who have a vote when I don't have a vote. Why don't we start counselling sessions and find out why they are in this situation? They have no business to be hungry and homeless." And so counselling sessions began at Central Methodist, and even though Myeza was not a trained counsellor, she quickly developed the skills. She had in fact trained and worked first as a teacher, then as an administrator at Baragwanath Nursing College, and she had also acquired some experience working with youth at the YWCA.

The church bought a house in Hillbrow, not far from the police station there, and this was where Myeza mostly saw the hundreds of desolate people who sought the church's help. "At least they could wash and have food there," she said. "Some would disappear for a long time and then come back. They would say, 'I got a job, but then my job finished. Now I'm back on the street and back to you.'"

During those early years, Storey was concerned about how to attract and encourage black people into what was ostensibly an all-white church. The city might have been changing but his congregation was not, despite his constant encouragement about everyone being welcome. Lindi Myeza was not only the first black employee at Central, she was also the first black member of the congregation. "I would get into church and the whole choir was white and the whole church was full of white people," she told me years later. "I was the only single black among this sea of whites. Come Holy Communion, I wasn't sure whether I should go forward or not, so I just sat there. I wondered what the whites would say. But one day I just got mad and went to Communion. The heavens didn't fall and there was no negative response."

It would be a good few years, 1981 in fact, before Storey could report that Central was truly a multi-racial congregation, with the baptising and receiving of their first black members, other than Myezi herself, although there were increasing numbers of black people attending services.

One of the first sermons Reverend Storey preached to an audience with a significant number of black people in it happened to be on 13 June 1976. He had been asked to conduct a service for about 60 staff of the South African Council of Churches which was under increasing surveillance and pressure from state security because of its opposition to apartheid's education policies.

On that day, he preached: "Your commitment to this struggle has brought unpopularity. You have suffered public smears by the South African Broadcasting Corporation and private persecution by the security police. Please know today that your stand has also brought the everlasting gratitude of countless 'little people' in this land who thank God for your caring… Racism is a disease of the heart; it is rooted in the fear that casts out love."

The white congregation wasn't too sure how they felt about this sermon.

In the sanctuary at that service was Winnie Mandela, Storey remembered. "I had no idea she was coming. She didn't publicise her movements in those days so as not to draw too much attention from the police."

Winnie Mandela was a life-long Methodist. She had been baptised in the Methodist Church and she and Nelson had been married in the Methodist Church in 1958 in her home village of Bizana in the Eastern Cape.

"It was the first time this bunch of whites had a significant body of black people sitting there," Storey chuckled. "The idea of Winnie Mandela coming into the church, the wife of the 'terrorist', was beyond most of my congregation, so a whole lot of them were pretty outraged."

Neither Storey nor his congregation could know that just three days later the political landscape of South Africa would change forever. On Wednesday, June 16, thousands of students in Soweto marched to protest at having to be taught in Afrikaans. Their protest was met with live ammunition from the police and the country erupted into violence. In the weeks that followed, it is estimated that over 500 people died.

The following Sunday Storey preached to a half-empty church. Some of the members hadn't shown up because they had been angered by the presence of black people in the church the week before, and with the content of the sermon. Others didn't show up because they were afraid. They stayed home in the wake of the violence, not wanting to venture into central Joburg.

This did not hold Peter Storey back, however. He was delivering on the promise he had made to the panel that had appointed him. "Last week I said that we had a choice between creating a real peace for all, based on facing the truth – or having people rise up against the violence that is breaking them. Some of you protested that those words were too dramatic. Now, we see, God help us, that they were not strong enough."

He went on to tell a story of the wife of one of the Church's ministers in Soweto that week who, even though she was surrounded by an angry crowd, had given refuge in her home to a white Afrikaner social worker who had been trapped in the midst of the violence. "She saved that woman's life at risk of her own," he said. "Hers was an act of courageous love and, given the role of Afrikaans in all of this strife, also an act of magnanimous grace. She incarnated our conviction that in Christ the dividing wall cannot stand."

In the days that followed, Lindi Myeza assisted many young people in Soweto, where she lived, and visited more than 300 people who had been affected by the violence, helping to arrange funerals and get coffins organized. She also helped hide Tsietsi Mashinini, one of the famous youth leaders in Soweto, and she did a lot of work with Tsietsi's brother Mokiti. "I used to hide Tsietsi in this house," she recalled, smiling slightly, when I went to see her at home. "I'd tell him to put on an apron and a *doek*. Make him sweep the yard. So when the police come, they will look for him and they will not see him."

Myeza and Central Methodist assisted over a hundred teenagers from Soweto who were not able to attend school while there was so much turbulence in the township. Myeza arranged for them to be taken into the homes of congregants and then to come in to the church each day for lessons and activities until it was safe enough for them to return home. She played a crucial role, a role for which she was voted "Unsung Heroine of the Year" by the readers of *The Star* newspaper in 1976.

Myeza continued to help young people in jail. "Even girls had been detained," she said. She would visit them and take them toiletries, items that people had collected for them. "Their parents wouldn't come anywhere near them," she said. "Their parents were afraid."

In all of this Myeza had Peter Storey's full support. Storey himself, along with several other church ministers, was arrested in 1978 for being part of a march to John Vorster Square protesting the arrest of a Congregational Church leader, and he was held for one night by the police. His conservative white congregation was dismayed. "They were concerned along the lines of, 'What if my mother had died while you were sitting in prison playing politics?'" Storey recalled. "'Who would have been at her bedside? How dare you get involved with things like that when you're a minister?'"

Another step towards turning the church towards the city came in the form of something quite different – the opening of a non-racial restaurant inside the church. Reverend Storey had been inspired by a similar idea he had seen at the Central Methodist Mission in Sydney, and Lindi Myeza's personal experience helped put the idea into action. The story begins when Myeza tried to find a place to eat lunch in 1970s Johannesburg, without much luck. Up the street from Central Methodist Church, in a big shopping centre on the corner of Pritchard and Eloff streets, there was a restaurant in the OK Bazaars but black people were not allowed to eat there. "I decided not to rely on hearsay and to see if it would happen to me," recalls Myeza. "I went upstairs, click, click, click, click with my heels. I just played dumb. You take your plate and go and dish. One black woman there said, 'Mama, you know, you are not allowed to eat.' I said 'Why?' 'No, no, no, it's for whites only.' So I said, 'If you say so, I'm also white.' So I dished my food, dished my food, thinking, What if they toss me out, how am I going to react? I think that woman told a manager. He said, 'Mama, you know, we are trying to make sure that we don't create trouble.' 'What trouble?' I said. 'Blacks are not allowed,' he said. 'Why are they not allowed?' 'Well, it's how it happens here.' 'Am I going to be allowed?' I asked. 'No, no, no, mama, the best thing, because now you've dished your food, let me help you go and sit at the corner.' 'In that case then,' I said, 'take your food,' and I gave him the plate. 'But you've dished,' he said. 'No, I don't want it anymore,' I said and I walked out."

She tried another restaurant, this time the one at John Orr's, another department store. "Click, click, click with my heels, I went upstairs with the lift. The cafeteria was filled with white people. I thought, Oh my God, this is what's happening in South Africa. Just when I got off the lift, the guy says, 'No, no, no, no, you're not allowed to come here.' 'We buy the same things downstairs,' I pointed out to him. 'Why can't we buy the same food?' 'It's the law,' he said. 'Whose law?' 'It's the law of the shop.' 'Who has put that law in place? I want to see it written.' 'No, please, please, I beg you. I might lose my job.' 'OK, if you're going to lose your job, let me go,' I said, and I left."

Myeza repeated the exercise in restaurants all over town – in Ellerines, the furniture store, at the Carlton Centre, and at coffee shops. Everywhere she went someone would ask, "*Wat soek jy hierso?* What do you want here?"

"In those days," said Myeza, "next door to Central Methodist there was a big hotel, Tollman Towers. It was a very prestigious hotel before they pulled it down and built the Johannesburg Sun. They wanted to know am I an American. So I said with a broad American accent, 'Yes, I am an Am-er-i-can. I'm from America.' Then someone said, '*Ai* man, this woman works next door,' and I was shown the door again."

Myeza decided if she couldn't have lunch in a restaurant, she'd try to eat lunch in a park. Opposite the Tollman Towers was Von Brandis Park, which is now the Smal Street Mall. Even in the park, black people were not allowed to sit and eat. They would have to go outside the park and sit on the street. "I got into the park," Myezi said, relishing the story in hindsight. "Sat down. Opened up my fish and chips packet. There were quite a number of tramps in the park. There comes a policeman. 'No, no, no, no, you are not allowed to sit and eat here.' 'But what about those guys?' I say. 'Can't you see they are white?' the policeman shouts. 'Can't you see that I'm black?' I said. 'Mama, please. Let us not cause trouble.' 'What trouble?' I say. 'The homeless people who come to me for food at the church, they can sit here, but I can't.'"

Myeza shared her experience with a leaders' meeting at Central Methodist. It confirmed for Peter Storey that there was a need for an open restaurant at the church. The large basement was not being used for anything at the time and so plans started moving forward to utilise the space and open a restaurant there. They would call it the People Centre.

The congregation was hesitant about the idea but despite their reservations and misgivings the People Centre opened in April 1978. One of the members of the congregation, Joan Rudolph, agreed to manage the place.

"The beauty of it," recalls Storey, "is that a lawyer could come from the Supreme Court and have lunch with clients of different races with ease, and at the same time a black street cleaner could come and order a very basic cup of soup. And both would be waited upon by one of our grey-haired white ladies."

In those days only those hotels in South Africa which were registered as international had permission to entertain black and Asian clients in their restaurants and the People Centre was the first truly multi-racial restaurant in Johannesburg. Even then, this was only because Central Methodist obtained a health certificate registering the church as a place where food was prepared. A health certificate was easier to get, Storey said, and they could obtain it without having to go to the other authorities. This didn't stop the authorities trying to close the People Centre down, however, but they didn't succeed. "Whenever the law came to try to intimidate us into closing the place, we just said, 'This is where we entertain our church people and some of our church people are black' and that was how we got away with it," said Storey. By 1981 the People Centre was serving more than 56 000 meals each year, which was over 200 meals a day.

"I remember an old white guy," Peter Storey told me, "with a very colourful vocabulary, who lived in a block of flats nearby. He started camping out at the People Centre. After a while, he made himself the unofficial, honorary welcomer at the door. A couple from New Zealand arrived one day. He was white and she was Maori. They couldn't find anywhere to sleep. None of the hotels would take them in so they came into the church. This old guy at the door said, 'You can stay with me.' Here was this white guy offering hospitality to a woman of colour and her white husband. I don't think he could have dreamt of seeing himself in that role three or four years before."

Storey saw the People Centre as the key to resurrecting the old spirit of Methodist hospitality. "The People Centre gave Central Church back to Johannesburg," he said. "It was the underground subversive integration of Central Church. Literally under ground."

Six

Offering Political Refuge at Central

DURING REVEREND STOREY'S leadership, about 200 white congregants, out of about 900, left the church, some because of his efforts at integration, others because of the content of his preaching.

"One day, the entire choir walked out." Storey smiled at the memory. "They had decided beforehand, if Storey mentions anything political, we're out of here. I didn't know what was happening behind me. The entire choir stood up. I could see my congregation waking up. I couldn't work out whether it was what I was saying or something else. To get out of the choir gallery and into the vestry, you have to do a sharp turn. God dealt with this whole issue because as this one guy turned to go around, his gown caught on the bannister and he was pulled backwards, and he bumped into the person behind him, who fell backwards into the person behind *him*. So there was this chaos. The congregation burst into laughter because there was this Keystone Cops thing going on behind me."

In the late 1970s and especially the 1980s, in addition to integration and the content of the sermons, there was a third reason that members of the congregation left the church. Central Methodist Church became a sanctuary for political organisations, for political meetings and for protest, and for many this was going too far. The church held a memorial service after Steve

Biko's death and a special service after the murder of Anton Lebowski, a political activist from Namibia. In an open letter in 1986, Reverend Storey wrote: "In apartheid South Africa, the Central Methodist Mission pulpit has been a voice for justice and reconciliation, and our sanctuary has been the venue for the great protest events over these tumultuous years. It was here that Mrs Winnie Mandela worshipped for the last time before she was banned, and here that Bishop Desmond Tutu was welcomed back after receiving the Nobel Peace Prize. It was here that black trade unions found the first venue for meeting, and here that the parents and family of detainees met for counselling and care."

In 1984 Storey was elected Bishop and leader of the Methodist Church of Southern Africa. At that time the position (now known as Presiding Bishop) was held in conjunction with one's parish duties so Storey remained at Central Methodist. He also became the Bishop of the District, which gave him oversight over many parishes in the Transvaal, one of South Africa's four provinces at the time.

In 1985 the name of Central Methodist Church was changed officially to Central Methodist Mission (CMM), reflecting Storey's outward focused vision. This shift from CMC to CMM indicated perhaps more strongly than anything else the move from a suburban mentality to an identification with the city, and from a white community to an inclusive community. In 1986 Central Methodist celebrated its 100th birthday along with the City of Johannesburg. At the time Bishop Storey said, "There is a sense in which the Central Methodist Mission enters its second century in not too different a position from that faced by our forebears at the very beginning – a frontier church in a rapidly changing situation."

In the 1980s Central Methodist offered office space in the building to a number of organisations. The Detainees' Parents Support Committee (DPSC) opened offices on the fourth floor, as did the End Conscription Campaign (ECC) – although the latter was called the Conscription Advice Bureau because it was illegal to promote conscientious objection.

The Action Committee to Stop Eviction (Actstop) also ran its operation out of the church. Actstop assisted tenants who were being evicted from apartment blocks in the inner city. It had been formed in 1978, mainly by Indian and coloured people who were being evicted from "white" areas under the Group Areas Act at that time. There was very little accommodation available in the townships set aside for Indian and coloured people so they looked to the city centre for a solution. This was the time, too, after the upheavals of 1976, when white people were beginning to leave the country, while others were moving from the city out to the suburbs. This resulted in numerous empty units in apartment blocks in places like Hillbrow, Joubert Park, Berea and the "inner city", as downtown Joburg came to be known. Some landlords turned a blind eye to the Group Areas Act because they wanted to rent their premises.

Evictions under the Group Areas Act continued. Actstop contested approximately 200 cases in court between 1978 and 1982. In 1983 the famous "Govender judgment" was handed down by Justice Goldstone, whereby the state was precluded from evicting people without providing alternative accommodation for them. This judgment was a watershed in Group Area legislation and resulted in the end of state evictions for a period of time. Actstop's success in halting evictions also contributed to its temporary demise but the organisation was revived in May 1987 when the pressure to evict black people from white areas in the city recurred. It remained active through 1990, when approximately 100 000 black people were living in the inner city and many landlords were demanding exorbitant rentals, but were not maintaining the buildings. Actstop worked with elected tenant committees in 76 buildings in the area to address issues of poor living conditions, including problems with lifts, electricity, plumbing and security. There were also problems of overcrowding, intimidation from landlords and harassment from the police. Ironically, 20 years later, in 2010, when Actstop had long since closed its doors, evictions in post-apartheid Johannesburg were still an ongoing concern. That was when Central Methodist established Peace Action, part of whose mission was to monitor evictions in the inner city.

In the early 1980s Lindi Myeza worked with Mohammed Dangor of Actstop to assist people who were being evicted from their homes in Fietas, just west of the city centre. The area had been declared a white area under the Group Areas Act so people who were classified as Asian or coloured or African had to be removed. Myeza remembers sleeping out on the street in solidarity with some of these people who had been evicted from their homes, and how Mohammed Dangor used to tease her, saying, "Lindi tells people that she slept with me in the street".

There were about 20 elderly people amongst the group Myeza was with, and she felt that they were too old and frail to be out in the open at night so she took it upon herself to let them sleep at Central Methodist. They slept in the Roberts Room, the first floor lounge and the chapel, and were there for some months. "They would come at night," said Myeza, "and during the day, they would go." She didn't tell anyone, not even Reverend Storey.

Given Central Methodist's outward focus, in the late 1970s and throughout the 1980s the church sent people out to the residential apartment buildings to visit the people who were living in the flats in the area around the church. There were over 100 such buildings occupied by black tenants within a six-block radius of the church and the numbers were growing. In 1981 the church visited 900 residents of flats in the city and its outreach teams encountered overcrowding, lack of electricity and passages flooded with sewage wherever they went. Of the 754 apartments visited in 1986, over 400 apartments had children living there with nowhere to go after school. This resulted in the recognition that there was a need for a pre-school and child care facilities in the city, and in June 1989 Central Methodist opened a day care centre, For the Love of Children, or FLOC. Initially, FLOC operated in another building on Pritchard Street, but then moved to Central Methodist Mission, where it continues to operate to this day.

Lay pastor David Ching was the man who led a team of fifteen people who continued the church's outreach work. He was also the caretaker at the church building and lived in the fourth floor apartment on the premises so he interacted with residents in the area on a daily basis. Ching observed that most of the residents around Central Methodist had a "refugee mentality", and he described them as "illegals" in terms of the Group Areas Act. He said they were exploited by landlords who assumed they would not complain for fear of being arrested.

Another result of Central Methodist's outreach work was engagement with the growing number of homeless people living on the street. Paballo Ya Batho (Caring for the People), a Central Methodist outreach programme, began operating in 1988 in co-operation with other churches in the area. At first, volunteers went out into the street to hand out soup and bread. Then it expanded its services to include blankets and clothing, medical care, counselling and advocacy support. Paballo Ya Batho also continues to operate today and volunteers depart from the church on Pritchard Street every Wednesday night.

Throughout the 1980s Central Methodist struggled financially to maintain its expensive building as well as its programmes and outreach efforts. In 1981 Storey reported that the Central Circuit, a group of five churches in the city, including Central Methodist, had a membership of

1 200 people. The fact that these members, many of whom were in the lower income bracket, were giving an average of R26 per month from their pockets was an indication of their commitment. All the same, this totalled only R374 400 per year for five churches, which was not a great deal.

A city church could not rely solely on funds from its congregation. Central Methodist's property was restructured to include three storefront shops in the Smal Street Mall for rent, and then, in 1984, during the construction of the Johannesburg Sun hotel next door, the developers offered to buy what was called the bulk or "air space" and transfer it to the hotel. They bought this space from the church for R325 000 and, as part of the deal, provided free parking for the staff and free Sunday parking in perpetuity for the congregation. When the Finance Secretary Ken Roberts co-ordinated the final payment of the church's debt, from its initial construction, in 1987, Central Methodist named the Roberts Room after him in gratitude.

While it certainly wasn't a money spinner, Central Methodist was given a block of flats in the city in 1981. It was around this time that the Sectional Title Act was passed, which allowed landlords to sell off flats as single units, a windfall for them, and some of them were ruthless in intimidating tenants into leaving so that they could sell individual apartments. If they were unsuccessful, they used the tactic of no longer maintaining the buildings. Peter Storey was vocal in the media about this state of affairs. "I made a song and dance about it in the press and on radio and I got a call from somebody who basically said 'I'm one of the people you've been bad mouthing. I own a block of flats and it's not as easy as you think. You can have my block of flats. Let's see if you can make a go of it.'"

Cornerstone House, with its 56 flats, was directly opposite Khotso House, the home of the South African Council of Churches. Storey wanted to show that a block of flats in the city centre could become a community where people cared for each other. Most of the tenants were elderly or on disability pensions but, Storey recalled years later with a twinkle in his eye, "I also owned a brothel for a period of time because one of the flats was being used for nefarious purposes".

By the late 1980s the increasing numbers of black people living in the city combined with the church's outreach to the surrounding apartments resulted in an increasing number of black people worshipping at Central. Given the falling numbers of whites coming through from the suburbs, Reverend Storey was pleased that this had resulted in Central Methodist becoming markedly non-racial. More significant changes were to come for the structure of the Methodist church, especially in terms of trying to redress its historic racism. In 1958 the Methodist Church had announced that it should be "one and undivided", but the Church had struggled to achieve this in practice. Most Methodists continued to worship in racially segregated congregations, or societies as they were called in the Church. There were three different societies at Central Methodist – an 8am, a 10am and a 7pm society. Each attracted a different mix of people. A group of societies together form a circuit. The Central Circuit was made up of the societies at Central Methodist as well as several other societies from adjoining areas such as Braamfontein, Bertrams and Victoria. In 1987 the Methodist Church of Southern Africa decided that circuits should be organised geographically instead of racially, as they had been in the past. What this meant for Central Methodist was that it was joined by black societies from other churches around Johannesburg – Crown Mines, Ophirton, Albert Street, and Cleveland. Ironically, to Reverend Storey this meant a setback for his efforts to build a "non-racial" image, but it did offer the opportunity for the different societies to work together and integrate in the future. In 1975 Ernest Baartman initiated the Black Methodist Conference (BMC) in order to improve the situation of black Methodists who were often excluded from decision making and in response to the white dominance and arrogance that continued in the Methodist Church. With its focus on promoting black leadership within the Church, the BMC continued its work through to the end of apartheid and continues its work to this day.

One day during a transport strike about 2 500 railway workers arrived at the church for a meeting. Their meeting elsewhere had been banned so Central Methodist had offered them the use of the church. Most of the men carried knobkierries. "You can come in here," said Reverend Storey, "but I will not have weapons in this church." He stood at the door, watching the men pile up the knobkierries in the foyer until there was a mountain of them, and wondering how on earth each man would claim his own knobkierrie afterwards. About 1 500 men gathered in the sanctuary, there were another 500 in the foyer, and another 500 in the hall in the basement. They were all singing. "And there was dear old Joan trying to run the People Centre," remembered Storey. Times were certainly changing.

Along with many other organisations and institutions in the rest of South Africa, Central Methodist was under assault from the apartheid state's security apparatus. There were numerous ways in which harassment affected the church. One of these was that the security police would regularly interfere with meetings that were held there. Murphy Morobe of the United Democratic Front said that Central Methodist was always willing to avail its facilities at short notice for a meeting. Police used to position themselves outside the building waiting for people to emerge from UDF meetings, SACC meetings and union meetings. David Newby, a minister at Central Methodist in the 1980s, recalled years afterwards that they had been particularly aggressive when Central Methodist hosted a gathering to mark the tenth anniversary of the Soweto uprising in June 1986 and threatened to arrest everyone who attended. When the press recorded a meeting or event, they would often surreptitiously hand the video cassette of their footage to Newby and replace it in the camera with a blank one so that the police wouldn't be able to confiscate their footage on the way out. There were other times when Newby would hide cassettes and documents behind the organ pipes in the sanctuary.

Central regularly received bomb threats. An unattended suitcase lying on the stairway would result in evacuating the building and calling the bomb squad. One day a white man walked into the building and placed a heavy-looking parcel wrapped in a brown paper bag next to the lift on the ground floor. At the time David Newby was holding a Bible study meeting with a group of women in Minor Hall in the basement. When he was told what was going on, he asked them to stay where they were while he went to investigate. Just as the bomb squad arrived, he saw the group of elderly women approaching. "We decided we would move to the chapel", one of them told Newby with a big smile as they all trooped slowly past the large object wrapped in brown paper, causing Newby's heart to drop. Fortunately, the "bomb" turned out to be rolled up sheeting, the threat a hoax.

Bomb scares eventually became routine. Someone would call the third floor office saying there was a bomb in the building. A member of staff would call the police to report the threat and then go around to alert people who were in meetings, and finally make an announcement at the People Centre. After a while people ignored them, said Newby, and simply went about their business.

There was an escape route from the window of one of the minister's offices on the third floor that people could use if the security police were after them. "I remember Andrew Boraine using that once," said Newby. "You could climb over the roof of the sanctuary, jump down onto the running track at the Johannesburg Sun next door, and escape through the hotel from there."

Even though hindsight gives these moments a lightness, these were tense times. Newby recalled that Reverend Storey could be quick to anger if he wasn't happy with someone's actions and, although he was a great crusader for human rights and justice, he was often autocratic. "He didn't have time to be consultative," Newby said. "It was his way or the highway." But Newby also recalled that Storey was humble enough to walk around the church at 10 o'clock at night with a step-ladder, changing lightbulbs.

In the early hours of the morning of 16 June 1988 someone painted graffiti on Central Methodist's outside wall, protesting against the DPSC and ECC whose offices were housed in the church. The church believed that it was the work of the security police. As Bishop Storey said at the time, "They wanted to smear us and some of the organisations we have sheltered and accommodated. They hoped to make it look as if some of these organisations would defile a house of God." David Ching wrote in the church newsletter, "We all feel very indignant about what has been done to God's house, but do we get as angry when one of our people is evicted from their flat?"

Storey responded by writing, "He's right, of course. We're angry about our building because we care very deeply for this sanctuary. Jesus also grew very angry when the House of God was cheapened, but His strongest anger was reserved for those who exploited people. He cared even more about that."

For many years Central Methodist Mission had provided a regular live national radio broadcast through the SABC and these broadcasts enjoyed a strong listenership. In 1988 Storey incorporated reference in one of his radio sermons to the church's amnesty candle, a candle with barbed wire around it, and a prayer for the victims of apartheid. In the middle of another sermon, one that included a Bible study on racism, Storey saw the little red light in the SABC studio suddenly go off. The public broadcaster had unceremoniously cut him off the air in an effort to frustrate Central Methodist's message. Two years later, after Nelson Mandela was released, Central Methodist was invited back on air. Storey enjoyed opening the service by saying, "As I was saying before we were so rudely interrupted…"

The assault from the security police hit fever pitch when Khotso House, the home of the South African Council of Churches in Johannesburg in De Villiers Street, was bombed on 31 August 1988. When the SACC staff arrived at work that morning after the explosion, they were redirected to Central Methodist. The headline in *What a Family!*, the newsletter of the Central Methodist Mission, read "Refugees at Central". Central Methodist took in the 100 staff members of the SACC after the bombing and gave them emergency offices and facilities. The newsletter report read: "Who would have thought that CMM would one day be a shelter for 100 Christians displaced from their 'home' by a bomb blast?" For some time, most of Central Methodist's halls were occupied by various SACC departments trying to reorganise themselves and continue their work. This scene would replay itself 20 years later, but this time the halls and rooms of the church building would be occupied by a different kind of refugee.

Reverend Paul Verryn was one of the SACC staff members who relocated to Central after the bombing of Khotso House. While he was stationed in Orlando West in Soweto at the time, he also worked for, and kept an office at, the SACC.

On the night that the bomb went off at Khotso House Verryn was on a late night flight from Cape Town to Johannesburg. He had left his car in the Khotso House basement and someone had given him a lift back to the building from the airport to pick up his car. First he went into his office to put down his files and write a report on his Cape Town meetings.

What Verryn didn't know was that there was an operation under way in the basement of the building that very evening. Eugene de Kock, a security policeman and the leader of a notorious death squad based at Vlakplaas, was in charge of the Khotso House bombing. He and his team gained access to the courtyard behind the building next door, which allowed them to scale a wall and drop down into a passage on the side of Khotso House where there was a door that led to the basement.

De Kock and his team carried into the basement 150kg of military explosives in eight rucksacks. They wore balaclavas and carried daggers and leather batons. Their plan was to place the explosives in the boot of a car to create the impression that it had been Khotso House property. But then a man walking past at street level was spotted peeping through a grille that had access to the basement. Although it was dark, De Kock was afraid the man might have seen them. He decided to abandon the plan to plant the explosives in a car boot. To expedite the whole operation, they placed the rucksacks next to the two lifts and fled the building.

De Kock and his team activated the explosives with an electronically timed switch. They had a second one if the first one failed, but it didn't. They got in their cars and drove towards Hillbrow to wait for the explosion.

Verryn realised that he was too tired to write his report that night and decided to go home. He took the lift down to the basement. He thought it was odd that the lights in the parking garage weren't on, as the guard usually kept them lit at that time, but he thought nothing further of it. He drove out of the carpark and onto the street. When he arrived home in Soweto, he received a message that Tom Manthata had called him to say that a bomb had exploded in the Khotso House building.

Three months after the bombing, a meeting at Wits University to protest the Delmas Treason Trial sentencing was banned. The gathering of close to 1 500 people was moved to Central Methodist as a prayer vigil instead. Reverend Frank Chikane from the SACC spoke. He said, "Those who are in chains would call on those of us who have our hands and feet free to use them to win our freedom." After Chikane, Reverend Alan Boesak approached the podium. While he was speaking, someone whispered in Storey's ear that the police were outside and wanted to come in. As Storey walked down the stairs to the foyer it occurred to him that while the police had been into the hall in the basement before, next to the People Centre, they had never been into the sanctuary. He stepped outside the front door to see an entire platoon waiting outside on the street wearing helmets and visors and holding guns. "I'm warning you," said Storey to the officer in charge, "if you go up there, that's a church. You're going to cross a line. It's not a hall or one of our rooms. It's a sanctuary. It's the sanctuary of God."

Without any warning, the officer yelled, "*Beweeg* - move!" and the men moved into the building. Storey ran in ahead of them, back up the stairs and into the sanctuary. Trying to remain calm, he interrupted Alan Boesak in the pulpit. "We're about to have visitors," he said. "Everyone keep still. We're going to say a prayer."

The officer followed Storey into the pulpit and readied himself to address the congregation. He had a gun on his hip. "I want them to disperse in three minutes," he said to Storey. Storey responded with a prayer. A long prayer. The policeman stood stolidly beside the three clergymen, Storey, Chikane and Boesak, with his hand on his gun, and waited throughout the prayer, looking slightly ill at ease. Meanwhile, a large group of police officers, in their helmets and visors, had lined up to face the congregation with their backs to the communion rail. Ken Roberts, finance secretary for the church, had had enough. He got up out of his seat, walked up to an officer and said, "Take off your hat. This is a church. How dare you wear a hat in church?" Two of the policemen sheepishly removed their helmets and put them under their arms. Storey finished his prayer. Then he told the meeting that the service had been declared an illegal gathering. "Please leave quietly," he said. "It would be easy for something to happen. Let's leave peacefully and with dignity."

Throughout the 1980s Central Methodist was a place of refuge for individuals, organisations, and political gatherings, often at great risk to itself. Inspired by the different aspects of this role and exploring its biblical foundation, Bishop Storey set down in writing his *Notes on Sanctuary*, in which he referred to several passages from the Bible, including Psalm 91:2, "God is our refuge and our fortress" and Isaiah 14:30, "The poor shall graze their flocks in my meadows, and the destitute shall lie down in peace".

"We need to be a sign and witness of this," Storey wrote, suggesting that spreading the word of God meant offering refuge to the poor and the destitute, already an important part of Central Methodist Mission's work. He also wrote: "We are called to protect foreigners and strangers" and "Jesus himself was a refugee in Egypt", demonstrating how strongly he believed that Central Methodist was a part of that heritage and that it had a responsibility to protect refugees, especially if they were seeking refuge from apartheid.

Storey was deeply disturbed by the fact that many people in inner-city Johannesburg were treated as aliens and were constantly under threat of eviction. It was Central Methodist's duty and his responsibility to reach out to them and offer them a safe haven.

Seven

The Tragedy of Stompie Seipei

In July 1988 Winnie Mandela's house in Orlando was burned down. Assuming that the apartheid security forces were responsible, Bishop Storey went to Soweto to offer her his support. When he arrived at what remained of the house, Mrs Mandela wasn't there. Neighbours told him that the house had actually been burned down by community members who were upset with her and also upset with a group of young men who lived on her property who had brought violent conflict into the community. This group called themselves the Mandela United Football Club. The neighbours told Storey that he would find Mrs Mandela at another residence a short distance away, and they gave him directions. There he met members of the Mandela United Football Club for the first time when they confronted him aggressively at the gate and would not allow him in.

If Peter Storey thought that his attempt to console her over the loss of her home had proved difficult, he would soon become embroiled in a much larger crisis around Mrs Mandela and the Mandela United Football Club, one that would involve Reverend Paul Verryn and the reputation of the Church itself. It would also shape the public's perception of Verryn for years to come.

The actions of the Football Club had already registered in other quarters. Journalist Nomavenda Mathiane had written about the Club and the Soweto community's concerns about it as far back as April 1987, but this had not caused much reaction at the time. Nelson Mandela was concerned about it, too. From Pollsmoor Prison he called for the formation of a committee made up of community leaders, and he tasked them with ensuring that the conflict between the community and Mandela United did not escalate. He asked them even to consider disbanding the club. The Crisis Committee, as it was called, included Reverend Frank Chikane, Reverend Beyers Naude of the SACC, Cyril Ramaphosa from the National Union of Mineworkers, Sydney Mufamadi from the Congress of South African Trade Unions, Sister Bernard Ncube from the Federation of Transvaal Women, and Aubrey Mokoena of the Release Mandela Committee.

In November 1988, just months after the Khotso House bombing, Paul Verryn was doing some work for the SACC in his temporary office in the boardroom at Central Methodist when Matthew Chaskalson, the son of human rights lawyer Arthur Chaskalson, and Ace Magashule came to see him. They brought with them a teenage boy. They told Verryn they were concerned about the boy's safety and were hoping he could stay with Verryn at his home, the church manse in Soweto, which was known to be a safe house for political activists. The boy's name was James Moeketsi Seipei, nicknamed Stompie, and he was fourteen years old. Stompie had already served time in detention for his political activities and the well-known Johannesburg lawyer Priscilla Jana was his attorney. Matthew Chaskalson worked in Jana's office. Not only did Stompie live in fear of the security police, he had also become the target of rumours that he had turned informer. Concerned for his safety in his home in Tumahole township outside Parys, a small town about 100km south-west of Johannesburg, Jana brought Stompie to the city and for a time he lived with Chaskalson, but they were still worried about his safety. Although the manse in Orlando was already quite crowded at the time, Paul Verryn did not hesitate. He took Stompie in.

Like the manse, Winnie Mandela's home was also a place where young acivists turned for support and accommodation. Some of the young men who stayed in her house were said to act as her bodyguards. Before it was burned down and she moved to Diepkloof-Extension, Verryn's and Winnie Mandela's houses had been a five-minute walk from one another, and, as Emma Gilbey describes in her biography of Winnie Mandela, "for a long time the relationship between the two houses was easygoing. Winnie even referred a number of youths looking for a place to stay to Verryn. And some who stayed with him eventually moved in with her."

Shortly before Stompie Seipei moved into the manse Paul Verryn had been made aware of another rumour that was doing the rounds in Soweto. This one was personal. It was rumoured that he was making sexual advances towards the young men in his care. It was Reverend Frank Chikane from the SACC who brought this to his attention, and Verryn was extremely concerned. He immediately met with his Bishop, Peter Storey, to discuss the rumours. Storey was sympathetic. As a single man in the ministry, one could easily become the target of such rumours. There were about 20 people staying at the manse at the time, which had three bedrooms and three beds. Some people shared beds, while others slept on the floor. Storey advised Verryn that in order to curtail the rumours, he should keep his own bed and bedroom strictly to himself. Verryn declined to follow this advice, however, revealing a stubbornness that would serve him well in some instances, but was also his Achilles heel. His view was that in such crowded conditions, to keep a bed to himself would have been "intolerable".

Just over a month later, on 29 December 1988, four young men were abducted from Verryn's home, and taken to Winnie Mandela's new house in Diepkloof-Extension. They were 29 year old Kenneth Kgase, Pelo Mekgwe and Thabiso Mono, who were both in their early twenties, and fourteen-year-old Stompie Seipei. A fifth young man, Katiza Cebekhulu, also left the manse with the others that day, but no one seemed to know whether he had gone willingly or not. What was clear was that Winnie Mandela, once she had admitted that they were indeed under her roof, was reluctant to let anyone have any access to these five young men.

A woman named Xoliswa Falati and her teenage daughter had recently moved into the manse. It is unclear whether she had been invited by Paul Verryn to assist with cooking and cleaning, or whether she'd needed a place to stay and had asked him for accommodation. Either way, she played a significant role in the household. Falati would testify repeatedly over the years to come that it was she who had expressed her concerns for the young men in the house and she who had gone to Winnie Mandela with these concerns. She feared that Verryn was sexually molesting some of the young men there. It was Katiza Cebekhulu who had first told her about this, she claimed.

Another motivator for taking the young men from the manse and moving them to Mrs Mandela's home may actually have been an argument over Stompie Seipei that Verryn had had with Falati. The rumour that Stompie was an informer had followed him to Soweto. Years later Verryn said he believed that Stompie had broken under interrogation, and that because he had broken, there was a suspicion that he was a sellout. Verryn had come home one evening to find Falati interrogating the boy. Stompie had been in a terrible state and Verryn had rebuked her strongly and instructed her never to do it again. At some level, given what happened soon afterwards, Verryn always suspected this altercation had sent Falati to Winnie Mandela. Falati herself was the subject of rumour at the time, too, with people accusing her, in turn, of being an informer. "This was a sure way of proving that you're not an informant – to victimise informants or would-be informants," Verryn said.

The abduction of the young men had taken place over the holiday period between Christmas and New Year so news travelled slowly. Verryn was away on holiday at the time, which contributed to the delay in a co-ordinated reaction from the Methodist Church. When Bishop Storey first heard about it, his initial reaction was that it could have been a misunderstanding. Reverend Otto Mbangula, Verryn's Superintendent Minister in Soweto, was also away. On his return, a steward in the church told him the young men had been taken by Xoliswa Falati and some members of the notorious Mandela United Football Club.

Winnie Mandela consistently refused access to the young men. Efforts by Aubrey Mokoena and a team from the Crisis Committee were in vain. Bishop Storey phoned Dr Nthato Motlana regarding the allegations Mrs Mandela had allegedly made against Paul Verryn to ask him if he could help. Motlana had been the Mandela family's doctor for many years. Motlana subsequently visited Mrs Mandela to try to discuss the allegations with her, and also to raise his concerns with her about her holding the young men in her house. His efforts to persuade her to release them also proved unsuccessful.

Then, in the early hours of Saturday morning, 7 January 1989, one of the young men, Kenneth Kgase, escaped while on sentry duty at the Diepkloof-Extension house. He fled straight to Central Methodist Mission on Pritchard Street, where he had previously worked part time. He arrived at about 6:30am and David Ching let him in. Kgase could barely talk. Ching phoned Paul Verryn who rushed to the church and took Kgase to Dr Martin Connell for a medical examination. That evening he took him to see a lawyer, Geoff Budlender, at the Legal Resources Centre. Then Verryn briefed Peter Storey.

Kgase said that Winnie Mandela had told the four young men, "You are not fit to be alive". He alleged that they had been assaulted by Mrs Mandela herself and then by members of her Mandela United Football Club. He reported that Stompie Seipei had been severely beaten but that he did not know where he was or if he was still alive.

Storey shared the feedback with Reverend Frank Chikane and the Crisis Committee and a delegation went swiftly to the Mandela house to confront Winnie. All she would say was that she was protecting the young people and that they had come to her at their own request. She declined to allow the group access to the youths, but then told them to return that afternoon. When they returned, Winnie's daughter Zinzi told them that one of the young men had "escaped", which they regarded as a significant choice of word, but she did let them inside. Pelo Mekgwe, Thabiso Mono and Katiza Cebekhulu were there. The group noted that Mekgwe and Mono had fresh wounds on their bodies and that Katiza Cebekhulu did not. All three confirmed that they were there of their own free will and that they had been subjected to sexual advances by Paul Verryn. Then Katiza Cebekhulu had a moment alone with the committee, and he admitted that they *were* being held against their will, and that they had been forced to tell the story about the sexual abuse. He said, "I'm going to die anyway, so I may as well tell the truth."

Storey and Verryn met with members of the Crisis Committee, who reported on their visit to Mrs Mandela and also questioned Verryn about the circumstances at the manse. Struggling with how to handle the situation, the Methodist Church considered the possibility of getting an interdict to force Mrs Mandela to release the young men, but the Crisis Committee decided to call a broader community meeting to discuss ways to resolve the crisis.

At the same time Albertina Sisulu, a leader of the United Democratic Front and wife of jailed ANC leader Walter Sisulu, sent a message to Bishop Storey warning him that Paul Verryn's life was in danger. Storey was reluctant to withdraw Verryn from Soweto but he was very worried all the same. He would have preferred that Verryn could just get on with his work, thereby making it clear that his Church had confidence in him, but in the end he believed he had no option and he ordered Verryn out.

In the meantime, Ismail Ayob, Nelson Mandela's attorney, paid a visit to Mandela in Pollsmoor. He returned with instructions that the young people should be released immediately – in fact he asked Bishop Storey to prepare accommodation for them – but still the release did not happen. Subsequent attempts by Ayob and again by Dr Nthato Motlana were in vain. Motlana had just returned from Lusaka, bearing a message from Oliver Tambo himself, the President of the African National Congress, saying that the young men must be released.

Then Oliver Tambo made a call to Reverend Frank Chikane, which was highly unusual. He told Chikane that he was very concerned about the situation and that if it had been possible for him to visit Mrs Mandela himself, he would have done so. He asked Chikane to visit her on his behalf. She would be expecting him, he said. Chikane interpreted Tambo's request as an instruction from above. The meeting lasted five hours and on 16 January, after two and a half weeks of uncertainty and negotiations, the young men were handed over to Dr Motlana. Motlana drove them to the law offices of Krish Naidoo, whom Winnie had apparently been consulting on this matter. Bishop Storey took Pelo Mekgwe and Thabiso Mono with him when he left Naidoo's office, but Katiza Cebekhulu stayed behind. It was not clear where Stompie Seipei was. In the meantime Storey gave Paul Verryn firm instructions not to communicate with the released young people in any way.

The broad community meeting that the Crisis Committee was organising happened to be set for the evening of that same day. There were about 150 people present at the Catholic Hall in Dobsonville, Soweto. The venue was kept secret. Those attending had to go to one location, be directed to another location and then sent to yet another in order to find the venue. Bishop Storey drove Mono, Mekgwe and Kgase to the meeting. In the car, the three young men told Storey that they never wanted to go back to the Mandela house, that they had been badly beaten when they were there, so much so that "our eyes could not see for a week". On occasion they had been assaulted by Mrs Mandela herself. They were worried about Stompie. And they also said they had been told to accuse Paul Verryn or be killed.

The meeting started at about 7:30pm. The space was packed. Most of the Crisis Committee members were there, as well as representatives from Soweto civic organisations and from Stompie's home town of Tumahole. A few representatives from different unions were there, too. In effect, it was a meeting of the Mass Democratic Movement, the new name for the United Democratic Front, which had been banned. There were also about ten young people there who had been living in the manse and who had been there at the time of the abduction. Paul Verryn was in the audience. Bishop Storey recalled a "sombreness" about this gathering. "There was a gravitas about it," he said, "and one had the sense that the people present knew they were dealing with a profoundly hurtful, painful situation and they conducted themselves... I think, with immense dignity and concern to discover the truth."

Reverend Otto Mbangula, Stewart Ngwenya and Sister Bernard Ncube led the meeting from a table at the front. The residents of the manse had put together a statement, which they had all signed, relating how the abduction had taken place, and they presented this statement to the meeting. Then Pelo Mekgwe and Thabiso Mono told their stories, confirming that they had been abducted, taken to Winnie Mandela's house and beaten, first by her and then by members of the Football Club. They also told the meeting that they had not been sexually molested by Verryn and that they had been primed to lie. While they were giving evidence, attorney Krish Naidoo arrived with Katiza Cebekhulu. They were accompanied by a member of the Football Club. "I have never seen such terror on people's faces," Storey said years later. "If the Football Club knew where the meeting was taking place, should the meeting continue at all or were we all in fact in danger?" It was well known that the members of the Club were always heavily armed.

When Katiza Cebekhulu was asked to give evidence he admitted to participating in the beatings. When he was asked why, he said, "They were being beaten and I also felt like beating them." Cebekhulu was then asked to describe the injuries Stompie Seipei, who was still missing, had sustained. He told the hushed gathering that the boy was "soft" on one side of the head and that he had been beaten so terribly that he had not been able to see out of his eyes. He had been picked up and dropped on the floor. He had not been able to walk.

Cebekhulu then alleged that Paul Verryn had lain on top of him on one occasion. Verryn was asked to respond to this allegation of sexual misconduct and he denied it. Someone from the Crisis Committee said that the only other person known to have made such an allegation against Verryn was Thabiso Mono, so the Committee asked Mono if he stood by what he had said previously. "I withdraw it unconditionally," said Mono. "I was forced to say it." Bishop Storey then informed the meeting that if there was any evidence of sexual abuse by Verryn he would have to institute proceedings against him, and he invited Thabiso Mono and Pelo Mekgwe and the nine other residents of the manse who were present to offer any allegations of any conduct unbecoming of a minister. Not a single allegation was made.

A young man named Thomas Nkosi stood up. He said that he had lived in the manse since 1987 and had often shared a bed with Paul Verryn. No hint of any misconduct had ever taken place. The other nine residents who were present at the meeting supported him in this statement. Bishop Storey turned to the meeting at large and asked again: "Does anyone here have any evidence against Reverend Verryn?" No one did. Bishop Storey then said, "I am not willing to proceed with any action against Mr Verryn on the basis of the evidence of one person who actually participated in the assaults on the other youths, and in my view is a totally unreliable witness."

Last to give evidence at the meeting was a young man named Andrew Lerotodi Ikaneng. He had once belonged to the Mandela United Football Club but had left. He told a long story of harassment by the Club, and said that on one occasion he had been chased by some of its members and nearly killed. He accused Jerry Richardson, the former coach of the Club, of trying to kill him with a pair of garden shears and leaving him for dead. He showed the meeting a fresh scar on his neck.

The Dobsonville meeting took a set of five resolutions. The first was that Winnie Mandela should be approached and instructed to produce Stompie Seipei. Second, all progressive organisations should no longer give her a platform. Third, the Mandela United Football Club must be dismantled forthwith. Fourth, Mrs Mandela should desist from creating an impression that she spoke on behalf of the people. Lastly, neither Krish Naidoo nor any other progressive lawyer in the country should act for her.

Some people at the meeting proposed a march on Mrs Mandela's house then and there, but Sister Bernard Ncube dissuaded them. The meeting closed after midnight.

On Friday, 27 January, eleven days after the community meeting in Dobsonville, the *Weekly Mail* broke the story about how four young men had been abducted from a local church, and one of them was now missing. Under the headline "Soweto Anger at Winnie 'Team'", journalist Thandeka Gqubule wrote: "Widespread grievances over the activities of the 'football team' associated with Winnie Mandela came to a head at a major community meeting in Dobsonville, Soweto, last week." The article outlined the sexual allegations against Paul Verryn and quoted Bishop Storey as saying the allegations had been investigated and had been deemed groundless. In Storey's view they were intended to deflect community anger away from the violent treatment meted out to the young people by their abductors. Xoliswa Falati was mentioned in the article. "Falathi [sic] seems to have clashed with the occupants of the house. She threatened to call in the football team to discipline them."

Local and international journalists had been trying to reach Winnie Mandela for her comment the day before the *Weekly Mail*'s story went to press, so she would have known the story was about to break. It was on Thursday or Friday that week, nearly a month after the abduction had taken place, that Katiza Cebekhulu went to the police station in Orlando West and laid a complaint accusing Paul Verryn of sexual assault. This was the first time that the police officially became involved.

The same Friday afternoon, medical doctor Dr Abu-Baker Asvat, a politically active man and leader of Azapo, who had a history of serving the poor, was murdered in his rooms in Soweto. Initially, the assumption was that the motive for the murder was robbery, but there was also some speculation about it being an assassination by political rivals or by the security police. That weekend *The Sunday Times* ran an article by Ezra Mantini quoting Winnie Mandela and drawing attention to a possible connection between the abduction from the Methodist Church and the murder: "Mrs Mandela said she had hoped Dr Asvat would be an important witness in complaints she had laid with the police involving allegations of ill treatment of boys at a church home in Soweto." The article quoted her as saying, "'Dr Asvat was the only professional witness who could back my story that the boys, who were alleged to have been kept against their will in my house, were in fact victims of abuse. I gave them shelter as it is my duty as a social worker.'" This statement implicated the Methodist Church as possibly having had a hand in the murder and of covering it up. Dr Asvat had apparently appeared anxious in the days before his murder and his family had received information that his anxiety was linked to the fact that he had examined the young men and that he had *not* seen evidence of sexual abuse. He had also insisted that Stompie Seipei be taken to hospital.

Years later the story in *The Sunday Times* still moved Peter Storey to anger. "It was so utterly bizarre even to suggest that the Church could be colluding with some murderer in order to get rid of evidence that might embarrass it. It was so absurd. It made us very, very angry."

By now the media around the world had picked up the story, and the Bishop was mindful of the sensitivity, but also mindful that Stompie Seipei was still missing. He tried to make this fact the focus of every interview he gave. He was very aware that Winnie Mandela was also speaking to the press but that her focus was on the sexual allegations against Paul Verryn. A piece in the *City Press* also mentioned Xoliswa Falati having been "given sanctuary at the church house after her home in KwaThema, Springs was petrol-bombed."

Storey and Verryn visited Stompie Seipei's mother in Parys. "It became clear to us once we met with her," said Storey, "that nobody had actually told her of events surrounding her son and we had to be the people who broke the news to her of the abduction and of the treatment which we understood Stompie had received, and of his disappearance. We indicated that while we could not give up hope, the outlook was very grim. And she spoke of her faith in God and the way that God had looked after Stompie in the past."

The search for Stompie continued. Finally, on 14 February 1989, his body was identified in a Diepkloof mortuary where it had lain unidentified and unclaimed for weeks. His throat had been slit and he had been left lying out in the open veld.

On 16 February, two days after Stompie's post-mortem, the Mass Democratic Movement publicly distanced itself from Winnie Mandela and the Mandela United Football Club. Murphy Morobe and Azhar Cachalia read the MDM's statement to a press conference, which was held in the Roberts Room at Central Methodist. The room was crowded with journalists and the mood was tense. The statement began by acknowledging Mrs Mandela's contribution to the struggle, before moving on to the "sensitive and painful matter" of the current crisis. "In recent years, Mrs Mandela's actions have increasingly led her into conflict with various sections of the oppressed people and with the Mass Democratic Movement as a whole. The recent conflict in the community has centred largely around the conduct of her so-called Football Club which has been widely condemned by the community. In particular, we are outraged by the reign of terror that the team has been associated with. Not only is Mrs Mandela associated with the team, in fact, the team is her own creation.

"We are of the view that Mrs Mandela has abused the trust and confidence which she has enjoyed over the years. She has not been a member of any of the democratic structures of the UDF and Cosatu, and she has often acted without consulting the Democratic Movement. Often her practices have violated the spirit and ethos of the Democratic Movement.

"We are outraged at Mrs Mandela's complicity in the recent abductions and assault of Stompie. Had Stompie and his three colleagues not been abducted by Mrs Mandela's 'football team', he would have been alive today."

In late February Bishop Stanley Mogoba, the Presiding Bishop of the Methodist Church of Southern Africa, who was senior to Bishop Storey, visited Nelson Mandela in Pollsmoor. Why couldn't Bishop Storey and the Church have acted differently, Mandela asked him. Why couldn't they have dealt with the matter pastorally? Why could Bishop Peter not have come closer to Winnie instead of it being discussed in the press? Bishop Mogoba explained that the evidence and the events as they had unfolded had made a simple pastoral approach impossible and that they had kept it out of the media and away from the police for as long as they could. Mrs Mandela had been the one who had broken press silence, he said, not the Church.

"I owe an apology to the Church," Mandela said then. "The fault is hers. I owe Peter an apology for what I've been thinking. It's an ugly situation."

Stompie Seipei was buried in Tumahole township on 25 February on a hot summer's day. Bishop Storey gave the funeral address before over 2 000 mourners who came to pay their respects and express their anger.

"There are moments in our history when all the tangled pain and violence and division and horror of our bleeding land seem to coalesce and confront us all. This is such a moment. As I stand here, I feel the burden of all the years, of all the suffering by so many people in so many ways. It's all here today, represented by this broken little body and this mother in mourning. This funeral is a parable of South Africa's pain."

Then Storey spoke directly to Stompie's mother: "Today you have the proud sorrow of a great funeral. You join the long line of grieving mothers who have buried their children amongst the vast throngs singing of freedom. But tomorrow you will be alone. And your son will still be dead. I am so sorry, mama."

Then Storey spoke to Stompie: "I did not know you well. You once sat in my office after a protest service at the Central Methodist Mission. There had been a march from Khotso House to the church. I thought you were lost – waiting for an elder brother perhaps. Then I was told that you were waiting for the security police to get tired of waiting downstairs so you could escape. I was told that you had led the march! And I looked at you and in my mind I cried, Dear God! What have we done? That a mere child, who should be playing marbles in a backyard somewhere or running with your friends in the veld, or chattering in a school room, is robbed of his childhood, and has the tired look of an old man already in his eyes… Your terrible and violent death was an unspeakable crime; and when I think of the way you died, I am deeply angry. But before your body was so brutally broken, your childhood was already dead. South Africa killed your innocence long ago."

Then Storey spoke to those gathered at the funeral: "Bow your heads for this child. Salute his courage. But do not injure him any further by using this funeral as a platform for revenge. If there are those who have come to stoke the fires of retaliation, you should go home, because you do him no honour… These past few weeks, as the facts of his dying have emerged, will be remembered as weeks of shame and of profound tragedy. These weeks have probed beneath the surface of South Africa's pain and exposed the deeper, hidden wounds these hateful years have carved into an oppressed people's soul – the erosion of conscience, the devaluing of human life, the reckless resort to violence, and the evasion of truth. There is a choice to be made today about these wounds. Either we will open them wider, or we will seek – for Stompie's sake, and hundreds more like him – to heal them."

Lastly, Storey spoke to the oppressive rulers of apartheid: "Yes, this tragedy casts an ugly stain on the struggle for freedom; but before you are tempted to take comfort in it, remember this: long before his life was so brutally taken, Stompie Seipei was already willing to lay it down. And there are millions like him. If a fourteen-year-old child will die for freedom, nothing can stop freedom coming. So, from this place of death and burial, hear this message: you will not kill the idea of liberty and you cannot bury the vision of a new South Africa."

Both Peter Storey and Paul Verryn maintained media silence as two cases made their way through the courts. First, football coach Jerry Richardson was charged with and convicted of Stompie Seipei's kidnapping and murder. The judge sentenced Richardson to hang. His sentence was commuted to life in prison and he served nineteen years before he died in prison in April 2009.

In Winnie Mandela's trial in 1991, Xoliswa Falati testified that she had brought the young men to Winnie Mandela's house, without Mrs Mandela's knowledge, in order to protect them from Paul Verryn. During the opening stages of the trial, Pelo Mekgwe was abducted and therefore unable to give testimony. Journalist Patrick Laurence linked the ANC to Mekgwe's abduction in an article in the Johannesburg *Star*, and was imprisoned and released on bail for refusing to reveal his source. Defence attorneys brought Kenneth Kgase and Thabiso Mono to testify that Verryn had made sexual advances toward them but Judge Michael Stegmann said that their testimony was so inconsistent and self-contradictory that they were clearly being used "as pawns in a game being played by Mrs Mandela and Mrs Falati".

There were those of the view that whatever Winnie Mandela might have done to these young men, it was outweighed by her enormous contribution to the struggle. Many people felt that the Mandela United Football Club had been infiltrated by the security police and that she had been set up, and cited the fact that Jerry Richardson had admitted that he worked for the police. Others believed that Winnie Mandela's trial would greatly damage the liberation movement.

The allegations against Mrs Mandela and her Football Club were not new, however, when the Stompie case came to light. Nomavenda Mathiane reminded readers of *Frontline* magazine in March 1989 that she had written about the Club two years before. "Members of the club were openly walking around Soweto with machine-guns over their shoulders and people in Soweto were mystified as to why the police were laying off," she wrote. "Now that the wheel has turned, it is sad to see the rush to descend like vultures, heaping all the blame on one pair of shoulders, as if shunning her will solve the problems."

During Mrs Mandela's trial her senior counsel, George Bizos, attempted to convey to the judge that the young men in question had left the manse voluntarily and that they were now lying for Paul Verryn in order to save his reputation. "The genesis of the allegations against Winnie Mandela may have arisen in order to divert allegations against Verryn," said Bizos in his closing arguments.

Paul Verryn was never called as a witness in the trial and he was not charged with any crime. Emma Gilbey's biography of Winnie Mandela suggests that "the trial was as much about his innocence or guilt as that of anyone in the dock... The dubious logic seemed to be that if Verryn was guilty of sexual misconduct then Winnie had to be innocent of the charges against her."

In his judgment, Judge Stegmann said "to imagine that all this took place without Mrs Mandela as one of the moving spirits is like trying to imagine Hamlet without the prince". He said that the prosecution did not disprove her alibi that she was out of town when the kidnapping and assault took place, but also said that there were inconsistencies between her testimony and that of the two corroborating witnesses. He also said that "she showed herself on many occasions to be a calm, composed, deliberate and unblushing liar".

Winnie Mandela was found guilty on charges of kidnapping and sentenced to six years in prison, but her sentence was suspended on appeal in 1993. Xoliswa Falati, who was charged in the same trial, was also sentenced to six years and served two years in prison.

For some 30 months, from the time of the original crisis through the Jerry Richardson trial in 1990 and Winnie Mandela's trial in 1991, Peter

Storey and Paul Verryn did not speak publicly about these events. However, the press continued to cover the story with headlines such as "Minister Abused Us, Say Youths", "Methodist Minister is Cleared", "Verryn: No Evidence of Sexual Misconduct", and "Minister Whose Morals Were Ripped Apart".

When Winnie Mandela's trial was over, Bishop Storey felt able to speak publicly at last. He used the platform of his official address to the annual Synod in mid-1991, where over 200 clergy and lay leaders from 75 churches of the Central District gathered. "For two and a half years and through two traumatic court cases, the Methodist Church has been constantly in the news. This is not the time to relate the crucial role played by our Church in securing the release of the surviving hostages, but I must address the persistent allegations about the moral behaviour of our minister in Orlando, Reverend Paul Verryn. These allegations not only caused him acute suffering but also brought the Church into disrepute. Our silence over this long period must not be misread: it would have been wrong to comment with court cases pending, or in progress. Now we can speak."

Storey continued: "Anyone tempted to believe the allegations – even on a basis of 'there is no smoke without a fire' – must reckon with the following questions: why did Mr Verryn report to me as early as October 1988 that rumours of this kind were being circulated about him, and seek my advice on how to deal with them? Why did those who say they were concerned about his alleged misbehaviour not ever report it to either his Superintendent Minister or his Bishop? Why did one of the kidnapped youths tell a delegation of top community leaders who visited them in captivity that they had been forced by assault to make these allegations? Why did two of the youths, on the day of their release, tell a meeting of 150 community leaders that they had been forced to lie about Mr Verryn? Why did at least ten residents of the Orlando West manse tell the same meeting that there had never been any impropriety? Why did Mr Verryn, in spite of all this, request an official Church Commission to examine the allegations? Why did that Commission, consisting of four ministers and a psychiatrist, find that none of the accusers accepted their invitation to give evidence? Why was the only charge ever laid against Mr Verryn – by a youth who participated in the kidnap and the assaults – investigated by the police and found to be groundless? Why did the judge in the trial of Mr Jerry Richardson dismiss the allegations against Mr Verryn? And why did the judge in this latest case [of Winnie Mandela] not only disbelieve those who persisted with the allegations, but also say that there had been a deliberate and protracted campaign against Mr Verryn?

"Nothing can undo the hurt done to an outstanding minister over these thirty months of hell, but what I can do is set the record straight and express my disgust at the ruthless way in which he was vilified for unworthy ends."

Reflecting back on the tragic events of 1989, it is clear that the Methodist Church held together through a major public crisis. Reverend Paul Verryn went to his Bishop immediately with concerns of the rumours about him. Bishop Peter Storey assessed those rumours and subsequent allegations and decided to support Verryn. Presiding Bishop Stanley Mogoba engaged in the crisis and stood by the decisions and actions of both Storey and Verryn.

Twenty years later, in 2009, the Methodist Church would once again face a major public crisis. Once again Paul Verryn would be at the eye of the storm. This time, however, the Church would not pull together. It would splinter apart.

Leothere Nininahazwe's office on the second floor, outside the gallery of the sanctuary. This room and another like it on the same floor, where Elizabeth Cheza slept, were formerly called cry-rooms where mothers could go with their babies during the service.

Meetings at Central Methodist / 2010

In July 2010, on the day after I had participated in my one and only karate class, I went to see Elizabeth Cheza, as we had arranged. We met in her room, the former cry room on the second floor. A bed and large chest of drawers took up most of the space alongside a small cooking area with a two-plate stove and a wooden counter-top balancing on several plastic buckets. I sat on a plastic chair and Elizabeth sat on her bed. She told me hers was a different life story from most of the other people who lived at Central Methodist. The fourth of seven children, she grew up in a big house. "We had two maids," she said. She married quite young and her husband worked at the University of Zimbabwe in the Sociology Department until he died in a car accident in December 2002. In 2004 Elizabeth came to South Africa looking for work.

Paul Verryn met Elizabeth when she was visiting a friend at the church, and he recognised her potential. She had completed O levels and she had a diploma in secretarial studies as well. She moved into Central Methodist in 2006 when there were a few hundred people living there. At first she lived in Minor Hall and other women made fun of her, saying, "There's no double bed for you here, honey." She kept telling herself, Soon I'll be leaving. Soon I'll be leaving. But Elizabeth stayed on.

Elizabeth worked at Central Methodist for two years with minimal income. She began to take minutes at the Friday night refugee meetings and also helped conduct a survey of residents to see what skills they had. When the Albert Street School opened in 2008 she was excited. The post of school secretary was offered to her and this allowed her to begin earning a regular salary which afforded her the little luxuries she enjoyed – nail polish, some new clothes, or getting her hair done. She went back to school herself in 2009 and began studying towards a diploma in business management. "It's not a fancy life," she said, "but I've been blessed. I'm a lucky person in this world. I've changed. I've become a stronger person. I'm not afraid of anything." I asked Elizabeth about her documents. She said that she had been renewing her asylum papers since 2007. "I've never been stopped by the police," she said. "It's not because I'm clever. It's not because I pray. I tell God – protect me."

Elizabeth often thought about going back to Zimbabwe. "Home is best," she said.

After Elizabeth and I finished talking, I paused at the other cry room to see if I could set up an interview with Leothere, but he looked busy so I didn't disturb him. I carried on upstairs to the third floor to see who might be at the Bishop's office. As usual, the waiting room was full. There were no seats left so I stood and leaned against the wall. As was often the case, Cleo was there, cleaning the windows with a rag and a big bucket of soapy water. "How are you today, my dear?" she asked. "I'm good. I'm good," I said.

One young man in the waiting room started chatting to me. He said his name was Dumisani and he told me that he was there to ask for a job teaching maths at the Albert Street School. He had grown up in Soweto and did four years at Wits medical school before he failed his fourth year, twice. "I'm going to reapply at UCT," he said. "I'm hoping for a second chance." Then, "Are you the Bishop's daughter?" he asked.

"Oh my goodness, no," I said. I couldn't contain my laughter. We must look alike, I thought. Cleo gave me a crooked smile. "Do you feel like a princess now?" she said.

I told Dumisani that in fact I was writing about the church. Another young man in the waiting room was clearly listening to our conversation. "I'm also writing about the church," he said. "I'm a journalist from Portugal and I'd like to interview Paul Verryn before I go home next week." He had been in South Africa for the Soccer World Cup. "I like Ronaldo as a player, but not his personality," he said.

As we were talking, I heard someone walking down the passage behind me towards the waiting room. I turned around to see a tall, thin man who had a fearful, fiery look in his eyes. "Is this Bishop Verryn's office?" he asked.

"Yes," I said.

Looking around at the 20 or so people squashed into the worn chairs and couches, the man asked, "Are you all waiting for him?"

"Yes, everyone here is waiting for him," I said.

"My name is Booker," he said to me.

"Ah, like Booker T Washington?" I asked.

His eyes warmed and he smiled. "Exactly," he said.

His full name was Booker Maseti and he proceeded to tell me and Cleo and anyone else who would listen that he had just lost his job in the Department of Community Development in the City of Johannesburg. "One minute you're trying to help people, the next minute you're on the street yourself," said Booker. "I've never been in this situation before and it's terrible. I need a place to stay."

"Are you a journalist?" he asked, and before I could give him much of an answer, he said, "I used to work as a journalist for *The Sunday Independent.*"

I was a little taken aback, and I wondered how this skilled, handsome man, who had worked as a journalist and a civil servant, had come to this point in his life. It was after 5:30pm by then so I started to get ready to leave. I said goodbye to Dumisani and the Portuguese journalist, but was aware that Booker was watching me closely. "Are you leaving now?" he asked.

"Yes," I said. "I've got to go."

"I'm also leaving," Booker said then, and he turned to walk down the passage and down the stairs.

"OK," said Cleo. She put down her rag. "I'm walking you downstairs. I don't trust that guy. He might try to give you a hard time."

"Do you know him?" I asked.

"Never seen him before," she replied.

I was touched by Cleo's protectiveness as she and I walked down the stairs together. We did pass Booker in the foyer but we kept on walking and went out the door and he didn't try to stop us or follow us. In fact Booker would become a regular resident at Central Methodist, and once he found his bearings there and began to recover from the trauma of his nights on the street, his regal manner and formal way of speaking would distinguish him from the other residents. I would see more of Booker Maseti.

Eight

Son of Soweto

In 1992 Reverend Paul Verryn was responsible for five congregations in Soweto, totalling about 2 500 people. His move to the township four years earlier had been a complete culture shock and it had had a major impact on his life. He discovered he had moved from a society which valued the individual above all to a society which valued community above all, and in the beginning it was a huge adjustment. "I think it was an existential crisis," he said. There were language barriers, too, especially at first, and he would have to rely on interpreters a lot of the time in his interactions with the members of his congregations. "It was one hundred per cent listening all the time," Verryn said.

There were many things to get used to, Verryn remembered when talking about those early days. For example, "I wondered why the *Te Deum* was sung for so long [in a township service]. I wanted to replace it. But it's the whole issue of respect, of the pace of life and dignity. There's a sense of affirmation of the community and that's the best thing about the black community – the sense of belonging." One of Verryn's favourite tasks was to give communion to the old, the sick and the disabled who could not attend church services. Several times a month he would visit their homes. Once he found a pensioner locked in a back room and had to wait until someone found the key so that they could take communion together. At another house, a woman lay close to death on a pink silk duvet. Her family took communion with her, probably for the last time.

It would be another five years before Paul Verryn would be called upon to take up the position of Superintendent Minister at Central Methodist Mission in downtown Johannesburg. Even then, he would continue to make his home in Soweto and commute into the city centre. The total of close to ten years of service in Soweto would also come significantly to influence his preaching when he moved to Central.

Almost every family in Verryn's parish had been affected by the violence in the 1980s and this reality greatly shaped his life and his work. Violence was on the rise again in the early 1990s, given the tensions and the political negotiations that were under way in the wake of Nelson Mandela's release on 11 February 1990 after 27 years as a political prisoner. Many of Reverend Verryn's congregants had fled conflict in Soweto, leaving their possessions behind. Some of them found refuge in the temporary corrugated iron shacks that became an informal settlement on the outskirts of the township and Verryn would visit them there and listen to their fears about violence. He saw first hand how traumatised some of these people were. One member of his congregation, for example, was suffering from hallucinations. The violence surrounding her had made her see the heads of her children nailed up above the door. He would do his best to console her, listening to her and praying with her. Often, when he was ministering to people in one place, he would be called to tend to other people in another. Once it was a distraught woman fearing she was about to be attacked, and often it was the Peace Action Monitoring Group that was monitoring violence in the townships. One morning he received a call to say that the daughter of a member of his congregation had been killed by unknown gunmen during the massacre of a Dobsonville family. He spent the morning taking grieving relatives to the mortuary. "Psychologically and emotionally the community is exhausted," Verryn was quoted as saying. "It's threadbare, and it's lost its tolerance. I think the sustaining features of *ubuntu* are hope, integrity, dignity and tolerance. When those start fraying at the edges you actually feel as if you are starting to lose the fundamental cement of this construction."

This was the climate and context that contributed to the actions of the Mandela United Football Club and the violence that ultimately killed Stompie Seipei. Paul Verryn was no stranger to it.

Even after Winnie Mandela's trial was over, Verryn's name continued to come up in the press and would do for a long time still. "I think [the trial] made me realise just how vulnerable I am," he said. "Now that it is over it feels like a reprieve from insanity – that's the depth at which I felt this thing. But I hope that it has given me a deeper perception of the difficult journey some people have to take and the ability to empathise more effectively with people who are struggling."

This empathy was something that Verryn was called on regularly to offer to his congregation. His manse was always filled with people wanting his advice and his help. But in turn, his congregation also gave him strength. "People supported me and they held my sanity together," Verryn said. "In my time of almost disintegration there were people who actually wept with my pain and prayed for me and for my safety."

While many of those close to Verryn in Orlando supported him, the broader public wasn't so kind and the sexual allegations lingered. Photojournalist Lesley Lawson interviewed Verryn and referred to this when she wrote about him in *Millennium* magazine in 1992. "It was publicly decided that Verryn was a homosexual; from there it was a short step to smearing him as a pederast. To make the mud stick, his accusers attempted to paint a Jekyll and Hyde picture of his life. A month after her trial, Winnie Mandela told a magazine: 'What kind of beast is this who wears a collar on Sunday and goes to preach to parents of these children, and preaches the word of God even to some of these children? At night he becomes something else… We are supposed to be murderers and kidnappers – all rubbish which is meant to shield this man. This whole thing stinks of such filth.'… But what chance is there of self-defense against a character assassination that relies on the existence of an evil shadow self? Verryn himself has refused to try."

Lawson continued: "There are many reasons for his silence. One is a wish not to hurt the homosexual community by a blunt repudiation. Even stronger, however, is his need to protect what very little privacy is permitted him by the nature of his work. His parishioners have access to him at all times and his house is permanently filled with all manner of refugees… For Verryn his sexual identity is one small part of his life that is truly private and he will defend that privacy at any cost. This position and the fact that he is single are the cause of years of calumny."

In addition to the injuries of the trial and the press coverage, it was the damage caused by violence in the community to which he ministered that greatly shaped his work life. In an interview with Irish writer Padraig O'Malley, in December 1993, their conversation focused on trying to understand the violence in the country. By then Verryn had completed six of his ten years of ministry in Soweto. He had also done a large amount of counselling, mostly for political prisoners coming out of detention but also for people who had been the victims of violence in the townships.

Verryn told O'Malley: "I think the exclusion and disempowerment of people for such a long time… the silencing of community feelings and people's aspirations has built up over the years… Secondly, a deep cause of the violence is the poverty and the enormous disparities that there are in the country… I think, thirdly, that there is a lot of thuggery in the wings of the political violence." Verryn also pointed to the violence brought against children in the mid 1980s when over 60 000 children were detained. "I think that another cause of the violence is the dissolution of the families and that cohesiveness which is very much part of the African culture in terms of extended families."

Verryn experienced violence directly in September 1993, just months before his interview with O'Malley. He had arrived home from a church service and was getting out of his car, carrying his stole and other vestments, when a voice said, "Give me the keys to your car," and he found himself staring at the barrel of a gun.

"I beg your pardon?" said Verryn.

A shot rang out, almost deafening him, but mysteriously Verryn was unharmed.

"Give me the keys or I'll kill you," said the young man who was pointing the weapon at him.

"Then kill me and it will be on your conscience with God," Verryn said. "I'm not going to give you my keys."

More shots rang out, Verryn ran into the house, and the gunman fled. When Verryn unfolded the vestments he was holding, there were bullet holes in the stole. Later, when Verryn took the stole to show Peter Storey, bullets fell out of the cloth.

Nine

Reverend Mvume Dandala and the Quest for Peace

REVEREND MVUME DANDALA succeeded Peter Storey at Central Methodist in December 1991. His five-year tenure there ran parallel with South Africa's political transition, another extremely turbulent period in the country, when violence was a continual threat and often a reality. The run-up to the 1994 elections was an especially fraught time.

On a Friday afternoon in late 1992 Reverend Dandala was working in his office at Central Methodist when the phone rang. The caller's tone was urgent.

"*Mfundisi*, the meeting tomorrow afternoon is going to be at the Pioneer Hall in Rosettenville," the caller said.

"I'm sorry, what meeting?" asked Dandala.

"The meeting with Mr Mlatsheni. The meeting to discuss the violence between the hostels in the city."

"I'm sorry, I'm not aware of such a meeting," responded Dandala.

"But the SACC told us that you are coming."

"Who at the SACC?" asked Dandala, still confused.

"Dr John Lamola," was the reply.

Dandala phoned Lamola, who said, "Ah, yes, *mfundisi*, I'm sorry. We met with them and we told them that we would ask you to chair their meeting. We forgot to ask you."

Dandala had other commitments set for the next day, however, and he phoned the caller back to tell him that even though the matter had been cleared up, he was sorry but he was unable to act as chair.

"*Mfundisi*," the man said slowly and deliberately, "if you don't come, there will be war."

The hostel system had been in place in Johannesburg for a very long time. Hostels were single-sex dormitories created by the apartheid government to house workers on the mines and in the city, the assumption being that these men were in the city temporarily and would return to their families in the rural areas and black homelands. In addition to workers from throughout South Africa, the hostels also housed men from other countries in the region, including Mozambique, Malawi, Lesotho, Swaziland and Zimbabwe.

During the period of political transition, a lot of the political violence happened around and within the hostels, and the development of the Johannesburg Hostel Peace Initiative was one of the signature projects that Dandala began at Central Methodist.

Throughout the 1980s Mangosuthu Buthelezi's Inkatha movement and the ANC-aligned United Democratic Front had been in conflict in KwaZulu and Natal, and thousands died in that conflict. After all political parties were unbanned in February 1990, followed by Nelson Mandela's release from prison, different parties vied for influence and this same tension was reflected in the city of Johannesburg. Inkatha officially became the Inkatha Freedom Party (IFP) in July 1990.The violence escalated throughout 1991 and 1992, especially with the proliferation of firearms. Some of the ANC township residents began to organise Self-Defence Units (SDUs), while many of the residents of the hostels, often thought to be aligned to Inkatha, established Self-Protection Units (SPUs). In addition the ANC alleged that there was a "third force", made up of government security forces and the police, which was responsible for fomenting the violence. Outbreaks of violence tended to accompany major political developments in the negotiations process between the National Party government and the ANC.

The Hostel Peace Initiative was not the result of abstract reflection within the Central Methodist Mission. "We didn't sit back and say, right guys, what other ministry does the city need?" said Dandala. "It just imposed itself on us. It was really a question of whether this church was flexible enough to respond to a crisis."

The programme forced Central Methodist to engage with migrants into the city because very few people in the hostels were from Johannesburg. As the programme grew, there were various reasons why Dandala had to travel far and wide. If there was a death, for example, the deceased's family would want the body to be taken back for burial in their home community, which was usually in a rural area. Some would go to prison. "I remember one guy, Mr Nzimande, was caught with a boot full of weapons, so he went to prison in Ladysmith," Reverend Dandala reminisced many years later, "so we all went to Ladysmith to visit him there. Some people asked me, 'Where are your boundaries? You are following people all over the country.' I would tell them, 'This is the reality of ministering to people in the city.'"

This reality was not new to Johannesburg, nor would the trend go away. Migrants had populated the city a hundred years earlier and there would be many more migrants to the city in the years to come.

Mvume Dandala first worshipped at Central Methodist when he moved to Johannesburg in 1986 to join the Missions Department of the Methodist Church of Southern Africa. When he and his family were deciding where to worship, his children made the decision: they liked the Sunday school at Central Methodist best. Five years later, at the end of 1991, when Bishop Storey became a separated Bishop, meaning he would continue his work without his own parish, Dandala was asked to succeed him as Superintendent Minister at Central. Dandala had mixed feeling about his new post. What can I try that Peter Storey has not tried, he asked himself. Two years into the job, running Central was still "the mother of all challenges," he admitted.

Dandala was not a stranger to challenges. He remembers a story that his uncle told him when he was a child to illustrate the importance of becoming a man who is not afraid of doing what needs to be done. "An *umnumzana* is a well-regarded community citizen because of what that person does," Dandala explained. "My uncle had a derogatory attitude toward what he regarded as 'gentlemen' who never wanted to produce anything but only consume. I didn't know the difference so he sat me down to explain it to me. He said an *umnumzana* will have sheep in his kraal. He'll look after his sheep when they are not well. And a 'gentleman' will come to *umnumzana* at Christmas with a rope to come and buy a sheep. *Umnumzana* will say 'There are the sheep in the kraal. I can sell you that one.' And point to the one that is on the other end of the kraal and the kraal has got mud this deep. And the *umnumzana* would say 'Unfortunately, I don't have any boys around here so you can go and catch it if you want.' My uncle said a gentleman will walk around not knowing how to walk through this mud to go and get the sheep. And my uncle said, 'Don't you ever be like that. Be an *umnumzana* who will walk through the mud for the sake of the sheep.'"

Born in 1951 in the small village of Dandalaville (named after his great-grandfather) in Mount Ayliff in the Eastern Cape, Mvume was the youngest of four children. He was close to and influenced by his father who was a Methodist minister. Reverend Killion Dandala ministered to very poor communities where men in the family were often migrant workers on the mines near Johannesburg. Dandala's mother was a strong and dedicated doer who reared her own pigs and chickens and grew her own vegetables.

Dandala's first visit to Central Methodist was at the age of 20 in January 1971. He and other young ministers had gone there to give their testimony regarding their calling to the ministry. "The idea of young black ministers going to an all-white church to speak about their calling had a huge impact," said Dandala. His first memory of Central Methodist, however, went back to the time of Reverend JB Webb and listening to great preachers from Central Hall on the radio. He remembers his father associating Webb with some of the pioneers in the opposition to apartheid. So when Dandala visited Central Methodist in 1971, when there were still separate ordination services for blacks and whites within the Methodist Church, it left an impression.

Dandala was ordained at the Central Methodist Church in 1977 by Reverend Abel Hendricks. His first appointment was with the Empangeni Methodist Church and he served there from 1978 until 1982. Then, from 1983 to 1985, he was Superintendent Minister of the North Circuit in Port Elizabeth, which at the time was the largest circuit of the MCSA. This was during the height of the political conflict between the United Democratic Front (UDF) and Azapo so Dandala was drawn into efforts at conflict resolution and peacemaking. "Molly Blackburn and Paul Verryn and I used to minister together when government was bulldozing people's shacks," said Dandala. During the first state of emergency in July 1985 he was detained without trial.

Dandala left Port Elizabeth in 1986 for a post in Johannesburg, leading the Missions department of the MCSA. He began the Malihambe Mission, a programme of sending black and white ministers to work in pairs, which at the time was groundbreaking but also dangerous. "We planned things so that they would go to a white community and then to a black community. Thirdly, they would go to either a rural community or a shanty town and together they would preach and come back. I don't think at the time that I had a sense of the impact of that programme," said Dandala.

This work would serve him well when he was invited to succeed Bishop Storey. "Peter Storey was there at the start of [South Africa's] transition as some white people started to depart the congregation. I was a member of the church at the time, so I watched Peter battling with that situation," recalled Dandala, "but when I came in after Peter there was just a massive exodus of white people. They just left. Sometimes I wondered did they stay because they thought they had to support Peter. Did they look at Peter as one of them and with my coming here, I'm not one of them, so they didn't have that obligation anymore?" Despite the exodus, Dandala was thankful for the strong support of several leaders remaining in the congregation. Among these were John Rees, Roy McAllister, Ken Roberts, and Janet Brodrick.

Dandala's sense was that the younger, white members of the congregation left because they felt that Central Methodist was not prioritising them, not as white people but as members. Dandala thought that they were looking for a pastor who would give them regular pastoral care and visit their families. "I didn't get the impression that they had any understanding or commitment to a church whose first priority was not its members, but the city."

At the same time a growing number of black professionals had begun attending the services at Central Methodist. Some of them worked in the legal offices that were situated around the church, as well as elsewhere in the inner city, and realised that there was a church in their midst. Many of them worshipped at Central on a Sunday only. This was not any different from the pattern established by many white congregants during Storey's time. Even so Dandala felt, just as Storey had, that the number of people from the congregation who were focused on the mission of the church, the commitment to serving the city, were few.

In the days when Peter Storey was trying to bring in more black people to the church, Lindi Myeza introduced Amadodana or the Young Men's Guild, which had its roots amongst black Methodists. Several years later, under Dandala, Myeza encouraged the development of the Women's Manyano at Central Methodist as well. These two organisations played a role in bringing in larger numbers of black worshippers.

Dandala found himself struggling to hold onto the dwindling numbers of white people in the congregation. "The moment I would hear that so and so was thinking of leaving, I would invest time to go and talk to them because I didn't want them to leave. I wanted us to retain our non-racial character," he said. "I believed it was important."

Peliwe Lolwana was a relatively new member of the congregation. Originally from the Eastern Cape, she went to study in the US and was based there from 1984 to 1990. When she returned to South Africa in December 1990, she and her husband started going to Central Methodist. It was convenient for them as they lived in Hillbrow to begin with and then in Bez Valley. The Lolwanas weren't very active at the church, however. Peliwe felt that it had a cold feeling to it. "There were lots of old white people. Even if there were only four whites left and a thousand blacks, we would do things the way the whites had always done it. I remember someone started a junior choir so then there was a black choir and an old white choir."

According to Dandala, the black people who were coming in "could easily have taken over and made it like any other township church," but he didn't want that to happen. "We wanted the Central Mission to keep the distinct cutting edge of ministries and a lot of white people who had been here had that experience. It was a question of sharing that experience with the newer members who were coming in. And for the newer members to bring in some of their experiences that would enrich this ministry. For me, when a good number of white people started moving, it was actually robbing the future of something that could have been unique."

With the dynamics of a changing congregation, Dandala struggled on many fronts. He wasn't sure how to pull the liturgies together or what music to play. The church was also battling financially. Dandala decided to spend R10 000 on a new sound system with microphones so that they could play guitars during the service. He gave a wry smile at the memory. "I think that was the last straw for old Ken Roberts," he mused. "He said, 'That's it. If that's how you're going to go with it, I won't stand in your way, but I'll go elsewhere.' I was forever very sad about that, a stalwart like Ken Roberts deciding to leave." There was no bitterness about Roberts deciding to move on, however. It had become more convenient for him to worship at a church closer to his home.

Another longstanding member, John Rees, said to Dandala, "'Mvume, we have to trust your leadership. None of us know what to do. Yes, this thing you're trying may fail but we have to decide, do we stick to the past or do we try to adapt to things as they are happening around us?' That was good," Dandala recalled.

In early 1993 Dandala made the difficult decision to close down the People Centre. By then non-racial restaurants were opening up all around the centre of the city and the People Centre was losing the unique nature of the hospitality it offered. It had always been subsidised, even at its highest point, and now it was time to let it go. In retrospect, the space would have been good neutral ground to have had available for meetings as political conflict in the hostels and other parts of the city escalated, but if Dandala regretted the decision afterwards, it was too late.

As a result of that one surprise phone call from one of the hostel dwellers, Dandala did, in fact, attend the meeting of hostel residents in Rosettenville at the Pioneer Hall. He arrived to find about 200 men sitting in two groups – Inkatha on one side of the hall and the ANC on the other. They were all openly carrying guns. Dandala asked who the leaders were and two men introduced themselves to him: German Mlatsheni from the ANC, who was the leader of the residents from Selby Hostel, and Jacob Dhlomo from the IFP, who was a leader at the Jeppe Hostel.

"We have called the Reverend here to chair our meeting," said Mr Dhlomo to the crowd. "We consulted between ourselves as leaders and agreed that he should chair."

Mlatsheni stood up to show he supported what Dhlomo had said. Then he turned to Dandala and said, "You can start."

"How should I start?" said Dandala.

"You can pray," Mlatsheni said.

"Pray for what?"

"Pray for the success of this meeting," Mlatsheni replied. "Use this passage from Isaiah. We've chosen it for you."

So Dandala prayed for the group: "Comfort ye, comfort ye my people, saith your God. Speak ye comfortably to Jerusalem, and cry unto her, that her warfare is accomplished, that her iniquity is pardoned; for she hath received of the Lord's hand double for all her sins… Prepare ye the way of the Lord, make straight in the desert a highway for our God. Every valley shall be exalted, and every mountain and hill shall be made low; and the crooked shall be made straight, and the rough places plain…"

Dandala sat down. "Right," he said. "What next?"

"We will give you rules for running this meeting. One of the rules is that there will be no blaming here. We will keep talking about the problem to find a solution to the problem. We are all wrong. We are all responsible. So it doesn't help anybody to remind me what I did or remind him what he did. Let's look for a solution." Then they said to Dandala, "If you fail, and we fight, you will die here with us."

That statement was about the outcome of the meeting, but it just as easily could have been about the sense of responsibility that Dandala felt for Central Methodist, for the city of Johannesburg and for the new South Africa. At this time of great transition and change, if everyone didn't pull together, the entire place would go up in flames.

The meeting continued for more than two hours until everyone in the room had said everything he wanted to say.

"Is there anybody else to speak?" Dandala asked, looking around the hall. There was silence. Dandala felt at a loss. "I don't know what more to say or do now because this is not in the church. If this had been in the church, I would have known what to say."

"What would you say if this was in the church?" someone called out.

"I would say let's share the peace. In church, when we've been having communion, we have this time to stand up and say Peace of the Lord be with you. And also with you."

"Let's do that then," said the man.

Dandala asked everyone to stand and share the peace with each other. Years on he described the scene that followed. "These guys knew each other before this war. As they look at each other, they recognise someone. 'Ah, you're still alive. How are you?' one said. Then another asked, 'Where is so and so?' 'No, so and so has died.' 'What killed him?' 'No, it was in this conflict.' Then the fellow started crying. An Inkatha chap crying for an ANC chap and an ANC chap crying for an Inkatha chap that he'd worked with. I just stood back and watched. It was incredible. This is the mission of the church, I thought. After about thirty minutes, I said, 'All right, let's sit down' and no one sits down where they had been sitting before. That was the breakthrough. After that, it was no longer them against us. The Johannesburg Hostel Peace Initiative was born in that moment."

Dandala gave a great deal of credit to Jacob Dhlomo, "an ordinary mine worker from Jeppe Hostel who one day took his life in his hands and decided that he would walk alone to their rival Selby Hostel to deliver a letter from his senior fellow residents at Jeppe, to ask his opponents at Selby how long they would continue killing each other for reasons none of them fully comprehended. From that gutsy initiative, the Hostel Peace Initiative was launched... at its highest point, this initiative involved no less than 50 000 people from 32 hostels in and around Johannesburg."

Dandala had landed himself a new job. He chaired the next meeting at the Pioneer Hall and, when the venue was no longer available to the hostel dwellers, the group decided unanimously (and without thinking to consult him) that from then on their meetings would all be held at Central Methodist Mission. "Not 'Can we go to Central?'" said Dandala. "But 'We will go to Central.'"

Meetings took place on Tuesdays and Thursdays downstairs in the hall. Once or twice the church was raided by people with guns looking for the meetings. "No one was ever killed," said Dandala, "but it could have happened. They were unidentified people. We didn't know where they came from. All we knew was that they were enemies of peace."

Just as Bishop Storey had done before him, Reverend Dandala struggled with the challenge of how little the congregation was involved with the outreach ministries at the church. While he would still have liked to integrate the two, he was hesitant to invite members of the congregation to the hostel meetings because of how delicate and sensitive the issues were. On occasion, there were special services for peace at Central and people from the Hostel Peace Initiative and the congregation would attend these, but they were the exception.

In the 1990s Central Methodist continued to be the place for special services. Chris Hani's memorial service was held there in 1993. When Dandala arrived at the church, Jeremy Cronin and Communist Party colleagues had already put up Party flags on the altar. Dandala was stern. "Jeremy," he said, "you know that this church is supportive of the struggle in every possible way. This church has defined itself in the front line of the struggle. But you also know our position regarding communism. We don't begrudge you guys for being communists but we certainly cannot have communist flags here."

During those years of transition and uncertainty, politically and socially, Central Methodist stood at the threshold of the old and the new. A special service was held to give thanks to those people who had made sacrifices for the liberation struggle. Both Walter and Albertina Sisulu attended that service. Some young people in the congregation heard the story of Robben Island there for the first time. Dandala asked people who had been in prison or detained for political reasons to come forward to the rail and then he asked the entire congregation to thank them and pray with them. Many people, black and white, famous and unknown, came forward. Dandala said, "That little service showed why it was important for me that we kept that non-racial face for this church. At that time, our church had a huge responsibility to contribute to the atmosphere for nation building."

Central Methodist also played a role in preparing for the first democratic elections in 1994 and here the remarkable skills of Lindi Myeza were invaluable. Myeza was still on the staff at Central, but she was now leading the church's outreach work. She realised that many people did not have IDs, which meant that they would not be able to register to vote. With the help of Home Affairs, Myeza led a campaign that resulted in Central Methodist Mission issuing more than a thousand IDs from the hall in the basement. Then she turned the foyer of the building into a voting station as part of voter education and training.

Just as Central Methodist was trying to cope with change and bridge the old and the new, so was the city. More and more businesses were leaving the city for the suburbs. Once influx control legislation was lifted more and more individuals were free to come into the city, the pattern of landlords abandoning the maintenance of inner-city buildings escalated, resulting in more poor people living in more crowded conditions. In an effort to engage with the changing needs of city dwellers, Central Methodist began a new ministry called the Urban Institute. It focused on moving people from life under apartheid to life as citizens in the city. It dealt with legal issues, housing, skills and language training.

"The city was changing drastically," Myeza recalled. "It was more black than white. The sad part is crime started coming into the picture too." Muggings of members of the congregation along the Smal Street Mall began to be more frequent occurrences.

Crime became an issue inside the church as well. Two speakers from the sound system in the People Centre were stolen, as was the wooden bench from the foyer and a red chair that had always stood near the lifts. The church newsletter noted wryly: "There used to be a time when nobody would dare to steal from the Church (they were too frightened or superstitious) – not anymore!"

In 1996 South Africa attempted to deal with the crimes of the past by establishing the Truth and Reconciliation Commission (TRC). Fazel Randera, a medical doctor who had treated many victims of apartheid, became a member of the TRC and in addition to his role as commissioner, he was also the co-ordinator of its Gauteng office. He was tasked with finding a venue for the first hearings that would take place in Gauteng. Randera approached Peter Storey and asked whether Storey thought that Central Methodist would be willing to host the hearings. Thinking that Randera meant the hall in the basement, Storey pointed out that it would only hold 500 people, which might not be enough space. Randera corrected him: the

TRC would want to use the main sanctuary, he said. "Isn't that going to be a problem for people of other faiths?" Storey asked. "Will people feel comfortable in a Christian church with a cross on the wall? Won't that give some people additional stress?" Randera responded by saying that during the struggle Central Methodist had identified with the oppressed and that the church had greater significance than a religious location only. It had sometimes been the only place where people could meet. As a professed atheist, not a practising Muslim, Randera decided that the church had a role to play in a secular society. He pursued the idea, with Storey's blessing.

Reverend Mvume Dandala agreed to host the TRC hearings and there was a special service at Central on the Sunday before they began. It was fitting that this service and these hearings were held in the sanctuary during Dandala's time there, as he believed that the church had a role to play in contributing towards nation building.

There were five days of TRC hearings at Central, from 29 April to 3 May 1996. As Randera remembers it, the church looked splendid, very well maintained. Many people made submissions to the Commission, which focused on human rights violations, giving people the opportunity, often for the first time, to tell their stories. Maggie Friedman made a submission about the murder of academic David Webster. Liz Floyd and others made submissions about labour activist Neil Aggett's death in detention in 1982. Sepati Mlangeni made a submission regarding her husband Bheki, an attorney, who was killed by the security police. He had received a parcel containing a cassette player which he believed contained evidence about apartheid atrocities. The parcel contained a set of headphones and when he put these on and pressed Play, the parcel exploded, killing him instantly.

Fazel Randera specifically remembers the case of Ahmed Timol who, in 1971, fell to his death from the 10th floor of John Vorster Square[2]. Timol's mother made a submission about her son's death. As she spoke Gujurati, there were times when Randera had to try his best at translation. He learned what trauma the translators went through by having to keep their composure while translating horror stories. He remembers choking up when Mrs Timol let out a painful wail while telling the story of her son's dying.

On one occasion President Nelson Mandela attended the hearings at the church and sat in a pew in the front row.

When Reverend Dandala was elected Presiding Bishop of the Methodist

2 the former name of Johannesburg Central Police Station

Church of Southern Africa his time at Central came to an end. Many were sorry to see him leave, amongst them Winnie Mandela. After the 1994 elections, she had become a minister in the new government and an MP and so she was based much of the year in Cape Town. Lindi Myeza remembered that "Winnie would come from Parliament to worship at Central Methodist, just to come to a good sermon from Dandala, and fly back to Parliament." But when Paul Verryn took over from Dandala, she said to Myeza, "I don't think I can come and worship here any longer. Please do understand."

Ten

Bishop Paul Verryn Appears before the Truth Commission

ELECTED BY 250 OF HIS PEERS at a Synod, on 6 July 1997 Reverend Paul Verryn was inducted as Bishop of the Central District, a post that Peter Storey had held for thirteen years. His congregation in Orlando, Soweto gave him a gift – a watch with a gold rim, black roman numerals on a white face, and a brown strap. The date was engraved on the back. As Bishop of the Central District, Verryn was now responsible for over 75 churches throughout Gauteng province. In addition to his new responsibilities at Central Methodist, and as Bishop of the Central District, Verryn also remained the minister of six congregations in Orlando for all of 1997 while the Church took time to find a successor for him there.

Essentially, he was doing three jobs, each one sizeable and carrying its own heavy pressures, and at times Verryn struggled to cope. "It was the Bishop of the District. It was Central Methodist. It was Orlando. In Orlando, there was a funeral every weekend, if not two. People were not interested in whether I had another responsibility or who I was in terms of my District."

Peter Storey was directly instrumental in arranging Verryn's appointment which, for Central Methodist Mission, he knew needed to be a strategic one. He was confident that Verryn was ready and able to handle it, although he was sorry to see Dandala go. Storey set up a number of interviews for Verryn with the lay leadership at the church and Verryn was duly invited to take up the reins.

According to Storey, Verryn was "a very thoughtful and powerful preacher with his own penetrating style" and he saw him as a bridge between a city church and the townships, given his years of experience in Soweto. Storey believed Central's strong engagement with the poor in the inner city should remain high in importance and he felt that Verryn's leadership would cement that engagement because this had also been the focus of Verryn's ministry in Soweto. "There was no question in my mind," Storey said, "that Paul would be a good public voice if Central was to remain a public platform. A voice in the city."

Verryn's induction as Bishop was conducted by Presiding Bishop Mvume Dandala at Central Methodist and attended by Bishop Storey. The new post meant that Verryn was responsible for 70 000 members in a very broad area, from Johannesburg and Soweto to Vryburg. When asked if he was concerned that his new post would take him away from the people, he answered, "I hope not. It is important that the distance between the members of the church and those with responsibility for administering it is reduced." He added, "We will struggle to deal with the pain of the past. Some relationships within the church are fractured and need repair. Many members are profoundly damaged by the past. We also need to explore a new way to deal with each other on an economic basis in society and in the church."

Just prior to his induction, Verryn was interviewed by Angella Johnson for the *Mail & Guardian*. Her opening words harked back to the topic that would seemingly forever be associated with the Bishop. "Paul Verryn is resigned to people harbouring doubts about his sexuality. Is he gay? That is perhaps the most frequently asked question whenever his name pops up in after-dinner conversation. Followed by debates over whether or not he did molest youths at his Soweto home, as Winnie Madikizela-Mandela[3] alleged to the world." She went on to say that "Ironically, although the allegation was expected to tarnish Verryn's image and derail his career, it is his accusers who have lost credibility and seen their reputations ruined by the scandal, while his continues to soar within the church."

When Johnson arrived at Verryn's third floor office for the interview,

3 after her divorce from Nelson Mandela in 1996, Winnie Mandela included her maiden name, Madikizela, in her surname

she found it a chaotic mess and Verryn and his secretary Tina having words about it. "Touch anything and you'll answer to me," she heard him say mock seriously. What followed was a frank and candid interview, with Johnson not avoiding the sensitive areas. She asked Verryn about marriage and children. "I'm married to the church," he told her, "and I've done a lot of nurturing of the children in my pastoral care." He said, "I can't blame people for thinking that I'm a paedophile… I'm not living in Cloud-cuckoo-land. It hurts but there's nothing I can do about it." There was a time, he confessed, when he wasn't sure he would have the resilience to recover from the allegations and trauma and continue his work. "I went into a black hole. Only the fact that I was innocent of any wrongdoing and my faith in God kept me going."

Verryn also told Johnson about meeting Nelson Mandela soon after Mandela's release in 1990, and she told the story in her article. Verryn was invited to tea with Mandela in Soweto. "I expected a much taller person," were the first words Mandela said to Verryn as he opened the door to him. They then sat down to tea which, somewhat bizarrely, was served to the two men by none other than Xoliswa Falati who was apparently working for the Mandelas at the time. Verryn and Mandela "talked politely about politics and religion. 'It was so British,' chuckles Verryn. 'We did not mention the Stompie affair. I just thought it a great privilege to be there.'"

At the conclusion of her interview, Johnson asked Verryn directly: "Are you gay?"

"I'm not going to enter into the thing of saying either I'm heterosexual or yippee I'm gay," was his response. "But the event certainly heightened my understanding of what it must be like to be gay… and victimised."

Later that year, Paul Verryn had another challenge to face. He had to make his own submission to the Truth and Reconciliation Commission. Special hearings were scheduled to discuss events of the late 1980s involving Winnie Madikizela-Mandela and the Mandela United Football Club. Verryn's life story had been inextricably woven in with Winnie's as a result of those events, the speculation around them and the court cases that followed. In 1997, as Paul Verryn was trying to move forward with his new role in the church, and as South Africa was trying to come to terms with its past, he and Winnie would meet again, this time face to face.

In her book *Country of My Skull* journalist Antjie Krog wrote that "The Winnie Hearings", as they were called, could be compared, as a South African media event, to the release of Nelson Mandela from prison

Vendor table outside Central Methodist Church, between the front door and the fence, August 2010.

Friday night refugee meeting, August 2010.

Men walking out of the sanctuary after a Friday night refugee meeting with cardboard boxes that will become their beds on the floor of the church, August 2010.

Central Methodist Church, corner of Pritchard and Smal Streets.

Joyce Gundu, head of the department of the primary school at Albert Street School, teaches a class in the sanctuary of Central Methodist Church, June 2009.

© Christa Kuljian

Ambrose Mapiravana, head of security at Central Methodist.

© Siven Maslamoney

Freedom Chivima, plumber and karate teacher at Central Methodist.

© Siven Maslamoney

Cleo Buthelezi, resident and staff at Central Methodist.

© Courtesy of Takudzwa Chikoro

Takudzwa Chikoro, student at Albert Street School and resident at Central Methodist.

© Denis Farrell, Picturenet

Men sitting on Smal Street during the police raid on Central Methodist Church, 30 January 2008.

© Tebogo Letsie, Picturenet

Crowd of people forced out of Central Methodist Church onto Smal Street during the police raid, 30 January 2008.

© Alon Skuy

Temporary tent camp in Gauteng after the xenophobic violence of May 2008.

© Museum Africa

Central Hall on the corner of Pritchard and Kruis Streets circa 1936.

© Museum Africa / Africa Media Online

Reverend JB Webb and his congregation getting ready to walk from Central Hall to the new Central Methodist Church building in 1965.

Courtesy Lindiwe Myeza

A painting of Lindiwe Myeza, staff at Central Methodist, done for The Star *in 1976 by Anna Zaleska.*

WHAT A FAMILY!

NEWS FROM THE CENTRAL METHODIST MISSION, JOHANNESBURG

NUMBER 31 OCTOBER 1988

As old as the city

CMM prepares for Anniversary

The people called Methodists have been witnessing to the love of God in Johannesburg for 102 years. From the day in July 1886, when John Thornhill-Cook, gold prospector and Methodist lay-preacher began holding services on his claim and begged for a minister to be sent, the record of Methodist witness has been one of innovative and deeply committed response to the spiritual and social needs of the mining camp, booming town and modern metropolis.

Now in 1988, when the city is facing its most challenging period of social change, the CMM is positioning itself to be the warm heart, the caring community in the city.

The priorities of evangelism, nurturing and discipling those who come into a relationship with God, caring for the children of the city and providing evening programmes for city-dwellers have been established and work already begun on making those dreams realities.

The care of CMM members continues with opportunities for worship, fellowship, learning and service.The importance of this care is reflected in the planned appointment of a lay pastoral worker in 1989.

The prospects for our 103rd year in the city promise to be exciting and we approach them from the context of a great Service of Thanksgiving to be held on Sunday 6 November at 2.30 pm. The President of the Conference, the Rev Stanley Mogoba will be the guest preacher and a special birthday programmme is planned for the children. Celebrations will continue informally over high tea after the service. (This will be the only service in the Mission on that day)

"Refugees" at Central

Central offers SACC temporary home

A few hours after the bomb blast wrecked Khotso House, the SACC was operating again from emergency facilities at CMC.

SACC staff arriving at the scene of the explosion were redirected to CMC and morning prayers went ahead as usual, this time in our Chapel.

For a few days most of our halls were occupied by various SACC departments trying to reorganise and then continue their work while they waited for the verdict on Khotso House. Slowly alternative accommodation for most departments was found and some documents rescued from Khotso House (staff being lowered through the roof by a Fire Department Vehicle !!)

At the time of going to press. only the Administrative section remained, sharing the CMC office and switchboard and Rev Paul Verryn's office occupying the Boardroom. The SACC have secured another building in Braamfontein and hope to move in from 3 October.

YOU
ARE
INVITED

Enclosed with this news letter is your invitation to the Anniversary celebrations. It would be helpful for catering purposes to know who will be coming. Please contact the Church Offfice at 337 5938 or leave your name at the Information Desk on Sundays if you will be joining us.

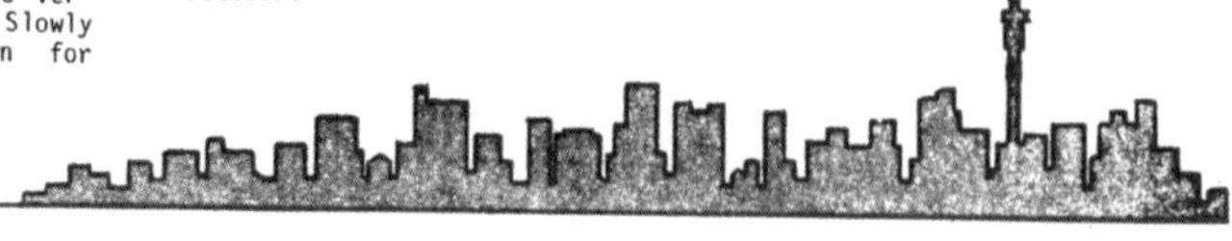

Page from Central Methodist Mission newsletter, What a Family!, *reporting "Refugees at Central", October 1988.*

A security policeman stands beside Bishop Peter Storey in the pulpit as he tells the prayer service for the Delmas treason trialists that it has been declared an illegal gathering. Reverends Frank Chikane and Allan Boesak stand behind him, December 1988.

Soweto anger at Winnie 'team'

Weekly Mail, 27 January 1989, article written by Thandeka Gqubule.

Tambo's help needed in 'ghastly situation'

City Press, 19 February 1989, article written by *City Press* reporters.

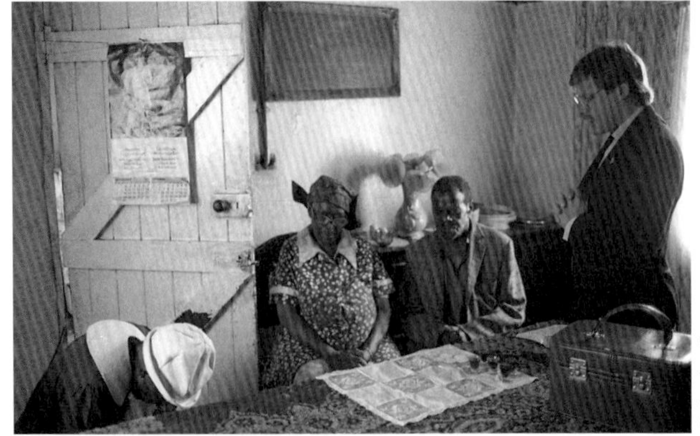

© Lesley Lawson

Reverend Paul Verryn offering communion to house-bound Soweto residents, 1992.

© *Jon Hrusa*, Sunday Times, *12 December 1996*

Reverend Mvume Dandala, 1996.

© *Raymond Preston*, Sunday Times, *27 November 1997*

Reverend Paul Verryn speaking to the media during the Truth and Reconciliation Commission, 1997.

in 1990. She recounted the statistics. "More than two hundred journalists from sixteen countries, more than twenty foreign television crews and one hundred news agencies from around the world have been accredited." The hearings took place in a recreation centre in Mayfair, just south-west of Johannesburg.

As the TRC transcripts recorded, on 25 November 1997 Paul Verryn's one-time employee and Winnie Mandela's erstwhile friend Xoliswa Falati was questioned by the Truth Commission. Hanif Vally was the commissioner in the chair.

> Vally: Your allegations regarding Reverend Paul Verryn came from Katiza Cebekhulu?
> Falati: Yes.
> Vally: Katiza said he lied.
> Falati: That's what I've seen on TV.
> Vally: That you had no source of information about Reverend Paul Verryn at all.
> Falati: That is why – you know when that thing was shown on TV. It was devastating.
> Vally: And you lied in court in the Richardson trial?
> Falati: Yes, I had to protect…
> Vally: You lied in court at your own trial.
> Falati: Yes, for the sake of protecting my leader. I had to lie to protect, that was our culture, to protect our leaders.

Later in her testimony, Falati continued:

> I want to ask forgiveness from Father Paul Verryn, to the public and to the world that I apologise to Father Paul Verryn. You know, he is a man when you're asking for one mile he takes you two miles. He has… [indistinct] the African children without expecting something from them. Unlike Mrs Mandela who… [indistinct] those who… [indistinct] like us and expecting something in return. Father Paul Verryn harboured us as destitute and displaced comrades from various places without expecting any gain from us.
> Chairperson: Thank you. Thank you.
> Falati: And I say I'm sorry to Father Paul Verryn and of course to those victims of assaults, brutal assaults from – the allegation from Katiza

Cebekhulu when Katiza was sent by Mrs Mandela, she has messed up with all our lives.
Vally: You maintained a lie against Reverend Paul Verryn for many years.
Falati: Pardon?
Vally: You maintained a lie against Reverend Paul Verryn for many years. He's the person who offered you sanctuary. He offered you a home when you didn't have a home and he could have also been regarded as one of your leaders. Yet you were prepared to maintain a lie which would possibly have destroyed his life. Why?
Falati: There was no choice. I've told you that when you are dealing with Mrs Mandela, yours is not to reason why. Yours is to do and die."

Katiza Cebekhulu testified before the TRC on the same day. The commissioner was Mr Joseph.

Mr Joseph: In regard to yourself, you had made allegations that Father Verryn had slept with you. Is that correct?
Cebekhulu: Yes.
Mr Joseph: And those allegations were false?
Cebekhulu: Yes.

To follow up, Paul Verryn's attorney Lisa Gerntholtz also sought clarity on this matter.

Gerntholtz: The allegations that you made about Bishop Verryn, you seem to vacillate between whether he raped you or whether he sexually abused you. Was there any truth in those allegations at all?
Cebekhulu: No, I even want to apologise to him for having made those allegations because they were not true and still are not true.

The day after Cebekhulu's testimony, on 26 November, Chairman Desmond Tutu began the proceedings: "We call Paul Verryn."

Silence. Verryn was conspicuously absent – "running a little late", apparently because he had gone to pick up Peter Storey as no one else had arranged a lift for him. When they did arrive, and Storey had his chance to speak, he addressed the TRC:

I want to thank this Commission… for the words of affirmation given

> to my colleague and successor as Bishop, Paul Verryn. In spite of the fact that the allegations made against him have been thrown out by two judges, the media has never used the name of Mr Verryn without associating him with the words sodomy or rape. I think that's disgraceful and I hope, sir, we've seen the end to that, and that this amazing Christian who served the people of this land will be able to walk from this place knowing he has been exonerated.
>
> And in connection with that, sir, I want to say that I admire him for the grace with which he has borne his burden. To my knowledge, sir, everybody who has publicly accused him of these dreadful misdemeanours has withdrawn those words except one – it is my hope that before these hearing are ended that last remaining accuser will use this opportunity to withdraw her words and to take back the accusations that she made against him.

That was not to be.

When Paul Verryn was sworn in before the Commission, he was questioned first by attorney Wim Trengrove about the circumstances at the manse in December 1988. Verryn told the Commission that he had been on holiday from 22 December but that he returned briefly on 28 December to find some tension at the manse between Pelo Mekgwe and Thabiso Mono. They were in the midst of an argument with Xoliswa Falati. She had threatened to discipline them by calling the Mandela United Football Club. Verryn said that he called the people involved together –

> … and we had a long discussion about what the problem was, and I left thinking that we had settled the issue, and that the young men had had a chance to express themselves and Mrs Falati had a chance to express her unhappiness about their lack of discipline, and that related, as I understood it, primarily to cleaning arrangements in the mission house.

Then Verryn asked for the opportunity to address Stompie Seipei's mother:

> I see that Mrs Seipei is in the audience here today, and the thing that has been most difficult for me is that, having heard the allegations, I did not remove him from the mission house and get him to a place where he could be safe, and I think that if I had acted in another way

> he could be alive today. And so I want to apologise to Mrs Seipei for my part in that.

Verryn then broke down in sobs. After composing himself, he asked for the opportunity to address Mrs Madikizela-Mandela:

> My – I don't know Mrs Mandela really. We've met face to face briefly in my mission house once, and my feelings about you have taken me in many directions as you can imagine. I long for our reconciliation. I have been profoundly, profoundly affected by some of the things that you have said about me, that have hurt me and cut me to the quick. I have had to struggle to come to some place of learning to forgive even if you do not want forgiveness or even think that I deserve to offer that to you. I struggle to find a way in which we can be reconciled for the sake of this nation and for the people that I believe God loves so deeply. And so I sit before you and want to say that to you.

The New York Times reported that "for the first time today, Winnie Madikizela-Mandela looked uncomfortable." The Chairman, Archbishop Tutu, asked whether Mrs Madikizela-Mandela wanted to respond. Her lawyer, Ishmael Semenya, said that she would "want to communicate with the Bishop" but not in the eye of the camera.

At that time, Ishmael Semenya had no idea that within a decade, he and Paul Verryn would become neighbours on Pritchard Street and that they would again become adversaries, but in a very different legal matter.

That afternoon, after the hearings and back in his office, Verryn was interviewed by the *Philadelphia Inquirer*, and he was asked to reflect on his life over the past nine years (December 1988 through November 1997). He said, "I think at a very early stage, I decided there was absolutely nothing that I can do about what people think. The invidious thing about this sort of allegation is that the more you protest, the more guilty you look. What this has done, it's been like poison gas in my life because I have felt I needed to be very constrained so that any kind of affection or warmth that I would show a child cannot be misinterpreted in any way whatsoever. It's not so much an attack on my character. It's an attack on my humanity, on my being."

Set of stained glass windows in the sanctuary depicting events in the life of Jesus.

Detail of stained glass window depicting Jesus washing his disciples' feet.

Meetings at Central Methodist / 2010

In August 2010 my mother-in-law and I went to the 10am service at Central. "It's a little bit unkempt," she said, "but the church is beautiful." Over 700 people were sitting in the sanctuary that morning and the choir behind the pulpit was in full voice. As opposed to the dimness of the room on a Friday night, today it was filled with sunshine. The first hymn was in Tswana: *"Ao! Modimo o' tletseng tshwaro, Ke tsile go go rapela; Mm eke simolola ka go re, Thapelo ga ke e itse; Ao! Morena wa me, O nthute. Go go rapela ka nnete."* A thumping beat was provided by each member of the choir holding a hard red cushion the size of a book in one hand and hitting it rhythmically with the other.

Paul Verryn began his sermon. "There are three things about Jesus that were quite radical. First, he didn't seem to have much stuff. He didn't have a computer, a laptop. Do you think he had a comb? Any deodorant? ... Second, he was a social misfit. The company he kept was disturbing. I don't know how he would have got on with the Pope. He was a little bit of a maverick." Verryn stayed behind the pulpit. "And thirdly, he died as a criminal," he said. "False charges were brought against him.

"What is the most critical issue facing South Africa, the region and the world?" The Bishop waited for an answer but none came. "It's the issue of poverty," he said. "It's difficult to gain access to the poor. The poor are off the main road. What was it about Christ that gave him access to the poor? I struggle with this. I get into my car each day and drive home. I can stop at the corner café and buy what I want to.

"There is something about the spirituality of the poor that refines our access to Christ. If poverty is going to be sorted out, who do you think is going to do it? The government? The taxman? How's it going to happen?" The congregation was silent. "No, it will be you," he went on, pointing at us directly, "and the churches and the NGOs that will do it. We have to save ourselves from a bloody revolution that will come because of rich and poor.

"And don't think that engagement with the world will leave you uncontaminated. Are there any sex workers here today? Please put up your hands?" Verryn looked up into the gallery and waited. "How many of you have raped someone?" he asked, as he cast his eyes across the pews. Then, in a softer tone, "And how many of you have been raped?" His next words came out in a bellow. "These are the issues in the inner city! We have become so refined, we are no earthly good. We have to engage in some rough stuff. That is the challenge to us all this morning."

On another occasion, in his office on the third floor, I asked Paul Verryn about his theology and how scripture had shaped his thinking. He sat on his grey couch, the fabric worn and shiny. I sat on the matching chair as I had done before. I had heard that the set may not have been replaced since this was Bishop Storey's office more than 20 years earlier.

"There is a very strong emphasis," said Verryn, "particularly in Luke's gospel, on a preferential option for the poor. There's quite a persistence of focus on the marginalised in the ministry of Christ. I don't think we can escape it." He jumped up and pulled a Bible from his bookcase. He carried it back to the couch and read: "Blessed are you who are poor for yours is the kingdom of God. Blessed are you who hunger now for you will be satisfied... Woe to you who are rich for you have already received your reward or your comfort." He looked up and said "And then you get the story of the Prodigal Son and the Good Samaritan and all the rest of it in Luke. So that's one emphasis."

My eyes were drawn to the Rembrandt painting of the Prodigal Son which was still on the floor, still leaning against the wall behind Verryn's desk.

"And then the belief that the essential gospel is for all and therefore that the doors of the church need to be open and welcoming," he said.

From across the room a light, airy, high-pitched chiming sound interrupted us. It was Verryn's cellphone. He walked over to his desk, looked at the screen and said apologetically, "Sorry, I have to take this." I couldn't help overhearing the conversation. He was talking to someone named Osmond about an eviction on the corner of Salisbury and Kruis streets. He kept the phone with him when he came back to the couch.

"Tell me about your open door policy," I said. "You welcome everyone, as we are all sinners, but how do you handle having thieves in your midst?" I asked.

Verryn leaned forward, his elbow up against the back of the couch.

"I have told the police many times, 'You must have rocks in your head if you think that I engender that kind of ethos within the church and welcome criminals. How on earth do you think I'm going to survive? Let alone whether the police help us or don't help us. I mean, you must think I have a logic that is so tortured that it's actually insane. Crime doesn't suit me. I want the best for what happens in this building. If you think that I welcome drug addicts and alcoholics and all the rest of it or if I welcome that kind of behaviour and that I'm quite happy with criminals finding refuge in the church, think again.'

"What the erudite... don't understand is that the poor don't come in a cellophane package. Sometimes the biggest challenge in their entire being is not whether they smell good like Estée Lauder but whether they have a morsel to take away the agony of their hunger. I think the real criminals in this country are the corrupt and those that manipulate their positions to extricate all sorts of unlawful possessions. In fact, I think that some of the wealth in this country is criminal. It's obscene actually.

"Not everyone in this building is 'good and clean and fresh, tra la la,'" Verryn said, imitating the jingle for a washing powder. "Not everyone in this building has a wonderful work ethic. Not everyone in this building is sinless, including myself... Yes, we face every conceivable social problem in this place. I also don't think that it's ideal that people should sleep on a cold floor on a wintry night. I don't think that's the ideal at all. We are right next to a 23-storey building that has got rooms and beds and bathrooms. This is the obscenity. The metaphor is right before you."

Verryn paused. I wanted to ask him more about the contradictions in the building, but those chimes started up again. It was Osmond calling back.

On another of my visits to the church, I brought some art supplies for Divine, the young man who had asked me for a drawing pad. I met him in the foyer and I gave him the pad and several drawing pencils. The next time I saw him, he showed me some of his work. He had sketched detailed drawings of birds and eagles, fantasy scenes, and people's faces. He told me how he loved to sit and draw, how it gave him some peace. He clearly found solace in his drawing and was proud of his work.

The next time I saw him, though, he looked down and dejected. He told me that someone had stolen his pad of paper and all his drawings. "Can you buy me another one?" he asked hopefully. Then he told me that he was planning to travel to Cape Town and hoped to find work there.

Some months later, I saw Divine again and he didn't look well. He said that he had gone to Zimbabwe and that he had come back over the border with a group of young men, all of whom had been shot as they were trying to cross, and all of whom had died. I wondered whether Divine's story was true or whether it was all in his head, and I was worried about him. In his hand he was holding a toy machine-gun that he had fashioned from some wire. He looked a lot more gangsta than when I had last seen him. He was wearing large shiny earrings and, to me, it didn't sound as if he was on very steady ground. Ambrose said to me that he thought Divine had experienced a lot of trauma in his life and that he might be mentally unstable. I had to wonder how Divine Love would find his way in this harsh world, and whether anyone really cared.

Eleven

Changing City, Changing Congregation

MVUME DANDALA HAD BEEN WORRIED about the departing white community from Central Methodist, but Paul Verryn wasn't as concerned. While Dandala would go to visit white members of the congregation if they were planning to leave and hope to dissuade them, Verryn's approach was different. "When they left," Verryn said, "I would just wave goodbye. I just didn't have the time. It sounds terrible, so uncaring, but I just was overwhelmed with the entire challenge. I was struggling to cope with a huge workload."

Peliwe Lolwana, who had joined the congregation in the early 1990s, remembered this contrast in the two men's styles. "Reverend Dandala used to say, 'If we lose white congregants, the church will fall apart.' Paul Verryn would say, 'Let them go if they want to go'." When Paul Verryn arrived at the church in 1997, Lolwana did not know him or his history, but she observed early on that he was starting to make some changes.

In mid-2000, Trefor Jenkins, a human geneticist based at Wits University, was one of the few remaining white people in the Central Methodist congregation. Originally from Wales, he had come to Johannesburg in 1963. When he first arrived in South Africa, he worshipped in a Methodist church in an affluent white suburb. He remembers the church's neighbours objecting to a congregation of black fellow Methodists using the same building because of their loud singing. Permission for black worshippers to use the church was subsequently withdrawn, under the argument that a population group that did not actually reside in the suburb could not use the church. In the early 1970s Jenkins and his family moved and started to worship at the Civic Methodist Church in Braamfontein under Reverend Peter Storey. When Storey moved to Central Methodist, the Jenkins family moved as well. Jenkins recalled that in the early 1980s "a positive effort was made to bring people together. The congregation, however, remained ninety-five per cent white."

Jenkins also recalled that Reverend Dandala "tried to maintain a balance and did his utmost not to frighten away white members", but Dandala continued Storey's tradition of a "city church", where the congregation came from a distance only for the worship and the focus of the church staff was on serving the city area.

The most dramatic change in the composition of the congregation to becoming predominantly black occurred, in Jenkins' view, during Bishop Paul Verryn's tenure, when changes in the style of worship were introduced. This included hymns being sung in a number of African languages and the service itself becoming very lengthy. "Many people didn't mind an hour or an hour and a quarter, but when it became two to two and a half hours, it was too much," Jenkins said. "With some, I am sure it was incipient racism that came to the surface in that situation and they felt threatened. Central was a white church and had become a black church."

The choir was another thing that was changing, from being predominantly white to becoming increasingly black. "Some of the choir people who liked their singing as they had done it over the years felt they were being swamped," Jenkins believed, "so better to go and join another choir in a suburb where they could sing the music they liked. The choir eventually came down to only two white members out of the forty or so."

Lindi Myeza remembered a definite "us" and "them" feeling, and she felt it was the white members who were the ones who were reluctant to embrace change or accommodate different traditions and cultures. "It would have been very good if they could have had a chance to learn our songs, when we have been singing their songs for so long. We have been singing their songs but they will not sing ours. They make no effort. Some even say anyway when they do come and we sing they think it is for their entertainment. We do not need to entertain them!" Like Peliwe Lolwana, she approved of

Verryn's efforts. Both women liked the changes to the service and the music, the combining of the two choirs, initiating more singing during the service, and having the congregation say the Lord's Prayer in Xhosa. "The church started feeling like the churches we grew up with," Peliwa said. Thanks to Paul Verryn, Myeza said, the congregation could now sing "the long *Te Deum,* the famous *Siyakudumisa*." This was a powerful statement about the direction of worship.

Jenkins believed that the black members of the congregation did not feel good about whites leaving and he felt sure that Verryn didn't either, but he never brought it up with Verryn, his reticence perhaps suggesting that it might have been a difficult topic.

It was of course conceivable that during his many years in Soweto, Verryn had simply settled into a rhythm of worship there that he was happy to carry forward at Central. The changing congregation was largely receptive of the changes he introduced and felt comfortable with them. In Verryn's view Central was a community that was going through the same sort of transition that South Africa was going through. This traditional white church was evolving into what, for many black people, was the new prestigious place to be seen. "It was very much a congregation in motion with no specific, clear-cut boundaries," he said. "The congregation, just as the city, sought to define itself. Who are we? Where do we fit in? What have we got to say?"

In an analogy borrowed from Bishop Storey, Verryn described the inner-city church and the suburban church as different bodies of water that required different approaches to fishing. "The real essence is that in a lake or a pond, the fish are always there and all you have to do is feel the nibble, whereas in the ocean, things are unpredictable. You can have a completely different congregation in an inner city from one month to the next. You're never quite sure if it's a rock that you're hitting or a fish or a current or whatever. The whole question of how you do your fishing and what you use for bait has got to be different."

Lindi Myeza's "us" and "them" comments could also have related to the change that was under way in South Africa more broadly at the time. Not only was change problematic for white people in places of worship, but also in places like schools and hospitals as these became more integrated. The trend of whites leaving when certain institutions became predominantly black repeated itself elsewhere in society. The process of adapting to different traditions and cultures and trying to be inclusive and accommodating was not easy, and by no means the norm. Myeza believed it showed that apartheid had succeeded in dividing people generally, and this was demonstrated and reflected in the church. "It is as if it planted deep-seated divisions and attitudes and a feeling of exclusiveness," she said, "and it is very sad."

As the shift continued, crime was becoming more of an issue in the inner city and this may well have been another factor in the flight of white congregants. Many of the white members had been accosted in the streets around the church, and Verryn himself had been mugged in Smal Street.

Peliwe Lolwana continued to feel comfortable at Central. Her grandchildren started going to Sunday school there and she and her daughter became more active members. And when, after 22 years of marriage, Lolwana and her husband went through a difficult time and were divorced in 2001, the church was a great support to her. "I wouldn't have survived without the church," she said. "Now I feel that it's a place where I belong."

There continued to be high profile services at Central Methodist under Bishop Verryn. On Saturday, 9 June 2001, twelve-year-old Nkosi Johnson's funeral was held there and was attended by more than a thousand people. It was less than a year earlier, in July 2000, when this young boy had spoken to the world at the World Aids Conference in Durban and became the symbol of South Africa's Aids crisis. "You can't get Aids by hugging, kissing, holding hands," he famously said to the thousands of people at the conference and watching on TV. "We are normal human beings. We can walk. We can talk." He said these words at a time when there was official government denial of the Aids epidemic, a refusal to roll out anti-retroviral treatment, and ongoing stigma of the disease. Nkosi's family was not able to afford the drugs that could have extended his life. He drew attention to the fate of poor, HIV-positive children.

The service at Central, which went on for three hours, included hymns in English, Zulu and Xhosa. During the service, Reverend Mvume Dandala, Presiding Bishop at the time, said, "I don't care what position you take in this debate on Aids. I don't care what position you take on anti-retroviral drugs. Just show this country, show these children some compassion." Outside the church, hundreds of Aids activists waved placards demanding better treatment for the millions of Africans suffering from the disease. Nkosi was one of close to half a million people who died of Aids-related illnesses in South Africa in 2001 alone. It would not be the last time the church would draw attention to the plight of the poor and the marginalised.

It was during this same period that Central Methodist first saw the impact of another challenge to the new democracy – the movement of people from conflict-ridden areas of the continent to South Africa.

Reverend Paul Mutombu was a Methodist minister in the Democratic Republic of Congo. He began offering refuge in his church in the DRC to people who had been traumatically affected by the conflict in that country. His generosity, however, put him and his family in danger and he was forced to leave. In 1999 he travelled to South Africa and arrived with his wife and five of his seven children. He went straight to Central Methodist Mission. His daughter Bibiche and her brother, the two oldest children, were in boarding school at the time, but they would arrive later on.

According to Bibiche, Paul Verryn first contacted the United Methodist Committee on Relief (UMCOR) in the US to make sure that her father really was a pastor and had worked for them for nine years, as her father had told him. Once his credentials had been verified Verryn hired Mutombu as a minister. The family was initially accommodated in Fatti's Mansions on the corner of Jeppe and Harrison streets, where the church owned a flat, but when Bibiche and her brother arrived, the Mutombus realised that the place was way too small. Verryn allowed the family to move into the apartment on the third floor at Central Methodist. While other staff had lived in the building previously, the Mutombu family was the first family of refugees to live in the church.

Reverend Mutombu began a 9am French-speaking service at Central Methodist for people from different French-speaking countries. The new congregation grew and he and his family were thankful for the community that the French service provided them. After two years in South Africa, Mutombu was diagnosed with cancer and within a year he passed away, leaving his large, young family behind.

"Bishop Verryn did everything for us," Bibiche recalled. "He bought the coffin for us. We went to bury my father in Congo and the Bishop paid for our transport. Bishop Verryn was the person who was there for us. He told us we could stay in the building and that we mustn't worry. He gave us shelter. He said we could stay there for free and that he was going to help us. And then we stayed."

By sheltering the Mutombu family, whether he realised it at the time or not, Paul Verryn's opening of Central Methodist Mission to provide accommodation for refugees had begun.

Twelve

The First Residents

THE FIRST TIME BRIAN MUZIRINGA walked into Central Methodist, in November 2001, he experienced the place as intimidating. "Very white-ish and quiet," was how he described it. "There was a man at the door – old man Basil – and there were beautiful benches in the foyer. I went up in the lift to the third floor to the Bishop's office. Tina de Rijke, his secretary, offered me coffee but I said, 'No, thank you'. There were flowers in the office."

Brian had been living on the streets of Johannesburg for months. When he first arrived in the city from Zimbabwe, none of the people he knew there was able to help him with accommodation. He was studying marketing at an institute in Braamfontein which focused on empowering the disabled. Brian was born in 1973 with a congenital disability. His legs were not formed properly so he couldn't walk. He had to crawl to get around, but somehow managed even to play soccer. At age eight, he had a double amputation at both knee joints, which allowed him to fit prosthetic legs.

Brian had heard that people in difficulty could sometimes make a phone call from Central Methodist, especially if they had to phone home, but the call he needed to make was to follow up on a job offer. He decided to take a chance. Luckily, Tina de Rijke said he could use the phone in the office. "When I said 'Thank you' to the Bishop," Brian recalled, "he didn't respond. I thought he was a bit scary and that he probably didn't associate with the public. That job never came through so I was a car guard for about R60–R80 a day. I was studying and it was hard to do my assignments at night. I was staying in the community of the streets on Loveday. My inner voice said to me, 'Maybe if I go ask that man at Methodist, maybe he can help me pay for shelter. Those shelters are congested but at least there's light at night.'"

Back in Harare, Brian had attended a multi-racial high school which did not cater for children with disabilities. He was bullied and he suffered from depression. He often wanted to leave the school but his parents encouraged him to finish his O levels at least, so he did, and then he went on to work in marketing. Brian was proud of his lineage. His maternal grandfather was of Zambian and Congolese descent and was a deacon in the Anglican Church. His paternal grandfather was a teacher who at one stage had taught Robert Mugabe. In 1999 and 2000, Brian became active in Zimbabwe in the National Constitutional Assembly (NCA), a coalition of civic organisations, including trade unions, student and youth groups, women's organisations and churches. The NCA opposed the government-proposed changes to the constitution that would put more power in the hands of the president. The NCA was successful in defeating the February 2000 referendum on the constitution, but Brian found the state's response concerning. It was also in 2000 that Mugabe began his controversial land reform programme, which included the occupation by war veterans of commercial farms. The crackdown against NCA members left Brian feeling that change was going to be very slow in coming in Zimbabwe, and he started thinking about a move to South Africa. Another factor was the growing shortage of foreign exchange which made it difficult to import the medical supplies he required for his prosthetic legs. He left for Johannesburg in 2001.

After trying to make life work on the streets, Brian went back to Central Methodist in January 2002 to talk to Bishop Verryn. Verryn asked him if he wanted to stay in South Africa or go back to Zimbabwe. Brian did not think he could risk returning to Zimbabwe because of his politics, so Verryn put him in touch with Judy Bassingthwaite at Paballo, the ministry of the church that worked with homeless people. She found a place for him at Cornelius House on Delvers Street. It was a good building with 24-hour security and a common lounge area. Each week he would make his way to the church to get money from Tina for transport and food.

A few months later Brian referred a friend of his, Shane Nzimande, who was also from Zimbabwe, to Paul Verryn. Shane was struggling to find accommodation in the city and Brian hoped the Bishop might assist him in the same way that he had helped direct Brian to Cornelius House. Instead the Bishop offered Shane accommodation at the church itself. There were two other Zimbabweans staying there at the time, doing painting and maintenance work.

"I felt lonely at Cornelius House," Brian confessed. "There was no one else there from Zimbabwe. Everyone was South African. So I started spending time with Shane at Central Methodist. Sometimes I would sneak in and stay with them for the night. One evening the Bishop came into the first floor lounge where they were staying. 'What are you doing here?' he asked. 'I'm visiting,' I said. 'This is a vulnerable place and you're vulnerable too,' said the Bishop. 'You must go back to where you're staying at Cornelius House.' He wasn't too happy with me."

By the end of the year, however, Brian was living at the church. "I even had Christmas dinner at the Bishop's house that year," he said.

Another early resident at the church was Leothere Nininahazwe from Burundi. He was 23 when he and his younger brother turned up there in March 2002. They arrived with nothing, knowing no one. "The place looked very smart," Leothere remembered. "There was a doorman who said, 'What can I do for you?' 'We need a place to sleep,' we said. 'The Bishop has gone out, so you can wait until he gets back,' said the man at the door. There was a long bench in the foyer, so we sat there and waited."

Leothere had been studying law at the University of Lake Tanganyika but the war in Burundi meant that he had to risk his life sometimes just to get to classes, which were often cancelled. Leothere described his background and that of his country. "The chaos started in 1993. The first democratically elected [and the first Hutu] President of Burundi [Melchior Ndadaya] was assassinated. The Tutsi majority was happy with the election but many rebel groups formed and the country went out of control. Then the acting President was killed a month later. There were machetes and spears everywhere. Opposing sides burned each other's houses. My mother was killed. She was a victim of the violence in 1993 when I was fourteen.

"My father worked for the agricultural department. He was offered a job in another province. Even though the rural areas were more dangerous than the capital city, he took the job. In 1998 he was killed too. He died in a terrible way. He had to choose between being cut by machetes and drinking poison. He chose the poison."

Leothere and his brother waited on the bench in the foyer of Central

Methodist for two hours. "When Bishop Verryn arrived, we went up in the lift with him to his office on the third floor," Leothere said. "We must have had sad faces. 'Are you hungry?' the Bishop asked. 'Eat first. Then I will hear your story, because it sounds like it's a long one.'"

Although Leothere's English wasn't very good back then, he managed somehow to communicate, and Paul Verryn was a patient and good listener. "We left home via ship," Leothere told the Bishop. "From Bujumbura to Mpulungu Port was four days on the water. We gave money to the captain but we had no proper arrangements. We weren't even sure of our destination. Maybe Lusaka. Perhaps we would go abroad from there. Maybe Canada. We had heard that they welcome refugees. We took a bus to Lusaka. Since we were a Catholic family, we looked for a Catholic church. We told them our sad story and that we wanted to carry on with our education. They told us to go to South Africa and to go abroad from there. So we made an arrangement with Rainbow Trucking to take us from Lusaka to Johannesburg. These guys were professionals. We didn't have any trouble at the borders. We spent a day in the truck in Harare. After a five day journey, we arrived in Johannesburg. The driver asked us, 'Where should I drop you?' We had no idea. We didn't know anyone.

"He dropped us somewhere in Kempton Park. We went to the Town Lodge Hotel and tried to phone the UNHCR [UN High Commission for Refugees]. We had passports but no visas. I thought that someone at reception would help call on our behalf but they didn't. We got a Telkom card and kept trying to get through, but our money was getting finished. Then another guest at the hotel heard our story at reception. He greeted us and assisted us with some calls. He suggested that we go to Jesuit Refugee Services. He put us in a metred taxi. We asked for his name but he said, 'Don't worry. I'm only here for a few days.' He was so generous. He was a mystery man.

"We arrived at Jesuit Refugee Services and they told us, 'We only assist people with documents. You should go to the Central Methodist Mission. No one else helps undocumented refugees.' They escorted us to Central. So that's how we ended up here."

Bishop Verryn listened attentively to the brothers' story. Then he told them there were three people currently staying at the church, two from Zimbabwe and one South African, and he gave them the choice of staying there with the others or being given accommodation at the church's centre in Soweto. They chose Central.

In those early days, when the church first started to provide accommodation, some members of the congregation were concerned. Lindi Myeza was among them. She and Paul Verryn had worked closely together at the Wits Council of Churches in the 1980s and even earlier, when Myeza was at the Wilgespruit Fellowship Centre and had sent young people to Paul's house in Princess for refuge. On this issue, however, they disagreed. "Paul was not always gentle with people," said Myeza. "He could be roughish." She was the only one, she claimed, who could, and would, stand up to him and he didn't always like it. "There were three Zimbabweans staying at the first floor. They would flush water during worship and burn their fish to smell. They would play their radio full blast. I went to Paul. I said, 'Paul, can you ask these guys to cook after we're gone? The service is only one hour. Paul, I don't think people are happy.' 'Yeah,' he said, 'you people talk about *makwerekwere*.' I said, 'I've never mentioned the word *makwerekwere*. All I'm saying is just ask them. They have the whole day to fry their fish. The Zimbabwean fish stinks. How can we worship, and hear the water flow and the doors bang?'"

When she got no joy from Verryn, Myeza went to see Presiding Bishop Ivan Abrahams, and repeated her complaint. Abrahams told her there was unfortunately nothing he could do about it unless more members of the congregation complained. "It's tantamount to gossip," he said. "Find out if you as a group can make a petition." She went back to the church and talked about the problem with some of the other members, and told them what Abrahams had said. Many years later, she was still indignant. "Before I knew it," she said, "Paul preached about me from the pulpit. 'I have official informers,' he said. That's when I walked out of the church. I took my bag and left. I cannot worship where there are informers talking about me. That's when I said, 'If you are worried about two of them, before you know it, there will be two thousand of them and you will not be able to handle them.' That's the last time I set my foot in Central."

This conflict illustrated parts of both Myeza's and Verryn's personalities. Verryn may have been inferring that Myeza was xenophobic – he remembers their parting, with less emphasis on the informer conversation and more emphasis on *makwerekwere*. In all likelihood Myeza might well have complained anyway, even if the culprits living in the church and playing the radio loudly during services were South Africans. She was a strong woman who didn't hesitate to take action as an individual, as she had demonstrated years earlier during the Soweto uprising and during her search for a place to have lunch in downtown Joburg. However, her comment about how the numbers would increase at the church suggests that she also understood the seriousness of the situation in Zimbabwe and that she feared the possibility of a large influx of people.

The clash also showed that Verryn did not handle criticism very well. For the most part, he had followed Bishop Storey's guidance through the Stompie Seipei saga, but there were other examples of his previous stubbornness under authority, such as his time in the military, when he did not appreciate being told what to do. Regardless of the motivations, this was one example of how someone crossed swords with Verryn and lost, a situation that would repeat itself again in the future.

The first time I contacted Lindi Myeza, in 2011, I called her at her home in Soweto. I learned that she had had a fall some years before and had had trouble with her hip ever since. She greeted my call with excitement, exclaiming, "Oh, Paul Verryn was here this morning to give me communion. What a coincidence!"

Despite Myeza's departure from Central in 2002, the 10am morning service continued to be full every Sunday. Most people had no idea there was a growing number of people actually living in the building, but there were some who were aware of the situation and weren't very happy about it. Some members decided to move elsewhere. On the whole, however, Sunday worship continued as normal.

Leothere Nininahazwe stayed on at Central. He started taking English classes at the Adult Basic Education Centre at the church, attending lessons in the cry room outside the balcony of the sanctuary on the second floor. After studying for about a year, the church hired him to assist with the English classes. He also began to attend the 9:30am Sunday service for French speakers in the chapel on the ground floor which had been started by Reverend Mutombu. He became a society steward for the church in mid 2003 and started working for the Urban Institute, the support programme that Reverend Dandala had started years earlier for newcomers trying to find their feet in the city.

"By the end of 2003, the place was starting to fill up," said Leothere. "Day after day, another one, then another one would arrive. There were about half South Africans and half foreign nationals. I decided it was time to rent a room. We found an affordable flat in Cornelius House on the corner of Delvers and Cornelius. My brother had a job as a car guard at the Fourways Mall. He would make about R60 a day. The Bishop wrote me a referral letter for Cornelius House. I needed that because the building was run by the Johannesburg Trust for the Homeless. I still felt like I was staying [at Central Methodist] because I was working there from early morning until the evening. I only went home to sleep."

Leothere took a number of different short courses, including home-based care and counselling. He met Peliwe Lolwana, who usually attended the 10am service on Sunday, and in conversation one day she told him that her sister needed someone to teach French at a Montessori school in Daveyton. The school took him on and Leothere taught there for several years while he continued to work at the church. In addition, he took on more and more work at the Urban Institute and by 2006 he was its director. The cry room became the Urban Institute's office. Leothere's brother went back to Burundi in 2005, but by then Johannesburg was Leothere's home. "The church has inspired me," he admits now. "It has opened up my mind. It often means working in tough conditions, but the Bishop always encourages me."

In 2004 the Methodist Church of Southern Africa, along with St Mary's Cathedral and Central Methodist Mission, established an organisation called Refugee Ministries Centre. The organisation was led by Emmanuel Ngenzi, who had already established himself as an important advocate for refugees in South Africa. Paul Verryn became the board chairman for the organisation. Other Methodist churches such as Berea Methodist, Bryanston, Kensington, and Trinity were involved and supportive as well. The Refugee Ministries Centre provided a walk-in service in the inner city from 2004–2010 before they moved to new premises outside the city in 2011.

The organisation focused on the influx of refugees into South Africa mainly from the DRC, Burundi, Rwanda, Ethiopia, Eritrea, Somalia, Pakistan, Algeria, Kashmir, and Zimbabwe. The centre built a strong reputation for working with government and other organisations to address the needs of refugees, first around documentation and then around human rights. Over the years, Emmanuel Ngenzi and Paul Verryn worked together closely.

The deteriorating situation in Zimbabwe after the March 2002 elections meant that more and more citizens of that country were leaving and heading for South Africa. The number of people staying at Central Methodist continued to rise. The elections were marred by violence and intimidation, and the opposition party Movement for Democratic Change claimed they were rigged. South African president Thabo Mbeki commissioned two judges, Sisi Khampepe and Dikgang Moseneke, to go to Zimbabwe to observe the elections. Their report when they returned was scathing. They spoke out vehemently against Mugabe for changing the Electoral Act in order to give the president, rather than parliament, the authority to alter electoral law. Mugabe also made changes to prevent challenges to election results, which would have great bearing on that country's 2008 elections. Despite this, the South African government and SADC did not speak out against the 2002 elections and Mugabe continued to hold power. By 2005 and 2006 there was growing suppression by his Zanu-PF supporters of any dissent in Zimbabwe.

Despite the new role that Central Methodist was playing in providing accommodation for the displaced and the homeless, it continued to hold special services. In January 2005 the church hosted a special memorial service for Makgatho Mandela, Nelson Mandela's son. Makgatho had died of Aids-related illnesses and within hours his father shared that fact with the world. This was an unusual step at a time when there was great stigma attached to HIV/Aids. *The Star* carried a report: "At a sombre and stately memorial service held last night at the Central Methodist Church in Johannesburg, politicians, struggle veterans and ordinary people came in their droves to pay their last respects to Makgatho… Conducting the sermon, Bishop Mvume Dandala said HIV and Aids was not a disease that singled out individuals, but one that attacked and obliterated communities and proud nations… Deputy President Jacob Zuma and cabinet members Trevor Manuel, Charles Nqakula and Nosiviwe Mapisa-Nqakula, Geraldine Fraser-Moleketi and Jabu Moleketi were among those present to mourn with the Mandela family. Two rows away from Mandela and his wife Graça was his ex-wife Winnie Madikizela-Mandela, flanked by their daughters Zinzi and Zenani."

In mid-2005 the Zimbabwean government implemented Operation Murambatsvina, a controversial government "clean up" campaign that destroyed shacks, backyard cottages and housing co-operatives, and forcibly removed people from their homes throughout urban areas. After a mission to Zimbabwe, Archbishop Ndungane, the Anglican Archbishop of Cape Town, submitted a report to the SACC, which described the operation as "inhumane". "In God's name, stop Operation Murambatsvina" was the SACC's response to the visit. The report estimated that between 800 000 and one million people were displaced during the clean up campaign. Some of the displaced people told the delegation that "they were given 30 minutes to pack their belongings, were loaded on trucks and dumped in a transit camp. They were told that they would be there for five days." By the time the SACC delegation visited, they had been there for a month. The delegation also visited Mbare township in Harare. "Almost every yard was filled with rubble from the demolition of structures. A considerable number of people who have been living in Mbare for many decades had their homes destroyed." Human rights groups said that in addition to losing their homes, many more people lost their livelihoods as well following the demolition of street markets and home industries.

The SACC decided to send a second mission to Zimbabwe, led by its chairperson, Bishop Ivan Abrahams, who was also the Presiding Bishop of the Methodist Church. This second mission included Bishop Paul Verryn. Upon return from the mission, Abrahams said, "I think a lot of these people are traumatised. There's a sense of numbness. It seems as if the government war on the poor is a kind of scorched-earth policy to drive people into submission. I just looked at the places from where the people were moved and it looked as if there had just been an air raid. [I felt] absolute outrage and immense anger." Abrahams also said that he hoped that President Thabo Mbeki would shift his official stance on quiet diplomacy. "It's just not working. This visit just reaffirmed that. To remain silent any longer would be scandalous to us. The credibility of all African leadership is at stake around what is happening in Zimbabwe."

It is worth taking a closer look at the history of Thabo Mbeki's relationship with Robert Mugabe, which has had bearing on South Africa's relationship with Zimbabwe and therefore on South Africa's reaction to Zimbabwean migrants. Their history goes back to before Zimbabwe's independence in 1980. At that time, Mugabe's Zimbabwe African National Union (ZANU) was aligned to the exiled Pan-Africanist Congress (PAC) of South Africa, not to the ANC. It was another Zimbabwean leader, Joshua Nkomo of the Zimbabwe African People's Union (ZAPU), who was aligned to the ANC, which was also in exile and operating under ground at the time. Most ANC members were devastated when Mugabe's ZANU won the election in March 1980. There were many ANC members in exile in Zimbabwe at the time who said they never felt welcome there.

According to Mbeki, the tension between the ANC and ZANU was largely the ANC's fault. In 1980 Mbeki believed it was his duty to help mend the relationship and he spent much of that year in Zimbabwe working out a deal that would allow the ANC's military forces to move easily through that country, giving them an important vantage point to apartheid South Africa. For various historical reasons, this deal fell apart and tensions remained between ZANU and the ANC.

There are some political commentators in post-apartheid South Africa who miss this history and make reference to the close relationship between the ANC and Mugabe's Zanu-PF as liberation movements. They are conflating the relationship between political parties and the relationship between Mbeki and Mugabe. In the family of freedom fighters, Robert Mugabe was like a father to Mbeki. This relationship would later have bearing on Mbeki's role as a mediator between Mugabe and Morgan Tsvangirai, the leader of the opposition MDC in Zimbabwe, whom Mbeki viewed as an outsider to the family of liberation politics.

Mbeki also stood with Mugabe when he came in for criticism from the West regarding the farm invasions which began in 2000. He believed that the West, especially Britain, was racist and was accusing Mugabe of wrongdoing only because he was victimising white farmers. As Mark Gevisser states in his 2007 biography of Mbeki, *The Dream Deferred*, "Mbeki had a point, of course," but Mbeki's racial reading of the Zimbabwe crisis "sometimes seemed to prevent him from acknowledging that Mugabe had strident black critics too, not to mention millions of black victims."

In addition to Mbeki's closeness to Mugabe, Gevisser pointed out that "Mbeki had many practical, logical reasons for his strategy of 'quiet diplomacy' [in Zimbabwe]. These included not wishing to precipitate a civil war and a flood of refugees across the South African border." Ironically, this reasoning would backfire on Mbeki. Gevisser suggested that Mbeki "put an ethnic spin on the threat of the refugee crisis in South Africa; such refugees would for the most part be Ndebeles [said Mbeki]" and that this would fan the flames of Shona-Ndebele conflict. As it turned out, Shonas and Ndebeles were both affected by events in Zimbabwe and both fled to South Africa. Ethnic politics became less polarised than they were in 1980.

The Mbeki-Mugabe relationship and the history between the two men would have a significant impact on how South Africa handled the situation, but the growing numbers of Zimbabweans fleeing to South Africa had an immediate impact on Central Methodist.

Penny Foley had been a member of the congregation at Central since her first visit to South Africa in the late 1980s. Originally from Australia, Foley's life would be shaped by the many years she devoted to the church. She enjoyed the evening service on a Sunday and remembers making soup so that those who attended the evening service could enjoy a warm mug afterwards. For several years, in the early 2000s, she made enough soup for 60 to 70 people on a Sunday. The number of people living at the church, especially Zimbabweans, started to rise in 2003 and 2004. By 2005 she realised there had to be between 200 and 300 people living in the church. "I couldn't make that much soup," she said.

Cleo Buthelezi remembers arriving at Central Methodist after dark one night in March 2005. She had spent two nights sleeping at Park Station with her two-year-old son Mihlali. An acquaintance had suggested that she go to Rhema Church for assistance, but then she got a call suggesting that Central Methodist might be able to help her. "I was in my own world," she said. "I had experienced a lot of trauma." She got into the lift and went up to the third floor. "As we were coming out of the lift, a man was ready to come in. 'We're looking for Bishop Paul Verryn,' I said. 'That's me,' said the man. He was running to a meeting, but he first went back with us to his office. Tina was there. She opened the burglar gate to let us in. Then the Bishop asked Tina if she could find some clothes for me and some food." Cleo and Mihlali spent the night in the church.

The next day Cleo got up and went to visit her cousin who was staying in Yeoville. Her cousin asked Cleo if she wanted to stay with her. "I thought it might be a bad idea," said Cleo. "I had an experience whereby my other cousin was supposed to take me in but it didn't work out because she was staying with another man. I didn't want to bother people. Rather I try and work out my own way. I decided to come back here to Methodist."

Cleo was born in KwaZulu-Natal in 1972, the youngest of seven children. She completed matric and went to the University of Port Elizabeth but was forced to drop out because she couldn't pay her fees. Towards the end of 2004 she got a call from a friend to take up a job as a receptionist in Johannesburg. She stayed with her cousin and her cousin's husband. Several months later, she lost her job and her place to stay, which is how she and Mihlali ended up spending two nights sleeping at Park Station.

After telling her story to Paul Verryn, Cleo moved into Central Methodist. To begin with she slept between pews three and four in the chapel on the ground floor. She would wake up in the morning, take Mihlali to the day care centre, FLOC, in the basement, and go looking for piece jobs. She managed to find a job on Sundays, selling *The Sunday Times* on the street in Roodepoort. One Sunday a woman who was driving by asked Cleo if she could come during the week to do her washing and ironing. "She asked me where was I staying. I told her that I was staying at Methodist. She offered to drive me here so that she could be sure that I was really staying here. And then she gave me work."

In those early days at Central Methodist, the residents were a small and close community. About fifteen people were sleeping in Minor Hall on the mezzanine floor and about 25 were sleeping in the chapel. A few others occupied the lounge on the first floor, but at that stage no one was sleeping outside the sanctuary on the first floor, nor on the second and fourth floors.

As the numbers of people living in the church grew, so did the expenses. Historically, Central Methodist Mission had generally relied on three sources of income: the rental from the two shops on Central's property, giving from the congregations, and donations, some of which were from public sources and others which were anonymous. In August 1997, just before Paul Verryn arrived at the church, Central Methodist established an investment with RMB asset management. This account grew over the years that followed and it was this account that saved the church from becoming technically insolvent.

In 2005 a new ministry was established at the church. This was the Ray of Hope ministry and it operated alongside the other ministries already based there: FLOC for child care, Paballo, which reached out to the homeless on Wednesday nights, and the Urban Institute. Ray of Hope held occasional meetings for residents of the church in the Roberts Room, and this forum became the time and place to discuss issues that affected those people living in the building, particularly around newcomers and how they might all try to help each other. "How should we welcome them, for example," Cleo explained. "We would talk about how best to try and help each other, how best can people be encouraged to take an initiative in their lives, to take themselves serious, rather than coming into the building and think that's the end."

In December that year Presiding Bishop Ivan Abrahams came to speak at the Christmas service at Central. Penny Foley remembers him saying, "I have never fully understood sanctuary until coming here tonight." Years later Abrahams recalled that Christmas and acknowledged that Paul Verryn and the refugee ministry had a hundred per cent of his support. "But who knew at that time," he said, "to use Byron's verse, that 'The thorns which I have reap'd are of the tree I planted; they have torn me, and I bleed. I should have known what fruit would spring from such a seed."

Thirteen

A Murder in the Church

"A Zimbabwean man has been killed at the Central Methodist Church in the Joburg CBD, where he and hundreds of other immigrants from all over Africa had sought refuge," *The Star* reported on 13 March 2006. "Andrew Khumalo was stabbed to death on Saturday, allegedly by a fellow Zimbabwean, apparently after a fight over clothing."

Paul Verryn had refused the newspaper's reporter entry into the church, but allowed himself to be quoted: "'There have been arguments, but we have never had this level of violence. This is huge. I am going to have a meeting with the residents to find out what happened. All we are trying to do is find a way in which we can provide hope and shelter to vulnerable people.'" *The Star*'s reporter tried to find out what had happened by talking to people outside the church. "A man who claimed to have witnessed the killing said there was blood everywhere. A knife-wielding man stabbed the victim several times. He fought back with his fists, but a few minutes later 'he dropped to the floor and died,' said the man who did not want to be identified."

Cleo Buthelezi said, "It was a shock. Seeing someone lying on the ground floor. It was very traumatic." Years later Verryn told me that Khumalo had witnessed the birth of his first child at about noon that day. By 8:30pm, he was dead.

During March 2006 the murder was not the only event at the church to receive press coverage. Central Methodist hosted a night vigil with Women Against Women Abuse (WAWA) to highlight the issue of violence against women. WAWA chose Central as the site for the vigil because it was next door to the Johannesburg High Court, where Jacob Zuma was due to stand trial shortly in an alleged rape case.

The following week Central Methodist held a memorial service for the granddaughter of Transvaal Judge President Bernard Ngoepe, who had been tragically kidnapped and killed. Many of Judge Ngoepe's legal colleagues and friends from the law offices in the neighbourhood attended the service. Advocate Ishmael Semenya, who was planning to move in next door at Pitje Chambers, spoke on behalf of the Johannesburg Bar Council. The child's "innocent face", he said, "is the one that will trouble the conscience of South Africans."

After Andrew Khumalo was killed inside Central Methodist, Bishop Verryn wanted to hold a meeting of all of the residents of the church to discuss the trauma, but realised that the numbers had grown so large by now that everyone would no longer fit in the Roberts Room. They would have to meet in the main sanctuary.

When Verryn reflected on the impact of the murder in retrospect, he said, "Initially, there was no formal expectation that they [the church residents] needed to come to church [services] at all. That became part of the way we were after the murder. I think I started realising, in actual fact, there was no cohesion in this community at all and that it was bordering on disorganised chaos. It was critical for us to put predictable markers in place." It was also as a result of this moment of taking stock that the set of rules was put in place for the residents at the church. On a Friday night the evening service was replaced by a "refugee meeting", which became the regular Friday night refugee meeting that continued to be held every week.

Verryn believed the refugee meetings were important because they provided a forum where the community had the opportunity to speak to one another, or just do simple things like make announcements. And if someone wanted to interview the community, then the community should have the right to ask questions and give permission. Another point of the weekly meetings, said Verryn, was to send the message that residents were "not just an object in this journey. You have the right to become the subject of your destiny and a decision maker about what you allow and don't allow. It's an attempt to show respect to the individuals, many of whom have had their self-respect destroyed."

In many ways the murder of Andrew Khumalo was a turning point for the church. Verryn not only set out new rules and held discussions with the residents, but he also organised a special meeting with members of the church societies to discuss conditions at the church. The meeting took place on a public holiday, Human Rights Day, on 21 March 2006. About 800 people attended. The issues of concern included cleanliness and health, drinking, and security.

Verryn also shared with the gathering how the process of accommodation at the church worked. He told them how he met with every new resident personally to find out their background and what had brought them to the church. Some people at the meeting spoke up and said, "It shouldn't only be *you* doing this, Bishop. This isn't just *your* church. You need assistance." Penny Foley was there and she does not recall that anyone spoke out against housing the refugees, but rather that people were focusing on questions of how best to house them and how to maintain order among the growing numbers.

Bishop Verryn did not always accept feedback graciously, and this was one occasion when he did not. What he took from the meeting was that the members were against the entire idea of providing accommodation and refuge. The meeting also marked another turning point, this one in the relationship between the congregation and the Bishop. "Ironically, it was the necessary opening up of a discussion about the consequences of providing refuge," Penny Foley said, "and it was also the closing down of the discussion. People went away from that meeting feeling that there was no point in speaking up. It was unfortunate that the meeting didn't provide the opportunity for more people in the congregations to have a little more ownership of the ministry to house refugees."

One family that had already engaged with the changes at Central Methodist, even before this meeting took place, was that of Ishmael and Bongi Mkhabela. Their family had worshipped at Central throughout the 1990s and had appreciated Mvume Dandala's cosmopolitan style, which they missed when Paul Verryn brought in a more orthodox, conventional style of worship. However, they had known Verryn for years, worked with him at the Wits Council of Churches and greatly valued and benefitted from his pastoral care. Ishmael Mkhabela had discussed the changes at Central with the SACC, Methodist ministers and church workers, and directly and indirectly put various suggestions forward to Verryn as a result. His background in community organising meant that he encouraged community participation in decision-making. He also worked on urban development and inner-city issues with the City of Johannesburg and he was respected as a grassroots activist who had a lot of wisdom about urban issues. Yet Mkhabela and Verryn didn't always agree on how best to structure the mission projects at Central. Mkhabela would generally promote organisational management and strategic planning. Verryn's approach, however, was more intuitive. Eventually, in 2005, the Mkhabelas chose to quietly retreat from Central Methodist.

The congregation could no longer ignore the growing number of residents at the church. People were no longer tucked away in nooks and crannies. They were using rooms to sleep in that the congregation expected to use as well, such as the Roberts Room, Minor Hall and the chapel. In fact the frustration level amongst some in the congregation was so high that they planned a protest one Sunday, complete with placards and toyi-toying. Oddly, or perhaps strategically, they chose a Sunday when Paul Verryn was away. The placards read: "Enough is Enough", "Down With Paul Verryn", and "Cleanliness is Next to Godliness". While those involved with the protest expected a disciplinary hearing, Bishop Verryn never spoke about it and took no action against them.

As the numbers of people taking refuge in the church continued to grow, so the utility bills for the church building went up and up. The debt to the municipality grew each month. That year, according to Penny Foley, Joburg Water advised the Bishop that Central Methodist would qualify for a free water allocation if he registered the church as a shelter and met certain requirements such as installing bunk beds. Nothing further came of this, however, and the debt continued to mount. By September that year, the church had been unable to pay its water bill for several months and had built up a debt of R146 000. For four days water was drawn from the emergency cistern set aside for use in case of a fire. At the time the monthly water bill was R25 000. Central Methodist negotiated a payment of R5 500 a month to the municipality to keep water flowing until a permanent agreement could be negotiated.

In June 2006, journalist Solly Maphumulo, who had written the earlier article about the murder in *The Star,* wrote another piece, entitled "Place of Worship Now a Den of Iniquity". The article began: "Murder in the cathedral has taken on new meaning for the once fashionable Central Methodist Church in Johannesburg. An immigrant has been murdered, drunkenness is rampant, fights are a problem, rape is not uncommon, theft is ongoing and overcrowding is a major cause for concern… But, say members of the congregation, conditions have deteriorated to the extent that it has become unsafe to go there. They claim people have sex in the church, that used condoms are left lying on the floor and that babies are delivered there. The toilets are blocked, and the place reeks of sewage. It has also become something of an informal market, with all sorts of items on sale by informal traders."

The article quoted Verryn as saying, "We can't put them on the streets. We have to find alternative venues. We have spoken to several people to try to find accommodation. The situation is appalling. I know the congregants are unhappy."

The article described a visit by *The Star* to the church at 8:15 one evening: "… the place was bustling with people of all ages: babies, toddlers, women, men, girls and boys. Underwear, napkins and clothes lined the stair rails. Residents had no place to hang their laundry so they placed them on the stair rails to dry. There was dirty water on the floor, the walls covered in grime, with piles of dirty blankets scattered around. The place smelled bad."

The article infuriated Bishop Verryn, especially the headline.

A week after *The Star* published its "Den of Iniquity" article, *The Weekender* published a piece on the church, too, but this newspaper took another view. Beneath the headline "Crowded House of Hope", *The Weekender* journalist said, "The church is doing its best to provide a safe and less squalid refuge." The article went further. "As the economic and political crisis in Zimbabwe has deepened, more and more Zimbawean refugees have flooded into the city. With many of them unable to obtain refugee status, the Central Methodist Church has become their only alternative." The article referred to the murder and the ways in which the church had reacted, with its new rules and nightly services. When asked about the complaints from the congregation, Verryn sighed and said, "The complaints are understandable. We have 700 people here. This is state-of-the-art worship architecture. It was not meant with this in mind. And it's not always clean. It doesn't smell good. The toilets are overworked."

Verryn said, "Part of the reason people come here is because the streets are dangerous. I don't think this is ideal, but it's better than the street. For people staying here, we hope they will find dignity and empower themselves. We try to help them empower themselves… On Sunday night I met a woman in her 60s, with gnarled hands, from Harare. All her children have died and she has to take care of her grandchildren. So she has come to SA from Harare to sell her crochet and knitting and asked if we could give her a place. That is a huge privilege, to house a saint like her."

At about the same time, in commemoration of World Refugee Day on 20 June, the National Consortium of Refugee Affairs, in collaboration with Lawyers for Human Rights and the Wits Forced Migration Studies Programme, issued a report outlining the difficult conditions facing refugees and asylum seekers in South Africa. The report applauded the tenth anniversary of South Africa's constitution, but then pointed out that "rather than finding safety from violence and persecution in the country, refugees and asylum seekers face administrative delays, extortion and the constant threat of deportation." The report applauded the fact that South Africa was not "warehousing refugees in isolated camps or detention facilities [but rather] encourages refugees to live in its cities, where they can work and contribute." It pointed out that the numbers of migrants in the country over all was estimated at fewer than 150 000. The report also found that in South Africa there were many factors preventing people from accessing their legal rights to proper documents and was critical of the fact that people had to sleep in queues outside Home Affairs offices as they waited days to file an application, that security guards and translators demanded money from them to get in the door, and that there were long delays and many cases of lost files. Despite South Africa's national constitution and international legal obligations, the reality for many migrants was police abuse and the denial of key social services, including medical care.

It was also around this same time that the City of Johannesburg began to express concern to Central Methodist about the city's by-laws not being adhered to and gave the church notice regarding health and safety by-laws in particular. Verryn had fire extinguishers installed and said that he was hopeful that the church would soon be compliant with council requirements.

Sometime in late 2006, after the nightly services and the regular Friday night refugee meetings had begun, Cleo Buthelezi heard that the Bishop was looking for her. "I went upstairs to his office on the third floor. People were starting to flood in so it was very difficult to get hold of the Bishop. You can sit all night waiting for him. 'I'm not going to do this,' I said, so I went downstairs again to sleep. He sent someone to come and fetch me. It was at night now, about twelve-ish. I went upstairs again. It was still flooded. I waited and waited. There were a lot of people sitting there that needed to see him and to tell him their stories. Then I went to my sleep again.

"Eventually, we saw each other. He told me that they need my help, that the lady who had been cleaning the area outside his office on the third floor was ill. He asked if I could come the next day at 9am. He asked me to clean the windows and mop the floor from the waiting room, down the passage, to where the lifts are. The lifts had stopped working. Someone else used to clean inside his office and the kitchen. So I made new arrangements for my other piece jobs." Cleo Buthelezi and her colleagues would have an uphill battle to try to keep Central Methodist clean.

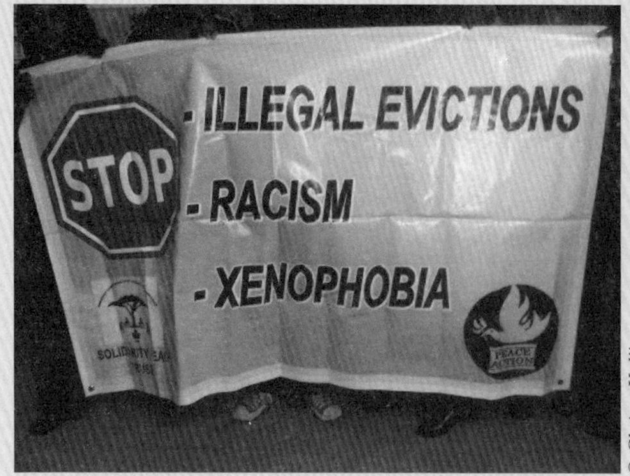

© Christa Kuljian

Banner for Peace Action and the Solidarity Peace Trust.

© Sam Wolson

Reymond Mapakata on the roof of Central Methodist Church.

© Alon Skuy

One of the "bad buildings" in Doornfontein in the city of Johannesburg that Evans Kuntonda and Christa Kuljian visited in October 2010.

Meetings at Central Methodist / 2010

In June 2010, Paul Verryn established a new organisation, Peace Action, to focus on monitoring human-rights abuses in the city centre. Peace Action monitored and intervened in cases of xenophobic tensions, illegal evictions, police harassment and arbitrary arrests. One of the first Peace Action meetings took place over a few hours on a Sunday afternoon, and I went along. The idea was for everyone to brainstorm about the future of the organisation and I was keen both to observe and to participate.

That was the day I introduced myself to Evans Kuntonda, the man who worked for Médecins Sans Frontières. I had seen him at a few Friday night refugee meetings, but we hadn't formally met or talked. The striking thing about Evans that Sunday, which also happened to be Father's Day, was that he clearly had a way with children. I had noticed this before but today it was especially striking. Throughout the meeting Evans was holding a toddler, a little boy who was about two years old. While he was standing up, while he was sitting down, as the child rested peacefully on his shoulder, as the child squirmed and fidgeted in his arms, Evans never once tried to palm him off on one of the many women at the meeting. He never got frustrated or looked like he wanted to hand over responsibility to someone else. He just kept contributing to the conversation in his working group and, eventually, the little boy settled down to sleep.

Evans arrived in South Africa from Zimbabwe in 2007 and lived on the streets for some months before moving into Central Methodist. He was one of the people who worked on the database of residents at the church and documented hundreds of personal testimonies of people who had sought refuge there. Evans worked with Bishop Verryn in May 2008 in the temporary camps that were set up after the xenophobic violence. It was then that he was hired by MSF as a field co-ordinator. He was also one of the few people to whom Bishop Verryn would delegate. Staff at MSF realised they were lucky to have Evans to negotiate between them and Verryn for decisions, even over uncomplicated things such as the placement of a new pipe in the building.

People described Evans as an inveterate networker, a connector, an organiser. He was also one of the very few people who could let Bishop Verryn know when he wasn't pleased with his actions, or indeed his inaction. Penny Foley once told me how Evans would get visibly irritated with Verryn for not paying attention to possible networking opportunities. There were times when Verryn would meet with or get a phone call from someone with real significance, someone who was in a position to assist the church or the refugees in some way, and Verryn wouldn't remember who they were or what the contact's name was. Evans would say, "Give me your phone. I'll find the missed call. I'll get hold of them."

As it turned out, Peace Action meetings were where I met and kept in touch with quite a few people at Central Methodist. In addition to meeting Evans that day, I caught up again with Cleo Buthelezi and we set a date for an interview. Other regulars at Peace Action included Brian Muziringa, Priscilla Manyere, Wellington Mukwamba, and Blessing Bissend. I also got to know Reason Machengere from the Solidarity Peace Trust through these meetings, where he was vice-chairperson.

Another Central Methodist resident who became an active Peace Action member was Reymond Mapakata. He was several years younger than Evans and he looked up to him. In contrast to Evans' sophistication and charm, Reymond was quiet and uncertain. Despite his shyness, Reymond and I got to know each other over many months, and we often walked to Peace Action meetings together. A group of us would meet at the church and walk the eight blocks down Kruis Street, past the Carlton Centre, and on to the Albert Street School where the meetings were held.

Although Reymond wasn't a very large person, he had a lumbering gait. He moved more like a long-limbed giraffe than a gazelle. Even when he was in a hurry, he looked like he was moving in slow motion. I saw him "run" up a flight of stairs once and he didn't bend his legs. He kept them straight and threw them out to the side, pushing off each stair to hoist the other leg up a few more. Reymond spoke in the same style that he moved. He often had a lot going on in his mind, but it always came out in slow, measured speech. He wasn't the kind of person you could imagine in a snappy courtroom debate or a high-speed police chase. But as luck would have it, Reymond would end up in scraps with the police more often than he'd like. He seemed to have a talent for getting arrested.

Reymond grew up in a rural village, Bikita, in Masvingo province in Zimbabwe, about 400km south of Harare. His father died when he was eleven years old so Reymond lived with his grandmother. He finished his O levels in 2000. He and his girlfriend Memory Taranhike had a son, Will, in 2002.

Bikita was arid and hot, Reymond said, and they couldn't rely on farming. "You have to rely on others who are working," he told me. "I had no job and no one to talk to." He took on odd jobs as a welder and a bricklayer and also worked for a while in Harare on renovations to the airport runway. In 2006 his second son, Willfred, was born and Reymond struggled to support his family. "We had no shoes and no trousers. We would see guys coming from South Africa with nice things," he said.

Reymond applied for a passport and tried to find work in the DRC and Botswana, and he even tried to import goods from Zambia for a time, but none of these avenues proved fruitful. He couldn't continue sitting at home and "waiting for a new day", he said, so in November he crossed the border into South Africa. He worked in Polokwane for a while in welding and construction but, as a casual worker, when the work dried up he was retrenched. At the end of 2007 he went to Johannesburg to look for work there and got a ride on a truck that was headed for the city. He was dropped off at Noord Street taxi rank and he lived on the street for many months.

Reymond was arrested for the first time in July 2008. The policeman who arrested him took his passport and refused to give it back. After his release, Reymond opened a case of theft at the Hillbrow police station but they never returned his papers. He continued to live on the street but soon he was arrested again. This time he was charged as an illegal immigrant with no asylum papers and sent to Sun City (Diepkloof prison). "One day they locked us in the cell. A man died that night and they didn't open up again until 8am. It was horrible." Reymond was at Sun City for two months and then released on 22 September 2008.

It was then that Reymond heard about Central Methodist and moved off the street. The Albert Street School had recently opened and he considered the possibility of studying for his A levels. As a 25 year old, an older student, he thought perhaps that further education would be the answer. "I was afraid of what had happened to me and I was thinking of my family back home." Shaking his head slowly, he said, "Memory got together with someone else because I wasn't sending money home to her. I'm a father failure."

Reymond devoted himself to his studies in 2009 and 2010 and he also discovered a new interest – film. He took a course with an Israeli film maker who had come to Johannesburg to make a documentary. Reymond started to have hope that after completing his A levels he could start working as an assistant in the film industry. The film maker gave Reymond a camera when he left, but it was stolen from the church.

Reymond was arrested for the third time in 2009. It was 8am and he had gone to the shop to buy bread. He was picked up for "loitering" and spent the weekend in jail.

He continued to volunteer and do small jobs for the various film makers and journalists who came to the church. One film maker, Richard Adams from New York City, was making a film about Central Methodist, and another, an African-American human rights attorney turned film maker named Isy India Geronimo, was making a documentary about homelessness in the inner city. One day, when Reymond was in Hilbrow, he was again picked up by the police. He called India Geronimo to let her know that he had been arrested. She went to Hillbrow to offer her assistance, but she, too, was arrested by the police. They weren't convinced by her American accent and wanted to see her papers. Both she and Reymond spent the night in jail.

A few days after his fourth arrest, I visited Reymond at the church and we went up onto the roof together. Reymond would often retreat up there for some privacy. He told me he was feeling very uneasy. "I'm not a criminal," he said. "I shouldn't have to run away. I'm a human being." The roof gave him a bird's eye view of the hustle-bustle of Pritchard Street. "I have to watch who's coming for me," he said. "Once they [the police] see you don't understand their language, it's a problem. It's worse if you don't have money in your pocket." With a melancholy look in his eyes, he said, "I'm still an able person. I want a better life, to be free, to support myself and my children. I think filming is going to help me. I want better skills in filming. I feel like I'm at the edge of life."

When Peace Action started monitoring human rights abuses, Reymond worked at the help desk in the foyer of Central Methodist, taking statements. He also worked with Peace Action to monitor the situation at the Home Affairs office in Marabastad, Pretoria. He had had to go there to renew his asylum seeker permit and had had a difficult time of it. He took the 4am train from Park Station to make sure he got to Pretoria early. When he got to Marabastad, it was after 6am, and he was told he was too late. He waited six hours but eventually accepted that he would have to come back the next day. "A police officer told people to go back to Zimbabwe as they are overcrowding in South Africa," said Reymond. He went back to Marabastad the next day and this time he was asked to pay a bribe of R400 but he didn't have the money. On his fourth visit, he managed to renew his papers, but only after giving an official his phone as a bribe. Once the official realised that the phone wasn't working, he got angry and said not to come back unless he had money next time.

Reymond related his experience to Peace Action and this helped to inform them about numerous abuses that were a daily occurrence at the Marabastad Home Affairs office.

Just as Reymond informed Peace Action about abuses at Home Affairs, and about his experience of being arrested by police on the streets of Johannesburg, Evans Kuntonda's work informed Peace Action and Médecins Sans Frontières about conditions in other buildings in the inner city and about the illegal evictions that happened there frequently. As the MSF clinic at Central Methodist began to receive more and more visits from migrants who were living in other buildings outside the church, Evans started to do outreach work to those buildings, and he led the effort to interview 500 people living in 30 derelict buildings in downtown Johannesburg.

One day in October 2010 Evans took me with him to visit one of those buildings. We met at Central Methodist and walked to the edge of the city to the east. Evans was wearing his white MSF jacket. Our destination was a building in Doornfontein, which was actually an old warehouse and not designed for residential occupation at all. At the time we visited it there were 500 people living there. On the ground floor were piles of rubbish creating rivers and lakes and we had to pick our way around the edges of the muck to get to where someone was living. Thin walls of plywood and cardboard had been put in place to create hundreds of small rooms. It was dark because there were no windows in this section and there was no electricity either. We opened a door. Inside sat a woman with her six-week-old baby. Evans had visited the woman throughout her pregnancy. He took the baby and held him while he chatted to her about her and the baby's health.

Afterwards we stood outside the building for a few minutes while Evans talked to another resident who was one of the community leaders. The residents were organising to resist eviction. They were also organising, with MSF's assistance, to develop a plan to clean up the waste that had built up in the building. It would be a big job. As we left, Evans told me, "Even without the problems in Zimbabwe, these buildings would still be filled. It's an issue of poverty."

Peace Action had a lot of work to do.

Fourteen

A Ray of Hope

Central Methodist's latest ministry, Ray of Hope, grew to become one of its largest during 2006 and 2007. The new ministry focused on the promotion and protection of the rights of refugees, asylum seekers and internally displaced people. The significant increase of asylum seekers to Johannesburg in 2006 resulted in Central Methodist providing accommodation to more than 700 people. It was then that the church began a range of programmes relating to adult education and training.

It was also in 2006 that Central Methodist started developing a database and issuing registration cards to all residents. Bishop Verryn still interviewed every newcomer personally, but other staff now took down information such as next of kin, educational qualifications and skills, and issued people with laminated photo IDs. Ray of Hope had a website designed and it was impressive: "Amongst the people that we host are school principals and teachers, accountants, mechanics, plumbers, carpenters, financiers, people with careers in marketing, journalists, politicians, and people from the medical professions... It is not a matter of skilled labour stealing the jobs of South Africans. In fact, the skills that have been driven into this country miraculously match exactly what is needed in our present economy... The intention is for individuals to gain independence and economic sustainability as soon as possible so that measurable contributions can be realised in an inner city that is exploding with potential and vitality."

The goal of the Ray of Hope ministry was to affirm the human dignity and restore the hope of asylum seekers, refugees and the displaced in the city of Johannesburg. Among the objectives of the Ray of Hope ministry listed on the website and also in a funding proposal written at the time was "to obtain, renovate and run a building outside the church that provides temporary and safe accommodation." This was significant given the challenges that were to arise a few years later to secure another building to accommodate the residents. There certainly were not sufficient funds at Central Methodist to consider such a purchase. Before Ray of Hope was set up the church would set aside resources under the Poor Fund, which was how Paul Verryn could assist people in need with small amounts of money for things such as transport and food. Once Ray of Hope was established, it operated within the Deaconess Society, which had begun its life as the Deaconess Institute way back in the 1890s. The Deaconess Society was a separate legal entity registered as a non-profit organisation, so it could raise funds independently, and for many years FLOC and Paballo had been its largest projects. The United Methodist Committee for Relief (UMCOR) (the same international organisation that Minister Mutombu had worked for before he arrived at Central Methodist) was a significant source of funding for Ray of Hope. For three months, from January through March 2007, it made an emergency grant that included support for food and meals, supplies for infants, access to clean water, and support for the Home Based Care clinic in the church. Despite the fundraising efforts for Ray of Hope, the resources of the Deaconess Society and Central Methodist were very limited in comparison to those held by the broader Methodist Church of Southern Africa, which collected funds from many sources.

Individual members of a congregation or society make contributions every Sunday. The societies make what are called "assessment" payments to the circuit. Each circuit makes assessment payments to its district, and each district makes assessment payments to the Methodist Connexional Office, which is the head financial office of the Church. The MCO administers insurance cover on church properties to the value of around R3 billion. It holds the title deeds and administers 1 400 properties. The MCO is responsible for paying salaries to about 1 200 employees and administers two pension funds and one provident fund. At the end of 2005 the pension and provident funds had a combined value of R712 million in assets. Clearly if anyone was going to buy a building, it was going to have to be the MCSA.

As the Ray of Hope ministry grew, Cleo Buthelezi spent a lot of time around the Bishop's office in her new job as a cleaner. At some point, she made the connection between Paul Verryn and Winnie Mandela and "put the pieces together", as she said. Cleo had a husky voice – she sounded like Tina Turner. "How can I end up being rescued by someone like this?" she said. "This man is well known and he's big in the country. You'll be scared one day just to walk into Zuma's office and start working for Zuma. It was something like that for me. I never thought in my life that I would work for someone who is well known and all that. *Eish*!"

Not long after she started cleaning the front office and the waiting room, Cleo was asked to start cleaning inside the Bishop's office as well and she was offered permanent employment. "In this office," said Cleo, "everything is there. You'll be working on that table where there is money that will be given to people that don't have money for food or money for transport. It's on the top of the table. In the drawer, there will be envelopes for people that are doing home-based care, the people who are doing the child minding course, the money for the cleaners. Here you are with your situation. It's like being taken from the street and then you go and work for the bank. It's a lot of temptation. But I managed. It's good when people trust you, especially when you are from a certain situation. If I had messed up one way or the other, I don't think I was going to be where I am right now. I've come too far."

In 2007 Cleo became more involved with the Ray of Hope ministry. Residents were still required to attend a service every night at seven and Wednesday night became a special healing service with communion. Cleo started setting up communion for that service. It was also that year that she began assisting with job placements for residents. "There was a couple that was looking for someone to work for them. The Bishop just called me and asked, 'Can you try and find someone that can work for these people?' I think he was listening to the way I was questioning them. I would ask them, 'What is she going to be doing for you?' 'How big is your house?' 'How many children do you have?' 'How much are you going to pay her?' He was listening. I think that's when he just *sommer* decided that I will do this placement thing. One day he just *sommer* announced in the church that if someone wants to offer someone a job, please you must make sure that they do it via the office, and you must make sure that Cleo talks to those people."

The community of residents put together a leadership committee at that time. At first it was led by a man named Saul Zvogbo. While Zvogbo had a large presence at the church, he later became a controversial figure, especially in the wake of the May 2008 violence and the increased influx of people at that time, and the donations that were being made to the church.

In December 2007 Médecins Sans Frontières opened a clinic at Central Methodist on the ground floor, with a separate entrance onto Pritchard Street. Just months earlier MSF had opened a clinic in Musina near the border with Zimbabwe and started operating mobile clinics to some of the nearby farms where many migrants from Zimbabwe worked. It chose Central Methodist as the site for its Johannesburg clinic because it believed it would be the best place to reach those migrants who were most destitute. Central Methodist was the place people went to when they had no other support or connections in town. MSF saw a pressing need to provide basic health services for these people. They would then be in a position to refer patients to the public health system for additional treatment if necessary. A key aim of theirs was to facilitate access for Zimbabwean migrants to existing health services in Johannesburg.

According to MSF's Eric Goemaere, who was involved in the initial negotiations with Bishop Verryn to start the clinic at the church, there were three issues that MSF wanted to clarify before they moved in. First, political independence was important to MSF. Second, MSF did not want to align itself to any religious denomination. Both of these issues were deemed acceptable. Third, MSF said it could see that Central Methodist was run as a "one man show", and this was a worry. After several appointments when they had had to wait for hours to see the Bishop because no one else could take any decisions, they were concerned. "Do you think this arrangement is ever going to work?" Goemaere asked Bishop Verryn. "If we have a divergence of opinion, how will this work?"

"Let's try and we'll see," was Verryn's reply.

"Actually, it worked better than we anticipated," said Goemaere.

Over its first year of operation, the number of consultations at the MSF clinic increased steadily, starting with 750 patients a month in early 2008 and reaching more than 2 700 patients a month in March 2009. The main diagnoses were respiratory tract infections, sexually transmitted infections, diarrhoea and gastro-intestinal conditions, and stress-related ailments. Every month MSF referred about 80 patients to other specialised clinics and services for the treatment of TB and other chronic diseases, ARV treatment and emergencies. They would make sure that a "social assistant" and a diagnosis referral letter would accompany their patients to ensure they received treatment. Without this assistance people would face major obstacles in Johannesburg's public health facilities and would often be turned away.

As in any overcrowded and unhygienic setting, MSF reported that "people staying in the Central Methodist Church in Johannesburg are exposed to a serious risk of communicable disease outbreaks. This risk is mitigated, at least in part, by effective collaborations between MSF and the Gauteng Department of Health. MSF carries out epidemic surveillance and prevention, and works with the Department of Health to intervene rapidly in case of epidemic outbreaks."

If the neighbours were beginning to notice the growing numbers of people living next door, they didn't say much at first. One letter to Bishop Verryn in July 2006, however, was a portent of things to come. The building next to the church on Pritchard Street was being refurbished to become Pitje Chambers, a new set of chambers for advocates. The new building had not opened yet but Ishmael Semenya, the founder of the initiative (and Winnie Mandela's lawyer during the TRC hearings), wrote to Verryn. Copies of his letter went to the Mayor, the Gauteng Premier, the South African Police Service and the Johannesburg Municipal Police Department. In it Semenya expressed concern about the increasing number of people living in the church and the volume of refuse this generated on a daily basis. Unauthorised hawking had begun in front of the church as well. He pointed out that he had attempted to secure a meeting with Verryn via his secretary to discuss the matter but without success.

It was remarkable how many institutions did *not* react to what was gradually turning into a crisis at Central Methodist, not at a municipal, provincial nor national level. Nor did the Methodist Church of Southern Africa itself seem overly concerned. The City of Johannesburg was not oblivious to the reality of migration into Johannesburg. The Inner-City Charter, which was finalised in 2007, acknowledged the fact of large numbers of migrants coming into the city and Mayor Amos Masondo opened a Migrant Help Desk that year (ironically, it had to take down its sign in May 2008 because of the xenophobic fears at the time), but these things were not very practical and went nowhere near getting a handle on the issues. The effort was important symbolically perhaps, but generally the city's support to migrants into the city was extremely limited in reality and the city was slow in responding to the specific situation at the church.

Despite the fact that both migration and housing were the responsibilities of provincial and national government, rather than municipal issues, the situation at Central Methodist had received limited attention from Gauteng province or from national leadership thus far. The Gauteng Department of Health did begin to work with MSF at the end of 2007, but this was already several years after residents had begun living at the church.

The extent of national government's involvement around migration was at the level of political negotiations in Zimbabwe, which involved the President and the Department of Foreign Affairs. In terms of other national departments, such as Social Development, Health, Education and Housing, their engagement with the issue of growing migration into the country was minimal. There was no unified national policy to which to refer and no cohesive strategy. In 2007 the Department of Home Affairs deported over 300 000 Zimbabweans. These deportations made clear that, despite the degenerating conditions in Zimbabwe, the South African government did not want Zimbabweans entering South Africa. A similar number were deported in 2008. The Department of Home Affairs did not take further action until July that year when it opened a Refugee Reception Centre in Musina in Limpopo province, close to the Zimbabwean border. Thousands of Zimbabweans fled there to seek asylum.

The City of Johannesburg's attention along Pritchard Street had been focused for some years on a project to upgrade public space. In 2007, together with the Johannesburg Development Agency (JDA) and some assistance from the private sector, they spent R12 million on revamping the area around the church and the High Court. The idea was to develop an attractive "legal precinct". The JDA laid unique paving, and installed benches and streetlights along Pritchard and Von Brandis streets and a modern red clock at the corner of Pritchard and Smal.

After the upgrade was complete, Bishop Verryn did receive an indication that the city was not happy with the situation at Central Methodist, and in October that year the city's manager of environmental health sent a letter to him, requesting that he comply with the city's by-laws, and "cease the overcrowding condition of the premises with immediate effect". The letter threatened legal action without further notice. Negotiations and correspondence between the city and the Bishop were still under way when, just a few months later, in January 2008, the police raid hit.

While the Presiding Bishop of the Methodist Church, Ivan Abrahams, was aware of the situation at Central, his focus was elsewhere and not on the crisis that was developing inside and around the church. Paul Verryn did not approach Abrahams for assistance; but nor did Abrahams step forward to offer it or ask many questions about what was going on. By the end of 2007, for the most part, Verryn appeared to be dealing with the situation, albeit barely, on his own.

It was then that Verryn developed the condition Bell's palsy, which is a disorder of the cranial nerve that causes paralysis, usually on one side of the face. There is no known specific cause of Bell's palsy and most people recover spontaneously. Strangely enough, while it didn't seem that 2008 would provide any relief from the high level of stress he was working under, Verryn recovered from his palsy the night of the police raid in January 2008. "What you find healing in that, I don't know," said Penny Foley.

Peliwe Lolwana, who had been out of the country for much of 2007, saw the crisis that was building at the church in 2008 as beyond her own skills and capacity. "I just continued to go to the service on Sundays between ten and twelve," she said. "Perhaps I chickened out, but I felt I couldn't do much. I do believe that it's the role of the church to look after the poor. Also, the church was there for me during my difficult time. Now the church was having a difficult time, so I didn't feel that it was the time to leave. I stayed. The only thing I could do was check in on Paul. I'd say to him, 'Let's go to the movies. Let's go have cheesecake in Rosebank.' I think he appreciated that, being able to get away from the church and all its problems for a few minutes."

Fifteen

The Thunderstorm Left Behind More than a Flood

If the neighbours, the City of Johannesburg and Gauteng province thought that the problems at Central Methodist would go away by themselves somehow, the shocking events of May 2008 left the church with an even higher number of residents and Bishop Verryn with an even greater conviction that he would not turn anyone away. When he reflected on the xenophobic violence, he said, "There is no doubt that the way in which we treat the stranger reflects our humanity; whether that stranger be from another country or whether those strangers be strange because they are poor is beside the point. If we are going to survive as a human race, we are going to have to reassess our fundamental value system."

Despite the levels of violence and displacement in May 2008, some of the residents at Central continued to find ways to continue with their day-to-day lives. One foreign film crew, who covered the xenophobia and visited the church during the time they were in the city, said, "Something of beauty and human connection has also found a home here – dance." In the space outside the gallery of the sanctuary on the second floor, a group of children gathered every day at 5pm to learn the steps of the waltz, the mamba, the cha-cha and the foxtrot. Twenty-one year old Beauty Mosutlhe, originally from North West province, had started teaching the children in the building after school.

Unbeknown to most people at Central Methodist, in the midst of the violence and the hardship of that time, a quiet love affair had begun to blossom there. Monica Chiwetu, the woman who had stayed in the Roberts Room under her blankets during the night of the January police raid, didn't know that only a few months later she would meet someone special. One afternoon before the dance class started, Monica was waiting for a friend on the second floor, looking out of the window outside the cry room where Leothere Nininahazwe had his Urban Institute office. Leothere had remembered meeting Monica once before when she had helped him carry donations up to the third floor. He asked Monica for her number but she didn't have a cellphone, so he gave her his number instead. "I just took his number on a piece of paper," said Monica, "and put it in my trouser. We saw each other again and started talking and then we went to the restaurant Kofifi, in Smal Street." By October that year, Monica was attending the Sunday morning French service.

Despite the efforts to continue life as normal in the wake of the May 2008 xenophobic violence, Bishop Verryn knew that the church was more than bursting at the seams. He also began to notice that there were a lot of children arriving at the church on their own, unaccompanied by parents or guardians. It was clear that many of the children were not going to school. There were a large number of qualified but unemployed teachers in the building, among them Alpha Zhou, John Manyani, Tafadzwa Gumindoga, Raphael Maisiri, and William Kandowe. That was when the idea for the Albert Street School was born. Along with Joyce Gundu, these residents became the first group of teachers.

"I wasn't there on the first day the school opened, but I was there on the second," said Joyce Gundu. "I began teaching grades one through seven, all in one class. There were about fifteen kids in the entire class. By August, there were lots more learners and two more teachers were hired. Even though the xenophobic violence had calmed down, we still felt vulnerable at Albert Street because there is only one way in and out of the school through the gate. Central Methodist felt more safe."

Joyce was born in 1982 in Chinhoyi, Zimbabwe. Both of her parents were teachers, but she never thought she'd follow in their footsteps. She went to the University of Chinhoyi to study art and design, but she got a teachers' diploma, too. Her plan was to work in textile design and she did work for Modzone Textile Company for six months. When things began to deteriorate in Zimbabwe, however, she had to leave her job. "In December

2007 my bonus wasn't enough to pay for bus fare to go to town and back to collect my salary. You had to queue forever to get your salary and then it was worth nothing."

Joyce decided to go to South Africa. Her parents were supportive and she had a passport so experienced no difficulty at the border. Her aunt was staying at Central Methodist so that was where Joyce went. Her aunt helped her get a job at City Market for a few months and then as a domestic worker in Mayfair. She also joined the security team at the church, but about six months later, when she heard about the plans for starting a school, she decided she would teach.

When Bishop Verryn realised that he had an emergency need for a school and a set of qualified teachers, his next challenge was to find premises. Immediately, he turned to the Albert Street Methodist Church, which was part of the Central circuit and about eight blocks from Central Methodist in downtown Johannesburg on Albert Street. It was an old building, constructed in 1893, and it was the first Methodist church in the city for Africans. From its early years, workers without basic education would gather at the church in the evening to learn how to read and do simple maths. Then a school was developed there for the children of domestic workers who couldn't attend white schools in the city. The Albert Street School operated for over 50 years, until 1958, when the apartheid government closed it down because it was a black school in a "white" area. In 2008 Albert Street seemed an appropriate place to reopen a school, this time initially to serve refugee children. The school was included with the other mission projects – FLOC, Paballo and Ray of Hope – under the Deaconess Society, which, as a non-profit organisation, could raise funds on its own. Early funding for Albert Street came from the United Methodist Committee on Relief.

When Joyce Gundu had first moved into Central Methodist in December the previous year, she slept in the vestry. "I come from a family where you stay in your own room," said Joyce. "I wasn't used to sharing a room divided by a curtain with strange people you don't know. It wasn't peaceful." However, it was really an outbreak of meningitis in the church in September 2008 that caused her to make a move. "It was terrible," said Joyce. "Children died. Tragedy Matsvaire and the other health workers from MSF were spraying and cleaning up." Joyce moved to a flat on the corner of Pritchard and Mooi streets and later into a room in Bertrams.

Moving out of the church did not deter her from working at Albert Street, however, and in time Joyce became Head of Department of the primary school. By December 2008 the enrolment for the primary school reached 200 children and the entire school had close to 500 learners. Most of them were unaccompanied minors – they had no parent or guardian with them in Johannesburg.

Takudzwanashe Chikoro (called Takudzwa for short) was one of those children. He was a teenager when he arrived in Johannesburg from Zimbabwe. Although he was eighteen, with his slight build and baby face, he looked much younger. The first time Takudzwa tried to cross the border, in March 2008, he crossed the river with a few other boys and then got lost in the bush and robbed by the "guma gumas", notorious gangs that roamed the border and preyed on those trying to cross. After two weeks the boys found themselves on a farm and got jobs harvesting potatoes for R15 a week. Takudzwa left the farm and went to Musina, but then he was arrested and deported back to Zimbabwe in early June.

On his second attempt, Takudzwa's crossing went more smoothly. This time he went by road and travelled directly to Johannesburg. He landed up at Park Station where he worked for a woman selling food who would give him a plate of *pap* as pay. Some weeks later, he met some learners from Zimbabwe who told him about the Albert Street School.

"At first, I didn't think it was a brilliant idea," said Takudzwa. "I wanted to keep working. But then I went to the Bishop's office [and talked to him] and I thought I should give it a chance. I expected the school to be big, with lots of kids, but it was small and everything was chaotic. I met Wellington and Edmore and Nkosinathi and joined them in a combined Form 3/Form 4 class. I guess what kept me going to school was the clothes and the food. At Albert Street, you got a school uniform and food every day at lunch. I started smoking in those days. The only thing I would 'eat', other than lunch, was cigarettes. Surprisingly, I did well in my assignments."

Takudzwa was born in 1990 and his life as a migrant began in childhood. His father died when he was seven years old and, less than a year later, his mother died in a car accident. He moved constantly, from relative to relative. "We were outcasts," he said, speaking of himself and his two older sisters. "We went to stay with my mother's relatives, but my uncle was so harsh and he was a drunkard."

When Takudzwa first arrived at Central Methodist, he slept outside on the street in front of DoRego's fast food shop in the Smal Street Mall. After a few weeks, he moved inside to the boardroom. "We used to go to MSF each week for counselling," he said. "They would give us toiletries. Evans would encourage us to study. MSF used to ask us if we wanted to go to the shelters, to the Red Cross, but I said no. Then at the end of the year, I moved to sleep on the fourth floor of the church. Me and some of the other guys had a bet. Who is going to be the best student? Is it going to be me or my friend Nkosinathi?"

At the same time that Takudzwa arrived at the Albert Street School in mid-2008, Central Methodist received large donations of food, blankets and clothing in the wake of the May violence against foreign nationals. For the most part, the donations were welcomed and passed on to those in need. However, there were times when people took advantage of the situation.

One day in July, William Kandowe received a text message from another member of the Central Methodist security team. About 110 bags of mealie meal, 50 bags of butternuts, each one 20kg, 20 five-litre bottles of cooking oil, and 20 bags of sugar beans, 50kg size, were being loaded from the church onto a bakkie in the street outside. "Do you know where all this is going?" the text message asked. William didn't know so he called Bishop Verryn to find out. The Bishop confirmed that he knew about the mealie meal. It was going to the camps, he told William.

The delivery, however, was diverted and it went instead to Park Station. Meanwhile, the police had received a tip-off: the goods were actually being sold at Park Station and certain church residents were the ones doing the selling. Saul Zvobgo, one of the leaders at the church and head of security, was arrested. Allegedly, another resident, Godfrey Charamba, was also in on the deal. At first the Bishop thought that William Kandowe was involved as well. He called William and said, "Go to Park Station. Look for Captain Makhubela." Then he warned him: "If you are involved, you will be arrested and locked up." William did as Verryn told him. He went to Park Station and found the police officer. The officer asked Saul Zvogbo whether William was involved in the theft and Zvogbo said he wasn't. Then William signed for the goods and they were returned to Central.

According to William himself, Saul Zvogbo pointed his two index fingers at William that day at Park Station and said, "Now we are enemies." Zvogbo was arrested and granted bail, and he returned to the church. Godfrey Charamba took himself off to Pretoria for a few days and was never arrested. William was afraid that Charamba and Zvogbo would try to seek revenge against him, believing that it was he who had tipped off the police, and he spoke to the Bishop about his fear.

For a long time, Saul Zvogbo had been in a position of some authority among the residents at the church and one of their leaders, not to mention head of the security team. In August 2008, after the theft of the donations, Ambrose Mapiravana was elected head of security in his place, which toppled Zvogbo from his prior position of respect and power. He was also let go from a security job that he held at MSF.

Theft was not the only social problem to emerge at Central Methodist. By now over 2 000 people were living in the church at extremely close quarters. Counsellors from the Sophiatown Community Psychological Services, amongst others, were brought in to provide counselling to some and to address the high level of trauma in others that was even more apparent now in the wake of violence in Zimbabwe and South Africa. The growing numbers of unaccompanied minors was also cause for concern, especially when these were young girls. The Gauteng Department of Social Development made visits to the church to assess the problem. Given the desperate situation of many of the residents in the church, some turned to prostitution. Others turned to begging on street corners. There were also serious health hazards to deal with. In November an outbreak of cholera in Zimbabwe put MSF on alert, especially when cases were diagnosed in Musina. They kept a close watch at Central.

Meanwhile the political instability in Zimbabwe was worsening. The March 2008 elections had effectively been stolen from Morgan Tsvangirai's MDC party. The government's electoral commission declared on 2 May that the March elections had been inconclusive, despite the fact that earlier projections were that the MDC had won. The commission stated that neither party had won a clear majority and a run-off election was scheduled for 27 June. The rising violence in Zimbabwe in April and May 2008 was severe enough to result in Thabo Mbeki sending a delegation of six retired South African generals to investigate. The generals reported back to Mbeki, but that report was never made public. Reports from Zimbabwean and international NGOs, however, stated that it was reasonable to accuse the Zimbabwean government of crimes against humanity and that there had been a systematic campaign of state-sponsored violence against the MDC.

The MDC originally agreed to participate in the run-off elections, but then withdrew as a result of many of its leadership being killed in the violence. Robert Mugabe declared himself President after a one-person presidential run-off. Conditions in the country continued their downward spiral. Unemployment went up to over 90 per cent. The country was hit with an inflation rate well into six figures. There was food insecurity and a near collapse of the education and health systems.

Despite these deteriorating conditions, South Africa's political leadership and government authorities largely ignored the thousands of Zimbabweans coming into South Africa, perhaps expecting them to adjust on their own without any targeted support or attention. The May 2008 violence in South Africa had resulted in the government providing some support for foreign nationals, but it was clear that this was intended to be temporary.

Many South Africans were concerned about the apparent lack of urgency in the South African government's response to what was happening in Zimbabwe. Thabo Mbeki's so-called quiet diplomacy towards Zimbabwe was widely interpreted as being easy on Robert Mugabe. In September, Mbeki brokered a deal where Mugabe agreed to form a government of national unity with the MDC but the talks stalled. The new president of the African National Congress, Jacob Zuma, described the situation in Zimbabwe as "untenable", but still there was little progress in effecting a change in that country. Not only was the South African government unwilling to be more aggressive with President Mugabe, but the fifteen countries that formed SADC were hesitant also. As one *Financial Times* article in January 2009 put it, "Critics say African leaders are still looking to the MDC to make concessions, rather than to 85-year-old Mugabe."

The violence in Zimbabwe prior to and in the wake of the June 2008 run-off elections had a particular impact on women. One Harare-based organisation was overwhelmed with reports from women who had been raped by members of Mugabe's ruling Zanu-PF party during the months of May and June. The organisation reached out to the New York-based AIDS-Free World, which undertook a series of investigative trips to the region with teams of lawyers to interview survivors of the violence. Their report was not released until December 2009, but they would find that there had been systematic rape in order to intimidate voters and members of the opposing MDC. Five days before the scheduled run-off election, when Morgan Tsvangirai withdrew, he stated that there had been a "systematic and widespread campaign of terror to intimidate the electorate into voting for Robert Mugabe".

Some of the women who survived this violent campaign found their way to Central Methodist Mission. One of the *pro bono* US attorneys from global law firm DLA Piper working with AIDS-Free World, Sara Andrews, interviewed some of these women. She described "a vacancy behind their eyes. They had been tortured physically and emotionally and lost total control of their world. They were just going through the motions of life." Andrews also attended a Friday night refugee meeting. She described downtown Johannesburg as an abandoned ghost town but said, "you knew you were coming on to something as you approached the church. People were everywhere. There was a huge gathering of people on the sidewalk. Inside, the church was chock full of bodies. People were standing around, buying food and eating dinner. Downstairs, people were sitting on the floor watching a football game. In one room, people had partitioned off sections with boxes and blankets. There were Bunsen burner stoves in the midst of all this. It was a chaotic environment. The person who showed us around, one of the residents, was proud to show that there was some order in the chaos, some systems in place. We were told that everybody was expected to leave the building every morning to look for work and that the place was cleaned during the day. I was surprised that there was any level of orderliness or cleanliness when so many people were confined to a building that was never designed to be residential."

Andrews said "some women seemed like they were in a coma and completely withdrawn. With others, it was impossible to believe that they were as dynamic and engaged as they were. The majority of the women we interviewed were professionals, leaders in their communities. They had been organising political demonstrations. These people were very impressive. They had been tortured in unimaginable ways. Yet they continued to wake up every day and seek food and shelter in the wake of enormous loss."

Many of the women who sought refuge at Central Methodist had been through tragic circumstances and some had suffered terrible abuse before they got there and were taken in by Paul Verryn. Soon, however, the Bishop would have to deal with allegations of abuse that were much closer to home.

On 30 September 2008 an SAPS team, led by Captain Shongwe, arrived at the Albert Street School. They arrested three teachers – Alpha Zhou, who was also the principal, William Kandowe, the deputy principal, and Tafadzwa Gumindoga. The charges against the three men were very serious: fraud, making petrol bombs, ATM bombing, child pornography, and rape. They were taken to Diepkloof prison, where they spent the next several weeks. William Kandowe's theory was that Saul Zvogbo had bribed the young girls who had made the rape accusations to do so as an act of revenge against him. One of the girls was the niece of Zvogbo's girlfriend, he said.

The men appeared in court on 13 October, and again on 21 October for bail hearings. Before setting bail, the judge dropped all of the charges against them except for the charge of rape. In Alpha Zhou's and Tafadzwa Gumindoga's cases, but not William Kandowe's, the rape charges were then changed to sexual grooming. The judge said, "I have twenty-five years' experience on the bench and I can tell when some counts go together and when others look fabricated. This collection of charges does not look right to me." Bail was set at R1 500 each and Bishop Verryn paid all three teachers' bail. The men returned to their positions at the Albert Street School and continued to teach there.

Just a couple of weeks' later, on 9 November, Tafadzwa Gumindoga collapsed outside the MSF clinic on Pritchard Street. An ambulance was called but by the time it got there, he was already dead. The cause of death was unclear, but it was debated amongst those who knew him. Some said it was suicide, others that he had been poisoned. William Kandowe believed that the stress of the allegations against the teacher had caused him to suffer a fatal heart attack.

On 11 November, William Kandowe and Alpha Zhou went to the Crown Mines refugee reception centre to have their asylum papers extended. When they arrived there, they were arrested, told that their papers were not in order, and taken to Lindela Repatriation Centre, a facility on the West Rand where undocumented foreigners were held prior to deportation. They were held there for over two weeks and then released.

Kandowe and Zhou appeared in court in January the following year and again in April to stand trial for, respectively, rape and sexual grooming, but on both occasions the complainants did not arrive to give testimony. On their third appearance, on 25 May 2009, when the complainants did not arrive for the third time, the magistrate dropped the charges and dismissed the cases.

It is difficult to recreate the details of the cases fully, especially as the complainants are no longer available to be interviewed, but one thing was for certain: gender violence and the abuse of young women were a reality in South Africa and Zimbabwe, and they were a problem at Central Methodist and the Albert Street School too. Men were in a position of power and influence and young girls were vulnerable. There was no doubt that some men were taking advantage of the situation. While Bishop Verryn believed that the men involved in this particular case deserved bail, legal representation and a fair trial, sending them back to teach at the school until their cases came to court sent the wrong message and failed to address the vulnerability of the girls at the church and the school. These might have been the first but they were not the last of the allegations of sexual abuse at Albert Street.

In early 2008, more than six months before the teachers' arrests, Bishop Verryn already knew that he had a problem. Reverend Kim Alexander, who had been based at Central Methodist for more than a year, and had been on the scene during the police raid in January, began to be concerned about the levels of domestic violence taking place amongst the residents of the church. With thousands of people living in dire circumstances, they needed help. When she saw an email from Penny Foley about possible funding to address gender violence, she decided to take action. She discussed it with Bishop Verryn and with his support she approached the Centre for the Study of Violence and Reconciliation to ask for assistance. Reverend Alexander asked Cleo Buthelezi if she would work with her and together they held a workshop at Central on gender-based violence and the law. Unfortunately, many of the migrant women staying in the church did not see the South African law courts as a possible recourse, given their vulnerable situation and meagre resources, so one workshop was clearly not going to be sufficient. Alexander and Buthelezi realised that they would need to design an intervention that would be more long term.

After the intense violence in May, with the assistance of the CSVR, they began a training programme. There were eleven people chosen for the training, which included information on gender-based violence, legal rights, and also practical skills such as listening and facilitation. The group met every Tuesday and Thursday for over a year through to July 2009 and the hope was that it would become a resource for others inside the building. As more people came to the church, many of them having suffered great trauma already, despite their best efforts, the challenges for the group became enormous. It became a case of a David facing a Goliath.

Part of Kim Alexander's work at Central Methodist included many forms of trauma counselling and damaged women often came to see her in her office. She remembers sitting at her desk one day in 2008 working towards a deadline. Someone from Paul Verryn's office put her head around the corner and asked, "Are you up for some counselling?" At first, she hesitated, but then agreed. A neatly dressed young woman was ushered in. Reverend Alexander invited her to sit down. The young woman's name was Beauty and she had tears in her eyes. She began her story by saying that she lost her job as a cashier in Zimbabwe so she came to South Africa to join her sister who was already in Johannesburg. They were both struggling to find work. "Our landlord told us that he knew a herbalist from Malawi who would give us muti and make us rich. We decided to take all our money to him," said Beauty. "The muti didn't work so we went back to see him again." With her eyes lowered to the floor, Beauty said, "He told me that he needed to sleep with me in order for it to work." She reluctantly agreed to sleep with the man, hoping that it would help. The sisters did not become rich, but Beauty found out that she was pregnant. She and her sister went back to the man's "rooms" only to find that he had left South Africa to return to Malawi. At this point, Alexander remembers feeling such anger that she found it difficult to continue. She remembers being angry not only at the man who took advantage of Beauty, but also at the power of superstition, and at Mugabe for his part in shaping this young woman's life, and at Mbeki for being silent on Zimbabwe.

Beauty was now destitute and pregnant, and concerned about her child that she had left behind in Zimbabwe. She leaned forward in her chair, the tears now rolling down her cheeks. She lowered her voice and said, "I give myself to men for money." She waited for the words to sink in. Then she said, "I don't want to but I have no choice." In a whisper, she added, "For as little as R20." Wringing her hands, she repeated the words – "I don't want to. I don't want to. I don't want to," her pain and her shame etched on her face. Alexander took Beauty's hands to pray but she struggled to find words that in some way might bring comfort or peace. She pleaded to God with great intensity, wanting somehow to offer a small bit of hope. After the prayer, they sat together in silence. Beauty's tears continued to fall.

"I've looked for work at all the shops," she said. "I've tried all the Chinese shops but they only offer R120 a week. That's not enough to cover my transport."

Alexander asked, "Would you like to return to Zimbabwe if you could?"

"No," said Beauty, "there's no chance I would find work in Zim. My only hope is to find work here."

Beauty didn't own a phone so Alexander took her landlord's number just in case she found a job to offer her. They hugged one another. "Come and see me again," she said. Beauty walked out the door and never did return.

Meanwhile, the church building was overflowing. In an article in the *Financial Times* a journalist observed: "Bishop Paul Verryn is about to lose his temper and it is easy to see why. Hundreds of desperate, often traumatised refugees, who have fled hunger, cholera and political repression, are camping in every inch of hallway and staircase at his Methodist Mission – including the narrow steps themselves. Two thousand or so people are staking out floor space in the building in a grim corner of central Johannesburg compared with about 1 300 a year ago, the vast majority of them from Zimbabwe, with another 500 on the streets outside."

In November 2008, Kofi Annan, the former UN secretary-general, Jimmy Carter, the former US president, and Graça Machel, the human rights advocate married to Nelson Mandela, were denied visas to enter Zimbabwe. All were members of The Elders, a global group that had been formed in 2007 by Nelson Mandela to promote human rights and peace. They insisted that their visit was not about forcing a power-sharing agreement in that country, but rather to assess the needs of Zimbabweans, many of whom were suffering from hunger and disease. When they were refused entry, the group went to Johannesburg and visited Central Methodist Mission instead to speak to men and women who had fled Zimbabwe and had sought, and found, refuge at the church. Once they learned that there were young people staying at the church, they asked to speak to some students. Amongst the students was Takudzwa Chikoro. The Elders came to the church in the evening after dark. Although the church was so full at that time that people were sleeping in the sanctuary, they cleared some space at the front and the three Elders sat in the front row and the students formed a circle on plastic chairs in front of them. Takudzwa remembers that their security detail was on guard.

He told The Elders his own story, why and how he came to South Africa. "Before they left," Takudzwa said, "they told us, 'We will see what we can do, but we don't want to promise anything.' People say that to me all the time. Visitors from Europe. Journalists from the BBC and the *Mail & Guardian*. I think it would be better to say nothing and then help if you can help."

Takudzwa's first name means "blessed by the Almighty". His surname Chikoro means "school" or "education" so in class when no one else answered a question, he said, the teacher would always call on him. That year he got nine prizes at the Albert Street School prize giving.

In January 2009, Kumi Naidoo and Nomboniso Gasa, two prominent South Africans, went on a hunger strike as part of the Save Zimbabwe Now campaign to draw attention to the crisis in Zimbabwe. They based themselves at Central Methodist Mission. Naidoo said, "As the stories get more heart-wrenching, the [SA] government position is incomprehensible to me." Archbishop Desmond Tutu, who was fasting one day a week in support of the campaign, became a more vocal critic of the government's approach to the situation in Zimbabwe, saying that South Africa had lost the moral high ground that it had won during the struggle against apartheid. Graça Machel said that she supported the fasting, too, and confessed that she had a heavy heart. "We can no longer stand and wait," she said.

Bishop Verryn made a statement which showed how the crisis in Zimbabwe was reflected in his church. "We are flooded," he said. "[The numbers] have gone through the moon and pressure is growing on what was already strained infrastructure. There is a reluctance to name the thing for what it is: a crisis that is creating a deluge of poverty."

The situation at Central was reaching breaking point.

PART TWO

Sixteen

"A Hostile, Complex Situation"

Rose Bond was the building manager for Pitje Chambers, the law offices on Pritchard Street next door to Central Methodist. For months, when Rose arrived at work before 6am, she couldn't get into the basement parking because people were sleeping on the ramp. She would hoot, wait patiently for everyone to move, and then inch her car down past the scores of people shaking out their blankets and moving their bags and belongings.

Then one day she had had enough and Rose snapped...

Rose had worked in the legal field for many years and she had helped open Lawyers for Human Rights with Brian Currin in Pretoria. She had known Ishmael Semenya, the founder of the Pitje Chambers Transformation Initiative, for many years. "Ishmael is like my brother," she told me once. "He called me back from my holiday when he was working on the Namibian constitution [in the early 1990s] and needed someone to type."

In the late 1990s, just as many businesses were leaving downtown Johannesburg, many of the advocates who kept offices in Schreiner Chambers and Innes Chambers across from the High Court on Pritchard Street left the area for new premises in Sandton. It was Semenya's brainchild to develop new advocates' chambers in the city centre. He and his colleague Andre Bezuidenhout of the Johannesburg Association for Advocates came together and formed the Pitje Chambers Transformation Initiative. They purchased a derelict building and approached Investec for financial support. The refurbishment of the building cost R26 million. In the tradition of Innes and Schreiner, the building was named after an attorney, and in this case also an anti-apartheid activist. Godfrey Pitje had served his articles with Oliver Tambo and Nelson Mandela.

The new chambers, with 56 members, were officially opened in May 2007 by President Thabo Mbeki. At the opening, Advocate Stephan du Toit said, "We as advocates in the city centre of Johannesburg are committed to the transformation of South Africa and we are here to stay." Sadly, several years later, Du Toit moved out of Pitje Chambers to offices in Sandton, too. His assistant said that he made the move because his clients weren't too keen to go to his chambers in town anymore.

Rose Bond said, "the neighbourhood was lovely in 2006 and 2007," but after the failed Zimbabwe elections in March and June 2008 and the xenophobic violence that had erupted in May that year resulted in an increased flow of migrants to the church, the area deteriorated rapidly. By the end of the year there would be over 2 000 people living in the church and close to a thousand sleeping on the pavement outside. Most of them were from Zimbabwe.

In August 2008 Rose wrote a letter to Bishop Verryn saying that there had been numerous complaints about strewn garbage and unhygienic conditions on the Pritchard Street pavement and that the "unsightly smelly mess" was attracting flies and rodents. She pointed out that people who were sleeping on Pritchard Street had no ablution facilities. "Faeces have been spotted in this area," she said frankly. "People wash themselves every morning in Pritchard Street, leaving the street and the sidewalk in a filthy, smelly state. They have no problem at all with throwing their waste on the pavement, urinating wherever they can, defecating in public, loitering for most of the day."

The letter also expressed concern about Central Methodist's fifth floor rooftop, which was visible from the upper floors of Pitje Chambers, and again Rose did not mince her words. "It is being used at all hours of the day for boisterous activities – blaring music, rowdy debates etc. This is causing disturbances to our members whose chambers overlook this area… [All of this] is reducing the area to a scruffy disgraceful place. I am sure you will agree that this is also not befitting of a place of worship."

Rose tried to enlist the assistance of the police. "'No,' the police told me. 'We can't come. We have a directive from the Mayor's office not to interfere because we'll get bad international media.'" So Rose called the Mayor's office herself to ask them when they were going to clean the streets. "We would have these frustrating conversations that would go on for weeks," she said. "For example, I would ask, 'When are you going to clean the street?' The City would say, 'We're waiting for delivery of ecoli cleaning chemicals.' Then I would say, 'OK then, we'll buy our own and do the cleaning ourselves.' 'No, but you have to use *bio-degradable* ecoli cleaning chemicals.' 'Where do you get *bio-degradable* ecoli cleaning chemicals?' 'You can't get them in South Africa. We are waiting for a shipment from China.' And so it went on. At that point," said Rose, "I wanted to put the phone down."

Rose was not alone. Other property owners in the Smal Street Mall were by now also very unhappy. They began putting pressure on the City, hoping that if they did the City would have to take action. The manager of DoRego's fast food restaurant on Smal Street, Veronica Mbuli, said, "Every morning we find urine, papers, stuff lying around." Her view on what should happen was clear. "To come here and sleep outside is not the solution. It's better to go back to their countries and fix the problem."

At the same time that Rose was becoming exasperated with Central Methodist, Zimbabwe was still in political disarray. After months of wrangling, Mugabe and Tsvangirai had agreed to a power sharing arrangement called the Global Political Agreement. Mugabe remained President and Tsvangirai was sworn in as Prime Minister. The Central Bank in Zimbabwe adopted South Africa's rand as an anchor for the virtually worthless Zimbabwean dollar. The hope was that there would be new stability and that the brain drain of skilled workers leaving the country would end. Despite this agreement, Mugabe and Tsvangirai continued to disagree on fundamental issues.

In late January 2009 church leaders of South Africa issued a joint statement expressing their concern for the continuing deterioration of the social, political and economic situation in Zimbabwe and calling on Robert Mugabe to resign. One of the signatories was Presiding Bishop Ivan Abrahams of the Methodist Church of Southern Africa. The statement said that SADC and the South African government had failed the people of Zimbabwe with quiet diplomacy and that Thabo Mbeki was no longer an appropriate mediator. Significantly, the statement ended with these words: "We commit ourselves to welcome and support our sisters and brothers from Zimbabwe who have come to find refuge in our country."

The City of Johannesburg also appeared finally to kick into gear. Nathi Mthethwa, the Director of Region F for the City, which included the inner city, distributed a proposed action plan to his colleagues. The plan set out timeframes for negotiations with the church, dialogue with affected businesses in the precinct, addressing service breakdowns, and addressing law enforcement challenges. His covering note stated, "It is imperative to mention that the challenges in the Methodist Church are escalating on a daily basis due to intricate problems in [our] neighbouring state of Zimbabwe, consequently the situation has become a 'national crisis'."

Phil Harrison was the head of the Department for Development Planning and Urban Management for the City. He and Ruby Mathang, a member of the Mayoral Committee and political head for Planning, took the lead and met with Bishop Verryn on 30 January. According to Harrison, it was at that meeting that Verryn requested that the City provide a building to which the thousands of migrants who were sleeping in and around the church could be relocated.

Ruby Mathang remembered that January meeting with Bishop Verryn and also that they had differed on the role the City should be playing. "Paul Verryn wanted us to provide housing for the migrants. That's not a City function. We can't manage a building," said Mathang. "We were on the side of the poor, but running a building is not the function of local government." Mathang differed sharply with Verryn on another matter, too. He told the Bishop that he should not take in any more people, but Verryn would not agree to this. "We will endeavor to give relief to these people," said Mathang, "but please don't bring another two thousand." Verryn's response was that he could not control the numbers of people arriving and that he couldn't turn people away either.

"I think we are at capacity," said Paul Verryn at the time in what seemed like an understatement. "But what criterion do you use for people who have got nowhere to go? Many people come to South Africa completely aware of the xenophobia that's in this country, completely aware of the fact that they are not welcome, but it's an escape from something that they consider is worse."

Despite the difference of opinion with the Bishop, Harrison and Mathang took up the task of finding alternative accommodation for the residents of the church. They identified the unoccupied Moth building on Loveday Street and estimated that it could accommodate 750 people. In February, Amos Masondo's Mayoral Committee approved a plan. Harrison found the funds to sign on the Johannesburg Development Agency to renovate the building. He also helped secure the commitment of Gauteng province to fund the building's ongoing management costs.

In the meantime the City's task team worked to implement several short-term measures. With growing health concerns, the Bishop agreed that the City should conduct regular health inspections at the church and provide fumigation services. The City also provided more regular waste collection and, in February 2009, installed a set of nineteen temporary toilets along Pritchard Street. "We thought we were doing a good thing with those toilets," said Phil Harrison ruefully, "but they became the main gripe." Rose Bond was of the opinion that the toilets made things worse. "It made it even more embarrassing to invite attorneys and clients to the building," she said.

In a "letter of protest" to Mayor Masondo, dated 11 February 2009, Rose Bond wrote: "We place on record our vehement protest to the lavatories placed on the sidewalk in Pritchard Street next to our place of business... This is causing chaos as it is greatly restricting pedestrian movement as the sidewalk is now filled with foul smelling lavatories. The faeces and urine stench emanating from the toilets is horrific, unhygienic and poses a health risk to our members and the public in general. Our members, tenants, clients and restaurants in the area are greatly affected by this attempted resolve. The Council has just compounded the problem... Numerous calls to the Metro Police requesting some resolve have been in vain. We demand that all Municipal by-laws be upheld."

On 13 February Nathi Mthethwa chaired a meeting at the Parktonian Hotel in Braamfontein. Invited to the meeting were all the stakeholders who had expressed their concern about the situation at Central Methodist. About 20 people from the City were there, as well as representatives from City Power, Joburg Water, and Pikitup, the waste removal company. Also present were managers from shops on the Smal Street Mall, including Captain DoRego's, the London Pie Company and Capello's restaurant, as well as property owners represented by the Central Johannesburg Partnership (CJP). Bianca Tolboom and Tragedy Matsvaire were there from Médecins Sans Frontières. As Bishop Verryn could not attend, Mary Metcalfe attended on his behalf, as a concerned friend but also as someone with significant influence. Rose Bond was there from Pitje Chambers.

Minutes from the meeting stated that Nathi Mthethwa opened the proceedings by introducing people in key management positions in the City who would be "spearheading the operations in solving the crisis at the church". He stated that the purpose of the meeting was to "look at key issues and find solutions to these problems with an achievable action plan" that would involve the City, the church and all the stakeholders.

Mthethwa recalled that the meeting was tense and uncomfortable. "There were different stakeholders with different interests," he said. "The City was perceived as a failed system that had failed to implement the by-laws. Potential investors in the area basically said, 'You guys are just idiots.'"

Rose Bond remembered the meeting and couldn't resist stating the obvious. "It was in a lovely [venue] with tea and beautiful snacks," she said. "And I thought to myself, we should have had the meeting at Pitje Chambers so everyone could have seen the garbage… and smelled the urine and the sewage."

Mthethwa said, "The guy from FNB [who had a branch on Smal Street] was so clean and meticulous. He said that he had his staff cleaning shit. It was terrible. Another guy from Capello's told the meeting, 'Shit is my new spice'. It was good that Bishop Verryn couldn't attend. If he had been there, he would have been eaten alive. I've never experienced such a hostile, complex situation. How do you strike a balance between a humanitarian crisis and the needs of business?"

Ruby Mathang remembered the day he visited the church with Mayor Amos Masondo. "That visit revealed the challenges. It was really touching to talk to people at the church and see their situation. We were very concerned about people sleeping on the streets. It strengthened our resolve to find a solution."

Nathi Mthethwa, in addition to his post with the City of Johannesburg, also held a post within the Communist Party of South Africa. He, too, was affected by a visit to the church. "I went once to an evening service," he said. "That was the only thing to make those people feel at home. As people, we are spiritual beings and the church played a crucial role in that. It was emotional. I would cry after leaving that church. I would go home to my own bedroom. It was hell."

While Mathang and Mthethwa were sympathetic to the plight of the residents of the church, they also wanted to respond to the concerns of business. The City did not have one unified point of view. Phil Harrison said that he witnessed many opposing points of view within the City on how to handle the situation, with some tending toward a humanitarian solution but others believing that enforcing the by-laws should be the priority. One urban researcher, Graeme Gotz, referred to the City bureaucracy as a "multi-headed hydra", while Lael Bethlehem, the director of the JDA at the time, said that the City of Johannesburg was like a Jackson Pollock painting with many painters. Everyone was throwing paint at the canvas at the same time.

Pitje Chambers became so frustrated with the City and the church that their next step was to institute legal action. In March they applied for a court order to compel the City to remove the toilets and the thousands of migrants from the church because their presence had become a health hazard. In her affidavit, Rose Bond was disenchanted and as candid as ever. "The Church and the municipality obviously have no reasonable plan to effectively address the plight of these displaced people, including housing them in a dignified manner… the displaced persons, the Church and the toilets have now totally destroyed the idea of a world class legal precinct that would lure practitioners back to Johannesburg."

Pitje Chambers also objected to MSF's clinic on Pritchard Street and addressed this by expressing concern that Central Methodist was not zoned to allow for a medical clinic on its premises. Rose Bond's affidavit stated that people had to queue on the Pritchard Street pavement because MSF did not have an adequate waiting area and that this was causing a health hazard. In reference to the restaurant on the ground floor of Pitje Chambers, Bond said, "Customers do not wish to dine in a restaurant in front of which untold numbers of ill people loiter on the sidewalk waiting for medical attention." She also listed and quoted from some of the City by-laws that needed to be enforced. "The Public Road and Miscellaneous By-Law states that 'no person may spill, drop or place or permit to be spilled, dropped or placed, on a public road any matter or substance that may interfere with the cleanliness of the public road.' The Public Health By-law states that a public health hazard includes 'unsanitary conditions, circumstances which make food and drink unhygienic or unsafe to eat or drink and circumstances which allow pests to infest any place where they may affect public health.'" Finally, the affidavit opposed the portable toilets. "To simply provide portable toilets to 4 000 displaced persons does not solve the underlying problem. It is akin to putting up a road sign 'Beware of the potholes,' and thinking that the potholes will disappear by themselves."

In his preliminary responding affidavit, Bishop Verryn said that the church was sympathetic to the problems faced by Pitje Chambers and the shopkeepers on Pritchard Street and the Smal Street Mall, but that "these problems are the direct result of the State's failure to observe its national and international obligations to provide shelter for homeless refugees and asylum seekers." The affidavit went on to state that "insofar as there may be any breach of any by-law, it cannot be relied upon in emergency situations where necessity would be a defence".

The City task team realised that they could not work in isolation. In Phil Harrison's opinion, the City had taken a progressive view toward migrants, but it was not only about the City. There was no clear national policy on migrants, no clear direction or framework in which to work. Mary Metcalfe helped to connect the team with Minister Sicelo Shiceka, who held the portfolio of Provincial and Local Government in the Cabinet. As a result, in March that year the task team became inter-governmental, which meant that now there was involvement at national and provincial levels. This expanded team was chaired by Yusuf Patel from the Department of Provincial and Local Government.

Patel knew that national government was not interested in creating refugee camps in South Africa. He believed that his role was to bring the different levels of government together to facilitate some immediate measures that would relieve the pressure on the church. The City had good intentions, he thought, but agreed that they didn't have the tools or the resources to deal with the situation on their own. Provincial and national resources needed to be pulled in. "This was a hell of a unfortunate situation," said Patel. "I had to build trust with the Bishop. He saw me as just another government official. The Bishop said to me, 'I know government wants to charge me with all of this and put me in jail.'"

The biggest political driver at the provincial level was the Gauteng MEC for Local Government, Dorothy Qedani Mahlangu. Mahlangu had been the provincial cabinet member who had led the process of setting up and then disbanding the temporary shelters in June 2008 in the wake of the xenophobic violence, so she was very familiar with the situation at Central Methodist. It had been Mahlangu with whom Phil Harrision and Ruby Mathang of the City of Johannesburg had negotiated the financial support for the ongoing management of the Moth building to which it was intended that residents of Central would be moved.

The inter-governmental task team was scheduled to meet at Mahlangu's office on 11 March 2009, but even before that meeting took place it became clear, as was the case with the City, that not every national department was on the same page either. The Department of Home Affairs announced that it was closing down the refugee reception centre which it had opened in July 2008 on the showgrounds in Musina. The centre was always meant to be temporary, it stated. At the same time Home Affairs was also considering granting special status to Zimbabwean refugees that would allow them to reside and work in the country legally. In April they announced a moratorium on deportations.

As a result of the closure of the refugee reception centre, Zimbabweans came into Johannesburg in even greater numbers – "about two hundred people in the last two weeks," Paul Verryn said, "seventy-one of them on Friday alone" – and when they arrived at Central Methodist, the Bishop did not turn them away.

Several Johannesburg papers reported that migrants from Musina were being given transport to Johannesburg by mini-bus taxis but no one was sure who was funding this. Rumours circulated that it was Bishop Verryn who was subsidising the transport but in fact it was the UN High Commission for Refugees. Dorothy Qedani Mahlangu was incensed. She accused the UNHCR of creating a crisis in Johannesburg. She met with their regional representative for South Africa, Sanda Kimbimbi, and they jointly announced that "the practice would be slowed if not stopped altogether and that Zimbabwean refugees from then on would be required to prove they had a place of residence or a job waiting for them in Johannesburg before they would be provided with transport". Kimbimbi said that many refugees came to Johannesburg in search of employment and that they "would now be advised that this would not necessarily be the best option".

Not only was Mahlangu upset with the UNHCR, but she also publicly criticised Bishop Verryn. "I don't think it's helpful for the Bishop to continue to do what he's doing under the guise that he's simply helping vulnerable people. I think he is exposing them to more danger. We are not condoning what he is doing. We condemn it. Any church, any community hall is not meant to be inhabited by people."

The argument continued to play out in the media. In the *Saturday Star* Verryn was quoted as saying that Mahlangu's statement was "absurd". "I don't think that in the midst of this gigantic crisis, where in fact people have got to work together, that we can point fingers and try to abdicate responsibility… We are not sitting with two thousand boxes in this place, which ultimately will be moved to another box. Some of these people are so vulnerable and fractured… We can interpret this as a curse and a nuisance, but in essence we're dealing with humanity."

Morgan Tsvangirai's Movement for Democratic Change sprang to Bishop Verryn's defence. "For Mahlangu to accuse a man of God, Bishop Paul Verryn, of exposing Zimbabweans to danger when he is actually providing us shelter is very regrettable," said MDC spokesman Sibanengi Dube. The MDC expected Mahlangu and the provincial government to complement, not complicate, Verryn's efforts and accused Mahlangu of insensitivity to the plight of Zimbabweans.

Her statements regarding Bishop Verryn, the church and the UNHCR notwithstanding, Mahlangu still had to co-operate with them, and she had to call on their assistance with the process of moving the residents of the church to other accommodation. Yusuf Patel said that although she was suspicious of the UNHCR because they had been busing people in from Musina, the UNHCR was also most likely to know how to count refugees and she was aware of that. In late March, while the Pitje Chambers case against the church was being negotiated, the UNHCR moved into Central Methodist and distributed tokens to approximately 2 500 people at the church who were eligible for relocation to other buildings, including the Moth building. Mahlangu announced that six buildings in and around Johannesburg had been identified as alternative accommodation. While 2 500 tokens may have been distributed, UNHCR knew that it was unlikely that there would be enough space at the other sites for all of those people.

Once the tokens had been distributed, 60 Home Affairs and local government employees took details from the residents of the church to establish who were the most vulnerable among them – women with children, unaccompanied minors, people with disabilities – and what skills each resident had. According to the UNHCR, only 1 800 of those who got tokens came forward for registration.

Some of the residents at Central said that they would not leave the church even if they were offered alternatives because they didn't think it would be safe. One woman, Charlene Mudiwa, pointed out, not unreasonably, that during the xenophobic attacks in May 2008 the church had remained safe and its residents protected. If xenophobic attacks happened again, she said, the new buildings housing foreign nationals would be the first places they'd go looking for them.

Freedom Chivima got a token and registered. He felt he didn't have a choice, being uncertain how long his plumbing job in the city would last. He needed to make sure he had accommodation.

Setting up the registration process was a rushed business because of intense pressure to deal with the situation quickly. Tension between the staff at the UNHCR and the City was often taut and sometimes tempers flared.

Lasting solutions were what needed to be found, however, and one thing was clear: these would only be found through the co-ordinated efforts of national, provincial and local government. Although most parties were in agreement about this fact, unfortunately, despite their individual efforts and good intentions, co-ordination was not working very well.

In mid-March the Smal Street Mall business owners put forward their own co-ordinated effort and lasting solution by erecting a heavy, metal, spiked fence between the church and the mall. This effectively closed off the pedestrian mall from 6pm in the evening until 6am the following morning and prevented people from sleeping on the pavement. The fence also created a barrier outside the front entrance to the church. Jason Brickhill, from the Legal Resources Centre, who was Bishop Verryn's attorney, immediately challenged this move. He questioned whether a portion of the fence wasn't on church property. It was also a fire hazard, he said, because it caused a bottleneck at the entrance of the church. In the event of a fire people would be trapped and in serious danger. The urgency of the Pitje Chambers case against the church took precedence for Brickhill over the construction of the fence, however, and he was not able to have more than a couple of meetings with the owners of the Smal Street Mall businesses and to pursue his line of objection. The fence went up and stayed up.

Reverend Kim Alexander remembered that the registration for new accommodation was still ongoing, even after the fence was erected. "People were pushing right up against it," she said. "I think that Paul thought people with disabilities who were living in the building would get hurt so he said, 'All those with any kind of disability – into the chapel.' Paul asked me to help count the people in the chapel. I walked in there and I just thought, Dear God, you are at work here. They were lame. They were blind. There was a man whose legs were maimed and who walked on his hands. I thought, In what other church do these people feel welcome? There's part of me that knows that Paul didn't handle things well, but there's a part of me that profoundly respects Paul's ministry."

During this period of conflict on the streets and in the press the team from the City of Johannesburg worked very hard to engage with the issues on the ground. Harrison, Mathang, Mthethwa, even Mayor Masondo, all wanted to find solutions. Although they had been slow to act, once the City became involved, it was continually looking for ways to collaborate. Gauteng province, on the other hand, took a more confrontational stance and viewed Central Methodist as a problem to be eliminated rather than a crisis that required careful resolution. Dorothy Qedani Mahlangu certainly took this view and Bishop Verryn did not trust that any of the government officials had the best interests of the church residents at heart.

In fact, at this point, Verryn's level of trust with people outside of government was also tentative. Even his relationship with a close friend took strain. Verryn had known Johanna Kistner for many years. She was the daughter of Dr Wolfram Kistner, a South African of German parentage who had been an activist under apartheid. Johanna was a psychologist and she headed up the Sophiatown Community Psychological Services, which Verryn had invited into the church in early 2008 when he recognised the need for trauma counselling after the January police raid. In December 2008, Kistner took several children who were living at the church to her home over the Christmas holiday. She had not informed Verryn that she was doing this and Verryn was outraged. They argued. According to Kistner, Verryn flew off the handle and screamed insults at her. Both their friendship and their working relationship were destroyed. While this personal conflict was one that did not play itself out in the media, in the year ahead Kistner's anger and Verryn's bull-headedness would affect the debate over the children who were being housed at Central Methodist.

As it so happened, in the more public conflict of the church, the City and Gauteng province, George Bizos of the LRC was in a position to help mediate and negotiate with the different parties involved, and at multiple levels, in order to avoid going to court. Bizos had worked on the Pitje Chambers case for a period of about two weeks in March and he had read Bishop Verryn's affidavit into the court record. After numerous emergency meetings, on 20 March 2009, on the High Court steps all parties reached agreement and Pitje Chambers withdrew its charges against the church. The City agreed to supply two security guards at the entrance and exit to Pitje Chambers, and to assign a dedicated team for refuse removal in the area. The City also agreed to remove the portable toilets along Pritchard Street and to keep the public toilets on the corner of Pritchard and Von Brandis streets open 24 hours a day.

The resolution of the Pitje Chambers court case did not mean that all of the church's neighbours were happy, however. Some of them were planning their own ultimate solution.

Carl Von Brandis statue on the corner of Pritchard and Von Brandis streets.

Meetings at Central Methodist / 2011

Sometimes I would go to specific meetings at Central Methodist, and sometimes I would go just to sit in the foyer and see who was there, and sometimes it would end up being a bit of both. One day in 2011 I went to a meeting in the chapel held by the United Nations High Commission for Refugees and Lawyers for Human Rights where the discussion was about issues of documentation. There were about 50 people there.

After the meeting I ran into Alois Mutenanhene and Moses Rombayi in the foyer. Both men taught embroidery and sewing up on the fourth floor. Alois was the man who had run away from the George Goch hostel to Central Methodist during the xenophobic violence in May 2008. He told me his wife Leona was pregnant again, now with their third child. In addition to sewing, Alois's friend Moses was also a gospel singer and he had a beautiful voice. I bought his CD, *Pindirai*, and was very impressed. Moses was looking to reach out to the growing South African gospel market and hoping to record another CD soon. If you were to listen to his powerful voice or look at his detailed embroidery work, you would never guess that Moses was struck with polio as a child and has struggled physically ever since. After we had finished chatting, Moses left the foyer, propelling himself forward with his crutches.

As Alois and Moses walked out of the building, Booker Maseti came in. I had seen Booker several times since I'd first met him in the Bishop's office the day he'd arrived at Central Methodist in July the year before. He told me, "From the outside, people think this place looks finished, but they would be surprised at all that goes on here. It's the lowest rung on the social ladder but a lot is happening." He paused and posed and then said, "You only get to gold when you dig through the dirt."

Booker always had something on the go or a big new idea he wanted to share. This time he informed me that he had started working at the Hub, which was a building in town that supported entrepreneurs. "It is an insult for those looking for a lavish lifestyle or an executive atmosphere, but it provides working space for entrepreneurs. We hosted Zanele Mbeki the other day," he said. "You should take a look at our website. I'm writing for the blog." I did have a look and not only did I find Booker's writings, but I also found a photo of him with Zanele Mbeki, Thabo Mbeki's wife and a former First Lady of South Africa.

I remembered that Booker had told me he used to work for *The Sunday Independent* so I went on line and found an article he had written about bikers in Soweto, his home town, entitled "Bikers Bonded by Burning Rubber of Freedom". Then I found a few articles from the City of Johannesburg website that quoted Booker in 2009 about increasing benefits for the poor when he was working on the Expanded Social Package in the city. That was the job he'd lost, which had led to him finding himself on the street.

Although Booker never went into details, he once told me that he had been estranged from his mother and his six siblings for the past few years. I was sure the circumstances were difficult, but I couldn't help thinking that his mother would want to see him. When he first arrived at Central Methodist, he slept on the stairs going down to Minor Hall and he said that some people were suspicious of him. Some believed he might be an undercover cop. He denied this but did admit to struggling with drinking too much. He was still looking for a full-time job. "When things go wrong in life, don't be afraid to hit rock bottom," he said. "That's where you'll find where you're meant to be headed. It steers the way for your next destination."

I wondered where Cleo was. It was always a good bet that she would be cleaning somewhere in the building, or working on paperwork in her room or in the office on the third floor. I would usually have to call her to find out where she was before we could connect. She was always busy, and today I couldn't find her.

When visiting the church I would often stick my head into the Roberts Room. Bishop Verryn had organised several exercise bikes in there for Freedom's karate students, and sometimes I'd find Freedom there working out. His latest challenge was to apply for Zimbabwean passports for himself, his wife and daughter and then apply for a work permit under the special dispensation at Home Affairs. He was hoping to be able to move away from applying for asylum permits every few months. He didn't know then what a long road ahead he still had – it would take another two years of effort to sort out the paperwork.

My other regular stop was at the help desk inside the front door. There was always someone sitting there. Often it was Reymond or Blessing, Wellington or Takudzwa.

I'd got to know Takudzwa through Peace Action meetings. He was one of those people who volunteered for everything. He had volunteered to be the head of the chess club and to co-ordinate the darts group. If someone wanted to start a newsletter, he would volunteer to help. If no one was holding refugee fellowship meetings, he would offer to take them over. At one Peace Action meeting, Takudzwa had volunteered to work at the help desk in the foyer. In fact, the two times I formally interviewed Takudzwa it was while he was working at the help desk. We would talk for a while and then we'd get interrupted when someone walked in to ask a question or report an incident.

One day, in March 2011, after finishing an interview with Takudzwa, I walked down to Von Brandis Street to see if I could find Esther Thomas, the woman who sold small items on the street there. It had been a while since I'd seen her. She wasn't at her usual spot. Sometimes if the harassment got too much on Von Brandis, Esther had told me she would move to another place on Pritchard Street, across from the High Court in front of Innes Chambers. That's where I found her today. She was sitting in front of what used to be Kids World. The shop was gone, the front gate was down, but the sign remained. Esther and I sat there together on her piece of cardboard. From this vantage point, we had a clear view of the comings and goings at the court.

Clients parked on the street to meet their lawyers on the front steps. Members of the JMPD stood around in orange and tan clusters. Attorneys walked by, dressed in black, some of them in gowns and pulling rolling bags along behind them, no doubt filled with legal papers. Journalists set up outside the front gate to catch a quote or a photograph as the attorneys and clients came out of the building after a case.

Esther told me that she had tried to see the Bishop on Saturday and Sunday, Monday and Tuesday that week. She wanted to speak to him about her documents. Finally, on Wednesday, she had made her way to the front of the queue and got to speak to him. He suggested that she go to Lawyers for Human Rights and ask them to review her asylum papers. She had followed his advice and LHR reassured her that all was in order but told her that she would have to renew on time because in August the special dispensation for Zimbabweans was going to end and the police would begin deportations again.

Before I could ask about her renewal, a man in black pants and a black shirt, holding a clipboard, walked towards us. "You cannot sell here. You must move," he said.

There was no one around us. We were bothering no one. "Why?" I asked him.

"Because shopkeepers pay a lot of money to maintain this place," he said. "You must go and sell on the corner of Kerk and Harrison."

"Kerk and Harrison? But that's –" Not waiting to hear the rest of my sentence, and with great speed, as if she'd had plenty of practice, Esther gathered her wares into her bag, pulled up her cardboard and started to cross the street. She headed back to her spot on Von Brandis and I followed her. I settled down beside her and we started talking about Zimbabwe again. "I don't know why they say there are no problems in Zim," she said. "There's no food. I couldn't go back to where I stay. We don't know when God is going to release Zimbabwe." Sometimes I wondered that too.

After the man in black had moved us on, I was reminded that the JDA and the private sector had spent a lot of money on the area around the High Court back in 2007 on new paving and benches, and installing the red clock at the corner of Pritchard and Smal. They had even polished the statue of Carl von Brandis.

The statue stands three metres high, and overlooks the corner of Pritchard and Von Brandis streets. Von Brandis was the first mining commissioner for Johannesburg and then became a magistrate and the most senior government official from 1886 to 1900. At his position on the western side of the South Gauteng High Court building, Von Brandis must have seen a lot over recent years, I thought – Winnie Mandela's trial in 1991 (when the building was called the Rand Supreme Court), Jacob Zuma's supporters dancing during his rape trial in 2006, and crowds gathering to watch the proceedings of Julius Malema's hate speech trial projected onto large screens outside the court in April 2011. And in 2009, when thousands of Zimbabwean refugees overflowed from Central Methodist on the other side of the High Court and slept at his feet, Von Brandis kept his steady watch. The plaque on his statue reads:

"He had the difficult task of upholding law and order in the fast-growing mining town of Johannesburg." By the way, Von Brandis was a migrant from Germany.

Seventeen

Death Threat Comes for the Bishop

Good Friday is one of the holiest days on the Christian calendar, marking the date of Jesus's crucifixion. Easter Sunday follows two days later, marking the date that Jesus was resurrected. In South Africa, the day after that, Easter Monday, is also a public holiday, making up a four-day Easter weekend.

Over the Easter weekend in 2009 Bishop Paul Verryn conducted more than the usual number of holiday services. That year the church was overflowing with people and the Bishop had been in almost continuous conflict with the City of Johannesburg and many of his neighbours. On Easter Monday, 6 April, he received a death threat over the phone. The caller, a man, said he had been hired by the shop owners in Smal Street Mall and that he had been given a car and a gun. The Bishop immediately filed a complaint with the police. He received a second call the following day. This time the caller claimed that the shop owners had given him the first instalment of his fee – R30 000. Verryn believed it was a blackmail attempt because the caller also asked him what he was prepared to do to save his own life. Verryn told the man he could not make a deal over the phone and asked him to meet him at his office.

Two men duly arrived. Posing as security guards, the police were waiting for them. They welcomed the men into the church and led them up to Verryn's office. There the men were promptly arrested on charges of intimidation and blackmail. While they still maintained they had been hired to kill the Bishop by local business owners who wanted the church closed down, Captain John Maluleke of the SAPS believed they were actually trying to extort money from Verryn for themselves. Either way, Verryn was extremely grateful to the police for their response and quick action, and while there was no love lost between the Bishop and the business owners around the church, he never did believe they had put out a contract on his life. Ambrose Mapiravana remembers that the Bishop asked the police to release the two men and declined to press charges.

At this time there were about 2 000 people sleeping inside the church and close to the same number sleeping on the streets outside. Residents who had received tokens from the UNHCR and had registered with Home Affairs the previous month waited patiently to be relocated.

The Gauteng government prioritised children, the sick and the aged for relocation, and Phil Harrison said the City's focus was more on getting the most vulnerable people off the street itself rather than moving those who had a place in the church building. There appeared to be some movement when, on 18 April, the first group of people was moved to My Lily Pot in Rosettenville south of the city, one of the six sites that had been earmarked for relocation. There were 131 people in this group, but they were only assured shelter for a period of three months. The temporary nature of this new housing was a concern to many of those preparing to make the move, as were the sites themselves. These were the Usindiso Place of Safety, Shaft 17 at Nasrec, Carol Farm in Randfontein, Wilgespruit Fellowship Centre in Roodepoort, and the Moth building on Loveday Street in town. Except for the Moth building and Usindiso, which was on Albert Street, the sites were all some distance from the city centre.

Property owners in the area around the church were now becoming desperate for the people sleeping on the street to be moved. As a group, they began to put pressure on their representative, the Central Johannesburg Partnership, to do something about it. The CJP oversees City Improvement Districts (CIDs), which are collaborations amongst property owners who pool their funds to improve security and keep the areas clean, bolstering the role of the local municipality. One internal email within the CJP in April 2009 read, "Please monitor the situation on the CID side of Pritchard Street". The "CID side" of Pritchard Street was to the south and included Innes Chambers and Schreiner Chambers. Ironically, the CID did not cover anything on the north side of Pritchard Street – the High Court, Central Methodist Mission, or the northern section of the Smal Street Mall.

CJP had attended that tense City meeting in February in Braamfontein and they had been looking to Nathi Mthethwa and the City of Johannesburg task team to solve the situation. Two months on not much had changed. Russell Thomas of the CJP later recalled that it was a terrible time. "It was horrible to see those poor people lying on the street," he said. "It was cold and there were babies there. I would come to work and I couldn't eat after seeing those people. It was like the Germans lining up the Jews. They were lying there in grey blankets. I thought they were dead. I couldn't get that picture out of my mind for months."

The pressure on the CJP from the property owners, who were paying levies to keep the place clean, did not let up. Cleaning the area along Pritchard Street each morning was a major task. Another internal email at the CJP took an optimistic view: "Refugees have moved from the Schreiner Chambers side. They are now sleeping on the Court side." Later that month the CJP met with management from Schreiner Chambers, their CID client on the south side of the street, to discuss the fact that people were still sleeping on the pavement outside their building. The meeting proposed a solution – a sprinkler system, with a timer to be programmed around the times the refugees trespassed on the premises. While a sprinkler system was never installed, manual watering with hoses did subsequently happen every night, and this did discourage people from sleeping on that section of the pavement. Lawyers for Human Rights represented the group of people sleeping on the street outside the church and the court, but they feared they might never again get a fair hearing from the High Court judges if they took action on their behalf.

MEC Mahlangu had tasked Russell McGregor of the Gauteng Department of Local Government with putting together a longer term plan to address the crisis. On 13 May 2009 he presented a draft plan to the inter-governmental task team. First he confirmed the need for the City of Johannesburg and Gauteng province to find medium- to long-term solutions for people, predominantly Zimbabweans, who were sheltered in and around Central Methodist. The proposal then stated that it would not be appropriate for government to provide shelter for this specific group of foreign nationals only, but that the project would need to address the broader challenge of temporary shelter for vulnerable groups in the inner city, South African citizens and non-nationals alike.

McGregor's plan focused on the Moth building as the pilot site for providing temporary shelter. This was the building that had been identified by Phil Harrison back in January, and for which he'd already secured management services and maintenance commitments from JDA and Gauteng province. McGregor proposed that the municipality would provide services such as water, electricity, refuse removal and maintenance, and that the management of the building should be funded by the Gauteng Department of Social Development. In addition, he said that the UNHCR and other UN agencies, the United Nations Development Programme (UNDP) for one, had also expressed willingness to fund the programme.

It was proposed that the daily management of the building would be contracted out to a qualified non-profit organisation which would report directly to the Gauteng Department of Social Development, and would be overseen by a board consisting of representatives from the contracted NPO, the City of Johannesburg, the Gauteng Department of Social Development, a UN agency, the SAPS, and the Central Methodist Mission.

By June there had been no further relocations of people to other buildings, neither from the street nor the church, other than the first group of 131 people who had been moved to Rosettenville. The inter-governmental task team was still working on getting the Moth building ready.

The Central Johannesburg Partnership was frustrated. The situation was worse than it had ever been and still nobody, it seemed, was really doing anything about it. Thousands of people were still living and sleeping on the streets.

Ironically, there was a building standing empty on the same block – Innes Chambers – right across Pritchard Street from the High Court. The National Prosecuting Authority had bought the building in 2004 with the intent of housing over 200 prosecutors there, but much of it had stood empty ever since. The delay in their moving in had apparently been caused by "technical problems" with the building's refurbishment, according to an NPA communications official. In the end the prosecutors set up office in Inner Court, a building on the west side of Von Brandis Street.

Innes Chambers was not the only building in the neighborhood that was largely unoccupied. The Johannesburg Sun Hotel, a complex with two towers, one 40 storeys high and the other 22 storeys, linked by a four-storey bridge with a pool deck and a running track, had been mothballed for years. It was right next door to Central Methodist on Smal Street. Over the years a number of buildings in the inner city had been abandoned by their owners, taken over by pirate landlords, and filled with people coming into the city from other parts of South Africa, and also other parts of the continent. Many of these buildings, called "bad buildings" by the City, were candidates for refurbishment.

In the middle of 2009 it was estimated that there were 600 000 to 650 000 Zimbaweans in Johannesburg. The Solidarity Peace Trust said that Central Methodist was only the "highly visible tip of a huge iceberg of Zimbabweans in Central Johannesburg".

At about the same time Médecins Sans Frontières assessed that more than 50 per cent of the Zimbabwean patients who attended the MSF clinic at Central Methodist were from outside the church, an indication that large numbers of Zimbabweans were living in other buildings in the inner city and that they had poor access to health care.

MSF raised another concern at this time: the plight of unaccompanied children. Over the past year MSF had witnessed a steady increase in the number of children arriving unaccompanied in Musina and at Central Methodist in Johannesburg, with a particularly sharp increase in numbers in the first half of 2009. As of May 2009 there were 150 unaccompanied children between the ages of seven and eighteen staying at the church. MSF warned that these children were extremely vulnerable and were exposed to many forms of abuse. They took their concerns to the Department of Social Development and UNICEF, and they provided a list of names and relevant details about each individual child. They also started a special counselling programme for unaccompanied minors and appointed three MSF counsellors to work with the children and give them emotional, educational and psychological support. "Despite the fact that key organisations and agencies are fully aware of the extreme vulnerability of this group," MSF stated, "no viable solution has yet been proposed or implemented."

Some of these children had lost both parents due to HIV/AIDS or other causes. Some had realised that their parents could no longer support them and these children had had to grow up overnight. By the time they found their way to Central Methodist, many of them had already been exploited. Some of them had been raped. One counsellor described the case of a 12-year-old girl who had been raped in Pretoria and had ended up at MSF at the church. "[She] got an infection and her behaviour completely changed after that. Once something like that happens to a child, you fear for more abuse."

At the same time that MSF was raising a flag about children in the building, Johanna Kistner of Sophiatown Community Psychological Services was doing so as well, although she took a different approach. In April 2009, together with several other children's NGOs, including Kids Haven and Big Shoes, she helped form the Johannesburg Child Advocacy Forum (JCAF). The Forum's main goal was to get all of the unaccompanied children moved out of the church and into shelters that they believed would be more appropriate for their needs, and safer for them. In June the Forum wrote to the Presiding Bishop, Ivan Abrahams, to express concerns about how Bishop Verryn was handling the situation of the children living at Central Methodist. Abrahams was as cautious as he had been with Lindi Myeza. "I can't act on hearsay," he said. "Put together affidavits about your allegations and then I'll see what I can do."

Kistner and the JCAF duly put the affidavits together. They also compiled a dossier of accusations against Verryn and submitted this to Abrahams in July. Abrahams passed the dossier on to the SAPS and the National Prosecuting Authority.

During this time, UNICEF began working inside the church building. By August UNICEF and the National Association of Child and Youth Care Workers (NACCW) had started training care-givers to work in the church to care for the unaccompanied minors. They had 21 people in their programme.

Meanwhile, another prominent neighbour of Central Methodist Mission had joined the fray. On 17 June the Deputy Judge President of the South Gauteng High Court, Phineas Mojapelo, sent a letter to the Johannesburg Metro Police Department, with a copy to the Mayor and the South African Police Service, on the subject of "Unacceptable and Dangerous Conditions in Public Streets Bordering the High Court Building". The letter lamented the presence of homeless people sleeping on the pavements, "no doubt joined by loiterers and others with criminal intentions." The National Directorate of Public Prosecutions had moved to the Inner Court building on Von Brandis Street by then and renovations were about to start there. This was sure to increase human traffic in the area, he pointed out. More than this, the area was "quite simply an eyesore and a haven for all manner of unsavoury and congested human traffic and behaviour." People no longer felt safe coming to the court and "no effort" was being made to enforce the traffic laws or the by-laws on trading and cleanliness.

The letter concluded with an appeal to the authorities for "intervention and immediate remedial action". Within a matter of weeks, the Deputy Judge President received a clear response.

Eighteen

Arrested for Loitering

ON THE EVENING OF FRIDAY, 3 JULY 2009, Daniel Sibanda[4] was asleep on the pavement on Kruis Street, across from the High Court. "I was awoken abruptly by someone who slapped my ear, and by the sounds of people shouting," he said in an affidavit to the court about the events of that night. "I was startled and thought that I was being robbed and attacked by some thugs on the street. When I looked up I noticed that the police were there... They told us to wake up and leave our bags behind. Some people were trying to put their shoes on and get dressed, but they were stopped by police officers and assaulted for taking their time."

Sibanda, a 46-year-old boilermaker from Zimbabwe, had been sleeping on Kerk Street for three months. He had been working for mining companies in Zimbabwe since he qualified in 1986 but in 2005 he was arrested because he was working for the MDC. Sibanda said that he was arrested again in 2008 and he was beaten and tortured by members of Zanu-PF. He was told that if he was arrested again, he would "disappear forever". That was when he decided to move to South Africa. Sibanda arrived in Johannesburg in March 2009 and first slept at Park Station for about a month before he was told about Central Methodist Mission. When he went to see if he could live there, it was too crowded, which was why he ended up sleeping outside

4 not his real name

on the pavement on Kruis Street. He applied for and obtained an asylum-seeker permit, but had not yet found permanent employment.

On the night of the arrests, sleeping not far from Sibanda was Michael Naidoo, a South African homeless man from Durban, who had been sleeping on Kruis Street for about nine years. "I was awoken abruptly by someone kicking me," he said. Naidoo had been disabled in a car accident when he was a child and he used a crutch to walk. He didn't have a job and had no living immediate family members. Naidoo said, "I have never been arrested in my entire life and I have always been a law-abiding citizen. I did not know that it was a crime to be poor and homeless. The police officer instructed all of us to wake up, leave all our belongings on the pavement and follow him into the police van. Other police officers arrived and were kicking people awake and pushing them into vans. When people refused to get into the vans, the police officers would assault them… I was afraid of being assaulted so I obeyed the police officer and climbed into the van, taking my crutch with me. I was afraid to ask the officer why I was being arrested because I noticed that when others asked the officers questions, they were beaten… During the arrest, I lost all my possessions, including clothing, a jacket, my shoes and my asthma pump. My identity document was also lost during the police raid."

The raid had been co-ordinated and planned jointly by the Johannesburg Metropolitan Police Department and the South African Police Service. When the police had raided the church back in January 2008, no one had been charged, and the general sense from the SAPS themselves, from the City and provincial government was that that raid had not been handled well. Eighteen months later, in July 2009, the level of frustration amongst the neighbours around the church had reached its limit and Bishop Paul Verryn was beside himself. As far as he was concerned, there had been no action on the part of government to assist in any substantial way. Despite commitments given by various stakeholders – the City, Gauteng province, and national government departments – no solution had been implemented. No alternative accommodation had been provided. While the Department of Home Affairs' moratorium on the deportation of Zimbabweans was still in place, the political and economic situation in Zimbabwe had not stabilised enough for people to return home of their own accord.

All Paul Verryn knew with any certainty was that his church was overflowing and people were suffering.

It was in this context that the police brought their significant resources, financial and human, to bear on the situation. Once again, it was the police who took action. It wasn't the only police action at the church since January 2008, but it was the largest.

When the police began their arrests that night, Evans Kuntonda had finished his shift at MSF but was still at Central Methodist assisting a pregnant woman who had gone into labour. As he was escorting the woman out of the building, he saw that dozens of police officers were busy rounding up the people sleeping on the street, using force if they resisted, and even using pepper spray on them. A JMPD police officer pushed Evans into the line with other people outside the High Court. "It was a commotion," he said emphatically.

Evans managed to phone his MSF colleague, Bianca Tolboom, at about 11pm that night. He told her what was going on and that the SAPS and the JMPD were using force. Tolboom immediately went to the church to see what medical support she could offer. When she arrived, she said, "there were police trucks and cars and police officials grabbing people and pulling them into the back of the police trucks. If people refused to climb into the truck, they were assaulted." She tried to ask what was happening and why the police were behaving that way, but was told only that the people who were being arrested would be taken to Johannesburg Central Police Station and if she wanted to ask questions she should go there.

Paul Verryn was out of the country that night attending a conference in the United States but Evans Kuntonda phoned him anyway. Verryn immediately phoned Commissioner Simon Mpembe, the station commander at Johannesburg Central whom he'd worked with before. Mpembe said he was no longer station commander there but told Verryn that he was aware of the operation under way on Pritchard Street. He referred him to Commissioner Ngwako Mashao, who was in command of the operation. The local shopkeepers and the High Court had been keeping up the pressure for the police to enforce the by-laws and remove the people who were sleeping on the pavements lining Pritchard Street, he said. Verryn phoned Mashao at once and requested him to halt the raid and release the people being held. Mashao refused.

Tolboom called two attorneys, Jacob van Garderen from Lawyers for Human Rights and Jason Brickhill from the Legal Resources Centre. Brickhill remembers that he was getting ready for bed that Friday night. "The police really have great timing," he said. All three of them arrived at the Johannesburg Central Police Station at about midnight. Tolboom requested that she be allowed to assess the medical needs of those who had been arrested but was told they were still being processed and she would have to wait.

Over 350 people were arrested that night.

Daniel Sibanda was distressed. "We were driven to the Johannesburg Central Police Station," he recalled. "The officers finished processing us at about 6am. I was put in a cell with sixty other men. We were given blankets but these were filthy and had lice. There was one toilet in the cell but it did not have toilet paper."

At 3am in the morning and again at 5am, on 4 July 2009, Tolboom tried to get permission to assess the people who had been arrested. The police refused. At 7am, Tolboom went home.

Van Garderen and Brickhill also waited at the police station throughout the night, and were also refused access to the people in custody. Evans Kuntonda was able to let Van Garderen know that there were a number of children in detention, and in fact Van Garderen had seen for himself some very young people being pushed into the police vans while he was outside the church. He had thought at the time they were minors.

On Saturday afternoon Tolboom went back to the police station and this time she took with her Dr Kerrigan McCarthy, a medical doctor who worked at the University of the Witwatersrand Reproductive Health and HIV Research Unit. This time a Captain Sibisi at the station granted them permission to assess the health needs of the people who had been arrested. While most of them had been processed by then and were in the cells, there was one group still in the waiting area waiting to be processed. Evans Kuntonda was one of them and, fortunately, he was given permission to help the doctors screen people who needed medical attention. They were given an empty cell in which to do these consultations. The MSF team was given access to a total of fifteen patients, six of whom needed treatment as a result of being assaulted by the police the previous evening. There was also a man on antiretrovirals who had lost his medication during the arrest. MSF provided him with a supply for three days and a referral letter in order to get further supplies. They also examined a 21-year-old woman who was four months pregnant, as well as a 58-year-old South African woman who was deaf and visually impaired. Tolboom presented a list of the fifteen people's names to Director Mashao and requested their release, although she was not confident that this would happen quickly. She was particularly concerned about Evans Kuntonda so she paid his admission of guilt fine of R300 to ensure his immediate release.

The next day, Sunday morning, Tolboom went back to the police station to follow up on the arrangement she had made with Director Mashao. To her dismay the officer on duty said she knew nothing about any arrangement. When Tolboom called Mashao he said that he had discussed the matter with Commissioner Mpembe but that no decision had been made.

Tolboom was called back to the police station in the afternoon. She was told that seven patients who needed further attention would be transported to the South Rand Hospital to see a doctor there but that "these patients would remain under arrest and hence be chained and handcuffed together. If it was found that they did not need hospitalisation they would be transported back to the station and put back in the cells." Tolboom wasn't comfortable with this prospect for patients who had gone through extensive trauma already so she decided to pay the admission of guilt fines for all of them, thereby securing their immediate release. Five patients were taken to hospital, and the pregnant woman and the older deaf woman were taken to My Lily Pot shelter.

Before she left the police station, Tolboom asked to see the register of names of all those people who had been arrested that Friday night. In total 367 people had been arrested outside the High Court building "for the criminal offence of loitering". They were all held in the cells over the weekend.

The Gauteng MEC for Community Safety, Khabisi Mosunkutu, issued a statement: "The issue here is not the foreign nationals who need shelter. The issue is the fact that there are hundreds of people living on the street in front of businesses and blocking the court entrance. When you have a situation where a judge can't get into the building because of people blocking the entrance, something needs to be done." Clearly, the letter of complaint from Deputy Judge President Mojapelo had turned into an order.

On Monday morning, 6 July, Van Garderen and Brickhill returned to offer assistance in representing the detainees in court. They were accompanied by lawyers from LHR, the LRC and the Aids Law Project, as well as a private attorney, Mr Ian Small-Smith, who had agreed to work on a *pro bono* basis. The attorneys attempted to speak to the prosecutor to say that in many cases the dockets they had seen were incomplete and did not identify the alleged offences and reason for arrest. They were also concerned that the loitering charge was inappropriate and should be withdrawn.

Van Garderen observed that the court and prosecutor had not prepared. "The incomplete files from the police were sitting on a chair and on the verge of falling on the floor," he said. Although the prosecutor expressed concern about releasing the detainees, he eventually agreed to withdraw the charges, seemingly because there was no actual basis on which to prosecute. Ultimately, none of those arrested was charged and, at Van Garderen's request, all detainees were released. He even managed to get the police to transport them all back to the church.

Daniel Sibanda was pleased to be released on Monday afternoon but he was angry, too. "I lost all my possessions," he said, "including clothes, a jacket, blankets, a Nokia 3110 cellphone and all my boilermaker tools. The tools that were lost were a combination set of 130 spanners, a 40 piece socket set, a 4 pound hammer, a tape measure, 3 steel rulers, 6 clamp sets, a line spirit level and a chalk line. The loss of my tools has been the most debilitating as it impedes my ability to earn a living."

Michael Naidoo had battled in the cell from Saturday to Monday without his asthma pump, which had been in the bag the police had forced him to abandon. Bianca Tolboom arranged to obtain another pump for him and she also advised that he move inside the church – which he did. "I have been living inside the church since the raid because the experience was very traumatising," Michael said.

Many Zimbabwean nationals continued to exist in limbo, between continual threat of arrest by the police for being undocumented and the Department of Home Affairs' slowness in implementing their plan to issue special documentation to Zimbabwean nationals in recognition of the conditions in their home country. The action by the police on the night of 3 July 2009 of swooping in and arresting people outside the High Court, which might be repeated at any time and without warning, or so it was feared, seemed to be entirely at odds with this plan and with the moratorium on deportations. These people may have been arrested for loitering but their only crime, actually, was to be destitute and without shelter.

People who lived in fear on the street were encouraged to crush their way inside the church for shelter.

Spokesman for the Johannesburg Metropolitan Police Department, Wayne Minnaar, offered little in the way of reassurance. The raid, he said, was part of Operation Chachamela (a Tsonga word meaning "walking on burning coals") and confirmed that the JMPD had been carrying out an order of the Johannesburg High Court to remove vagrants from in front of the court building. He said that people could expect follow-up operations to ensure that they complied with the city's by-laws. Operation Chachamela's plan was to clean up the city in preparation for the 2010 Soccer World Cup for which South Africa was the host country and which was a year away. Minnaar also said that about 100 women and children were not detained during the raid that night, but released on a warning.

On 6 July 2009 *The Star* reported: "There is no national political solution on the cards for destitute Zimabweans sleeping on Joburg's streets, but city officials are trying to house them, while metro police plan to continue arrests." The spokesperson for Home Affairs, Ronnie Mamoepa, was quoted in the same article, saying that Home Affairs was not involved in the raid. "The solution is to resolve the situation in Zimbabwe," he said.

Phil Harrison of the City of Johannesburg said the July raid "came as a surprise", while Jack Bloom of the Democratic Alliance noted: "It is tragic enough that so many Zimbabweans sleep on pavements in the bitter cold, but police harassment adds to their ordeal. This situation has been allowed to get out of hand because it was ignored for so long by all levels of government."

Days after the July raid there was another development. Gauteng province reneged on its commitment to fund the ongoing costs of the Moth building. They decided that provincial budget cuts meant that they would no longer have the resources. Mayor Masondo, Phil Harrison and Ruby Mathang were left without funding. The Mayor wrote to provincial MEC Mahlangu to say that the City had already spent R9 million on the Moth building and that expectations from the media and the church were high, but to no avail.

Contradictions abounded, not only between the national Department of Home Affairs and the police, but also between the police, the City of Johannesburg and Gauteng province. It had been four months since residents at the church and on the street had been registered by Home Affairs and local government authorities in anticipation of being given alternative accommodation. The City and the provincial authorities had said they were preparing to move them. Now the residents were losing faith that the City was ever going to find them somewhere else to live. Why would the City have told them they were preparing accommodation for people one moment, and then go and arrest them the next? Who were they supposed to believe? Where were they supposed to go? The right hand, which was the City trying to move things forward, didn't appear to know what the left hand might do next.

Meanwhile, the JMPD was resolute. People could expect more raids. They would do their job.

The relationship between Central Methodist Mission and the police was complex. While the church condemned the raids and violent behaviour of the police, the security team at the church needed the police to provide back-up for them in cases where criminals were at work in the building. A front page headline in the *Sowetan* in late July 2009 read "Church Haven for Gangs". In doing research for his article, the writer said he had been "guided around the hidden corners of the church" and was grateful to have had a guide who could explain how things worked there. "Many people have fallen victim to these gangsters but are too scared to tell Verryn. These gangsters engage in criminal activities outside and then come here to hide. No one challenges them because everyone is too afraid. The dark nooks and crannies of the cavernous church are such that even by day I would have felt unsafe without [a guide]. He said the gangsters were called the Sowetans and that they spent most of their days hanging around the stairs at the back of the church. Residents said the Sowetans seldom bothered them in the church and conducted most of their activities outside. Verryn said he knew about the gang and had on several occasions tried to rid the church of the criminals. 'The police arrest them but we find them in the building again,' Verryn said. 'I don't understand it.' He said he had an agreement with the police to patrol the church at least once a week… 'Criminals are not welcome in the building,' Verryn said."

In the same month as the raid, July 2009, the Albert Street School celebrated its first birthday. The school's enrolment was 523, and 110 of its learners were unaccompanied minors. Wellington Mukwamba, the head boy from Zimbabwe, spoke at the anniversary party, looking very smart in a blue suit. A large cross and "God is Love" was painted on the wall behind him. "This school saved us from child labour and abuse," said the lean teenager to the hundreds of children and visitors who attended. "Imagine you are ten years old. Imagine your parents have HIV. You are in a country where systems have collapsed. You sleep in the streets and have no food. Then you arrive in Johannesburg and you can't get access to normal schools. Central Methodist Church opens its doors. We will never forget this." Mukwamba bowed towards Bishop Verryn, who was seated at a plywood head table that was covered with a white lace table cloth. "Thank you, Bishop," he said. "Thank you, donors. Thank you, teachers."

It was a festive occasion. The speeches were followed by several presentations. Freedom Chivima put his karate students through their paces. Another group performed to kwaito music, followed by ballroom dancing. The children cheered and applauded each performance. White, blue and purple balloons swayed along the gallery above.

The Albert Street School would go on to excel in the dramatic arts later in the year when some of its learners participated in the Hillbrow inner-city drama competition, the theme of which was "I am a human being and I belong". The Albert Street learners wrote a script about an albino boy who was ostracised by his community. They had previously written a play about their journey from Zimbabwe and xenophobia, so they decided to choose another issue that needed the spotlight. Takudzwa Chikoro played the role of the albino boy's grandfather. "My character thought that it was a taboo for an albino to be born into the family. He thought he had no choice but to chase his daughter and her albino son away." The Albert Street School's play won first prize.

After the presentations, Bishop Verryn stood up to congratulate the school. "Study hard," he told the children. "Remember that the time you learn is not only in the classroom. Start reading. Read so that your mind will expand." Elizabeth Cheza shouted out, "We are a baby! When a baby reaches its first year, there is joy in the family." Bishop Verryn then blew out the candles on the big white birthday cake.

July 2009 brought sadness as well. Bishop Verryn bade farewell to someone who had brought great pain to his life but to whom he had offered forgiveness. Xoliswa Falati died on 15 July. Some time earlier, she had walked into Paul Verryn's office and asked to reconcile. "I think it was inconceivable at one time for her to make the shift, but what happened was that she came to my office and apologised for everything that she had done," said Verryn after her death. "She said she had been so unkind and that she had betrayed me, and that she had known that once she was released from prison, she would eventually come back. Her confession and her humility, not her humiliation, gave her such a profound dignity. So much so that once our friendship had been restored, it became a seamless garment."

In an interview with Janet Smith for *The Star,* Verryn suggested that Falati had been ostracised from certain ANC comrades after she had testified against Winnie Mandela before the Truth and Reconciliation Commission in 1997. "It seems her big fault was giving that evidence against Winnie. It was seen as an unforgivable thing at the time, yet there was something really sad about her displacement."

Not only did Verryn conduct a memorial service for Falati at Central Methodist and preside at her funeral in KwaThema, he also performed the last rites for her before she died. For some months, Falati had been living on the fourth floor of Central Methodist in the Home Based Care facility there.

In the same interview with Janet Smith, Verryn revealed that he, too, had come to some resolution with Winnie Madikizela-Mandela. They had had a chance encounter at a Cosatu conference a few years earlier. Verryn said the meeting was "just wonderful. I was standing with Jessie Duarte and Sydney Mufamadi and others, and there was certainly a tension in the group as she arrived, because of me. But she and Jessie greeted each other and then she turned to me and gave me one of those huge, generous hugs of hers, and I really felt that in that moment a repair had happened. It was a very, very good moment for me."

There were still 3 000 people living in and around Central and the JMPD maintained a regular presence there. And, as they had warned, they regularly raided the area outside the church and routinely confiscated the goods being sold by the vendors near the entrance. Evans Kuntonda personally witnessed another raid on the evening of 20 August that involved more than six JMPD vehicles and approximately 50 officers. No one was arrested on that occasion, but the police confiscated goods from vendors.

By this time Kuntonda had been working for Médecins Sans Frontières for more than a year and he held a special position in the Central Methodist community. He had influence within MSF as he was on staff there and he also had a strong relationship with the Bishop. There were some people who disliked Kuntonda because of the access he had to Verryn, but mostly he was well liked.

On 30 July, at about 3pm, five Zimbabwean women and their children were sitting on benches in front of the High Court. A group of SAPS officers told the women, "We don't want to see you here. We are tired of you. Go back to your country". The officers debated among themselves whether to arrest the women. Eventually, one of them said that the women could go but warned them that if they were caught sitting on the benches outside the High Court again, they would be arrested.

The enforcement of the by-laws was disturbingly reminiscent of the days of the pass laws during apartheid when the movement of people in the cities was strictly controlled and public areas were for one race exclusively. Sitting on a bench in a public area, like Lindi Myeza had tried unsuccessfully to do in 1970s Johannesburg, had been legal for all races by then for more than fifteen years.

Lawyers for Human Rights wrote letters to the JMPD and SAPS requesting that arrests in the area cease. When they received no response,

LHR proceeded to issue an application in the South Gauteng High Court requesting that the High Court declare that the arrests on 3 July 2009 were conducted unlawfully. It also requested that the SAPS and JMPD be prohibited from conducting further operations in the area, that the by-law criminalising loitering be declared unconstitutional and invalid, and that the government be compelled to engage meaningfully with those seeking shelter at the church in order to find solutions. The concern was expressed that Operation Chachamela would continue through to June and July 2010, the months of the World Cup. The aim of the application was to "prompt the City of Johannesburg and others within government to develop more appropriate policies to deal with those living on the streets".

Ironically, on the same day that the application was presented to the High Court, 30 October 2009, the church would receive another unexpected set of unwelcome visitors. These visitors would arrive unannounced in the early hours of the morning when the thousands of residents were fast asleep. This time, it wouldn't be the police.

Nineteen

Sexual Favours for a Toothbrush

"A SON THROWS HIMSELF AT HIS father's mercy. The son is a ruin, his head balding, his clothing ragged. He kneels and buries his face in his father's breast. The old man, white bearded and scarlet caped, looks down at his son with tenderness and love. Their monumental figures glow in a pool of light, reflected on the faces of spectators in the impenetrable darkness."

David Smith's article about Central Methodist, published in *The Guardian* in early September 2009, started by describing this image, its reference the framed reproduction of Rembrandt's *The Return of the Prodigal Son.* This painting was leaning against the wall in Paul Verryn's office on the third floor, and I would notice it too, still there, seven months later on my first visit to the church and many subsequent visits. The biblical image of homecoming and forgiveness was appropriate, given Verryn's policy of never turning anyone in need away, but the image was also ironic. Like the prodigal son who betrayed his father and returned for forgiveness, there were men in the building who had betrayed Verryn's trust. There were men in the building who were taking advantage of some of the young girls who had sought sanctuary there.

Smith's article went on to describe what he observed in the church – the clutter and squalor, the stench of sweat and urine, the peeling paint and the cracked tiles. He wrote that the Bishop estimated that there was one death every two weeks there, with the winter months being especially harsh.

Screenings for HIV and tuberculosis at MSF had gone some way towards staving off disaster but alcoholism, gang crime and violent feuds persisted.

Most of the approximately 3 000 people who were staying at the church, according to an August report by MSF, were male. There were 44 women registered with them for reproductive health services, 60 pregnant females and 100 children under the age of five. From January to July 2009 MSF found 103 suspected and 36 confirmed cases of TB. With funding and co-operation from Gauteng province and the City of Johannesburg, MSF conducted a mass TB screening campaign in August and 826 people were tested over four days. They identified 20 new adult TB cases and seven new paediatric cases, which confirmed suspicions that tuberculosis infection rates at Central Methodist were high.

Verryn was quoted saying, "'Every conceivable social problem that you could imagine is here, from child abuse to stealing to sex on the steps. It happens. It can be testing, but on the other hand there's a huge possibility. To begin organising and garrisoning the potential of people in this place can be exceedingly rewarding. There is huge hope looking for a home…' Verryn added, 'The World Cup next year is becoming a pain in my neck because everybody wants the city to be clean and beautiful and spick and span. We need to get rid of the cockroaches who are poor and shove them into some corner because that's not what a world class city really looks like. If they could smudge us into oblivion it probably would be the happiest day of the bureaucrats' life.'"

In September allegations of sexual abuse at the church and at the Albert Street School surfaced in the media. On the morning of 14 September, Talk Radio 702 aired an interview that one of its journalists, Micel Schnehage of *Eyewitness News*, had conducted with a girl from the school in which the girl claimed that adults were offering to buy young girls toiletries in exchange for sex. "Toiletries are gold," the child said. "You can't report it because you think, who's going to buy you toiletries again?"

Also in September, new allegations were raised against William Kandowe, the deputy principal at Albert Street, who had been accused of rape the previous year. Kandowe caught wind of this. "I packed my small bag," he said, "my change of clothes and my Colgate. I was ready for the police." Bishop Verryn phoned Kandowe personally as soon as the allegations surfaced. Verryn said bluntly, "'Tell me the truth. If you are using my office to do bad things, I will not support you.'"

The Methodist Church set up a commission of inquiry to investigate the sexual abuse allegations. Pending its report, this time Verryn suspended Kandowe from his post at the school. He also confirmed that multiple cases of sexual abuse had been reported to the police. Of the toiletries for sex claim, he said, "We have not been aware that there is such a desperate scramble for toiletries. We have tried to meet those needs. It's shocking that people get sexual favours for a toothbrush. This is sick."

Reverend Kim Alexander urged Verryn to move the young girls out of the building immediately. "They're just sitting ducks," she told him.

"Where?" he said to her. "Tell me where?"

Alexander said she would approach Jay Bradley at the Usindiso women's shelter to see if they could take the girls in. Usindiso was on Albert Street, in the old pass office building, down the road from the Albert Street School. "I cannot leave these girls in this building for one more day," she told Bradley, who said that Usindiso would take them but would only be able to house them on a temporary basis. It was better than nothing and Alexander set about organising the move. Afterwards, when it became clear that the girls were going to be moved from Usindiso into foster care, Alexander brought some of them back to Central Methodist. This move became controversial at the public hearings that would in time be held by Molebatsi Bopape of the Gauteng Legislature's Health and Social Development Portfolio Committee. Jay Bradley would claim that it was Paul Verryn who had wanted the girls back at Central Methodist and Reverend Alexander would say this was a lie.

Following the Talk Radio 702 story about sexual abuse allegations, David Smith wrote another piece for *The Guardian* in the UK, in which he stated that a teacher at the Albert Street School had been suspended as a result. He quoted Paul Verryn saying he feared the problem was widespread. The article also said that "an anonymous letter sent to Verryn claimed that the man had approached a girl and asked her to be his girlfriend and to sleep with him. The girl rejected his advances, after which he allegedly 'made life difficult for her'". Verryn took the claims very seriously, Smith wrote, saying that even the vaguest allegation needed to be examined. "'Normally, you assume someone is innocent until proven guilty. Here one has to assume guilt until innocence is proved.'" The article also said that Verryn had admitted he would be surprised if it was only one teacher. "'I think it's more than one and not just teachers,' he said. 'It's men generally.'" He also said that the children staying in the church had been carefully counselled about their bodies being sacred, and how nobody had the right to touch them. They were also told to speak up if somebody did interfere with them.

The Star newspaper contacted Verryn on 17 September and asked him whether any of the girls involved in the sexual abuse allegations had been moved to the Usindiso women's shelter. Verryn declined to answer the question and instead referred the newspaper to the Presiding Bishop of the Methodist Church, Ivan Abrahams.

The annual conference of the Methodist Church of Southern Africa was always held in mid-September and this year the delegates assembled in Pietermaritzburg in KwaZulu-Natal. The gathering of ministers from around the region was abuzz with discussion about what was going on at Central Methodist. Ivan Abrahams convened a small group to craft a communiqué condemning the neglect, exploitation and abuse of children. The statement said: "We affirm the gracious courage of CMM in opening the doors of their church to the thousands of displaced persons who, as a consequence of social instability, fear or destitution, have turned to the church for help." The statement defended Central Methodist for providing sanctuary to the vulnerable, but suggested that the impact of doing so had been overwhelming. It went on to confirm that allegations of abuse had been brought to the attention of the Church leadership and that Abrahams had appointed a committee to investigate the allegations further. He had also reported the allegations to the Department of Social Development and to the National Prosecuting Authority. "By so doing, the Presiding Bishop met both his statutory and moral obligations in terms of transparency, accountability and responsibility," the communiqué said. "We urge the relevant authorities urgently to complete their investigations and to report their findings to the Presiding Bishop."

In November 2010, over a year later, I set up a meeting with the Presiding Bishop. We met at his office. The headquarters of the Methodist Church of Southern Africa was in a cream-coloured stucco double-storey house on a one-way road that ran parallel to the highway near Eastgate Mall. The headquarters had previously been situated on Rissik Street in the city centre but concerns about safety in the inner city saw its relocation in 2003. Ivan Abrahams was originally from the Eastern Cape. He was in his mid-fifties and was tall and fit. He looked like he could have been a rugby player, but he told me his sport was actually long-distance running.

I asked Abrahams about his decision to go to the authorities in 2009 when the sexual abuse allegations at Central Methodist began to emerge in the media. In fact, he told me, he had gone to the police and the NPA months before the media began reporting on the issue in September that year. "The breaking point came with the ongoing allegations of abuse," he told me. "I had meetings with the organisations raising the allegations – Big Shoes, Kids Haven, etc. I asked them, 'Why are you coming to me?' I told them I couldn't take action without legal affidavits setting out what they were saying. They came back to me with affidavits. Then I did report the allegations to the police and to the National Prosecuting Authority."

I asked Abrahams to tell me more about the process of reporting the allegations.

"I met with the [provincial] MEC of Safety and Security and the Police Commissioner," he said. "They said they were coming to the meeting in a dual capacity. They were in their political posts but they also said, 'We are members of your Church.'" Abrahams sat up straighter in his office chair and paused for a minute. "Then they threatened me," he said. "They said, 'What if everyone in the Methodist Church knew what was in these documents?'" The pitch and pace of his voice started to rise. "'What if they knew about these allegations? Wouldn't you be in trouble? Shouldn't you do something?' That's when I said, 'Go to hell. Why don't *you* take action?' My colleagues who were with me said that I was rude. I told them they should have defended me."

Abrahams compared the situation with him and Paul Verryn to Obama having to fire his general in Afghanistan. "He had to fire him because of all the pressure," he told me. "I kept hearing people say, 'You have a rogue bishop.'"

I asked Abrahams whether he could share any documentation with me that would help me understand the evolution of events – correspondence between himself and Verryn, for example, or the dossier from Johanna Kistner and the Johannesburg Child Advocacy Forum that he had submitted to the NPA, or perhaps various resolutions taken about Central at the national conference in 2009.

"All journalists want to sensationalise this story," was all he would say. "We don't release information for the integrity of the Church."

The official statement released in September 2009 by the Church covered all fronts. While the statement did not attack Bishop Verryn personally, it did make it clear that the Presiding Bishop could not be blamed. As far as Abrahams was concerned, he had turned the matter over to government institutions and in doing so he had done his job. Now it was time for them to do theirs.

Aside from the sexual abuse allegations, the overall crisis at Central

Methodist Mission had been building for a long time and could hardly have gone unnoticed by the broader Church. As developments unfolded and the situation threatened to spiral out of control, the lack of intervention or action of any kind from any quarter, including from the Methodist Church itself, was certainly a contributing factor to the crisis. The situation at Central Methodist was complicated and difficult and it raised difficult moral questions. Until the Presiding Bishop was forced to take action in mid-2009, it appeared that Ivan Abrahams' *modus operandi* had been to stand back and do nothing. From Abrahams' own viewpoint perhaps it was better to do nothing rather than take action that might create another set of problems. Paul Verryn certainly had had no doubt in *his* mind. Taking action, despite the consequences, was better than doing nothing.

Abrahams saw his own and the Church's involvement differently. The Church did take action, he told me at our meeting in 2010. "I have no doubt that Paul's initial intention was good. But the other issue is that Paul Verryn was the custodian of that church on my behalf. The property was in my name. If someone brought a civil suit to the church, we would be bankrupt."

Another question that needed to be asked, I thought, was one of accountability and how accountability plays itself out within the Church. A minister, as far as I knew, was accountable to a bishop. A bishop was accountable to the Presiding Bishop. In the absence of engagement between a Presiding Bishop and a bishop, as appeared to be the case with Ivan Abrahams and Paul Verryn, who was to be held responsible? And if there is a vacuum of leadership, who is to be held responsible when important issues are at stake? In the face of general inefficiency and incompetence – and this certainly appeared to be the case as far as many quarters in government were concerned when it came to the crisis at Central Methodist – how should the Methodist Church have dealt with the decisions that were made by Bishop Verryn if the Church and the Presiding Bishop were of the view that they were problematic decisions?

Although Abrahams could not say so in the Church's public statement, privately he was fuming. Although he denied it, there were many people who believed that there were personal tensions between Abrahams and Verryn that had been left untended. Abrahams, it was said, felt injured by the fact that Verryn had not called on him for authorisation for anything he was doing. He saw Verryn as a loose cannon. Probably, Abrahams should have confronted Verryn directly with his concerns years earlier, and it was not clear why he did not.

Bishop Verryn, however, was not an easy person to confront, and he believed strongly in what he was doing. He would argue keenly for his point of view and it was well known that he could be a formidable opponent when his mind was made up. There were many people, inside the Church and outside, who would not have wanted to criticise Verryn for fear of his reaction.

Reverend Ross Olivier, who had known both Abrahams and Verryn since the 1980s, was amongst the group that helped draft the statement at the MCSA conference in Pietermaritzburg. Olivier was reluctantly drawn into the situation with the MCSA and Central Methodist on two fronts. First, Olivier was asked by Abrahams to field any questions from the press that might come up as a result of the communiqué. Second, Olivier was asked to chair the commission of inquiry that had been set up by the Church to investigate the sexual abuse allegations at the Albert Street School and to advise the Presiding Bishop on how to handle them. "We didn't have the capability to investigate these things," Olivier told me much later. "I took the decision that if these allegations had been made, then you had to report them to the appropriate statutory bodies such as the police, the Department of Education and the Department of Social Development."

During the same time as the conference was being held, in late 2009, Central Methodist commissioned an independent evaluation of the Albert Street School. Mary Metcalfe had been assisting the school with teacher training and she helped identify and acquire funding for the evaluation from the Open Society Institute of Southern Africa. Howard Summers, who had run an educational consultancy for many years, was contracted by OSISA to do the job. The evaluation was conducted between 1 September and 30 November. William Kandowe, the deputy principal, was suspended at the time and the principal, Alpha Zhou, was Summers' main contact. The evaluators relied on documentation, interviews and classroom observation.

The final evaluation report was completed in November 2009 and it was thorough. The school had grown rapidly from the start, it stated, because of its open door policy of accepting students who did not have documents. Enrolment currently stood at 534 learners. There were sixteen classes and 21 teachers. Although the school was started because of concern for unaccompanied minors at the church who were not going to school, that group of children now comprised only 25.7% of the school (137 children). South African learners made up another 26.2% (140 children), and the remaining 48% were foreign nationals whose parents or care givers had settled in Johannesburg.

Teachers were paid a stipend of R3 500 per month and, under difficult circumstances, they were doing an admirable job. In fact the school was doing remarkably well, despite facing major challenges, including few financial resources and inadequate facilities. There were teachers for all subjects, the administration staff ran an organised office, and the school had registered for the Cambridge Curriculum. Summers found the principal, Alfred Zhou, to be open and committed. The learners all had school uniforms. It was also praiseworthy that the school was able to keep so many learners off the streets. The evaluation had particular praise for the school's management. "The vision and the passion of the School Management Team are evident. They appear to have the interests of the learners at heart and see the school as a well-knit community."

The evaluation did express concern over the lack of appropriate space for the school and the fact that several grades had started to hold lessons at Central Methodist, which meant that they were using space for teaching that was used for sleeping and accommodation at night.

It also noted "overcrowded/makeshift classrooms, inadequate furniture, few serviceable blackboards, no text books, no library, no internet facilities, no science room or equipment, no teaching resources, inadequate toilet and drinking water facilities, no playground area for break times, and no sporting facilities". The school needed money and the report on this score was frank. "If the school cannot get a massive injection of funds, then it raises the issue of whether the school should continue."

The school currently received funding from the United Methodist Committee on Relief (UMCOR), the Dutch Embassy and World Missions Possible, but the lack of financial resources was still a challenge.

Although the Albert Street School was not yet registered with the Gauteng Department of Education, negotiations were under way. Howard Summers later said, "I got the sense that the Department of Education was supportive. They didn't come in with Casspirs to tear the place down."

The evaluation did not ignore the allegations of sexual abuse. "Following on from press reports relating to sexual abuse at the school, two learners made allegations of sexual abuse in the open section of the learners' questionnaire. This was reported to the Bishop who has informed the SAPS. Another allegation of sexual abuse was made at the Parents' Meeting held on 28 November 2009. The principal told the parent concerned to report the matter to the police."

Over all, despite the problematic areas, Summers was impressed with the Albert Street School and he did not recommend that the school be closed. “On the contrary,” he said.

This generally very positive evaluation of the school, however, did not do much to change its negative public perception. The sexual abuse allegations continued to hover above it.

Washing line in front of the stained glass window in the sanctuary.

Meetings at Central Methodist / 2011

For many months I had heard about Mr Tony but so far I hadn't met him. He had lived in the building for over a decade but didn't attend Friday night refugee meetings or work with Peace Action so our paths hadn't crossed naturally. He had been described to me, however, so when I first saw him standing in front of the church behind the palisade fence, I knew it was him. After that, whenever I saw Mr Tony, whether he was sitting alone observing the goings on, or walking through the foyer, he always looked as if he had wandered onto the wrong film set by mistake. His rounded salt and pepper beard matched his curled mustache. He walked slowly and used a crutch as a result of a stroke, but he was always impeccably dressed. I wondered who ironed his shirts. How did he always manage to look so manicured? He struck me as an old-fashioned gentleman in the middle of chaos.

Mr Tony Bansi was born in the Democratic Republic of Congo. He left the DRC as a teenager and travelled to the United States to live with a cousin and he finished his schooling and went to university there. "I won't tell you my age," he said but he did tell me that he left the DRC at thirteen or fourteen and that was in the late '50s or early '60s, so I reckoned he must be close to 70 years old.

No one could tell me exactly what year Mr Tony had arrived in South Africa, but it was likely it was in the late 1990s or 2000. He had previously met Ivan Abrahams from the Methodist Church in the US and he stayed with him for a few days when he got to Johannesburg. Abrahams referred Tony Bansi to Paul Verryn as he was interested in migration issues. In addition it seemed that Mr Tony was exploring the possibility of remaining in South Africa for some time. One day when he was visiting Home Affairs, he had a small stroke. It's likely that the issues he was dealing with there were stressful. Not long after that, he had a second stroke while he was on the ground floor at Central Methodist. This time the stroke was so severe that he couldn't move. Verryn and others helped get him to the hospital.

When he had recovered enough to be discharged, Verryn offered him a place to stay at Central in a room behind Minor Hall. Mr Tony took up the offer and has never left.

"I still ask myself why didn't I go up there," Mr Tony said to me, pointing to heaven. "It wasn't my time. I've *been* up there. There was a big door. People in white garments looked at me. 'You're not coming in,' they said. 'It's not your time.'"

For twelve years Mr Tony has lived in the room behind Minor Hall, observing the changes as the building has evolved. Every day he gets up and makes his way through Minor Hall, walking slowly through the room that is crowded with women and babies, mattresses and blankets, buckets and piles of clothing.

One day, we sat down in the sanctuary to talk but on that occasion Mr Tony only gave me bits and pieces of his life. He was lucid, but there were moments when I couldn't follow his story very well. He said he got married in the US and his wife Margaret was a teacher. They had two sons and two daughters, Tony, Claude, Margaret and Janet. He told his children, "Look after your mother. Don't let anyone into my bedroom," and he went to South Africa. He said that about six years before, his wife had wanted to come and visit him in Johannesburg, but he had told her, "You'd better not."

"When I get well," he said to me, "I will go back."

"Aren't you well now?" I asked.

He held up his crutch. "Look at this," he said. "When I don't have to walk with a stick, then I'll be well."

When I told Mr Tony that I was writing a book about Central Methodist, he said, "Everyone will want to read that book. Make it simple and write the truth."

As we slowly walked out of the sanctuary together, he said, "I like the Bishop, but something happened in his head. Do you think he's helping Zimbabwean people? It's good to help people who are poor and needy, but in doing so, you have to be very careful. I hope God will forgive him."

Every Wednesday Mr Tony went to sit in the Bishop's office for help from the church. A man named Justice Khanyile, who worked for many years as Central's building manager, once told me that he often spent time with Mr Tony. Sometimes he would help him to buy vegetables. Mr Tony was a vegetarian. "Do not eat meat," he told me, "not even eggs." Justice kept an eye on Mr Tony. Sometimes they would watch wrestling together on television. "I don't like to see such a distinguished old man living in this place," Justice confided one day.

I asked Mr Tony if he ever thought of moving out of Central Methodist. "That would mean that I'd have to change my address to live outside of this environment," he said. "Then I would be lonely. I don't want to be lonely in an apartment by myself."

Another person whom I met and saw regularly at Central Methodist was Elizabeth.[5] She was a rotund woman who was never without her baby on her back and her three-year-old daughter holding onto her leg. I never saw Elizabeth without those two children attached to her. Elizabeth was often one of the first people I greeted when I arrived at the building because she sold small goods outside the church on the Smal Street Mall. In winter she sold gloves and ear muffs. In summer she sold socks or alice bands. She would always ask me about my children and I would ask about hers. She and her husband lived in the first floor lounge, which was set aside for married couples. One day she told me that she had taken her daughter to the doctor and discovered that she had had a small stroke. The doctor referred Elizabeth to a specialist, but for some reason, she had to miss the appointment and some months had gone by. She asked me, "Should I go back to the original doctor, or do you think I can go straight to the specialist to ask for another appointment?" I told her I thought she could go to the specialist and ask to reschedule. Over time I would learn what additional traumas Elizabeth faced and what a strong character she had.

5 Elizabeth requested that I not use her surname

Twenty

"The Horror that We Saw"

In the early hours of the morning on Friday, 30 October 2009, Molebatsi Bopape, the chairperson of the Gauteng Legislature's Health and Social Development Portfolio Committee, paid an unannounced visit to the Central Methodist Mission. She invited the police and the press to accompany her. Once again the residents were rudely startled out of their sleep. This time they were blinded by police torches and photographers' cameras flashing in their eyes as they struggled up from their blankets.

Ambrose Mapiravana was asleep on his mattress in the boardroom. He got a call from one of his security staff at the front door to tell him that this delegation had turned up. "I met them in the Roberts Room," said Ambrose. "The police that were there, they knew me but because they were under orders, they didn't speak to me. They were in the building for about two hours. I stayed at the front door until they left."

By the time the sun was up, Molebatsi Bopape's impressions were on air and in the newspapers.

"We will make a recommendation to close the church after witnessing the horror that we saw this morning," said Bopape. "If I could have it my way, I would close it down today. If another infectious disease has to break out in that church, it would be a disaster… it's a ticking time bomb. I wonder if the Bishop realises what he is exposing these people to. Can you imagine what goes on at night on the floor where young 14-year-olds and

15-year-olds sleep? Children are being exposed to abuse, babies are sleeping on the floor, the place is so filthy that we couldn't even breathe."

She announced her intention to hold a public meeting the following Friday, 6 November. Bishop Verryn and his management would be invited to appear before the committee, and NGOs, as well as representatives from the City and Gauteng province were welcome to participate so that they could all work out a way forward.

Democratic Alliance Gauteng spokesperson on health, Jack Bloom, who had been part of the delegation, agreed with a co-ordinated approach by local, provincial and national government, but maintained that the current crisis at the church wasn't the root of the issue. "Primarily," he said, "it is a foreign policy problem concerning internal conditions in Zimbabwe that has led to desperate people seeking shelter at this church. The option of a properly-run refugee camp for Zimbabweans should be considered seriously."

Bopape was less diplomatic. Her comments in *The Saturday Star* were direct and brutal. "Most of the mess in that church has been created by Bishop Verryn. We are now faced with a disaster here."

Verryn's response was disdainful. He said that Bopape was passing judgement on an issue that was complex and about which she knew nothing. "They didn't tell me they were coming here," he said, "and she didn't even have the decency to speak to me." He said he had no issue with her closing the church "as long as she has got an alternative for the worshippers and the people."

Bopape remained adamant about what would *not* happen next and why. "The government will not fund any centre to house these people because it will serve to encourage more people to do the same thing," she said. She did not need to hear Verryn's side of the story because it was already clear that there was a crisis, nor did she need his permission to visit the church. She went above Verryn's head and appealed to the Methodist Church. "The Church leadership has to come to the party because they have allowed Verryn to create this monster. You cannot have four-month-old babies growing up in such a place. We could not even breathe while in that church because of the bad smell, so how do you expect children to live healthy lives?"

Jack Bloom pointed out that the comments Bopape was making to the press were her own personal views and not those of the Portfolio Committee. He wanted the committee to arrive at a considered decision and also to allow Verryn the opportunity to respond. "The committee does not have powers to decide," he said, "but to influence decisions. The situation at the church is highly undesirable, but we need a considered decision. This monster was created by the government failing to provide an alternative."

The moral outrage that Bopape expressed at the living conditions at the church was understandable. Unfortunately, her care and attention came rather late. The situation had been brewing for a long time but this was the first time the committee had actually shown interest in addressing it.

Certainly, none of the residents at Central Methodist *wanted* to live in an over-crowded situation with no privacy and few sanitation facilities. They were not living there out of choice, but because of the circumstances they faced and because Bishop Verryn had opened up the church and invited them to live there. The church had responded to a humanitarian crisis to which few others had responded.

The Portfolio Committee had every right to be concerned about the church and to co-ordinate their oversight function, but to conduct a visit in the middle of the night, without consulting anyone within the church and bringing not only the police but the press with them, understandably gave the visit the sense of a raid. And for people already traumatised and vulnerable, it was yet another bad experience. Paul Verryn's consequent anger was just as understandable.

Molebatsi Bopape made her statements to the media on the basis of one visit to the church, a visit which had taken place after midnight. Why had she not rather held off on commenting until a more thorough, longer-term engagement with the church had been explored? It seems as if she had made up her mind on the matter before she had even set foot in the building.

On the Monday after Bopape's surprise visit, Professor Tinyiko Maluleke, President of the South African Council of Churches, and General Secretary Eddie Makue issued a media statement on the situation at Central Methodist Mission. The SACC's view was that it would be easy to turn Central Methodist into a villain but that this was the wrong way to look at it. "This church has tried to do what government should have done, what every South African should do, what every other church should do, i.e. welcome the destitute, provide care for the sick, provide shelter to the homeless."

Presiding Bishop Ivan Abrahams and the Methodist Church of Southern Africa also made a statement, in which their actions to date were re-stated: they had reported the issue of unaccompanied minors to the Department of Social Development at provincial and national levels. They had referred the alleged sexual abuse to the National Prosecuting Authority. They were waiting for feedback. The MCSA also said that they had exceeded their resources at Central Methodist and would welcome intervention from all relevant government departments. They called for the urgent implementation of sustainable solutions.

Paul Verryn was invited to attend the Portfolio Committee's public hearing set for Friday 6 November. He informed the committee co-ordinator on the phone that he would not be able to attend the hearing because he was chairing a meeting of the Church Unity Commission on that day. On Thursday, 5 November, Jason Brickhill, representing Bishop Verryn, sent a letter to Molebatsi Bopape requesting that the meeting be rescheduled and that they find another suitable date, but the meeting went ahead. Reverends Kim Alexander and Khanyisile Nduli from Central Methodist and the Albert Street Church were in attendance. Many allegations arose at that meeting. The press coverage focused on a statement from Sizakele Nkosi-Malobane, chairperson of Gauteng province's Safety and Security Committee, saying that she had made her own "unannounced and disguised visits to the church" and that she had seen "some kids having sex publicly with their boyfriends" there. She also claimed that there was a great deal of crime inside the church, so much so that members of the church congregation felt unsafe. She herself had been "asked to pay R5 at the door to gain access to the building".

More questions were raised at the meeting about the conditions in which children were living and attention was focused on the deteriorating condition of the building itself. One quote that received attention from the press was from Reverend Kim Alexander. She asked the gathering whether people thought God cared more about a building than people. "I have not seen the government trying to help the people living at the church all these years," she added. "The church is in debt by over a million rands in water and electricity bills. Where has everybody been for the past three years? South Africa has failed these people."

Godfrey Charamba, a long-time resident at the church, was also present at the meeting. Charamba had not always stuck to the right side of the law himself and had been in trouble with Paul Verryn before, but he was a loyal supporter of the Bishop. He told the meeting that many of the church residents trusted Bishop Paul Verryn and that if they were to be moved, they would want him to be involved. This prompted one of the NGO representatives, Susan Black, to say that she smelt a "cult in this unconditional love for Verryn".

The meeting concluded with a plan to set up a task team which would get to grips with the problems arising out of the situation at the church and also ensure that children were moved off the premises as a matter of urgency.

A second public hearing was scheduled for the following Friday, 13 November. Again Bishop Verryn had a diary conflict. He attended the start of the meeting at 9am but had to be at a Finance Committee meeting of the SACC by 10am. Chairperson Molebatsi Bopape was aware of this, but was still very upset when she called Bishop Verryn to speak and discovered he wasn't there. Later she said, "the whole country is waiting for resolution of this issue that has been compounded by one person. It's simply unacceptable."

Again allegations were put forward that Verryn had become a cult figure in the church. Jack Bloom was one person who voiced this concern. "Verryn's superiors in the Methodist Church need to seriously investigate whether he has built up a cult following at the church and how this affects attempts to relocate the refugees." Representatives from NGOs at the meeting claimed that children were being prevented from moving out of the church.

When asked by the media for his response, Verryn said, "There's no way I'm running a cult. I will be horrified if people start thinking of me as a cult figure." He also disputed claims that the church was preventing children from moving. "Right at the beginning we were concerned about the safety of the young girls, that they be moved, but they have told me they don't want to move to Usindiso because they were previously discriminated against during an earlier stay there. We've got to look for something better. I certainly didn't influence them [to refuse moving from the church]. The children have been cared for wonderfully by the [Central Methodist] community and they feel this is home for them. I still don't think it's ideal and will continue to look for a place that's willing to co-operate with us. I think the church is being victimised. Clearly there's a political agenda. I have been absolutely clear. You need more accommodation. I must tell you there are another 30 000 to 50 000 people accommodated in the utmost squalor [in this city]."

Bishop Verryn had not done himself a favour by missing the Portfolio Committee's first two public hearings. While he may have been angry with Mrs Bopape and did not want to give her control of the situation, he also gave the impression to an interested public that he wasn't taking the hearings seriously. Verryn was a complex person in this regard and he seemed genuinely not to care what people thought of him. While his ability and determination to stand up to a self-serving politician was admirable, at the same time he came across as arrogant and stubborn.

A third public hearing took place on 20 November. This one Bishop Verryn did attend. He participated throughout and had prepared a submission to the Portfolio Committee which addressed many of the allegations that had been raised in the previous two hearings. First, the submission addressed concerns about children living in the building, including their living conditions, the absence of educational and recreational facilities, alleged sexual interaction amongst teenagers and offers from various NGOs to provide shelter for the children.

Central Methodist, his submission said, "had already engaged in a plan, working with the National Department of Social Development… to remove vulnerable children from the building" and he asked the Portfolio Committee to support this initiative that was already under way. The submission conceded that the conditions at the building were not ideal and required urgent attention, but contended that the Portfolio Committee had not fully explored the reasons why so many people were living at Central Methodist, especially in light of the closing of the camp in Musina in March and the police raid in July. The submission stated that as of 19 November, there were approximately 70 children, 50 babies and 40 unaccompanied minors living at Central Methodist. The church had separated the girls and pre-pubescent boys from the teenage boys, who were now required to sleep in their own separate areas. Children living at Central Methodist were vocal and were encouraged to speak up about any concerns they had during structured opportunities that were organised on a regular basis with various caretakers, including two ministers, Reverends Alexander and Nduli.

The submission provided a summary of the set of activities that were routine and regular at Central Methodist and the network of organisations that were working with the church. Pre-school-age children living at the Mission attended a crèche and preschool, FLOC, in the building. School-age children attended Albert Street School. Children were supervised after school by 22 child care workers who had been trained by the National Association of Child Care Workers, working in association with UNICEF. The Solidarity Peace Trust donated 460 meals a day to the schoolchildren at a cost of between R15 000 to R18 000 a month. After-school activities included drama, ballroom dancing, soccer, netball, karate and a book club.

Verryn's submission to the Portfolio Committee pointed out that the much publicised partnership with the City of Johannesburg to provide the Moth building as an alternative venue for those living at Central, with priority given to women and children, had stalled. This, he understood, was because the funding was no longer available, even though "draft lease agreements had already been exchanged at that point and are still in the possession of the Mission".

As for the City's approach to migrancy in general, there was a sign of movement in October 2009 when the Johannesburg Migration Advisory Committee held its first meeting. The plan was for the committee to meet quarterly and to bring together leadership from the City, the Department of Home Affairs, Foreign Affairs, Education, the migrant community, NGOs, academia, the SAPS and the private sector in order to address the major challenges posed by migration into the city.

Ironically, the wrangle between Verryn and the Portfolio Committee seemed to help bring the focus back onto the plight of Zimabwean asylum seekers at a time when there was growing fatigue on the topic. The City's task team, which had been in place since January 2008, and the inter-governmental task team that had been meeting since March 2008, had yet to achieve anything lasting and concrete in ten months of operation. Russell McGregor, who chaired the task team, and who had proposed a plan in July to pilot a model project for dealing with migration and homelessness in the inner city, was still hopeful that it would move forward. According to him, the relocation to the Moth building had stalled due to a lack of money for a service provider. In actual fact, McGregor's task team had been inactive for months.

In another related development, Dorothy Qedani Mahlangu, who had been responsible for setting up the temporary camps after the xenophobic violence in May 2008, was moved from her position leading the Gauteng Department of Local Government to head the province's Department of Social Development and Health in May 2009. Given the growing debate about the children at Central Methodist, Mahlangu and her department were on a collision course with Paul Verryn as well.

Now the proposed new task team, to be led by Molebatsi Bopape herself, intended specifically to address the needs of the children staying at Central Methodist as a first priority. A tug-of-war over these children, about 50 of them, was about to begin.

Twenty-one

The Debate over the Children

A South African media analyst, Theo Coggin, said at a 2009 donor conference that "the mainstream media is interested in scandal, hostility and disasters as these are what make the news. In more general terms, it's interested in sex, scandal, politics and sport."

In the Central Methodist Mission and the Albert Street School combination, the media found not only sex, but also sex in a church, which is seen as particularly scandalous. While the concern about sexual abuse from many was sincere, some people believed that the unintended result of focusing on these allegations was to take attention away from the broader issues of 3 500 refugees in desperate need of accommodation, services, and support. Yusuf Patel, who chaired the inter-governmental task team, was of this view. "Why didn't they [the Department of Social Development] focus on the broader concerns? If they had kept their eyes on the big picture, and the social implications of the flow of thousands of people into the country, they could have solved lots of problems. Instead, they got focused on the needs of 50 unaccompanied children."

While not everyone agreed with Molebatsi Bopape and the Portfolio Committee that the church should be closed, there were valid concerns about the children's situation. Bianca Tolboom and others at MSF had already expressed this concern and while they had hoped that Bishop Verryn might have taken more decisive action, they did not want to be aligned with those who sought to condemn him.

Different media sources took different approaches to the story. Micel Schnehage of Talk Radio 702's *Eyewitness News* team spoke regularly about Central Methodist and the sexual abuse allegations.

A South African monthly journal, *Noseweek*, specialised in exposés and revelations, and liked to tilt at authority, especially self-important authority. In Bishop Verryn and Central Methodist Mission, they might have thought they had found a perfect target. Their October 2009 issue included a story about the church entitled "Abuse or Mercy". It began at the crowded church entrance. "Here hawkers are grilling fish and mealies, meat curries bubble on paraffin stoves and vetkoek are piled on huge enamel plates. But it's not the food you smell first. It's the stench of stale urine, sweat and crap that hits full on. As the *Noseweek* team passes through the throng at the entrance, cops begin beating a man about the face – apparently he lives in the church and they've just arrested him for theft. *Noseweek* is here to investigate allegations of rape and child abuse, gangsterism and sex for favours, and we quickly learn that all this is indeed happening at the church – and more."

The journalist seemed disarmed by Bishop Verryn's frankness, however. "An evidently exhausted Bishop Paul Verryn, who presides over the house-of-worship-cum-ghetto, conceals nothing. 'This place teeters on the edge of violence on a daily basis,' says Verryn, who acknowledges that he may no longer have the control he once exercised over the shelter. 'It's a moveable feast and there are days when this place is in a state of utter chaos.'"

The piece went on to describe the situation related to unaccompanied minors and the differing points of view. "The most vulnerable in this overcrowded squalor are 110 unaccompanied minors, as well as other children, including 70 babies and 50 toddlers. The children are at the centre of a battle between Verryn and the Johannesburg Child Advocacy Forum whose members include representatives of Childline, Sophiatown Community Psychological Services, Big Shoes, Usindiso, Kids Haven, CoRMSA and Save the Children UK."

Noseweek conducted some in-depth interviews with some of the organisations involved. Liebe Kellen, a social worker and colleague of Johanna Kistner's at the Sophiatown Community Psychological Services, was blunt. She said Verryn had lost control of the situation, which did not comply with the Child Care Act. "Maybe Verryn wants to be this all-encompassing father figure," she told *Noseweek*, "but it is not working – to the detriment of the children who are sheltered there." Verryn fired back, suggesting that Kellen may have had a personal axe to grind, given that she had removed children from the church without his permission, or the consent of the church, and had subsequently been barred from the premises. As a result of that incident, Verryn now only allowed government agencies and UNICEF to work with residents of the church.

UNICEF child protection specialist Heidi Loening-Voysey took the view that the untenable situation was a result of South Africa's social systems already being overwhelmed before refugees began arriving in large numbers. Her role was to work with the Central Methodist Mission to ensure the environment was child friendly and safe, and UNICEF was training people "to look out for abuse, to prevent it and respond to it". The child care workers helped ensure the children's quarters were cleaner, that children were under adult supervision all the time, and that children got their fair share of the food, and that the food was nutritious.

In the end, the *Noseweek* article suggested that there was too much finger-pointing at Verryn and the church and not enough action. "Verryn appears to be doing the best he can," it concluded, "rarely leaving the church before 3am as he staves off a tsunami of challenges, as he attempts the impossible – to bring order to violent chaos."

While all this was going on and Verryn was constantly in the press regarding the unaccompanied children at the church, the Bishop was continuing with his work elsewhere in the inner city of Johannesburg. He continued to visit some of the most vulnerable people in other buildings, many of which were completely derelict. In late 2009 he was working closely with Médecins Sans Frontières. "Many of the buildings that poor people live in in the inner city make this place [Central Methodist] look like a five star hotel," he often said.

One evening, after dark, he visited the Chambers building with Evans Kuntonda. It had no electricity and no water and was accommodating more than 1 000 people at the time. Verryn and Kuntonda held a meeting by cellphone light with Lazarus Kinhara, chairman of the Zimbabwean blind community, many of whom begged at the city's main intersections. "I find it incredible that we were led into the building where *I* can barely see anything, by a blind man," Verryn said. "How can we pretend we are a church and ignore the most vulnerable in our society?"

Various people continued to clash with Bishop Verryn over the children at Central Methodist. Not only had he fallen out with Liebe Kellen and Johanna Kistner of the Johannesburg Child Advocacy Forum, but he also had something of a power struggle going on with Lorraine Cock of the Gauteng Department of Social Development, which had been working hard to find ways of moving the children to other shelters.

The conflicts always seemed to be struggles over power and authority. Each person involved believed that he or she was doing the best thing for the children. There were many observers who felt that Bishop Verryn could have handled things differently had he been willing to delegate more and relinquish some control over the situation, but that was just not his style. The clashes got ugly. Lorraine Cock believed that she was so disliked at the church that someone deliberately dented her car when it was parked in front of the building on Pritchard Street one day.

The media coverage continued to veer from admiration to dismay, sometimes reflected by a single reporter. Beauregard Tromp of *The Star* covered the situation at Central Methodist and wrote several articles about it in late 2009. The first, in September, celebrated the role of the church and saw it as under attack from the City. "Sometimes on a Friday, sometimes on a Wednesday, a game plays out in front of the Johannesburg High Court. Babies are bundled up, hair extensions jammed into plastic bags and playing cards stuffed into pockets… by the time the high pressure hoses start blasting the sidewalk its temporary residents have long since scattered… With no hint of subtlety, the City has decided to make life as uncomfortable for the mostly Zimbabwean refugees who throng around the High Court most days." The article said, "the church has become more than just a safe haven. It is a place where people come to network and [it] forms the cornerstone of a community where everything from job-seeking to Latin American dancing takes place."

Less than three months later, Tromp wrote another article, this time about the underbelly of Central Methodist. He interviewed a group of teenage boys whose friends had prostituted themselves at the church for cash. The article described young women trying to kill their babies so that they could look for men or turn to prostitution, in order to survive. It also said that the principal at the Albert Street School had girlfriends amongst his students, "flashing some cash and sealing the deal with a date at the local KFC… to make the teenagers feel 'special'."

Reflecting on the complexity of the situation, the day after publishing Tromp's disturbing article, *The Star* published an editorial that pleaded "Solve Harmful Church Crisis". It said the crisis required a "delicate and collective approach from the government and civil society," but applauded the role that Central Methodist had played for decades as a beacon of hope and a refuge for the destitute, harkening back to the 1980s when it had offered a safe haven to people facing political persecution, and more recently, to Zimbabweans fleeing dire economic circumstances.

The editorial described the debate raging over the children. "Unfortunately, the most vulnerable among us often attract predators. The overcrowded conditions at the church, and the numerous atrocities which have come to light in recent years, invariably involve girls, women and babies." The newspaper said that the threat by the Gauteng Legislature to close the church without providing an alternative seemed ludicrous. It called for the church, NGOs and government to work together and to put an end to the bickering "which has seen slander, rumour-mongering and outright undermining of each other".

Just days before the Tromp article and the editorial appeared in *The Star,* a group of civil society organisations issued a statement in which they pledged support for Central Methodist and Paul Verryn. Initiated by Lawyers for Human Rights, the Legal Resources Centre and the AIDS Law Project, and issued on 8 December, the statement was endorsed by close to 40 organisations. A press conference was held in the sanctuary at Central Methodist. Evans Kuntonda of MSF spoke. "This place is not a solution, but I don't know where there is a solution." Other speakers included Cleo Buthelezi and Takudzwa Chikoro, who was still studying at the Albert Street School.

The statement commended the work of Paul Verryn and Central Methodist over the past several years, saying that the church had given people a sense of community and provided them with networks that had linked them to health care services, skills development, educational opportunities, recreation and work. Nevertheless, the situation at the church was not sustainable. While the group welcomed the concern of the Gauteng Portfolio Committee, it urged against arbitrary evictions or unfair processes. If the church were to be closed, the people staying there would not "miraculously evaporate". They would be dispersed and forced under ground into places where they would be less accessible.

The group of signatories called on the government urgently to provide alternative accommodation and social assistance. They called on the national Minister of Social Development to establish a task team with full-time staff and clear terms of reference to find alternative accommodation. They called on the Minister of Home Affairs to lead a national dialogue about how best to assist Zimbabwean migrants in South Africa. They called on the South African government and SADC to engage with the Zimbabwean government, and they welcomed the appointment of new mediators in Zimbabwe from South Africa.

The depth and variety of the signatories to the civil society statement, which included, among many others, Amnesty International, Cosatu, the SACC, CSVR, Islamic Relief, Jesuit Refugee Service, and CoRMSA, reflected the complexity of the situation. It was precisely this complexity that the grandstanding politicians obscured. Several journalists did not allow them to get away with it.

Eusebius McKaiser wrote an article in *Business Day* entitled "Wicked Irony in Politicians Painting Themselves Saviours". It began, "There is something abhorrent and disturbingly ironic about the Gauteng legislature's portfolio committee on health and social development trying to take the moral high ground in answering the tough humanitarian question of what to do with Zimabwean refugees at the Central Methodist Church in downtown Johannesburg. Removing children from the site seems to be their hasty short-term solution. A longer-term solution is not clear but a recommended closure is not ruled out. What is ironic and abhorrent about all this is the shameless attempt by the politicians to rock up with moral platitudes at hand and, with the help of a bevy of broadcast journalists, send out a message of deep and genuine care about the refugees' well-being. How convenient – as if the crisis happened overnight and they did not or could not have reasonably been aware of it. The truth is that the nature and causes of the unfolding humanitarian crisis in downtown Johannesburg are more complex."

McKaiser identified "continuing political instability within Zimbabwe and continued ill-considered state responses to refugees within SA's border" as the two major causes of the crisis. He said, "Verryn and the CMC have made mistakes… Further it is possible that the CMC could have been more vigilant and open about potential abuses that such an undesirable space might enable. But to conclude from these facts that a quick visit, some tough words and removal of children to an unknown place will solve the underlying drivers of the crisis is unforgivably short-sighted."

A similar point of view was put forward in *The Star* by journalist Heidi Holland, the author of the book *Dinner with Mugabe.* She described Paul Verryn as a "holy man obeying the highest Christian commandment to love his neighbour in a country where xenophobic violence looms ever more menacingly in view of 2009 stratospheric job losses. Verryn opened his church and offered radical hospitality to thousands of refugees from tyranny-torn Zimbabwe when no one else in South Africa would protect them. How outrageously hypocritical it was of the Gauteng legislature's portfolio committee on health and social development to pitch up at the church recently and portray themselves as morally concerned about the hapless refugees when the entire government has been utterly indifferent to their plight. It is years and years past the time for South Africa's authorities to act humanely and acknowledge that, but for Paul Verryn's imperfect intervention, the lives of those in the overcrowded church would have been even harder."

Hermann Reuter of MSF wrote in the *Mail & Guardian* that it was clear that the church could not deal with the challenges of migration and migrant accommodation alone. "The church has become like an ambulance – visibly exposing a dilemma and raising the alarm… But the ambulance is not the problem and it cannot be dealt with as such… The government wants to deal with the church in isolation from the broader challenge… [and to blame] Paul Verryn for somehow creating this situation."

At my meeting with Presiding Bishop Ivan Abrahams in 2010, when we had talked about his role in going to the authorities with the allegations of sexual abuse of some children at the church and at the Albert Street School, he had said, "Everything came to a head with the children." In November 2009, he told me, the Church was making plans to assist the Department of Social Development with moving the children but there was a reason they hadn't followed through. "Some people said that there was militia in the church, that there were guns in there," he'd said. "I asked the DSD and the Advocacy Forum, 'Have you made security arrangements?' They said, 'No.' We had buses and gift bags ready for those kids, but we didn't proceed because of concerns about security.'

When I talked to Johanna Kistner of the JCAF in May 2010, she was still angry and frustrated by events. "Our experience with the Central Methodist Church has been a very painful one for me and colleagues from other organisations. We believe that there is a massive failure on the part of the church (not only the religious leaders in the CMC, but also in the MCSA), the state and society in general… We know that perpetrators of sexual abuse remain installed in positions of power. The sense of betrayal is very deep and our understanding is that we are dealing with a cult which defies any attempt at demystification." Kistner went on to say that no one had had the stamina to see things through. "We have worked with children who have left the church for over two years now and so we have quite a good sense of what is happening there and yet have been rendered powerless, as so many others, to do anything about it. This plays into the cult of Central Methodist, They think it is the only place that is able to keep the children safe."

In the tense environment when Central Methodist, Paul Verryn and the issue of the children were under continuous media scrutiny towards the end of 2009, Lorraine Cock and the Gauteng Department of Social Development continued to try to relocate some of the children from the church. Takudzwa Chikoro said there were a series of meetings to plan what would happen and that he attended some of these. "Lorraine Cock thought I was the rudest guy ever," he said. "I would say to the social workers, 'We know of children who are living in Joubert Park and on the streets in Hillbrow. What about them? I'll show you where they are.' Their response was 'We are not here to debate with you'." Takudzwa said the social workers would come and take one or two children away at a time and they didn't know where they were being taken. "We were frightened," he said, "because we would hear that someone had been taken away, and he would be gone."

Officials from the Department had made an arrangement to pick up some children on Monday, 7 December at the Albert Street School but when they went in through the front gate, the children ran away, hopping over a back fence. The *Sowetan* spoke to some of the children. They told the newspaper that the social workers were rude to them and threatened to remove them by force if they refused to go. They said they had also heard that staff at the shelters were xenophobic. Howard Summers, who was working on the evaluation of the Albert Street School at the time, put it another way. "Some of those kids had walked from Zimbabwe. No wonder they didn't want to go to kiddies' haven."

In late November and early December it appeared that Bishop Verryn and the DSD were almost playing a game of hide and seek with the children, with the DSD on the one hand persisting with their plans to take the children away and Verryn and the children resisting their efforts on the other. After the children had run away from the social workers on 7 December, Verryn moved them temporarily to the premises of an organisation in Sandton. Then he decided to resettle them at a Methodist community centre in Soweto. The children remained there over the holidays and into the new year.

Given that it was now the government's stated intention to move the children out of Central, Bishop Verryn, with the guidance of the Legal Resources Centre, decided to put forward an application to the court for a curatorship for the children. Verryn believed it was essential that someone sufficiently experienced and independent be formally and legally empowered to protect their best interests. Jackie Loffell of the Johannesburg Child Welfare Society proposed well-respected children's rights lawyer Dr Ann Skelton from the University of Pretoria to serve as the curator.

On 21 December, the Presiding Bishop Ivan Abrahams sent an email to Paul Verryn in which he opposed the bringing of an application to have a curator appointed. If Verryn persisted with this route, he warned, there would be consequences. "You will leave me no alternative but to initiate disciplinary action if you pursue the court application."

Verryn immediately withdrew from the court proceedings and the Aids Law Project took over the application. Despite his withdrawal, and unbeknown to the Bishop at the time, Abrahams proceeded the next day, on 22 December, to submit a complaint to the District Disciplinary Registrar of the Methodist Church. This was the initial step towards internal Church proceedings against Paul Verryn.

Jason Brickhill recalls the last time he spoke to Ivan Abrahams. It was Christmas Eve 2009. He wanted to encourage Abrahams to support the application to have a curator appointed. He told the Presiding Bishop that this was not a political move and advised him that it would be in the best interest of the unaccompanied minors at the church.

Ivan Abrahams was not convinced.

Twenty-two

Suspended

ON 18 JANUARY 2010 AN ENVELOPE WAS delivered to Paul Verryn's secretary Tina de Rijke on the third floor. Tina opened the envelope to find inside a Notice of Disciplinary Enquiry, including a charge sheet, addressed to Paul Verryn. The notice instructed Verryn to attend a disciplinary enquiry of the Church's District Disciplinary Committee (DDC) on 1 February 2010. It was signed by Jeff Matthee of the legal firm Malherbe, Rigg and Ranwell. Matthee was the attorney to the Methodist Church of Southern Africa.

The charge sheet contained two charges:

1) You are charged with contravening the provisions of paragraphs 5.10 read with 5.9 of the Laws and Discipline of the Methodist Church of Southern Africa in that during or about December 2009 you instituted, alternatively caused to be instituted, alternatively participated in the institution of legal proceedings for and/or on behalf of the Church, alternatively a structure within the Church without the authority and/or without same being instituted in the name of the Presiding Bishop and the Executive Secretary.
2) You are charged with failure to comply with, alternatively obey a lawful instruction received from the Presiding Bishop in that you communicated with, alternatively granted interviews to, the media, alternatively representatives thereof, despite having been expressly instructed not to do so.

Verryn was certain he was being charged for something he hadn't done, but before he had a chance to react, he received another envelope, on 19 January 2010. Inside this one was a notice of suspension. The letter stated that the Presiding Bishop had been informed of the charges and that he had "no alternative" but to suspend Verryn from exercising all ministerial functions and official responsibilities. The letter was signed by Reverend Vuyani Nyobole, the Executive Secretary to the Presiding Bishop. Verryn wasn't in his office when the suspension notice arrived, so Tina called him and read it to him over the phone. "I felt numb," he said when he recalled that moment.

What led directly to the delivery of these two envelopes was a written complaint that Reverend Nyobole submitted to Jeff Matthee on 22 December 2009, the day *after* Presiding Bishop Ivan Abrahams had sent the email to Paul Verryn opposing his involvement with the application for a curator. The complaint requested that charges be laid against the Bishop. Jeff Matthee was not only the attorney to the Methodist Church of Southern Africa. He was also a District Displine Registrar (DDR) for the Church. The fact that Matthee had taken on both roles simultaneously would prove to be significant in the final outcome of Paul Verryn's suspension.

According to the *Laws and Discipline* (basically, the constitution) of the Methodist Church, the DDR decides whether a complaint demands the laying of a charge and a hearing. As a DDR, Jeff Matthee was in the position to make that decision. Again according to the *Laws and Discipline*, in responding to a complaint, the DDR must consider, amongst other things, whether a breach of the Church's constitution has been alleged, whether all means of pastoral intervention and counselling or mediation have been exhausted, and whether the alleged offence damages the integrity or good name of the Church.

In his introduction to the eleventh edition of *Laws and Discipline,* published in March 2007, Presiding Bishop Ivan Abrahams highlights a section of chapter eleven regarding how to discipline members and ministers of the Church: "The true spirit of Methodist discipline requires that it be exercised in harmony with the Grace of Christ, with tenderness, patience and fidelity, seeking rather to win Members (and Ministers) back to Christ than to discontinue them."

This was not the approach Abrahams chose to take in disciplining Paul Verryn.

After the written complaint on 22 December 2009 and before the serving of the charge sheet on 18 January 2010, the DDR did not communicate with Verryn regarding the possibility of counselling or mediation, nor did the DDR discuss these matters with Bishop Peter Witbooi, who had just taken over as Bishop of the Central District, and was now responsible for Paul Verryn as a minister in his district. Verryn had stepped down from his role as Bishop at the end of November 2009 and all of this came to a head shortly afterwards. In December, for the first time in twelve years, Paul Verryn therefore became "only" the Superintendent Minister responsible for Central Methodist Mission but no longer for the entire Central District. Peter Witbooi succeeded Verryn and took up the post as Bishop in December 2009. Some suggest that the Presiding Bishop, Ivan Abrahams, waited for this moment before taking action against Verryn.

Around 6 January 2010, Jeff Matthee did communicate with the Legal Resources Centre and proposed a meeting to set up a "line of communication" between the LRC and the MCSA on matters relating to litigations by the Central Methodist Mission. At the time, he identified himself as the MCSA's attorney, but he did not reveal that he was also the DDR, nor that he was reviewing a complaint against Verryn.

There had been one other significant development in the interim. On 5 January 2010 Dr Ann Skelton was appointed curator for the children at the church and she began her investigation immediately.

After reviewing the contents of the two envelopes, Paul Verryn believed that the two charges against him were without merit and that his suspension, therefore, was invalid. On 20 January he wrote to Reverend Nyobole suggesting that the suspension was not in compliance with the laws of the Methodist Church. He also wrote to the Convenor of the MCSA on 21 January requesting mediation and arbitration of the dispute in accordance with the internal dispute resolution system of the MCSA. He pointed out that it would have made sense to have had a further exchange of correspondence or a hearing about the charges before the suspension was imposed.

Jeff Matthee addressed this question in a letter to the LRC on a Malherbe, Rigg and Ranwell letterhead in which he said, "Alternative interventions, as prescribed within the *Laws and Discpline* of the MCSA, were considered prior to determining that the complaint demands the laying of a charge." He also stated that "in all the circumstances, we respectfully submit that the process of mediation or other pastoral intervention would not be appropriate."

Verryn later said he found the omission "bewildering and regrettable", and added, "It is quite contrary to the ethos of the MCSA".

On 21 January 2010 the Methodist Church posted an announcement on the home page of its website. "The Methodist Church of Southern Africa would like to confirm that the former Bishop of the Central District, Paul Verryn, has been suspended. He has been charged with transgressing the *Laws and Discipline* (*L&D*) of the Church. The hearing will be held on the 1st of February 2010 in Johannesburg, facilitated by the District Disciplinary Committee, which is appointed in terms of the *L&D*. In terms of the *L&D*, the committee is to meet within a period of 21 days after receiving the charge. This committee has the power and duties to impose a sanction it deems fit. The Central Methodist Church will continue to run under the new Bishop, Peter Witbooi, who is responsible for the administration of the District." The contact person listed on the statement was Mr Bongani Khoza who was an attorney with Malherbe, Rigg and Ranwell along with Mr Jeff Matthee. Khoza told the media that Verryn "has been suspended and charged in an internal process". He would not disclose the reasons for the suspension.

Because there had been no public clarification on the charges, inevitably there was media speculation, some of it assuming that Paul Verryn's suspension must have been in relation to issues of the sexual abuse of children at the church who were under his care. On 22 January, *The Star* published a piece entitled "A Dark Cloud Over Verryn". The author was again Beauregard Tromp. In its opening lines the article included an odd reference to Paul Verryn's past. "A renowned former anti-apartheid cleric, Bishop Paul Verryn has been suspended from the Methodist Church while the intelligence services are investigating various claims against him and the Joburg CBD mission. Church officials confirmed that the bishop, who was based in Orlando West, Soweto, and worked with, among others, Winnie Madikizela-Mandela, had been suspended from all activities within the church, but refused to divulge details."

The article quoted Ivan Abrahams as saying that he was "deeply distressed" that Verryn could have brought a legal application in the name of the Methodist Church, as the Presiding Bishop was the only Church official empowered to take legal action on its behalf.

The reference to Madikizela-Mandela was not taken up anywhere in the rest of the article, but it was explained in a second piece by Tromp several days later under the title "Ghosts of the Past Come Back to Haunt Brave Bishop". "It has been twenty years since Verryn had to listen to testimony after testimony of young boys who, in graphic detail, spoke of how he had allegedly sexually molested them. Then, Verryn was thrust reluctantly into the spotlight at the trial of Winnie Madikizela-Mandela and others in relation to the murder of 14-year-old Stompie Seipei in 1988. The defence, led by acclaimed human rights lawyer George Bizos SC, centred on whether allegations of boys being sexually molested by the 'white priest' were true. A few years earlier, Verryn had been placed in charge of the Orlando Methodist Church, where he quickly built a reputation among the community for harbouring political activists and youth sought by the police."

The article omitted to say that the charges against Verryn were subsequently shown to be false.

Micel Schnehage of Talk Radio 702 reported: "Central Methodist Church's Reverend Paul Verryn has been suspended but the church said structures will be put in place to ensure the mission is run properly. Verryn was relieved of his duties earlier this week, on unspecified charges. Last year, *Eyewitness News* revealed that children were being forced to prostitute themselves at the church to survive. Most of the people living there are Zimbabwean refugees. The suspension of Verryn came as little surprise."

Also on 22 January, the LRC issued a statement to try to clarify the situation. They expressed concern that media reports were linking Verryn's suspension to allegations of sexual abuse and particularly that there had been no attempt by the Presiding Bishop or any legal representative of the Methodist Church to correct that speculation. The LRC took it upon itself to clarify the two charges, neither of which had anything to do with sexual allegations past or present, and both of which were in fact of a procedural or technical nature – "entirely unrelated to any of the grounds that emerged from media speculation". The first charge related to the institution of legal proceedings for the appointment of a curator to safeguard the interests of unaccompanied minors living at Central Methodist. The allegation was that Verryn had instituted such proceedings without authority and without doing so in the name of the Presiding Bishop or Executive Secretary. The second charge related to Verryn allegedly making media statements after being instructed not to do so. In view of the second charge, Verryn would not personally issue a media statement. The statement said that Verryn had requested mediation of the dispute between himself and the Presiding Bishop.

Bongani Khoza responded on behalf of the Church's legal representatives, saying that "it was wrong for Verryn to suggest the matter was between himself and Abrahams." He said that the Presiding Bishop had referred the matter to the District Disciplinary Registrar Jeff Matthee and that the decision to charge Verryn had come from him, Matthee, not from Ivan Abrahams. "The Presiding Bishop had nothing to do with it. How he is now seen as having a personal vendetta against Verryn is mind-boggling," Khoza added.

One prominent member of the congregation at Central Methodist was quoted as saying that "the Methodist Church was assassinating Verryn's character" and called on ordinary Methodists to rise up and challenge the church leadership. "When have you ever heard of a church publicly announcing the suspension of one of its ministers?" the member said.

The Aids Law Project, the organisation that had been the applicant for the legal curator after Verryn withdrew, also made a statement, calling for accuracy in reporting on Bishop Verryn. They, too, expressed concern about the misleading impression created by the media that the disciplinary charges were related to the allegations of sexual abuse. They said that Verryn made the application for the curator "in the midst of swirling accusations of abuse of children at the CMM, the children's fears of being relocated, and also to ensure that the process for relocating the unaccompanied minors was done properly and with their well-being and access to psycho-social care in mind." Once the MCSA expressed its opposition to Verryn's proceeding with the case, the Bishop had taken no further action. The Aids Law Project had intervened and became the applicant in the case. Finally, they pointed out that all parties involved, including the government, had welcomed the appointment of Ann Skelton as curator.

"The suggestion that Bishop Verryn has been doing all he can to keep the children at the CMM is false. Various media reports have referred to an 'application' or 'interdict' brought by Bishop Verryn that the unaccompanied minors should not be removed from the CMM. No such application was made. The facts are as follows: An application to appoint a curator was set down for 22 December 2009. However, the Department of Social Development requested a postponement until 5 January 2010. An undertaking was given by the Department that no further steps would be taken in respect of the removal of the unaccompanied minors during this time."

On 23 January, after seeing the coverage of Verryn's suspension in the media, a woman named Wendy Landau, whose friendship with Verryn went back many years, decided to set up a Facebook page called Friends of Paul Verryn. By the next day the page had 140 friends and by February over a thousand. At its peak it had over 1 600. "He's one of the top church people of our generation," said Landau. "What he's going through is horrendous. He's got feelings. He needs to know there are people out there rooting for him." The Facebook page read, "By joining and participating in this page, we endeavor to work together in consultation with each other on ways to speak out publicly about our concerns and support." Comments posted on the page ranged from support to accusations of conspiracy. Landau said that many of the commentators were disgruntled Methodist members and ministers. "There's a real hunger in the Methodist Church to express concern," she said. "It's a fight for the soul of the Church."

Two trade unions, the municipal workers union Samwu, and the metalworkers union Numsa, came out in full support of Paul Verryn. Samwu's spokesman Stephen Faulkner said that the two charges were without substance and should be withdrawn and that an apology should be offered. Numsa's spokesman Castro Ngobese said that Numsa was concerned that Verryn's suspension formed part of a broader agenda to discredit his social standing in society and that the bourgeois media had been co-opted to prosecute Bishop Verryn through public opinion.

One striking article in the *Mail & Guardian* asked some penetrating questions. "A power struggle in the Methodist Church? A pre-World Cup clean-up cloaked in official hypocrisy? Or the reining in of a gung-ho cleric who has made almost as many enemies as friends?" One section of the article, under the heading "Old whispers, old wounds", referred to reports of child abuse at the church. It quoted MSF and Usindiso as stating that none of the allegations pointed to Verryn, "yet the cloud of suspicion of sexual abuse has hung over Verryn for 21 years, almost to the day. This was when, in 1989, Winnie Madikizela-Mandela accused him of such." The piece concluded: "There is no evidence to show that Verryn is, or ever has been, involved in sexual misconduct with minors. Yet at a time when he is back in the glare of a controversy, not all of it flattering to his pastoral or professional style, it seems the old whispers just won't be silenced."

Verryn's congregation and the entire Methodist community heard about the suspension via the media, either on the radio or in the papers. There were significant implications, including the fact that other ministers would have to take up some of Verryn's duties, giving the annual January Covenant service, for example. Some people in the church who didn't like the fact that Verryn had offered residence at the church for so many years were pleased about the suspension. Neither Bishop Witbooi nor Presiding Bishop Ivan Abrahams, however, ever came to Central Methodist to discuss their minister's suspension with the church's congregants.

Verryn's disciplinary hearing scheduled for 1 February was set to be heard by three ordained ministers and four lay members of the church. At the end of January, however, the Convenor of the MCSA postponed the hearing indefinitely and decided instead that Verryn would face his seniors, Presiding Bishop Ivan Abrahams and District Discipline Registrar Jeff Matthee, in an arbitration. The arbitration proceedings would be conducted by a panel convened by the Methodist Church of Southern Africa.

On 5 February 2010 Abrahams questioned in a letter the Convenor's rationale for his decision to turn to arbitration. He referred to his own decision to refer the complaint to Jeff Matthee, the DDR, and to suspend Verryn. "In both instances," Abrahams wrote, "the authority granted me is unfettered and unrestricted. All that is required is for me to have properly applied my mind in this matter. I am satisfied that I acted as required. There is no incumbency on me to provide reasons for my decision in this regard, nor am I prepared to provide such. Nothing in the *L&D* [*Laws and Discipline*] requires or compels that I do so. I shall not compromise the Constitutional authority of the Office to which I have been appointed to uphold."

The Convenor responded ten days later, explaining his rationale and the nature of the arbitration panel. He directed both Verryn and Abrahams to sign the Arbitration Agreement and ordered, against Abrahams' will, that the arbitration process proceed. The arbitration panel took up their task in mid-February, but it would be months before they made their final decision.

Twenty-three

Ann Skelton to the Rescue

When Dr Ann Skelton, the Director of the Centre for Child Law at the University of Pretoria, got the phone call in December 2009 asking if she would be willing to act as a curator for unaccompanied minors at Central Methodist, she didn't know what she was in for. She had never met Paul Verryn. She didn't realise that her appointment would play a role in his suspension from the Church. She didn't know that she would be thrust into the role of breaking up a fight between feuding parties. She didn't think that she would be driving back and forth from Pretoria to Johannesburg on a regular basis for the next two years. But Skelton wasn't one to shy away from a challenge.

In her no nonsense style, Skelton dove straight into the task. It was her mandate to assess the options and determine what was in the best interest of the 56 children placed in her care. In just over a month she gathered and analysed an enormous amount of information. She consulted with the children. She consulted with all the other relevant role players in the church. She consulted with the NGOs that were involved and with the various government departments.

"There was a need for a curator," Skelton told me, "because things were gridlocked. The Gauteng Department of Social Development was ready to get a court order. Paul Verryn was concerned about the fears and phobias of the children. Some of the members of the Johannesburg Child Advocacy

Forum seemed panicky. There was a stand-off. There were such extreme views in this case. There were hair-raising and outrageous claims. I had to stay neutral and focused. I confined myself to my court mandate and could only make findings that were substantiated."

Skelton once told me that in her view it had not been wise for "the Church to go half-cocked into legal proceedings and send a suspension letter. The naming of me as a curator as the reason given for Paul Verryn's suspension was just ridiculous. All parties agreed that I could be neutral."

Clearly, Skelton's presence did bring some sanity to the situation. On 8 February 2010 she submitted her report to the South Gauteng High Court. Her findings and recommendations were widely respected. She had walked into a ring of fire and come out the other end unscathed.

The first thing Skelton did was speak with the children directly. While she had been named the curator for 56 children, she took on 16 more who fell within her mandate. She met with them at the Soweto Community Centre and was immediately impressed by how articulate and confident the children were. She asked them why they were so resistant to being assisted by social workers who were trying to move them to shelters. They offered several reasons. First, they said that they had frequently experienced xenophobic and what they called "racist" attitudes from social workers and other professionals. Some had been told that they had "left their rights behind at the border," that they were expecting to be treated better than South African children, that they "do not have the right to say no," and that if they persisted in refusing to go into care they would be deported.

One vital issue the children raised with Skelton was the issue of their education. A number of them were doing O and A levels through the Cambridge system. They felt that this option was superior to doing Matric. The fact that they could access this system free of charge at the church was a matter of great importance to them. As one boy said about living at the church, "It is not that we do not like to be comfortable. Everyone would like a nice place to stay and all that, but we are committed to getting our education. If we have to sleep in a bad place but we are getting a good education, we can cope."

Skelton asked the children if they were happy with their move from the church to the Soweto Community Centre. They acknowledged that they felt safer there, that the place was cleaner and that they received better food. There was also space for them to play soccer and to feel safe outside. One major improvement was that they could work on their homework more easily at the Centre, something that was very difficult for them to manage at the church.

Skelton's report had a long section that reviewed both national and international laws relevant to unaccompanied minors. It included the South African Constitution, the United Nations Convention on the Rights of the Child, the African Charter on the Rights and Welfare of the Child, the South African Immigration Act, The Refugees Act, The Child Care Act, and the Children's Act. She also reviewed the distinction between existing policies in South Africa and what was happening in practice.

Skelton's report reviewed some of the history of the church and how it had come to house so many people. It said that there had been unaccompanied children at the church for some time and that the Provincial Department of Social Development (DSD) had known since 2005 that there were unaccompanied children at the church.

She confirmed that in many cases the children had made the journey to South Africa on their own and had had to walk "dauntingly long distances" to get there. Others caught lifts with strangers. These children had already been exposed to exploitation and sexual abuse and some of them had been preyed upon by gangs at the border near Musina. Girls were particularly at risk. While the children were offered assistance with documentation and transportation to Johannesburg, these arrangements often involved rape or transactional sex.

Skelton sketched out a timeline leading up to her appointment that shed light on events in late 2008 and 2009 and the difficult relationship between the government and the church. In October 2008 the Gauteng DSD had sent a social worker to Central Methodist to investigate the circumstances of the children there. The social worker identified which children were unaccompanied and briefly assessed those she could find, although some were working on the street so they were not assessed. The social worker's recommendation had been that the DSD should keep its doors open to assist any unaccompanied minors who might need assistance. Skelton wrote, "This passive approach had little effect, as only a trickle of children actively sought assistance of their own accord."

By January 2009 there was concern for the growing numbers of people living at the church and the DSD embarked on a more pro-active plan to assist the unaccompanied minors that were among them. They developed an internal policy framework and set up a database so that they could begin to move vulnerable adults, mothers with babies, youth and families away from the church. In April that year UNICEF joined the effort to assist.

By June the relationship of co-operation that had developed between Paul Verryn and the DSD had become tense. Despite the strained relationship, the work continued. UNICEF and the DSD entered into an agreement with the National Association of Child and Youth Care Workers (NACCW) to train and support child carers at the church who would carry out assessments of the children and identify the need for family tracing and reunification or other support. They would also develop a model for independent living for adolescents for whom family tracing or placement in a children's home was not an option.

In August 2009, 21 carers were contracted by the Central Methodist Mission to undergo the NACCW training. Médecins Sans Frontières employed three counsellors at the time to provide ongoing support to the children as well. The care givers developed a register of the children and moved the unaccompanied children to a designated area on the fourth floor of the church. Some 25 children were moved to other places of safety or shelters, but some of them ran away and some later returned to the church on their own. Trying to work with children *in situ* had been agreed upon and seemed for a while to be working. Skelton observed that "Trust between the parties was tenuous, there were setbacks from time to time and a sense that efforts were being subtly undermined, but viewed overall, this was the furthest that the parties had ever journeyed down the road towards a solution."

Skelton's report made very clear that the unannounced oversight visit by members of the Portfolio Committee on Health and Social Development from the Gauteng Legislature had had a very negative affect on the children in the church. "Their trust in the adults trying to help them – already at low ebb – was destroyed," she said.

Ironically, the DSD had at all times had the power to take police into the building to assist in the removal of children, as this was authorised by law. However, they had consciously avoided such a "heavy handed" approach. Although the Department had not been party to the night-time visit by the Portfolio Committee led by Molebatsi Bopape, the children nevertheless believed that it was the DSD that had brought the police into the building.

Skelton once told me, "There's the problem of one arm of government not knowing what the other is doing." Referring to the unannounced visit, she said, "– and then they go blundering in. The politicians messed up. That visit struck the match. The children couldn't distinguish between that raid and the work of the DSD. The DSD didn't take an aggressive approach, but the Portfolio Committee did. I doubt whether they had the authority to do it."

When I asked Skelton what else she thought had contributed to the crisis in late 2009, she said, "First, there is no overall system. The problem starts at the border, at Musina. The DSD could intervene at that time. But by delaying and letting kids come through to Johannesburg, it becomes problematic. The DSD delayed too long in Joburg." She described the provincial DSD as "sensitive but dithering".

She continued, "Then, a lot of the issues occurred because the City wasn't prepared. Also, the City's paradigm right now is cleaning up the streets [for the World Cup], rather than caring for children. There used to be a steady trickle of unaccompanied minors. Now there are none. The inner city is patrolled by the Displaced Person's Unit. The kids may have moved to Melville and Milpark because they've been swept out of the inner city." Skelton paused, and then said, "Basically, good prevention work from the City, the DSD, and the province could have helped avoid a crisis."

Skelton made one further comment to me about what contributed to the situation. In her opinion it was the overall policy at the Department of Home Affairs at that time, while there was a moratorium on the deportation of Zimbabweans. "What message are we sending?" she said, her voice rising in exasperation. "'Come to South Africa. We won't deport you. We'll give you temporary asylum papers. But if you beg, we'll take your children away. Come to South Africa, but we won't give you work permits.' My waiter at a restaurant the other day was a Zimbabwean air traffic controller. Can you believe it?" Skelton paused, frowning slightly. "There are nurses and teachers. Our overall approach is so ambiguous. We should rather say, 'Don't come,' if we are not going to help people live a decent life here."

Skelton's February 2010 report stated that after the unannounced oversight visit at the church and the public hearings, the national and provincial departments of Social Development met with Bishop Verryn to discuss plans for the removal of the children. The plan was for social workers to meet with the children to discuss their assessments and their possible relocation. By this time, however, the children were no longer co-operative for a number of reasons, some of which she had heard first hand. The children were often given inadequate support at some of the places they were moved to, especially, apparently, at Siyakhula, a shelter near Orange Farm. This was not surprising as none of the staff at Siyakhula was trained in child and youth care.

Also complicating matters was the fact that some of the professionals had given the children the impression that they only needed to go to the shelters if they wanted to, and also that they would be taken to see the shelters before they were permanently moved there. Not all professionals agreed with this approach, and children felt cheated or betrayed when they were told they could not choose, or when their placements were not carried out in the way they had expected.

Skelton acknowledged that despite the challenges, staff at DSD and various NGOs invested enormous time and effort in trying to solve the problems, especially once the allegations of sexual abuse surfaced, but that "as their efforts were thwarted, they became highly frustrated." It was around that time that DSD started to issue warnings that they would approach the High Court to get an order allowing them to go into the church to remove the children by force, assisted by police if necessary. Central Methodist was in the media spotlight throughout.

It was at this point in mid-December that Bishop Verryn put forward an affidavit to support an application to have a curator appointed. In Verryn's affidavit he stated that many of the children had already left the church and were staying at a Community Centre in Soweto, which also belonged to the Methodist Church.

Skelton's report concluded that, ideally, the unaccompanied children should not have been allowed to gather at Central Methodist in large numbers in the first place. Due to the fact that they had remained there for a long time, however, they had bonded with one another and with other adults there, which created a dynamic that made it very difficult for outside professionals to work with them. The children experienced "bungled efforts to assist them in a negative way".

Skelton cautioned that the children should not be seen as a homogeneous group for which one single solution could be found. She recommended that each child have an individual plan worked out for him or her. She expected that many of the younger children and the older girls would be taken into the care system and placed in shelters or in children's homes. She found, however, that a number of the children, especially those who were around sixteen and seventeen, had enjoyed high levels of autonomy for a number of years and were resistant to the idea of being taken into the state child care system. In Skelton's view, these older children were unlikely to benefit from the care system. Nevertheless, she found the majority of the teenagers to be highly motivated to complete their education and she said they would need assistance with that.

The report found that the allegations of sexual abuse of the children at the Albert Street School were sufficiently alarming to have "required a more robust response." Skelton saw that several criminal investigations had faltered and that there were stories of lost dockets and complainants who had disappeared. "These do no credit to those whose job it was to investigate this matter," she said. She also believed that Central Methodist could have done more to distance itself from the alleged perpetrators. The fact that Paul Verryn had paid bail for the alleged perpetrators and had not suspended the men pending internal hearings had sent an "unfortunate message". However, she stated that the internal disciplinary hearings did not result in any findings against the alleged perpetrators, and also that the police investigations did not result in prosecutions because the original complainants could by then no longer be traced. Under South African labour law, without a disciplinary finding of guilt or a criminal conviction, dismissal of the alleged perpetrators would not have been possible. Skelton did write to the Acting Head of Public Prosecutions about the criminal cases, but she did not have a sense that these would proceed.

When I asked Ann Skelton many months later for her impressions of Paul Verryn, she said that she was concerned that he and the broader Church had not taken enough action to address the exploitation going on at the school. She also said, "He's been falsely accused before. Perhaps he feels those men were falsely accused. More should have been done to root out those men from the school and that wasn't robustly done. However, I don't think he's an abuser."

Skelton recommended that the children in her care not continue with their schooling at the Albert Street School in the long term because of the repeated allegations of sexual abuse there. However, she did suggest that they continue to attend, accompanied by a child and youth care worker, until an alternative arrangement could be found for them either with a tutor or at another school. While she found this a far from ideal solution, she believed it was important to avoid any interruption of their education.

"Whilst Paul Verryn and the Central Methodist Mission have come in for a lot of criticism about the conditions at the church and the exposure of children to danger," read the report, "the fact remains that the church was providing shelter and assistance to a group of children to whom little or no assistance was (initially) being offered by the State."

As for Paul Verryn, Skelton said he "definitely has something special about him, something charismatic. People either think he's a demon or a saint. He's flawed and he knows it. He knows he has a temper. He's complex.

But can you say that what he's done with the church is wrong? No. What would we have done in South Africa if the SACC hadn't taken sides during apartheid? Can you be religious and partisan? Yes."

Skelton found from the people she interviewed that the general view was that Paul Verryn's lack of co-operation ultimately undermined the attempts by the state and NGOs to move the children to more appropriate places. Nevertheless, she recognised that Central Methodist's initial response of providing shelter, food and education was "a human response to a real crisis that had been created by an incoherent policy regarding unaccompanied foreign children". The problems relating to the children at Central Methodist, however, were "symptoms of a much wider problem relating to the lack of a properly resourced and co-ordinated system for the management of unaccompanied foreign children in South Africa."

The report's recommendation was that the children who were living at the Soweto Community Centre should be permitted to remain there, and Skelton recommended that the Provincial Department of Social Development register the Centre as a shelter so that it could receive government support of, at that time, R26 per child per day.

Skelton's report went on to provide further recommendations for the broader group of unaccompanied foreign children in South Africa who continued to arrive in the country, mostly from Zimbabwe through the border point near Musina. An improved system was needed if it was going to be possible to ensure that further children did not gather at the church – or any other informal, unregistered shelter.

The Wembly Reception Centre in Selby, south of the city centre, should begin receiving children as soon as possible. The management of unaccompanied foreign children was a national competency for the national department of Social Development and an unfair burden on the provincial budgets and resources of Limpopo and Gauteng provinces. Skelton suggested that the national DSD consider seeking UN assistance with the further development of services for this group of children. Also, she made recommendations to several other government departments, including Home Affairs.

Skelton received six written submissions from NGOs and government commenting on her report. In response, she prepared an addendum dated 1 March 2010. She stressed the importance of an ongoing monitoring mechanism and recommended that a meeting of all responsible parties should be convened by the provincial DSD. Skelton continued to hold meetings in the interest of the children in her care for the next two years, far beyond the mandate of her appointment, but she felt it was her duty to follow each of these minors until they reached eighteen or were safely placed with families or in alternative care.

It was Ann Skelton, in her capacity as curator, who helped to end the immediate crisis of the unaccompanied children at the church, and her report put the situation in an important national and international context. Whether her report – which Paul Verryn believed was "balanced and wise" – would have any impact at all on the broader situation at Central Methodist was uncertain. Everyone was still waiting for the arbitrators' decision about Paul Verryn's suspension. Would they uphold it or set it aside? It would take some weeks before they would find out.

Divine Love and Christa Kuljian talk in front of the High Court, Pritchard Street.

Meetings at Central Methodist / 2011

One day in mid 2011 Cleo Buthelezi was watching the news in her room on the second floor when she saw a story about a woman in Saudi Arabia who had been arrested for driving. It struck Cleo as a terrible injustice that women should be restricted for cultural and religious reasons. She started thinking about how women who lived at Central Methodist were constricted in many ways, and also for cultural reasons. She decided she wanted to hold a workshop to discuss these issues and she chose August, women's month. I made one or two visits to the church to meet with Cleo and talk to her about her ideas, how she might organise the workshop and whom she might invite. At first she thought about inviting external speakers from other NGOs, but then she decided to focus on participants from within the building only.

On the day of the workshop, Cleo set up plastic chairs in the Roberts Room and made sure that she had some snacks and drinks for after the workshop was over. About 20 women attended, including two of the ministers who were working at Central Methodist at the time, Reverend Mahlakahlaka and Reverend Sibiya.

Just before Cleo welcomed everyone, she asked me to hold her cellphone for her so I put it in my bag. Then Cleo opened the workshop and started the discussion. The conversation moved from women's health to cultural expectations of women in marriage and with children. The two ministers spoke about their experience in the ministry as well.

Just as the workshop was ending, I had to excuse myself to leave. I couldn't stay for snacks because I had to pick up my daughter for an appointment. I dashed out of the room and drove through town to Rissik Street, past Park Station and on towards Braamfontein. While I generally try not to talk on the phone while I'm driving, when my phone rang and I saw that the call was from Central Methodist, I answered it. It was Cleo. "You forgot to give me back my phone," she said. "Can you come back?"

"Oh shoot," I said. "OK, I'll come back."

I quickly made a call to my daughter to tell her that I was running late. I passed Park Station, turned left onto Wolmarans, and as I turned left again onto Harrison Street to head back into town, I drove straight into a police road block. I was still on the phone. A policeman motioned for me to pull over. "I gotta go," I said to my daughter. Shit, I said to myself. Now, I'm really going to be late.

The officer said, "Ma'am, you know there's a R500 fine for talking on your cellphone while you're driving?"

"Yes, sir, I know," I said. "I'm sorry. I had to make a call because I was running late and I had to drive into..." Before I could finish my sentence, someone from behind the policeman was waving and saying "Hey, Christa. Hello."

The policeman turned around, and I got a better look at who it was. Divine Love stood there, smiling broadly. I hadn't seen him in many months. He looked great. He had a red bandana wrapped around his head, and he was wearing fresh new blue jeans. He didn't look dragged out and run down like he had the last time I'd seen him. He was selling something.

"Hello, Divine," I said. "Long time. How are you?"

"I'm good. I'm living here in Braamfontein now," he said.

The policeman looked at Divine. The policeman looked at me. "Do you know this guy?" he asked, clearly perplexed.

"Yes," I told him, smiling, "I do."

The policeman hesitated. He looked at me and then at Divine again before making up his mind. "OK, you can go," he said to me. "Don't talk on your cellphone." And he moved on to stop someone else.

"When will I see you?" asked Divine.

"Do you ever come to Central Methodist anymore?" I asked.

"When will you be there next?" he said.

"I think I'll be there on Friday for the Friday night refugee meeting."

"Maybe I'll come then," he said. "Do you have R5 for me?"

"Yeah, I think I do," I said. I put down my phone, found a R5 coin and handed it to him. "How is your art?" I asked. "Are you still drawing?"

"Yes. I've got a drawing of you," Divine said.

"Bring it on Friday," I said. I waved goodbye to Divine and drove back to Central Methodist to give Cleo her phone. I couldn't get that chance meeting at the police road block out of my mind. What should I make of it, I wondered. A bit of Divine intervention perhaps?

I never saw Divine Love again.

Twenty-Four

"Is this Boat Going to Sink?"

On 27 April 2010 the arbitration panel, led by Peter Le Mottee, announced its decision. The panel had decided to set aside the suspension against Paul Verryn. The decision was conveyed to Verryn by email two days later.

The decision, however, was based on a technicality. Because the Church's legal advisor, Jeff Matthee, was also the District Disciplinary Registrar for the MCSA in the case against Verryn, Le Mottee said this amounted to a conflict of interest that led to a reasonable apprehension of bias.

On 4 May the General Secretary of the MCSA, Vido Nyobole, sent out a broader email announcement that confirmed that the arbitrator had set aside the charges and Reverend Verryn's suspension "on a technicality". Nyobole pointed out that "the merits of the case were not dealt with, which means that Paul could be charged again by another District Disciplinary Registrar should the Church pursue the matter".

In contrast to the announcement of Verryn's suspension in January 2010, the announcement of its lifting received virtually no press coverage. Two years later people were still asking the questions – What had Verryn been doing since he was suspended? Was Paul Verryn still at Central Methodist?

In fact Verryn continued to work at Central Methodist throughout the three months of his suspension. He went in to the building every day, saw people in his office as usual, and chaired the Friday night refugee meetings. For those three months the only thing Verryn did not do was preach any sermons. The lifting of the suspension allowed him back into the pulpit.

Friends of Paul Verryn celebrated the ruling, but one posting on the Facebook page suggested that the celebrations were premature. "Sorry to disappoint you – and everyone else who is celebrating the fact that Paul's suspension has been lifted. I think quite differently on the matter," wrote Brian Sandberg from Durban. He urged people to read the statement from Vido Nyobole of the MCSA more closely. "The General Secretary's wording almost seems to call into question the validity of the arbitration process by seemingly implying that the technicality was 'somewhat frivolous'. So, is Paul truly 'free' again? Personally, I think absolutely not and that merely the bell has sounded for the end of Round One."

One person who was not happy with the ruling was Presiding Bishop Ivan Abrahams. He decided to put forward an application to the High Court appealing the arbitrators' decision. Although it was unusual for Church matters to be heard in a public court, he was hopeful that an appeal would reveal that the arbitrators had gone beyond their mandate. Others within the Methodist Church, however, had stood by Reverend Verryn throughout. The Synod of the Central District met in May 2010 and noted that it had been deeply concerned at Reverend Paul Verryn's suspension and was further concerned that the Executive Secretary indicated the possibility of further charges against Verryn. The Synod passed a resolution of support for Verryn and affirmed its belief in his ministry. It called for a public apology by Church officials for "the high-handed and arbitrary actions" taken against Verryn and asked for a public statement about the motivations for these actions, as well as a clear declaration that the MCSA would not pursue any further charges.

In September that year the annual conference of the MCSA was held in East London. Questions were raised from the floor about where things stood in relation to Paul Verryn's suspension. This resulted in a small committee being put together to present a way forward for the Church. The committee was chaired by Bishop Ziphozihle Siwa and it included Reverend Ross Olivier, who had helped draft the communiqué on Central Methodist the year before. The committee proposed a number of steps to the conference for resolving the matter, among them asking Presiding Bishop Abrahams to withdraw the application he had made to the High Court appealing the arbitrators' decision. According to Ross Olivier, "Conference unanimously adopted the resolution." Perhaps one could say that this was the end of Round Two, but at the time it wasn't clear how many rounds there would be.

After the suspension was lifted, in mid-2010, the number of people living in the church had come down to under a thousand. This was quite a drop from a year earlier, just after the July 2009 police raid, when the number had risen to over 2 000, largely because everyone who had been sleeping out on the pavement had moved inside. I asked Freedom Chivima and Cleo Buthelezi why they thought the numbers had come down. Cleo said that people became worried when the Bishop was suspended in January 2010. "They didn't know what would happen or if the place would close," she told me. Freedom said he thought that "word had gone out that it was too crowded," and that fears about xenophobia also played a part.

It was the church and Bishop Verryn who supported Freedom in training further in karate. While he was teaching karate at the church, he was also training at Solly Said's karate gym in Fordsburg. In April 2010 Freedom earned his black belt. Despite the uncertainty at Central Methodist, Freedom was thrilled he had finally met his goal.

Soon after he was reinstated, in June 2010 Verryn established Peace Action, with the purpose of monitoring human rights violations. Peace Action set up the help desk in the foyer of Central Methodist so that people could report abuses, generally by the police, but also by Home Affairs. There was also some anxiety that xenophobic violence might return in the wake of the Soccer World Cup that was shortly to be held in South Africa. Many people were saying to foreign nationals, "Once the World Cup is over, we are coming for you." In addition, as Johannesburg wanted to present itself as a World Class African City – the motto on many billboards – there were ongoing efforts by the police to "clean up" the city.

I asked Phil Harrison from the City of Johannesburg about the City's vision for a World Class African City. He said that the City's current official policy document, the Growth and Development Strategy of 2006, called for a "World Class African City for All". Unfortunately, the "for all" was dropped from the city's letterhead and from every banner and billboard throughout the country during the World Cup and therefore from the City's consciousness.

The fact that the number of people living at Central Methodist was down substantially was good news for Rose Bond, the building manager for Pitje Chambers. She was pleased that the portable toilets on Pritchard Street were gone, and that she could make her way down the ramp to the parking garage in the morning. Rose and Cleo met for the first time at Wits University on 17 August 2010 when I gave the Ruth First Lecture there, entitled "Making the Invisible Visible: A Story of the Central Methodist Church". For several months afterwards, they worked together on a cleaning programme for the area around Pitje Chambers, Central Methodist and the High Court.

In August and September that year, after the World Cup had been and gone, residents at Central Methodist were still uneasy about the future. There was a lot of talk at the time about whether things were going to change. Over the years, Verryn had periodically warned residents that he would close the church to them as a result of bad behaviour. Sometimes he would get so angry with the conditions in the church – the toilets, the drinking, the fact that people were destroying church property or not cleaning up after themselves – that he would threaten everyone that he had had enough and they were going to have to leave. Now he had started to raise this possibility again.

Another reason for this pervasive feeling of uncertainty was that Verryn was planning a trip to the US to teach and give sermons at the First Congregational Church in Old Lyme, Connecticut, a church he had worked with for many years. He was going to be away for a full three months, but he hadn't yet shared with the residents exactly what his plans were or exactly how long he would be gone. People wondered if the government or the Methodist Church leadership would take the opportunity to close the church down while he was away.

Despite Verryn's term as elected Bishop coming to an end in December 2009, the name "Bishop" stuck and everyone in the building still called him that. One day I had a long talk with Ambrose Mapiravana in the foyer. He was slumped dejectedly at the help desk and he had a very long face. I stood next to him for a few minutes looking out the front door. "The Bishop gave me two weeks' notice," Ambrose said. "He says he is going to move everyone out of the building and I need to be prepared."

"Do you think he's serious?" I asked.

"Ag, he's been threatening for years. People don't believe the Bishop, but I dunno." He shook his head and looked down at the floor.

"Do you think he's frustrated with the situation in the building? Do you think he's tired?"

"Yes," Ambrose said, sighing. "What do you do when you're hitting your child because you want her to be disciplined but she laughs at you? You want her to feel pain but she's laughing. The vendors are a problem. They sell through the night. If someone's walking from Faraday to Park Station, they stop here at Smal and Pritchard to get cigarettes. The Bishop says over and over at the refugee meetings to stop selling at 10pm but no one listens. He says the doors need to close at 10pm but it's so hard to implement."

The foyer was relatively quiet in the middle of the afternoon. Several people were sitting on the stairs behind us. A man walked in and asked Ambrose, "Where can I find Bishop Verryn?"

"He's not in," said Ambrose.

The man turned and left and we returned to our conversation.

"The Bishop wishes he'd never opened up this church to anyone," Ambrose said gloomily. "Just like God wishes he never created mankind. Man is making too many problems for him."

Ambrose wasn't the only one who was anxious. On another occasion, Cleo Buthelezi and I had a similar conversation. We were sitting together on the steps near the front door. "Is this boat still on the sea?" she asked. "Is this boat going to sink? Are people going to jump?" I looked enquiringly at her, waiting for her to continue. "I feel like it's too quiet," she said. "We are waiting for the government to do what they want to do. Believe you me, it's a little bit scary. Change is scary. You never know where change is going to leave you." On an earlier occasion I had asked Cleo if she ever thought about moving out of the church. "I only want to part ways when things are on smooth ground," she said. "The Bishop is having a hard time because he's helping other people. I know some people don't see it like that. But he has taught me that I can make it, that I can believe in myself. He has changed my life to see that life is about other people."

I asked Father Mike Nyamarebvu at the Solidarity Peace Trust what he thought would happen if Central Methodist closed down.

"It would be a tragedy," he said forthrightly. "There is a haven there. There is a network there. The Bishop has an open door policy and that confounds us. But anyone who is in distress can go there. That is the only haven we know of. With due respect to SPT, we have not been able to offer a haven in the same way." Father Mike continued, "If it's not there, it will be catastrophic. Government doesn't have the capacity. The UN has let people down. Other shelters don't take foreigners. There's a huge amount of work being done there educationally and in terms of training. The plight of the poor is reduced by that place."

Another development that had people feeling uneasy was some discussion that had been going on at Médecins Sans Frontières about changing their way of doing things. In late 2010, MSF found that only 10–15 per cent of the visitors to the clinic came from Central Methodist itself. The majority were coming from numerous slum buildings in the inner city. MSF announced at several Friday night refugee meetings that they were going to be doing more work with mobile clinics. Residents were concerned that the clinic in the building might close down.

As MSF began running the mobile clinics throughout the city in 2011, it cut back on the hours that the fixed clinic was open until it did, in fact, close down completely. By the end of June 2012 it would close the mobile clinics as well. These decisions were shaped by the fact that the organisation was struggling on two fronts – how best to develop a model of care to address a chronic humanitarian challenge in the city (rather than a single acute emergency), and a crisis of funding given the prevailing economic problems in Europe.

A few days after our conversation in the foyer, I got talking to Ambrose again. I asked him if he was ready to leave the church. He shook his head. "No, with the help I get from the Bishop it will be unfair for me to walk away," he said. "As long as the refugee ministry continues, I will be with him. I've learned from him that life is best when you are among the poor, not among the rich. I must assist him the best I can. Now that the Bishop is away, I've told everyone to stop gambling and drinking and smoking. I tell them, if the church people see this, they will blame the Bishop. So things are quiet now."

Despite the networks that existed at Central Methodist and the community of people who lived there, there was a definite sense that none of it would carry on if Verryn wasn't there to hold it all together. Given his lack of propensity to delegate, not much happened while Verryn was away in the US. He did keep in touch with his office staff and the other ministers, but Friday night refugee meetings were suspended. Peace Action meetings proceeded with the support of MSF, but many decisions were put on hold.

Despite Verryn's firm handle on authority, there was also a sense that people stayed on because there weren't a lot of alternatives out there. Although the church wasn't in the headlines anymore, it was still playing a vital role in many people's lives.

Twenty-five

The Tip of the Iceberg

In mid-2010 there was still uncertainty about whether residents of Central Methodist would ever move into the Moth building. It had been eighteen months since the idea had first been proposed by Phil Harrison and Ruby Mathang of the City of Johannesburg. Was there any chance it might still happen? I heard that Russell McGregor could help me with the answer. McGregor had chaired some of the inter-governmental task team meetings about Central Methodist in 2009 and had continued to work with the City, the province and national government on the plan to relocate people from Central into the Moth building. He also chaired one of the public hearings held by Molebatsi Bopape after her unannounced visit to Central Methodist in October 2009.

Originally from the Western Cape, McGregor was first employed by Gauteng province in 2005 as the director of the Community Development Worker (CDW) programme. It was while he was in that post that Dorothy Qedani Mahlangu pulled him in to help organise the temporary shelters for refugees after the xenophobic violence in May 2008. Mahlangu contacted McGregor again in March 2009 when things hit crisis point with Central Methodist. She asked him to represent her at the meetings of the inter-governmental task team.

Because the task team needed administrative capacity in order to function, McGregor was seconded to national government in September

2009 – working for the Department of Cooperative Governance and Traditional Affairs (COGTA), the old Department of Local Government, which led the committee. Yusuf Patel, in that same national department, welcomed McGregor's assistance because the department recognised that it needed a dedicated person to help engage with the growing crisis around CMC and to co-ordinate the involvement of various people at national, provincial and municipal levels.

By the time I visited McGregor, in July 2010, he had been working on issues of migrant housing for two years. We met in his Johannesburg office, which was large and airy but empty. There was nothing on the walls and only one or two books on a shelf. No personal assistant. No kettle. We sat at a bare round table near the window.

McGregor clarified that he was still working in national government and that he had been asked to lead a programme called Strengthening Communities of Diversity and Peace, which was funded by the European Commission and United Nations Development Programme. Central Methodist Church was one of the pilot sites for the programme. "There is a notion, which is not true," said McGregor, "that foreign nationals and South Africans are arriving in their hordes and causing problems in the city." He said the programme had three objectives: to explore the lessons learned from Central Methodist, to address gaps in migration policy, and to address capacity building needs within government to deal with migration. "I'm confident we can do a lot in the next six months," he said.

"When you say 'we' do you mean you'll have staff working with you?" I asked.

"No, we'll advertise for consultants and other groups to do the work."

When I asked how much money the EC and the UNDP had committed to the programme, McGregor hesitated and I had to ask him again. He was chewing very hard on his right thumb nail.

"There should be around R15 million to work with for the period February 2010 through January 2011," he said. "Hopefully they will consider an extension if things go well."

I asked if he had something I could read about the programme, and again he seemed not to have heard my question so I changed direction.

"And how are things with the Moth building?" I asked. "Weren't there plans for people to move in over a year ago?"

"When the Gauteng DSD said in July 2009 that they could no longer fund the management of the Moth building, it threw everything into disarray," said McGregor. "The City had renovated the building at its own cost. They got everyone excited. Then there was no money." He adjusted his glasses. "We recently got an agreement to fund an NGO to manage the Moth building at R6 million for six months. Now we have to get the City to sign a contract."

I was certain the city would be hesitant to sign if they knew that the UNDP money would run out in a year. Then they'd have to fund the management of the building themselves. When I pointed this out to McGregor, he agreed and said the NGO would have to produce an exit strategy. There's only funding until 2011," he admitted, "but we want the National Treasury to commit funds and the provincial department of Social Development should be involved. It can't be left to the City." McGregor had given a presentation to the Mayoral Committee and their concern was financial sustainability. Also, they were opposed to people staying permanently in the Moth building, the intent being to help people only for a period of months until they moved on somewhere else.

McGregor said that he wanted people from Central Methodist to start moving into the Moth building in the next month or so. He wanted Molebatsi Bopape and Paul Verryn to serve on a board to oversee the building. He mentioned how the year before the Department of Home Affairs and the UNHCR had registered 2 500 people from the church but he also acknowledged that the old list wouldn't be accurate any longer. "We'll have to get everyone interviewed and screened again," he said.

I asked McGregor what he thought were the lessons from Central Methodist. His view was that what had happened there showed up the shortcomings of government and civil society and that neither had the organisation to find solutions and co-ordinate efforts. He felt that government and civil society didn't work together, or even worse, that they were fighting with each other over who should get the credit. McGregor looked down at the smooth, empty table in front of him. "If government is not providing a service, how can it attack someone who is? How can you criticise and then your own buildings are derelict?"

I knew that the City of Johannesburg was struggling with many derelict buildings. At the time that MacGregor and I talked, however, I imagined that the Moth building was still standing empty, newly renovated, and waiting for the residents of Central Methodist to arrive. As I would find out later, this was not the case.

As I got up to leave, I was struck by the similarities between Russell

Zapiro cartoon, 1 April 2007.

Zapiro cartoon, 26 June 2008.

© Christa Kuljian

Three buildings on Pritchard Street: the High Court on the left, Central Methodist Church in the middle and Pitje Chambers on the right.

© Paul Jeffrey

Sign on the palisade fence that went up on the Smal Street Mall in front of Central Methodist in March 2009. Someone scratched out the word "No" on the second line.

© Austin Andrews/MSF

Temporary toilets placed on Pritchard Street in March 2009.

Rose Bond, Building manager, Pitje Chambers.

Dorothy Qedani Mahlangu, Minister in the Gauteng Provincial cabinet.

Ann Skelton, legal curator for unaccompanied minors at Central Methodist.

Ivan Abrahams, Presiding Bishop of the Methodist Church of Southern Africa.

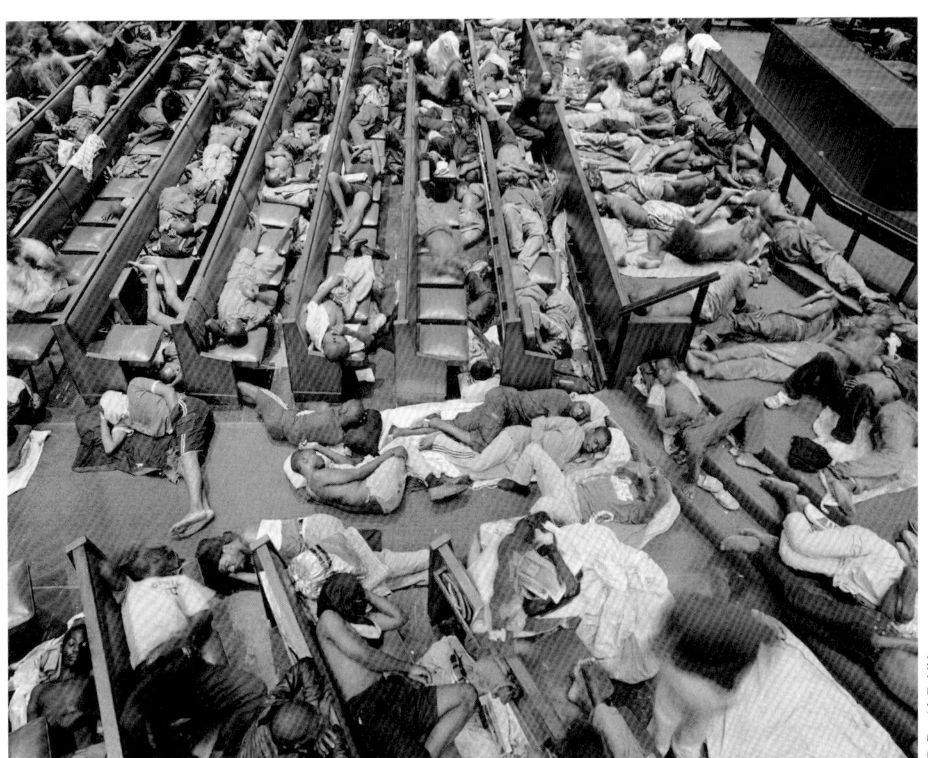

Refugees from Zimbabwe sheltering in the Central Methodist Church on Pritchard Street, in the city. 22 March 2009.

© Austin Andrews / MSF

People sleeping on the stairwell, Central Methodist Church, March 2009.

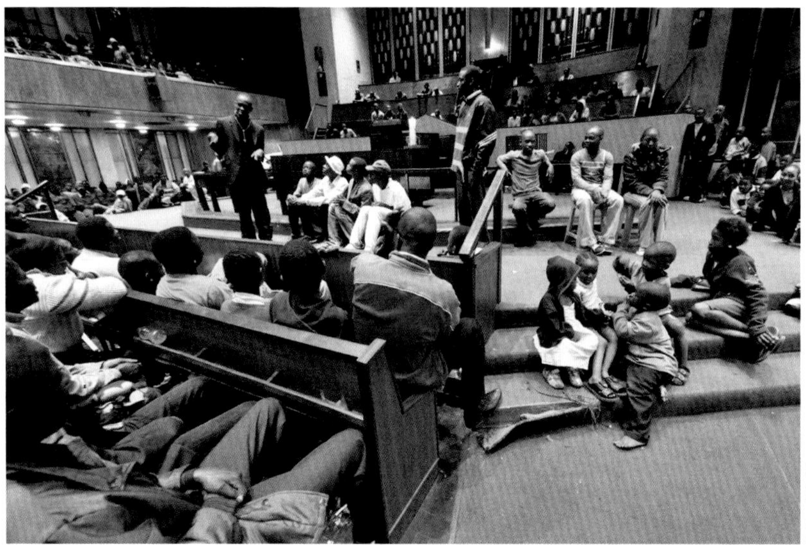

© Paul Jeffrey

Preforming an educational skit during an evening service in the sanctuary, Central Methodist Church, June 2009.

A mother presents her baby to Paul Verryn for baptism during an evening service in the sanctuary, Central Methodist Church, June 2009.

The Moth Building.

© Christa Kuljian

Asylum seekers queue at 6am at Marabastad Home Affairs office in Pretoria.

© Christa Kuljian

Asylum seekers queue outside Marabastad Home Affairs office.

© Christa Kuljian

Man wearing green overalls and wielding a sjambok leads asylum seekers across the street.

© Christa Kuljian

Reason Machengere of Solidarity Peace Trust and Ishmael Kauzani of Zimbabwe Youth Wing talk with Yahyah Kasseem after being told by Home Affairs officials to leave and come back the next day.

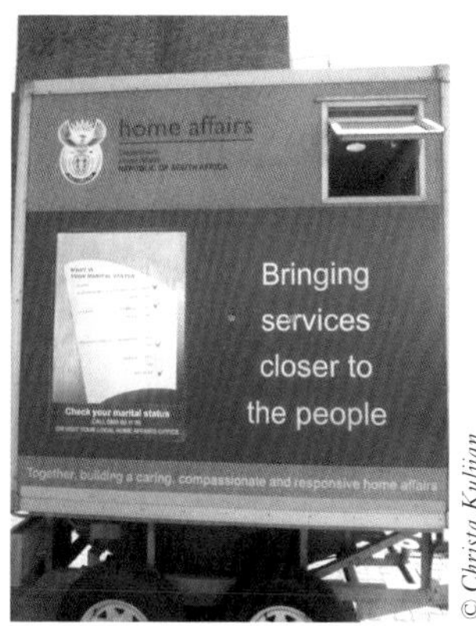

© Christa Kuljian

Home Affairs caravan outside Marabastad Home Affairs office.

Procession into the sanctuary at wedding ceremony, Central Methodist Church, 28 August 2011.

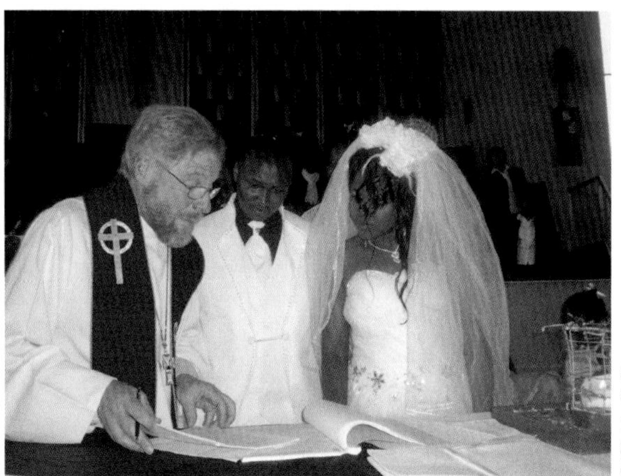

Paul Verryn officiates at wedding of Leothere Nininahazwe and Monica Chiwetu, 28 August 2011.

Monica Chiwetu and Leothere Nininahazwe at wedding reception in Braamfontein, 28 August 2011.

McGregor and Paul Verryn. They both had control over purse strings and were overseeing large processes that affected large numbers of people. Both of them wanted to achieve something important with their work. Neither one of them was focused on building or managing an organisation to get the work done. Neither one looked to be very good at delegation. But that was where the similarities ended. McGregor was a lone ranger. He was in an empty office with no staff, taking on major national programmes on his own. He was concerned with his accountability to everyone above him in positions of power – the EC, the UNDP, COGTA, Gauteng province, the Treasury – but he did not seem to have shown great accountability to those who relied on him from below.

Verryn, on the other hand, was a pied piper, working in an office that was filled to the gills, surrounded by thousands of people, taking on big problems with a never-ending queue of the destitute at his door. He showed his greatest accountability to the individuals who arrived on his doorstep, to the refugees and the homeless. He showed little accountability to those in positions of power – those in the City, the province, the private sector and the Church. The only force above him to whom he felt any kind of accountability was God.

The challenge of moving people from Central Methodist to more appropriate accommodation could never be seen as an isolated problem. It was part of a much larger problem of housing in the city. Russell McGregor and Paul Verryn had both articulated the need for temporary housing in the inner city, housing where people could stay for three to six months, find their feet and then move on. Such housing simply did not exist. Thousands of migrants moving into the city were staying in derelict buildings and, with nowhere else to go, not moving on. As the Solidarity Peace Trust had put it, Central Methodist was the "highly visible tip of a huge iceberg in Central Johannesburg".

In 2010 Evans Kuntonda and a team of four others from MSF conducted field work for a survey of 82 buildings in central Johannesburg in which an estimated 50 000 to 60 000 people were living in appalling conditions. While MSF called them "slum buildings", others who were working in urban development in Johannesburg used the softer term, "bad buildings". MSF's team interviewed 500 people living in 30 of the buildings. The majority of the residents were from Zimbabwe, but there were also Malawians, Tanzanians and South Africans among them. The spaces were badly overcrowded and sub-divided so that each floor felt like a warren of rooms. Sanitation was very poor or non-existent and there was little access to clean water. In many of the buildings, there was no system to manage waste. Evans Kuntonda told me that close to 40 per cent of the residents shared a water tap with more than 200 people and that about 50 per cent of the residents of these buildings shared a toilet with more than 100 people.

Another dynamic that had an impact on housing in the city as well as on the story of the Moth building was evictions. Evictions had a long history in Johannesburg. Forced removals were a strong feature of apartheid and people were often moved out of the city for racial segregation planning purposes. Lindi Myeza, back in the early 1980s, had helped give people shelter who had been evicted from their homes and Actstop had been working on this issue in the city for over a decade. Inner-city evictions continued in the post-apartheid era. One conservative estimate is that 10 000 people were evicted from inner-city buildings in Johannesburg between 2002 and 2006 in order to make way for municipal plans for gentrification. Several major court cases reviewed municipal responsibilities to provide emergency housing. While provincial governments held the funding for emergency housing, municipalities were obligated to address the needs of people threatened with evictions from buildings owned by the City or by the private sector. This obligation was not always met.

In early 2010 alone, MSF and Evans Kuntonda witnessed evictions from four buildings which housed over 1 000 people in each. These evictions always happened in the same way – private security companies, one in particular known as the Red Ants, and sometimes policemen, were sent by the owner to chase residents out of the buildings with violence, using sticks and, on occasion, rubber bullets. Once evicted, the residents were not allowed to go back inside to collect their belongings, which were then thrown out from the windows onto the street. MSF reported that no strategy was proposed for the relocation of the residents. In the hours following an eviction, people would try to contact friends or relatives to find refuge in other buildings. For many days after one of these evictions, hundreds of people were still sleeping on the pavements in the middle of the city. Although some people believed that these evictions were linked to the City's clean-up effort in advance of the World Cup that year, the evictions didn't necessarily imply an upgrading of the buildings as a result.

As it turned out, a group of South Africans who had been evicted from another building in the city, an industrial building in Carr Street in Newtown, had been living in the Moth building since November 2009.

The City of Johannesburg had moved them there. I found this out when I called Walter de Costa from the Displaced and Migrant Persons Support Programme, the organisation that Russell McGregor suggested could manage the Moth building. My intention was to find out from De Costa how things were going. He told me that 250 people were already living in the Moth building, but he wasn't too concerned because he said the building had the capacity to house 700. "It would be good to get people from Central Methodist Church in there now," he said. "Then it would be an integrated facility rather than only being for foreign nationals, because of xenophobia." De Costa said the UNDP had the money, but they were still waiting for the Mayoral Committee in the City to sign the contract.

De Costa wasn't the only one to mention the resentment that housing Central Methodist residents, most of whom were Zimbabwean, might cause in the Moth building. I spoke to Dorothy Qedani Mahlangu from Gauteng province in September 2010 and she was frank. She said, "I didn't agree with the Moth building. So many people in South Africa are without proper shelter. Government can't be seen to focus on foreigners. It won't be justifiable. It would mobilise xenophobia."

Initially, it was unclear to me why the City had decided to move the people from Carr Street into the Moth building. I subsequently learned that the City had had an incentive. A private property developer called Chestnut Hill Investments had been trying to evict people from Carr Street since 2008 in order to convert the building into retail space ahead of the 2010 World Cup. In August 2009 Judge Neels Claasen of the South Gauteng High Court ordered the City of Johannesburg to provide temporary accommodation for the 140 residents of Carr Street. To sweeten the deal, the court ordered Chestnut Hill to pay the City R1.5 million to help with the the relocation costs and to support job training for the residents.

The city had more than one reason to consider moving the Carr Street people into the Moth building. Lael Bethlehem of the Johannesburg Development Agency (JDA) was one person who put pressure on Phil Harrison and the City to move them there. She felt strongly that the new Carr Street development was important for the City. In addition, the City and the JDA had just spent a pot of money renovating the Moth building and had been left high and dry by provincial government on the management costs. No one wanted the Moth building to stand empty, and this did provide one option for solving the problem of Carr Street at no additional cost to the City, at least not initially. While neither Phil Harrison nor Ruby

Mathang had the power to authorise the move, they did believe it made sense. Someone – the Mayor, the City manager, or the head of housing – gave the go ahead for the City's legal department to negotiate with the court and so the move went ahead.

Phil Harrison once told me that he thought the judgment on Carr Street had been a good one, i.e. for the developer to pay the City to relocate people. However, he also pointed out that the unintended consequence was that it also made it easier for a private developer to evict people. There is yet to be a clear and consistent legislative framework on evictions. Unfortunately, government policy on housing is also confusing, with varying responsibilities at national, provincial and municipal levels and no truly clear or cohesive strategy.

I also heard from Phil Harrison and the head of the City's legal department Pieter de Klerk that the Mayoral Committee's original agreement to refurbish the Moth building had included a requirement that 25 per cent of the residents be South African. This requirement was never reported in the media, but was included because of the concern on the part of government that they would be seen as giving preferential treatment to foreign nationals, and a fear that the building could be vulnerable to xenophobic attacks. Phil Harrison and Ruby Mathang thought that moving the Carr Street residents into the Moth building would help meet that requirement.

I asked Leslie Mogoro, the head of Housing for Region F (the inner city) why the City of Johannesburg had moved other people into the Moth building and not the residents from Central Methodist. He said, "I'm just an operational guy. I don't know." What he *could* tell me, though, was that the Moth building was unique in that it was the only building that the city managed itself and that the City spent R3 million a year on the running costs – water, electricity, cleaning. When I asked Mogoro whether any funding came from Gauteng province, he said, "No, the province has never given us money for transitional or temporary housing. We have put in quite a few applications, but nothing has been forthcoming. We finance the Moth building from our own operational budget."

Russell McGregor continued working on the Central Methodist pilot project for another four months, hoping that the City would approve the deal. Then, perhaps out of frustration, in November 2010 he closed down the project and left the National Ministry. "The Ministry wasn't functioning," he said over the phone, "so it wasn't possible to move the programme forward."

"And the funding from the UNDP and the European Commission?" I asked.

"You can't bring in the funding if nothing's moving," he said.

MacGregor returned to his previous post with Community Development Workers (CDW) at Gauteng province. His work with migration, xenophobia and housing solutions had come to an end.

I still wasn't fully satisfied with why people from Central Methodist had never moved into the Moth building. The failure of the provincial Department of Social Development to follow through on its commitment to fund the management costs of the building did not fully explain it. Russell McGregor's shift back to the province and the failure of the international funding to come through didn't completely explain it either. While Phil Harrison and Ruby Mathang from the City of Johannesburg agreed with the relocation of people from Carr Street into the Moth building, they may have originally thought that people from Central Methodist would move in as well. After all that media coverage about efforts to find alternative accommodation for people at Central Methodist and all the efforts of the inter-governmental task team, there must have been another good reason why no one from Central Methodist had ever moved in? Also, if the City was willing to take money from the private sector in 2009 to help with funding temporarily, why were they hesitant to do the same with the money from the EC and the UNDP in 2010? Was it a decision based on fears of xenophobia? Was it bureaucratic inertia?

What was clear to me was that the story of the Moth building was a story of government dysfunction. It was a story of how all levels of government – municipal, provincial and national – could not pull together to address the temporary crisis for some 2 000 people. In addition, however, there was one small aspect of what happened there, one belated reason that contributed to the fact that no one ever moved in from Central Methodist. This one possible explanation came to me only after I made a visit to the Moth building myself. In fact, it was quite simple.

In April 2011 I had an opportunity to visit the Moth building with Paul Verryn. Verryn had been invited by the Centre for Applied Legal Studies to assist with a tenant committee election there and I asked if I might go along. The building was in a cul de sac at the end of Loveday Street, on the corner of Rissik overlooking the railway line. We drove from Central Methodist in Verryn's canary yellow Honda Jazz through a drizzling rain and quite a bit of traffic, but we actually managed to get there, spot on time, at 2pm.

"You don't know how miraculous this is," said Verryn.

We walked through the raindrops, up a few wet steps through the security door, past several people in the small lobby through to the meeting room at the back. It was a large room, almost three times as big as the Roberts Room at Central. It was in good condition with a grey cement floor, freshly painted salmon-coloured walls and rows of grey and salmon tiles. I could tell that the Johannesburg Development Agency had been at work there.

Morgan Courtenay of CALS greeted us and introduced Michael Eastman, an advocate, and a man named Makwatla Pale. About 30 people were sitting and standing around three rows of grey metal tables, chatting and waiting for the tenant committee election to start. Kids were running around. Babies were crawling on the floor. On two walls of the room, sheets acted as room dividers between rows of beds. Some of the tenants had moved into this room from the basement, apparently because of flooding down there.

"OK, let's get started," said Courtenay.

Verryn opened with a prayer. "Let us pray that we will listen to each other and make progress. Let us pray for those whose lives are in trouble." A clap of thunder emphasised his words.

Courtenay asked the gathering, which had grown to about 50, to break into three groups – one for each building that was represented. The residents who had been relocated from Carr Street had been joined by evicted tenants from two other City-owned buildings, Chancellor House and PG Alexander. Verryn proposed that the tenants from each of the three groups elect three people for a total of nine to serve on the tenant committee. The drizzle turned to a downpour which started making a racket on the roof.

"Can you hear me?" shouted Verryn. "We need nominations from Chancellor House. Who proposes?" A man in a red Vodafone shirt pulled another man outside who had had too much to drink. "Who seconds?" persisted Verryn.

I looked around me. At the other end of the room, two panels were missing from the ceiling and a waterfall was now pouring through the gap. A pool of water started to form on the floor and a stream began to flow towards us.

"Are you prepared to stand?" asked Verryn. A man in a white button-down shirt translated into Zulu. "When I call your names, will you please stand!" Verryn had resorted to shouting in a gallant effort to be heard over the din on the roof. The drunk guy walked back in. Morgan, Makwatla and Michael walked around gathering all the small pieces of paper with the votes written on them.

"These are the names you have chosen," said Verryn. The stream from the other side of the room had now formed a pool under our feet. With his left hand on his hip, Verryn chewed on a blue pen he held in his right. "Write three names on the paper. Don't write four because then the paper will be spoilt." Some people started to leave. "No, please stay. You must stay!" he called after them. "You can vote."

The rain had let up a bit and there was a cool fresh feeling in the room. I gave my pen to the people sitting next to me. One woman said, "It's better today. Last week, the water was up to that line." I looked to where she was pointing and there was indeed a water mark on the wall, about ten centimetres above the floor.

Michael Eastman, the advocate, counted the ballots and the votes. After the election was finished and the new committee of nine was named, Morgan Courtenay spoke to the group. "This building is obviously no good," he said. "We want your stories to put in the court papers, so please stay and speak to us."

"Where are you going to take us?" asked a young woman in a black *doek*.

"We can't say. We have to wait for the City to tell us."

Courtenay later told me that CALS had sent a letter of demand to the City to fix the building – its broken windows and leaking ceiling – or move the residents to appropriate alternative accommodation.

The R1.5 million payment from Chestnut Hill Investments was meant to be used by the City within 12 months from November 2009 to facilitate job skills programmes to help the residents to find work. Eighteen months later, in April 2011, residents of the building maintained that there had been no registration for any programmes and that no job training had ever taken place.

After the tenant election, a woman who lived in the building offered us a tour. We went up to the second floor with her, which was for the male residents. It was much smaller than I expected. It was one large open room that was divided by sheets and bunk beds. I had expected doors off a hallway with rooms for families. The first floor for women was the same – one large open room. Here there were no divisions, no privacy. What had the city intended with their renovation? It didn't look as if this building had been set up for residential use at all. (Leslie Mogoro later clarified for me that the renovations had been done dormitory style for the potentially large number of Zimbabwean residents. The intention had never been to house families and couples in separate spaces.)

"What is the capacity of this building?" I asked Morgan Courtenay.

"There are about 300 people living here now," he answered. "The capacity is contested. The City says it's 750 but we think it's at its peak now."

Given what I had seen, I agreed with him. After the province had reneged on its funding, after people from Carr Street had moved in, and after national government had been unsuccessful in co-ordinating the international donors – perhaps there was one more reason the plan had fallen apart. Perhaps the City had completely misjudged the capacity of the Moth building. Perhaps there just wasn't enough space.

We went down into the basement, which was completely flooded. As Verryn waded through inches of water, he said sarcastically, "Russell McGregor must have been promoted from provincial to national for the stellar job he did with this building."

A recent *Mail & Guardian* article about the Moth building said that "with the third floor least affected by flooding, the scene and mood in this dormitory is that of an indoor refugee camp. Sheets are fastened around clusters of bunk beds to forge a measure of privacy and there are two colonies of these 'tents' in an approximately 300 sqm room. In the cramped and unventilated space, a cast of characters clashes daily." One resident reported that tempers flared and that theft was so bad you could be robbed while you were asleep.

Sometime later, I called Morgan Courtenay at CALS. I was interested to find out how it had happened that he'd asked Paul Verryn to help with the tenant election. Why would CALS have imagined Verryn might be happy to assist in a building that had been earmarked two years before for residents of Central Methodist? It turned out that Courtenay had only recently joined CALS and hadn't been aware of the history. "When I realised that elections had to be held at the building, I didn't want people to think that CALS was biased or that the elections were rigged," he said. "I asked people at the Legal Resources Centre if they knew of someone who could help. They told me that Paul Verryn had provided oversight for many such elections in buildings throughout the city. Paul mentioned something about the Moth building history in passing when I first called him, but he didn't elaborate."

It certainly looked like the chance of anyone ever moving into the Moth building from Central Methodist was close to nil. As we drove back to the church that day, Verryn said, "They aren't organised. The only thing they have in common is their drinking. That building has no soul."

Twenty-six

Conflict within the Methodist Church

EVEN THOUGH THE IMMEDIATE CRISIS AT Central Methodist seemed to have passed, the debate continued within the Church about Paul Verryn's role there.

The theme of the church's annual conference in September 2010 was "An Invitation to the Round Table". In his opening address, Ivan Abrahams said that "a round table is a good metaphor and a helpful egalitarian image and vision of the Church." He went on to say that "We must intentionally open our doors to *migrants* and in the process be renewed, enriched and transformed. We are called to offer hospitality to *strangers* and *exiles* (Leviticus 25; Rom 15:7). The call of Christ to welcome strangers is central to the gospel message (Matt 25:31–35)." In nearly 250 pages of documentation in the Methodist yearbook that covered 2010 there was no reference to Central Methodist Mission's welcoming of strangers, however, nor to the challenges it faced, nor the debate it engendered. There was no reference to Paul Verryn's suspension and the arbitration that had followed.

The difficult relationship between the Presiding Bishop and Paul Verryn, while not articulated publicly, was an open secret. Reverend Peter Storey told me that Verryn had received many votes in the election for Presiding

Bishop in 2003, the year in which Reverend Ivan Abrahams was elected. Storey and Verryn hadn't seen each other for a long time and they went on a walk together during the conference held that year in Pretoria. Verryn shared with Storey his feeling that there had been some rigging of the votes. Having lost elections to become Presiding Bishop three times himself, Storey's reaction was to say to Verryn, "This is taking your suspicions a little bit too far."

Six years later, when the crisis at Central Methodist was in the headlines, Storey said he was amazed that despite Bishop Verryn and Presiding Bishop Abrahams being within a mere two miles of each other, there was absolutely no communication between them. "I thought this was utterly unworthy of a church like the Methodist Church and its leadership," he said.

Bishop Peter Witbooi, who had been a minister in Bosmont for many years, took over from Paul Verryn as Bishop of the Central District in December 2009. Almost two years later I met with him at his parish at St Johns United Church in Parkmore, Sandton. Tall and dapper, Witbooi had a thin moustache and wore rimless glasses. He was wearing a double-breasted blue jacket and grey slacks and his manner was relaxed. I hoped that he would shed some light on the conflict within the Church and I asked him for his view of what had happened at Central Methodist.

"What Central Methodist Mission has done for me," said Witbooi, "is expose the government's unwillingness to deal with migrants. I would have expected that those who were in exile would have catered to those from the region." As for his predecessor, he said, "Paul Verryn is very serious about his understanding of the gospel. When the first two people asked to stay [at the church], Paul didn't think it would evolve to thousands. If Paul had a choice between a building and human beings, there is no choice. If he got the money, he would buy another building."

Witbooi leaned back in his large armchair. "Once Paul makes up his mind on something, bulldozers won't stop him. I think there is strong support within the District for Central Methodist and also for the school. Albert Street had a pass rate in 2010 second only to St Johns with their A and O levels." Alpha Zhou, the principal at the Albert Street School, had resigned from his post in early 2011 and moved to Cape Town. William Kandowe, deputy principal at the time, took over from him and was still in the position of principal.

I asked Witbooi to talk about the allegations of sexual abuse at the school.

"Paul reported all of them to the police," he said. "The Presiding

Bishop gave the entire file to the NPA." He paused and then added, "The best thing that happened was the appointment of the curator, Ann Skelton."

"What did you think of the decision to suspend Verryn?" I asked.

"The Presiding Bishop should have taken action while Paul was still Bishop. By waiting until Paul stepped down as Bishop, it gave the impression that he waited for that moment. That period of the suspension hurt Paul deeply. The Church is his family. I think he was treated very unfairly. At the conference in Pietermaritzburg, Ivan asked Ross Olivier to speak to the media about what was going on. That helped to get Paul out of the firing line, but Paul was on the coal face. He felt that if there were allegations against him personally in the press, he had to respond."

Witbooi admitted that communication within the MCSA was a problem. "We don't have enough face to face communication in the Church," he said. "There was a long paper trail of correspondence, but emails and letters don't always work. I think this could have been sorted out if they had just come together over a cup of coffee." He smiled. "Paul makes us mad," he said, "but quietly we admire him. We wish we could have the guts to do what he does." He paused. "If I were him, would I have done the same or would I have said, 'No, sorry, I can't help you'?" He didn't answer his own question.

When I had met with Presiding Bishop Ivan Abrahams in his office in November 2010, I had asked him about the lifting of Verryn's suspension and what he had felt about the artbitrators' decision to do this.

"This is not a quarrel between Paul and me," he had replied. "There was no need for mediation. The arbitrator went beyond his mandate. It's as if a South African judge calls for the death penalty when it's not in our constitution. The arbitrator has got to make a decision if it's right or wrong, but he cannot offer a remedy, especially when the remedy has no place in our constitution, the *Laws and Discipline*. If he says there's a perception of bias, and this whole thing hangs on there being a perception of bias, then send it back and let it be looked at again. Don't offer a remedy by lifting the suspension."

Despite the difference of opinion on this issue within the MCSA, Presiding Bishop Abrahams did follow the recommendation of the committee in East London in November 2010, and he did not continue with court proceedings. However, the Methodist Connexional Office, which the Presiding Bishop chaired, sent a letter to Bishop Peter Witbooi in November 2010 recommending that Superintendent Minister Paul Verryn be removed from his post the following year. While the letter may not have carried any legal weight, it indicated that the conflict within the Church over Paul Verryn's role at Central Methodist was still simmering.

A year later, in December 2011, when Ivan Abrahams had announced his decision to leave MCSA, and take on a new post as the head of the World Methodist Council in the US, I met with him again. On this occasion our meeting was more casual. We had lunch at a café. It was a warm day and he arrived in a Hawaiian-inspired, short-sleeved blue shirt. "Ah, you look relaxed," I said.

"No, it's all a show," he said. "I'm stressed. I was packing this morning for our move, but I thought I'd better take a shower before coming over to see you."

I ordered a lime and soda. He ordered salmon and cucumber on rye.

"Why did you decide to leave the MCSA?" I asked him.

Abrahams was frank. "I needed a change," he said. "One's just bone weary. I'm tired of the crap, you know. I've asked all my predecessors, where is the joy in heading a big organisation like the Methodist Church and nobody, not Stanley Mogoba, not Mvume Dandala, nobody can tell me. And also, the Central issue has just been so taxing, so draining. I've also come to the end of my term. I could have done another term but I just thought, no, no, no, enough of the dysfunction. I just don't have the energy to continue."

"What was most difficult for you about all the issues at Central Methodist?" I asked.

"There has been no commitment. There's a swathe of files, larger than what you can believe, from our Church leadership, executive leadership, bishops, to the municipality leadership, provincial leadership, national leadership, institutions like the police, NPA, national intelligence. The paperwork is a mountain and I have not pursued any of it. In fact, I saw the woman who is on the case at the NPA two weeks ago and I just decided not to raise it anymore because I'm totally disinterested... Some people have been very disingenuous, claiming that it is a personality issue between myself and Paul. And he has ridden on that... But again, I want to reiterate: I'm cutting ties over here. It's not a personal issue. This institution is going to have to answer when everything comes to the fore."

I wondered whether Abrahams thought that one day Central Methodist would come back to haunt him in some way. He had told me previously that he had been very supportive of Verryn and Central Methodist back in 2005.

As it hadn't seemed, to me at least, that there had been much engagement from MCSA at Central Methodist between 2006 and 2008, I took this opportunity to ask him why.

"Why didn't the Church intervene earlier to address the challenges at Central Methodist?" I asked.

"There is no doubt that what started off as something very noble and commendable," he began, "has degenerated into an absolute catastrophe, just in terms of human dignity." He was clearly thinking about Paul Verryn. "If I can speak of any relationship cracks," he went on, "as the head of the Church, surely one has to enquire and that was not very welcome. I want to say categorically that there is a deep underlying racist issue going on here. Had these refugees been white, had the pastor in charge been black, we would have dealt – " He left the sentence hanging, unfinished, and I waited quietly for him to speak again. The next words came out in a rush. "But for some reason, everybody seems… acts like he's untouchable and everybody relates to him like he's untouchable, which is very, very sad. I'm sorry if it seems as if this thing has been personalised. But the record speaks for itself."

Since Abrahams had already left his post at MCSA when we spoke, perhaps he felt more at ease and able to speak his mind. It wasn't the first time I'd heard the accusation that race had played a role in the situation at Central. I had heard that this issue had come up at the annual Church conference in Lesotho in September. I'd asked Verryn about it myself. Referring to the discussion at that conference, he had said, "Is it because they're black people that we are prepared to let things go like this and if it was white people it would be different? I don't know what colour they think I am." "What would you say to that argument?" I had asked Verryn. "I would say you clearly don't understand the problems of poverty and who is affected most by poverty in this country. And you are playing to an audience. That's what I'd say. When you yourself have not even had the decency to try to see if there is anything you can do about the place and how do you know what the conditions are in the church and what's happening at the church if you haven't come?"

Ivan Abrahams put forward another reason to explain why things had fallen apart within the Church, one that was to do with Paul Verryn specifically. "This was not the first or second or third time that Paul had unilaterally been a law unto himself," he told me. "With the police raid on the church, I only heard the day afterwards. It was an absolute dismissal of the authority of the Church. Not having the courtesy to say, 'Hey, this is happening over here.' It splashed on my television screen. Again the Bishop is the saviour in the whole thing. Another thing that has been consistent in all my dealings with him is that he is always the victim."

I asked him for his view on why there had never been any resolution to what had happened at Central.

"My disillusion is with the Church," Abrahams said. "I had at least hoped that we would have the moral high ground to deal with this thing. For the last year, I've just decided, let me have some distance from this thing and see how it pans out."

"Can you help me understand what happened internally within the Methodist church?" I asked.

Once again Abrahams was candid and direct. "In a nutshell, it is a lack of commitment. People don't really wrestle with these issues. There are many things at play. It's race, it's gender, it's class, it's foreign nationals. It's a strong white male holding the whole thing together. I don't know. People just get tired. There's just a lack of resolve," he said.

"How does the line of accountability work?" I pressed him. "Can you describe the structures and how they work? And do you believe that they *are* working?"

Abrahams did not hold back. "It's actually a contradiction, because whenever we've gone to court and the judge has looked at our governing document, they will ask, 'Who is this Presiding Bishop? Because he has more authority than the Pope.' All authority devolves from the Presiding Bishop." Abrahams paused and then said, "If I could reinvent and live my term over again… I think I would go by the book more and allow the book to look after me. But it is consultation and a collaborative leadership style that I think has been the undoing of many things that could have been done by decree." His bitterness was painfully apparent. "The church folks crucified one," he said. "The church folks hit seeming inertia by trying to collaborate."

Then Abrahams started speaking in the voice of what I assumed were the "church folks". In a high-pitched tone and shaking his head, he said, "'We're trying to do this thing with integrity so it's a win-win situation' … 'The greater cause is the cause of Zimbabwean refugees' … 'Yes, there are some casualties but let us see how we can operate in a restorative way.'" He sighed and then went on in his own voice, "It's in trying to do all of that that I feel burnt."

I went back to discuss Paul Verryn and, knowing that we were running out of time, asked Abrahams if he was still upset that the arbitration panel had overturned Verryn's suspension.

"Our Church's senior counsel was prepared to take this thing further," he said. "But again, do you want to go to the High Court? It will go to Bloemfontein to the Appeal Court. It would be three years later. Do you want to be caught in such a protracted battle? For that reason, our conference offered a remedy."

Abrahams was finished with his meal and his lift had arrived. I wished him well with the new chapter in his life in the United States. As I waved goodbye, I thought about a quote I'd noticed he had at the foot of his emails when we'd been emailing each other to set up our meetings. Beneath his signature was this line: "True leadership is like gentle wind on a field of grass. A soft gentle coaxing breeze has the whole field swaying in one direction, whereas a violent wind has the whole field in disorder."

Twenty-seven

Life (and Death) Goes on Inside Central

At the end of 2010 there were still over 800 people living at Central Methodist Mission. While the church was no longer in the headlines, journalists from around the world continued to visit on an almost weekly basis. The violence in Zimbabwe had subsided, but fears remained of what would happen when a new election was scheduled in that country. New arrivals continued to seek accommodation at the church. Day to day work continued with the Albert Street School and with Peace Action.

On Christmas Eve that year Elizabeth Cheza passed away.

There wasn't consensus about what had caused Elizabeth's death. Cleo Buthelezi, who had visited her at Selby Hospital, said that she had cut her finger with a staple, that the cut had become infected and that the infection had spread. It was possible that Elizabeth's immune system wasn't strong enough to fight it off. Bishop Verryn, whose name Elizabeth had written down as her next of kin, later told me grimly: "Selby Hospital is a mortuary. No one comes out of there alive."

I remembered our karate class together, and Elizabeth's enthusiasm for her work at the Albert Street School. I remembered Elizabeth taking notes on Friday nights, small and compact and always managing to look fabulous, in her silk shirt and a jacket, or in jeans and polished boots. I felt very sad about her passing. Friday night refugee meetings wouldn't be the same without her.

Cleo moved into Elizabeth's old room and she was glad to have the private space. She and Taurai had had a daughter, Sandy, in 2009 and her son Mihlali was now nine years old. "I've moved into 'the mansions'," she told me. As Cleo well knew, there was a hierarchy of space at Central. For the people sleeping in a common area, there was no privacy. As soon as you moved into a room, no matter how large, there were certain privileges that came with it, such as greater access to electricity. The smaller the room, the greater the privacy.

One morning in January 2011, Cleo and I sat chatting on two white plastic chairs outside her new room. We talked about how shocked and sad we were that Elizabeth was gone. Then we talked about Leothere and Monica, whose relationship had begun and blossomed at Central, but who had suffered a tragedy that holiday season. The couple had been planning to get married on Christmas Day. Leothere had met with Monica's uncles and paid bride price earlier in 2010. Everything was in order and many relatives had already arrived in Johannesburg for the occasion. On Christmas Eve, Monica and Leothere were at the Albert Street School, where the ceremony was to take place.

A few months later Monica herself would tell me what had happened that day. "We were cleaning and setting up for the next day," she said. "I was just sitting and I started bleeding badly. There is a fire station next to Albert Street, so Leothere took me there to check me. They asked, 'Did you eat something today?' I told them I had tea in the morning and pap in the afternoon. They called an ambulance for me and we went to Joburg Gen where I had been going to the ante-natal clinic. It was after 1am when the baby was born. It was a C-section. The baby was 730 grams. He didn't have an incubator, but he needed a feeding tube and was in intensive care and breathing with a machine." She stopped for a minute. "We named him Trésor," she said. "French for 'treasure'. We didn't manage to do the wedding, but that was fine. We could postpone the wedding."

Monica spent five days in the hospital, but after she was discharged they kept the baby there. "On the 30th," she said softly, "he passed away. The Bishop did the baptism and the burial. We had a chapel service for him. To be honest, it's like I was mad. It was as if I lost my mind. It was too hard for me to accept."

Cleo shook her head as we talked about Monica and Leothere's sadness.

Then Freedom Chivima came to join us and he pulled up another plastic chair. He was wearing a blue overall jacket and a black beanie. I thought he looked ill. He had lost weight and his eyes and cheekbones were more prominent than usual. Only days earlier, he told me, he had lost his job, the only job he had ever had in Joburg as a plumber, the job that he had found three years earlier, in January 2008.

"The police were looking for me," he said. "My boss told them that I had stolen a basin. The police left a message for me with my wife so I called them back. They said they were downstairs from my place, so I went down to speak to them. They told me to get into the police car and one guy said, 'Should we put him in the boot?'

"I spent one night in jail. I sent an SMS to my boss and said, 'This is not humane. I did not steal the basin.' Two other guys I work with were in jail too. They got us a lawyer who helped us to be released."

As we were talking a young man walked by. He was dressed like an urban rapper, with his jeans hanging down below his boxers. Freedom watched him go and then said, "When I was a teenager, I used to dress like that, with a cap turned to the side. School days were the best, when you didn't have big responsibilities." He looked down at his hands in his lap and said, "I was raised in a Christian home. Just like Job, I arrived on earth with nothing. God gave me everything I have. If he wants to take it away, he can."

Cleo tried to joke Freedom out of his gloomy mood. Punctuated by her powerful laugh, she said, "Ah, little brother, this was your first time in jail. It will make you a man," but Freedom barely smiled.

It's possible to sit in one place at Central and see everyone you know in the building walk by. As Freedom, Cleo and I sat talking, Bishop Verryn walked up the stairs towards us. He, too, looked thin and drawn. As he got closer, I thought he looked as if he might even have had a stroke. He seemed to be shaking slightly, but he greeted us all, smiling widely. I later learned that over the holidays he had been diagnosed with diabetes and a serious thyroid problem. "I have to eat a lot of little meals," he told me when I had a chance to chat to him. Another time, much later in the year, Verryn and I met for one of our interviews in a coffee shop in Rosebank. He ordered apple crumble and ice-cream. "Isn't that against the rules?" I asked him, mindful of his diabetic diet. "Who cares?" he answered. I ordered vanilla ice-cream with chocolate sauce and we both tucked in. After about 45 minutes we were still talking. The waiter came over to us to see if we needed anything else. "How was that vanilla ice-cream and chocolate sauce?" Verryn asked me. "It was good," I told him. He looked up at the waiter. "I think I'll have one of those," he said.

In addition to his recent diagnosis over the 2010/2011 holiday period, Verryn had also been involved in a car accident the week before my conversation with Freedom and Cleo outside Cleo's room. Fortunately, he had not been injured. Ambrose Mapiravana had an opinion on this. He said, "When things are going badly and you have an accident but you are not hurt, it means that you are going to be OK."

I had heard that it was in early January that the letter reached Verryn from the Connexional Office, via Peter Witbooi, recommending that he be removed from his post, so he must have been feeling pressure from within the Church. I had also heard that Verryn's response had been, "If Ivan wants me dead, that's fine. Give him my corpse. He'll be happy."

As Verryn walked away from us, Cleo turned to me and said, "They are trying to get rid of Paul, but he is like a rash. He's stubborn. It's hard to get rid of him."

Two days later I attended the Friday night refugee meeting, which that evening was focused on police action in the area. Verryn's face was still drawn. His cream shirt and brown pants were hanging on him but his voice sounded stronger. "No matter how someone treats you, don't think you're rubbish," he told the residents. "You are made in the image of God." Instead of Elizabeth, this time it was Cleo Buthelezi sitting beside Verryn taking notes. She looked beautiful, I thought, dressed all in black. Before the meeting started, she had asked me if I wanted to introduce myself again to the refugee meeting. Not waiting for my answer, she said, "No, no, you don't have to." Then she looked at me and smiled. "Have we adopted you," she said, "or have you adopted us?"

Freedom reported back on karate classes with enthusiasm. He looked a hundred times better. Somehow his love for karate had pulled him back from his feelings of despair. In the next several months, Freedom met with a union attorney, attended three meetings with the Commission for Conciliation, Mediation and Arbitration (CCMA), and tried to claim three months of his salary for unfair dismissal. His employer never showed up for the meetings, so in the end Freedom was left with nothing. Fortunately, his wife Lakidzani was working at a pre-school in Fourways, so her income helped the couple cope. Freedom tried to make ends meet by taking on part-time plumbing contracts and driving jobs. His karate classes continued every evening in the Roberts Room from 6–8pm.

Takudzwa was there and as energetic and active as ever. He still ran the chess club and the darts group. Despite being diagnosed with tuberculosis in 2010, he recovered and finished his A levels at Albert Street School. He hoped to study law at the University of South Africa (UNISA) in 2011. Unfortunately, his future was uncertain because UNISA told him he could not register based on his A level results alone. He needed his O level results as well, which were proving hard to obtain from his former school in Zimbabwe. In the meantime Takudzwa worked at the help desk and monitored evictions and abuses for Peace Action. His ultimate goal, though, was to become a lawyer. "I'd like to be the leader of my country," he said. "I can be president but I have to fight for injustice first. I come from the grassroots. Mandela was a lawyer. He didn't have rallies to say please vote for me. He fought for injustice first."

At the following Friday night meeting, Reverend Verryn, looking even stronger, said, "This Sunday at the 10am service I will give some space for a discussion of the congregation's concerns. We are one [the congregation and the residents]. You can imagine you are separate but you're not. I want to find a way of ending the moaning." His audience was attentive. "Let me give you a little bit of a vision," he went on. "When Zimbabwe is free and South Africa is free, wouldn't it be wonderful if we built relationships to build southern Africa? If it doesn't happen here, we might as well burn this place down. If there is a God, this has got to be possible."

At the Sunday service, wearing his white robes, Verryn preached to a filled sanctuary. "You can kill your relationship with God stone dead if you give and it's only about money. If you do that, then the way that you are engaging becomes a dead habit. I have a profound commitment to Jesus. His politics are superb. We cannot ignore the poor. We have to recognise how each of us can make a difference."

At the end of his sermon, he said, "I came out of the pulpit now because I want to hear concerns from you. This is a family time to discuss your concerns, about the building, about toilets. Zimbabweans are our flesh and blood. This place is a barometer and I can tell you the numbers are increasing from the rural areas of Zimbabwe. But I want to open this space for you."

One person stood up and said, "The broken chairs in the sanctuary are a concern for this congregation."

"We should modernise the sanctuary," said another. "It would be good to have screens to display the hymns."

Verryn nodded. "The school doesn't take place in the sanctuary anymore," he said, "so we can work on these things."

"As we refurbish," said a man from the back of the sanctuary, "can we move the Zimbabweans to Randburg and Bryanston?"

"This is an inner-city church," Verryn replied. "We can't close the doors, unfortunately. No, that's not possible."

"With everyone sleeping with their blankets on the floor here, it's not the House of God." This came from a woman with an orange head wrap.

"That depends on how you view the House of God," Verryn said drily.

A woman in a white blouse offered to get a quote to do some restoration at the church. Then Peliwe Lolwana stood up and announced, "If anyone is interested, we do want to form a refurbishment committee. Please see me after the service."

Verryn closed the service with a story that he had told me before and that he in turn had borrowed from Peter Storey – the story of the suburban church and the city church, the dam and the sea. It was worth hearing again. "The features of a city church are different from a suburban church," he said. "In a suburban church, it's like fishing in a dam or a pool. It's quiet and calm and you know what to expect. In a city church, it's like fishing in the sea. It's often turbulent, always changing, and you never know what you'll find there."

Peliwe Lolwana chaired a meeting of the newly formed refurbishment committee in March. The committee organised a day to clean the sanctuary – Saturday, 9 April 2011 – and invited the entire congregation and all of the residents. Cleo brought Jik and Handy Andy and Jeyes Fluid. Peliwe wore jeans and used a mop. Zandile Dotwana, a member of the choir, recalled that there were over a hundred people there that day. "It was wonderful. Everyone was cleaning and washing the walls."

The committee met again the following Saturday in the sanctuary. This time the focus was the toilets. "I've been coming to this place for years," said Peliwe. "I don't even know where the toilets are. I just hear that they are bad. I've long disciplined my body not to need the toilet here, but I feel sorry for those with young children."

The group sat in front on the right side of the sanctuary near a stained glass window that overlooked the vestry. Through the frosted window, you could see the shadow of clothes hanging on a washing line.

The discussion turned to fundraising. "I went to CTM and Builders Warehouse," said one woman, "to ask for supplies. I brought a letter from the church. They asked, 'Is this that church on Pritchard Street? Are the people still staying there?' You could see their facial expression change."

"A letter is probably not sufficient," responded Peliwe Lolwana. "People don't know this church and where it's coming from. The challenge with this church is that our pockets are uneven. It's hard to raise collection to make things function. A benefactor is paying the salaries of the ministers. The best we can do is try to build a giving spirit."

Afterwards I dropped in to see Cleo. She told me that not everyone in the church was happy that she had moved into Elizabeth Cheza's room and started taking notes at the refugee meetings. "Sometimes I don't know whether I'm South African or a refugee," she said. "Sometimes the South Africans talk to me like I'm one of them. Sometimes they talk to me like I'm not. I feel I belong with the refugees. If I was working in a company, I wouldn't be happy. I feel I'm the chosen one. I have a purpose. I see what has happened to me as a blessing, not a curse."

Although many people lived at the church for a time and then moved on, there was still a sense of community amongst many of the residents. And news within the community often travelled fast.

In late February I received a text message from Reymond Mapakata. "I'm afraid Evans is at critical point," the message said. Assuming it was Evans Kuntonda he was referring to, I texted back, asking, "Do you mean he is in the hospital?" "Yes!" came the response.

When I called Reymond, he couldn't tell me what had happened. "Evans fell this morning," he said. "The Bishop just got back from the hospital and he says he's in critical condition." I wondered whether Evans might perhaps have had a stroke. I called Penny Foley, the circuit steward at Central, but she wasn't sure what had happened either. She told me some people were saying Evans had attempted suicide. Later she sent me a text saying that it seemed Evans had taken a very large dose of an insecticide. "They are giving him huge doses of stuff to turn it around," her message said.

I was shocked. Evans was such an active, engaged member of the community at Central. Why would he have done this? I had received a friend request on Facebook from him. On my computer screen were two options: "Confirm" or "Not Now". The request had been there for weeks but because I was not often on Facebook, all the friend requests and notifications had gone untended. Evans' profile picture was the Zimbawean flag, bright and proud, as if the Zimbabwe bird and the stripes of green, gold, red and black represented hope for the future.

I got to the Brenthurst clinic on Tuesday, 1 March for the 7–8pm visiting hour. About 30 people from the church showed up to visit Evans in ICU and went in two by two. The first two came out weeping. I washed my hands with pink steriliser and walked in with Prince, another resident at Central. Evans was awake. His face was swollen and distorted and his left eye was completely closed. There was tape over his mouth but I couldn't tell what it was for, or what it was holding in place. Evans' body was covered with a sheet so I couldn't tell if his body and arms were also swollen. He recognised us. He followed our movements with his good eye. After Prince had had a private moment with him, I stepped up to the side of the bed and took his hand. He couldn't speak but he looked into my face with deep intensity, as if to say, Yes, I know you. I recognise you. I'm glad you are here. I want to stay alive. I said, "I'm so glad to see you," and he squeezed my hand and nodded. I told him, "You are a special person, a giving person. People need you so you must get well."

Evans died at 4:10am on 4 March 2011. At the memorial service in the chapel later that day Ambrose said, "The pillar is gone and the building is crumbling. Now we all have to stand up." Tragedy Matsvaire, Evans' MSF colleague, stood up and said that MSF should hire Priscilla, the mother of Evans' child. "She is suffering. She is in pain. She has lost Evans. She is smart. She is hard working. If I were in charge, I would hire her to take his post."

Evans once shared with me his hope for the future. He told me that during the 2008 Zimbabwe elections, cellphones had been distributed to the voting stations so that people could report on events. He had been one of the people to receive those phone calls in South Africa to independently gather the election results. Telling me this in late 2010, he said, "During the next election, I want to be on the ground reporting. I don't want to be the one in South Africa getting phone calls."

If I had accepted Evans' friend request on Facebook, would I have learned more about his life, I wondered. Some of the details about his early life had never been very clear, apparently. Penny Foley had once told me that his parents had died young and that Evans was brought up in a Catholic orphanage. Yet his obituary, written by his employer, Médecins Sans Frontières, said that after high school Evans had joined a Catholic seminary to train as a priest but that he was not able to finish because of his father's death in 2003 when Evans was 23. I had also heard that his mother was still alive. Was he abandoned as a child, or did he spend time away from his parents, but didn't want to reveal the full story? Were there other complicated family dynamics that came into play? Was this one of the reasons why Paul Verryn was so fond of Evans and took him under his wing?

What we did know was that Evans Kuntonda arrived in South Africa in 2007. An article written by an MSF colleague, Jonathan Whittall, said that Evans had lived on the streets for some months before he moved into the church. There he had worked on the database of residents and "documented hundreds of personal testimonies of Zimbabweans who had sought refuge… He had a comprehensive understanding of where people were fleeing from and why."

Evans and his partner Priscilla Manyere moved out of Central Methodist into a flat in November 2009 and in December Priscilla discovered she was pregnant. Their relationship was often difficult, however, and Evans could be possessive and competitive, even holding Priscilla back from a possible job at the University of Johannesburg. She held a degree in sociology from the University of Zimbabwe. She went back to Zimbabwe to live with her parents for a while after the baby, Shammah, was born, but she returned to Johannesburg when Evans went into hospital.

Jonathan Whittall from MSF had shared his flat with Evans for a couple of months and said it seemed that his phone never stopped ringing. "Someone from the building needed to go to hospital – they asked Evans to accompany them; someone else needed advice on applying for refugee status and Evans understood the system; a group meeting was being held in Yeoville on xenophobia and he was required. MSF wanted him to get more information on a possible eviction in one of the slum buildings and his network was extensive. Two people had been arrested outside the church, a mother and a child. Evans was needed to bail them out."

There were times when Evans was quoted in the press, including the time, in December 2009, when he spoke at the press conference when 40 civil society organisations signed a statement in support of Bishop Verryn and Central Methodist. In December 2010 Evans read a blog about migrants and anti-racism in Italy. The blog said that anti-racism movements and labour movements needed to work together. Evans responded, saying, "We have a lot in common when it comes to migrant labour laws here in South Africa… because locals are saying migrants are taking their jobs. My wish will be that we start to pay solidarity with you in Italy."

Evans could be described as charming and competent and reliable and compassionate. He worked hard. "But it wasn't always clear what his personal goals were," said Penny Foley. "Did he want to continue organising buildings in the Joburg city centre? Did he want to enter the ministry? Did he want to enter politics?"

Just as there was some uncertainty about his early life and what direction he might have wanted to choose for his future, there remained uncertainty about his death. In the week after Evans died there was lots of talk in the building about whether he had in fact been murdered. On the Friday night after his funeral, Paul Verryn said, "Last week we went through agony in this building with Evans' death. This week, there has been a party of gossip, of talking, of accusations. If you are talking, I will send the police to you to see what you know. If you've said he was murdered, you must know something. His death does not give you the opportunity to degrade and dehumanise him. We gossip happily in the corridors. We need to talk about this openly. Who would like to ask questions?"

Mr Dumas, an older, South African resident of the church, stood up and said, "We would like to know the result from the doctor. What did the doctor say?"

Verryn responded, "The death certificate said that he died of bilateral pneumonia. The poison perforated his oesophagus and infected his lungs. Blood tests showed a high level of amino phosphate, a poison used on plants and on mice."

Verryn went on to talk about suicide and how none of us can hold ourselves above Evans' action. "Counsellors have said that sometimes a person gets so low that the only decision they have is to end their pain. If this was the decision that Evans made, we need to respect that. I have often got to the point where I didn't want to live anymore. My sister – she is dead now – but I remember my sister once asking me, 'Why aren't you talking?' I said, 'I'm not talking because I'm struggling to keep myself alive in my head.'"

Verryn said, "As a minister, I have failed. Evans was like a son to me. I ask myself, why couldn't he come to me and cough out his anger? I feel anger at his death. I feel guilt. I feel sorrow."

Both Elizabeth Cheza's and Evans Kuntonda's deaths were a big blow to the community at Central. I had been away when Elizabeth passed away over the holidays, as had many others, and I missed her memorial service. Weeks passed before I went back to the church and heard about her death so it was hard to absorb. Evans' death came just over two months later and, in contrast, for me it was much more immediate. Regardless of the circumstances, the community was still reeling from one death when it had been hit by another.

Jonathan Whittall wrote, "Whatever the specific reasons were for Evans to take his own life – the roots are all the same. Evans' untimely death was ultimately a consequence of the dire political situation in Zimbabwe that has forced so many to flee as a matter of survival. Evans was political and so, too, was his death. Evans carried not only his own heavy burden, but also the past and present burden of many of his countrymen who sought the quiet strength and direction that was his hallmark."

What happens to someone's Facebook page when they are no longer living? I let the friend request stay up for months. If I clicked on "Confirm" that would mean I would have access to his Facebook page, which didn't seem right now somehow. Finally, I clicked on "Not now". It didn't mean I didn't want to be Evans' friend. It meant I had to say goodbye.

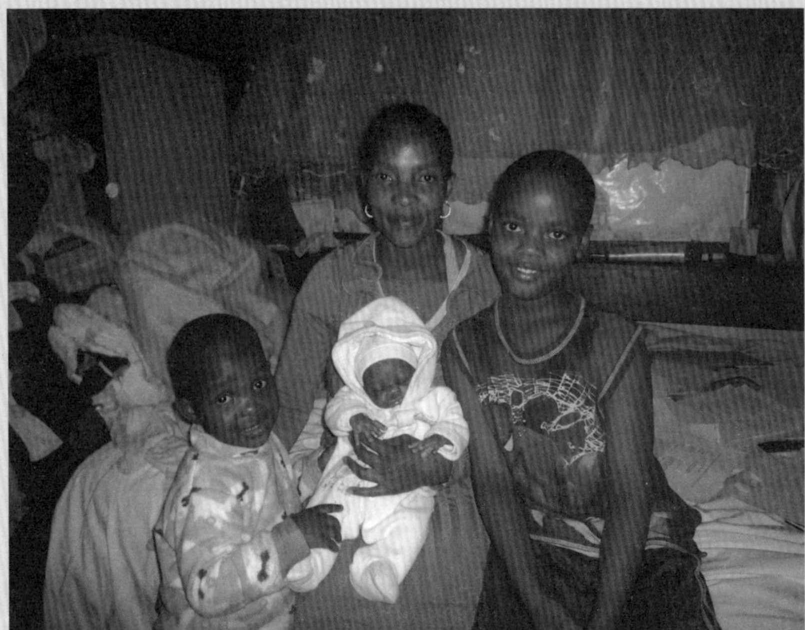

© Christa Kuljian

Cleo Buthelezi in her room at Central Methodist with her children. Mihlali is nine. Sandy is three and Mercy is a new-born, November 2011.

© Christa Kuljian

Women's Manyano celebrate Mercy's first birthday at the 10am service in the sanctuary, November 2012.

Meetings at Central Methodist / 2011

It was a Monday, and I had just finished an interview, so I decided to stop by Cleo's room. She was lying on her bed, clutching her pillow and looking distraught. "They are going to arrest me. The police will come and get me. I'm going to jail."

"What happened?" I asked.

And Cleo proceeded to tell me what had happened the day before – Sunday, 13 November 2011.

"It was about 1 o'clock. I was working in the Bishop's office," she said "when I got a call on my cell from Reverend Mahlakahlaka. She told me she was with a young woman with a baby in the foyer and they were looking for a shelter. 'How do you get to that shelter over on Albert Street?' she asked. I told her how to get there and thought that was the end of it. Then I walked downstairs with the Bishop and when we got to the foyer, Reverend Mahlakahlaka was still standing there. She told me, 'This is the woman I was talking about.' The Reverend told the woman, 'This is Cleo' and asked me to walk her over to the shelter that keeps mothers with babies. So I took her there and came back.

"About forty-five minutes later, that woman came back, and she was looking for me," Cleo went on. "She found me in my room and told me that the shelter was full for the night and that they told her to come back the next day for a referral. Then she asked for something to eat and I made her food. She told me she was from Mpumalanga and that she had come to Johannesburg several days ago. She gave birth the day before. Then she asked if she could wash so I made an arrangement for her to shower up on the fifth floor. I asked Takudzwa to take her up there and she left her baby with me.

"The baby was quiet so I didn't really mind her being with me. But then I realised it had been close to two hours. I called up to the fifth floor to find out where that woman was. They said, 'Oh, she left long ago.'

"I was shocked. That woman left the building and she left her baby with me. She didn't leave the baby with just anyone. She decided she could trust me and she left her baby with me."

Cleo was clearly very distressed. "They're going to put me in jail," she said again.

"Why do you think that?" I asked.

"Because if they find me with this baby, they're going to think I stole the baby. I'm going to have to go register this baby with the police," she said.

"Well, that's a good idea," I said. "You must register what happened with the police."

Then Cleo and I walked downstairs to where Sibongile, the head of FLOC, was caring for the baby. She was tiny, only two days old, and wrapped firmly in a blanket.

Over the next few days, Cleo took care of all the paperwork. She reported the abandoned baby to the police. She took the baby to the hospital to make sure she was in good health and that she got a yellow card for her immunisations.

Bishop Verryn thought it might be possible for someone from the church congregation to adopt the baby, but Cleo wasn't too keen on that. She had had a miscarriage in August and she thought that perhaps it was a sign from God that this baby had been left with her. She was giving serious consideration to keeping the baby herself.

A few months later, Cleo had made up her mind. She decided to keep the baby. She explained why. "I have to take care of her," she said, "so that if her mother ever comes back, she will find a healthy baby girl." Cleo gave the baby the Zulu name Samkelisiwe, meaning "a gift that you receive and accept". Her English name was Mercy.

Women's Manyano is the women's organisation within the Methodist Church that Lindi Myeza brought to Central Methodist many years earlier. When they heard that Cleo was going to keep the baby at Central they decided to offer their support. Every month they bought food, clothing and nappies for Cleo and Mercy.

It had been several months since I had last seen Elizabeth, the woman who used to stand in front of the church in the Smal Street Mall with her two children, selling small items. She pulled me aside one day and told me that she had lost a baby, a baby girl who had been stillborn. I felt terrible. I hadn't even realised that she had been pregnant. "There was a while when I couldn't afford to send her body back to Zimbabwe for burial," said Elizabeth. "The Bishop wanted to help but didn't have any money. Eventually, he helped me and we buried her."

As if that wasn't enough to cope with, Elizabeth faced another big problem. Her husband was physically abusing her. She asked if we could sit down and talk. She said, "I'll talk to you like a social worker." She told me that she went to Johannesburg Central Police Station and she found the office that dealt with domestic violence. "They helped me," she said, "and they've set a court date."

"Didn't they give you a hard time because you are a foreign national?" I asked.

"No, they were only concerned about the domestic abuse," she replied.

Some weeks later, after the court date had passed, I saw Elizabeth again. I asked her how it had gone.

"I didn't get there," she said. "But my husband has settled down now. Everything is OK."

The next time I saw Elizabeth, she wasn't standing in the Smal Street Mall. She was behind the palisade fence, one child on her back and the other holding onto her legs as usual. Elizabeth was reaching through the vertical metal bars of the fence, holding out multiple pairs of socks for sale, shaking them hopefully to the people passing by. "Three for R10," she offered.

"Why is everyone selling from behind the fence?" I asked her.

"The JMPD told us we have to stand here now," she replied. "We don't have any choice. They know we don't have documents, so they can tell us what they want."

It was humiliating – a row of people waving their hands through the bars. When I left the building that day, I felt like I was leaving Elizabeth in prison.

Over the couple of years that I had been getting to know the stories of some of the thousands of people who had passed through the doors of Central Methodist, I was struck again and again at the adversity and challenges they had to contend with, and how somehow they managed to pick themselves up and carry on.

Reymond Mapakata was certainly one of these people. As a result of his correspondence with the film maker Richard Adams in New York, Reymond had managed to land another film-related opportunity in September 2011. He worked for several days in Rosebank at the Tri-

Continents Film Festival, assisting the organisers with logistics. Afterwards, he made an arrangement to meet the director of the festival to explore other work opportunities. He didn't make it to the appointment because he was arrested – for the fifth time in four years.

At about 5:30pm, he had been walking with three friends to go to a shop to buy food. "We met with the police with a convoy of cars and a big truck," Reymond wrote in a statement after the incident. "They blocked our way and told us all to lay our hands on the truck. They searched us all over while they were pointing guns at us. I had a photocopy of my asylum seeker permit. One of them told me that it works in Zimbabwe, not in South Africa. Four of us were pushed into the truck because they said we were illegal migrants and were loitering. We did not have time to talk as they were pushing us into the truck and beating us with a baton stick. We spent four hours going around town while the truck was loading foreign nationals. People were loaded until it was overloaded. We were squashed in the truck. We could hardly breathe."

At about 7:30pm on 29 September I received a text message from Reymond. "I'm arrested," the message said. Then he sent me another one. "They asking for R300 bribe." I called him and he said that Bishop Verryn had sent a church staff member, Mafika Dlamini, to help him. Mafika took Reymond's original asylum permit to the station but it didn't help. I got another text message. "They are charging me with gambling now."

The next morning Reymond was taken to the Westgate courts. He sent me another text. "I'm out now. How is your day? I'm OK." I called him to find out what had happened. "I didn't have the bribe they wanted, so they kept me overnight," he said.

"And what about the charge of gambling?" I asked.

"That was just a strange thing at the police station," said Reymond. "After they saw my permit, they charged me with gambling because they wanted to lock me up."

~

On 12 November 2012 Mercy celebrated her first birthday at FLOC at Central Methodist with chocolate cake. The day before, a Sunday, she was warmly held high by the members of Women's Manyano during the 10am service for everyone to admire. She was whisked up to the pulpit where birthday presents and a cake were waiting for her, and the whole congregation sang. Cleo beamed from the sidelines, sitting with Mihlali, now ten years old, and her three and a half year old daughter Sandy.

Cleo often spoke about how proud she was of the young mother who had left Mercy at the church. "That girl could have killed that baby, but she didn't. She could have taken the baby to a dumping site and run away. But she didn't. She brought Mercy to me."

Twenty-eight

Sjamboks at Marabastad

"WE DON'T WANT YOU HERE. We want this area clear," said a man with a sjambok as he hit us on the legs. It was before dawn and still pitch dark outside the Marabastad Home Affairs office in Pretoria. The man walked on, giving the same treatment to others queuing in the veld, and leaving us with our jaws open. Incredulous, Reason Machengere from Solidarity Peace Trust turned to me and said, "We've just been beaten with a whip."

The motivation for our trip to Marabastad in August 2011 was to accompany Mr Yahaya Kassim to apply for an asylum permit. Since the Crown Mines refugee reception centre in Johannesburg had closed on 1 June that year, Zimbabweans in need of an asylum permit now had to travel to Marabastad in Pretoria. Reymond Mapakata had reported his bad experience at Marabastad to Peace Action and ever since then I had been interested in getting there myself. When the opportunity of going with Mr Kassim had presented itself, I was pleased to be able to travel to Pretoria with him and Reason and Ishmael Kauzani of the Zimbabwe Youth Wing.

Kassim had a letter from the Movement for Democratic Change in Zimbabwe and an affidavit setting out his circumstances. On 5 August, the *Daily News* from Zimbabwe reported that "Kassim, who is MDC-T youth chairperson for Ward 11 in Mbare… sustained severe facial burns after a group he identified as Zanu-PF youths trailed him to his friends' home in

Mbare." Now Kassim was staying at Central Methodist and being assisted with medical care and support by the Solidarity Peace Trust.

I took a picture of the crowds waiting to gain access to the office before there was any light. The flash attracted three sjambok-wielding men. "Why are you here? Are you with the media? Why are you hiding yourselves?" they demanded.

"We aren't hiding ourselves," said Reason. "I am from a human rights organisation. I've come to assist this man – Yahaya Kassim. What queue should he be in?"

One of the men whisked Kassim away, hoping perhaps that if he got him in the queue, we would be happy and leave. Another of the men with a sjambok said, "Three of you came here for one guy to get his papers? I suspect you. This sounds very suspicious to me."

"Are you all working for Home Affairs?" I asked.

"No, we work for the police," said one man with a black leather jacket and a sjambok.

"Why don't they give you uniforms?" I asked.

"Because we are fighting crime here. There is too much theft and you can't fight crime in uniform," he said.

"Why do you need a sjambok?" I asked.

"Because these people don't listen," he said. "Home Affairs only wants to see one thousand people each day. We put people in queues of fifty each and line them up near the road [DF Malan Drive]."

The remaining people were in two long winding queues of about another 1 000 people further back from the road, one for men and one for women. All of them were applying for or renewing asylum permits, which meant that for economic or political reasons they had been forced to leave Zimabwe. For various reasons, these people were not in a position to apply for a study, work or business permit under the Zimbabwe Documentation Project (ZDP), the process which Home Affairs began in 2009 to make sure that all Zimbabweans in South Africa had proper documentation.

I counted over 50 babies in the women's queue alone. I spoke to one woman who told me she had got there at 5am that morning. "I don't have much hope of getting inside today," she said. A man named Memory told me that people spend the night at Marabastad, burning tyres and cardboard to keep warm in the bitter cold, because they know that is their only chance to make it into the right queue and into the building. "It's the worst at 2:30 or 3am," he said. "These guys use their sjamboks to wake us up. Then they start collecting bribes and putting people who can pay into the first queue."

At the end of the queue was a tout managing the process without a sjambok. Speaking in Shona, Reason told her that he wanted to help someone get an asylum paper and asked if she could help him get to the front of the queue. She offered to put him up front for R150 – R75 for her and R75 for a police officer to facilitate. Reason said he would come back to her. She gave him her name and phone number.

It was 6:20am and the sun was rising behind the Pretoria skyline. Marabastad was only a few blocks from downtown Pretoria. Later, when the sun was up, you could see the Union Buildings in the distance. Some of the group of 1 000 at the front were being led across DF Malan Drive. They were not walking across the street. They were running. The men with sjamboks had told them to run. The thwack, thwack of the sjambok against legs and buttocks turned my attention to the back of the queue where a man was hitting people, seemingly for no reason.

There was a police van parked outside the Home Affairs office on the corner of DF Malan Drive and Struben Street. We walked past it as we watched the people running across the street. They continued to run along the perimeter fence of the Home Affairs property. Women with babies on their backs were running. Young men and old men were running. Instead of foreign nationals applying for papers from Home Affairs, they looked as if they were in military training at an army camp.

They were the lucky ones, we discovered. They were inside the gate and on the premises of Home Affairs. Hundreds of others would wait outside in the veld for another day or more. Inside the gates, there was continued commotion. The thwack of the sjambok sounded again and again. People ran from one side of the yard to the other. By then it was close to 7am. Except for the one police van parked on the corner, we hadn't seen anyone involved who was in uniform and clearly and officially from Home Affairs or the SAPS. My guess was this was so that both institutions would be able to deny they had anything to do with this harsh treatment.

We waited in the veld across the street from the front gate, observing what was going on. A man in green overalls and a dark blue beanie, carrying a sjambok, counted a pile of notes. He handed some of the money to a woman at the front gate, who was wearing a blue Best Secure Security jersey. The sign next to the front gate read: "Together, building a caring, compassionate and responsive Home Affairs."

After 8am, not knowing exactly where Yahaya Kassim was, Reason called him. Kassim said he was with the group that was sitting on the pavement inside the Home Affairs yard. Hoping that he would make progress, we went into downtown Pretoria to buy breakfast.

In April 2009 the Department of Home Affairs had implemented special dispensation for Zimbabwean nationals. They had halted deportations and allowed Zimbabweans to remain in South Africa without documentation for a period of six to nine months. Then, in September 2010, Cabinet announced that the special dispensation would soon end. The setting up of the ZDP sought to relieve pressure on the Asylum Seeker Management system, but the data that Home Affairs had at that time was not very reliable. According to the department's estimates, there were approximately 1.5 million Zimbabweans in the country.

Jacob Mamabolo, the head of the ZDP, announced that by the deadline of 31 December 2010, Home Affairs had registered a total of 275 762 applications, which suggested that many Zimbabweans had not applied for work or study permits, and continued to rely on the asylum seeker process. As a result of the backlog at Home Affairs in processing the applications, taking fingerprints and gathering supporting documents, Home Affairs extended the moratorium on deportations until 31 July 2011.

Freedom Chivima had applied at the Harrison Street Home Affairs office for a work permit in December 2010 but more than six months had gone by and he hadn't yet received a text message on his cellphone to say that this had been granted to him. In the meantime, he had to keep renewing his asylum permit so that he wouldn't get in trouble with the police. Freedom's friend Shephard Zikuyumo did receive a text from Home Affairs so he went back to follow up, but the queues were incredibly long. "Can you imagine?" he said. "I spent two nights on the street, just to put my finger in the ink."

There was a high level of tension at Central Methodist and Peace Action about what would happen after the 31 July 2011 deadline. Some people thought that the police were dusting off the police vans and that Home Affairs was getting ready for mass deportations to Lindela Repatriation Centre. It turned out that August was a grace period for Zimbabweans to regularise their documents. This made sense because of the logistical delay at Home Affairs, and the department said it would make an announcement when the grace period was over. Many people remained on edge, wondering when the knife would fall. Before the special dispensation, Home Affairs had deported an estimated 15 000 undocumented Zimbabweans each month from the holding facility outside Musina in Limpopo.

The Gauteng SAPS spent R350 million a year on immigration policing, a costly and ineffective management of migration. I wondered whether Home Affairs had considered recording every foreign national entering and departing South Africa and allowing them to reside in South Africa for a specific period. That way, police and government departments would be in a better position jointly to plot out a strategy for managing migration, or at least to formulate a plan based on accurate data.

When we got back to the Marabastad Home Affairs office just after ten that morning, there were still hundreds of people waiting in the veld along DF Malan Drive. We walked along Struben Street and over to the area where Kassim was sitting. By now the sun was high and it was hot. Reason tried to pass a banana, naartjie, two donuts and a drink to Kassim through the fence. The security guard nearby said, "No, you can't give him anything."

"Why not?" asked Reason.

"They aren't allowed food," said the guard.

"But they aren't prisoners," said Reason.

About 20 minutes later, security guards told Yahaya Kassim and his group of about 200 people that they would have to leave the premises. They would not be seen that day. They would have to come back tomorrow. One woman with two small children tried to negotiate with the guards. I couldn't hear what she was saying but the tone of her voice and the look on her face showed that she was about to cry, desperate not to be turned away. A man showed the guards his prosthetic leg, but they didn't budge. "Go," they said, pointing to the gate. "Go."

Reason and Ishmael talked through the fence, trying to understand. "Why are you telling everyone to leave?" Reason asked.

"We are understaffed," said one female guard.

Not able to speak much English, Kassim had survived multiple traumas – first being burnt on the face, then spending ten days in hospital, and having to leave his wife and two children behind in Zimbabwe. Now he was having to negotiate South Africa's Home Affairs' bewildering logic.

Reason decided he was going to try to speak to the manager of Marabastad Home Affairs. He went to the front gate and I went with him. We were stopped by a guard at the gate and another man, in a brown Home Affairs shirt, called to the man from behind us, "They are prohibited. Those two are prohibited."

We moved away but Reason tried to continue the conversation through the fence. Whether it was Reason's attempts to be rational and speak about the work of his organisation and Kassim's plight, or whether it was my presence as the only white face around, two guards engaged with the conversation – the man in the brown Home Affairs shirt and the woman who had said they were understaffed. "We are from a human rights organisation," Reason told them. "We are helping this man with medical care. We brought him here and he needs assistance." Eventually, they let Kassim back onto the premises at about 11:15am. As I walked away from the gate, I was pleased that Kassim had been allowed another chance that day, but I thought about all the thousands of others who didn't have an advocate, who were treated without respect.

Three hours later, Reason called Kassim to find out about his progress. He was going to have an interview, he reported. An hour after that, at 3:30pm, the electricity went out in the building and he was told to come back the next day to finish the process. After close to ten hours, Kassim still did not have his asylum paper. He did have hope, however, that it would be issued the next day.

After going back to Marabastad for another long and difficult day, Kassim received an asylum document, but he was told he would have to renew it after a month. Memory, the man who had slept overnight in the veld, wasn't so hopeful. Without someone arguing his case, and with no money to pay a bribe, he had been sliding to the back of the queue for more than a week. "Please help us," he said to me. "Please tell people what is happening at this place."

Twenty-nine

The Axe and the Tree

THERESA CHIRIPITI, WHO LOOKS TO BE in her fifties, is sitting in a circle of people telling them her story. She wears a light blue, long-sleeved dress and a black knitted cap. She speaks with confidence and broad gestures with her arms. Her words, spoken in Shona, are translated with sub-titles on the screen: "They closed the door," she says. "The ones who held me were juveniles. One of them said, 'Why don't you beat her?' Then another answered, 'No. Just rape her and leave her.'" Chiripiti begins a high-pitched weeping as she tells the story and she lowers her arms and her face to the camera. She covers her face with her hand and says, "Someone says, 'She is too old to be raped and tortured and held hostage by children like you.'" Through her tears, she says, "After that… I started having problems… with my health," catching her breath with sobs after each few words. "I don't know if I got sick because of the many boys that raped me," she says, and then she breaks down completely.

We watched Theresa Chiripiti tell her story on a large white screen at the front of the sanctuary. She was in a documentary film called *The Axe and the Tree*. It was late morning on a week day and the sanctuary was filled with residents of the church and visitors and children from the Albert Street School. Reverend Paul Verryn had chastised the children earlier for fidgeting and giggling, but after this *gogo* had told her story and wept, there was silence in the hall.

The documentary had been made in late 2010 and it was about the impact of the electoral violence in Zimbabwe in 2008. The film followed the work of the Tree of Life, a local NGO that conducted community healing workshops in Zimbabwe. It followed the stories of four individuals from Harare who had survived beatings, torture and rape.

Howard Varney, from the International Centre for Transitional Justice, explained. "We decided to make this film to bring home to audiences around the world the stories of Zimbabwean victims of torture and organised violence. The voices of Zimbabweans have been drowned out by incessant state propaganda. We are of the view that more can be done to hold the state to account. The stories in this film speak of unimaginable horrors, torture, targeted murders and rape as a weapon of war. We hope that by the world hearing these stories Zimbabwe will be held to the benchmarks that the Southern African Development Committee has called upon Zimbabwe to adhere to."

The film's title was taken from a Shona proverb that says "the axe may not remember, but the tree that has been chopped will never forget".

Many of the residents at Central Methodist Mission were living with traumatic memories. One day in May 2011, a few days before I saw the film, I was chatting to Cleo again outside her room on the first floor. A tall, well-built man in his early thirties came up to us and waited for us to finish talking. I thought he wanted to speak to Cleo, but in fact he asked to speak to me. He said that Priscilla Manyere and Takudzwa Chikoro had told him that I was working on a book and he wanted to tell me his story. He turned around, lifted up his shirt and showed us his back. His skin looked as if it had melted, with ridges and welts across the width and length of his back. He told us that he couldn't reach down to tie his shoes. "Once I lie down," he said, "I can't get back up on my own."

It turned out this man, whose name was Thomas Kanuwera, had met Reason Machengere and Father Mike at Solidarity Peace Trust and they had offered him medical care and psycho-social counselling. He was on their list of political refugees. SPT had arranged a safe house for Thomas in Kimberley where he could recover without anxiety, but he came back to Johannesburg for medical care, and because he was lonely. Now he was living in the SPT room on the ground floor of Central.

I arranged to meet Thomas the next day in the foyer. With difficulty, he sat down on a red plastic chair and he told me his story.

Over a year before, in April 2010, Thomas met a friend of his, Bana[6], at a shopping centre in Harare. Thomas had travelled with Bana in the past and knew him through work. They started a conversation about politics and Thomas said something to the effect of "I'd rather vote for a baboon instead of Mugabe". Thomas could see that Bana was irritated by this statement but they stopped the conversation, parted ways, and he didn't think much more about it.

Later in 2010 Thomas found a job as a driver in Brits, near Pretoria. On 29 August, while Thomas was sleeping, someone knocked on his door. Thomas got up to open it and was pulled outside by a group of people. He believed that Bana was amongst them. They poured diesel all over his back. "I could see them using burning paper to set me alight," he said. "I can remember thinking, I'm burning. I'm burning. Then I couldn't feel anything.

"A white man named Chris from next door comes to switch off the fire," Thomas continued. "He calls the ambulance and I go to the Brits hospital and then I am transferred to Klerksdorp. When I gain consciousness, I ask the nursing sister, 'What time is it?' and she answers me. Then I ask her, 'What time did I come here?' She runs out of the room and comes back with other nursing sisters. They look at me as if I am crazy. I think I have been there for a day. They tell me I have been unconscious for a month and a half.

"At first I can't eat. I keep smelling diesel.

"The police come. They ask me if I know who did this to me. Then they catch Bana. But they say he is out on bail. I am afraid to go to Brits to get my things because I think he might find me. I wonder, How is a foreigner given bail without bribing the police?

"Then, still in the hospital, I get a call from the investigating officer in Brits saying that Bana is dead. The policeman says, 'He's dead so there is no case anymore. The case is closed.'

"I spent six months in hospital. I left in February 2011. My wife and my son and my mother are back in Zimbabwe. They haven't been able to visit me because they don't have the money. I want to get working again so that I can go to them or send them money to come to me."

A few days later, I saw Thomas again in the foyer at Central. As he walked in the front door, he looked stronger than he had done the week before. We greeted each other and shook hands. He showed me that he could bend over

6 not his real name

and demonstrated by picking up a small plastic packet from the floor. "Soon I'll be able to tie my shoes," he said with a smile.

At Friday night refugee meetings, Reverend Verryn often spoke about the impact of trauma. During a sermon in January 2011, he told a story about how it was possible to be imprisoned by a traumatic memory. "Some time ago now, when the TRC was still operating, the Commission went into the Vaal area and when they went there, the hopes of all the people in Sebokeng, Sharpeville, Boipatong, all those townships, were raised high. Here was a chance for them to speak out about things they had kept secret and quiet for a long time. Unfortunately, the Commission could only be there for a week and the tension and the mood of those townships was a deep concern. I had been involved in counselling political detainees and ex-political prisoners for quite some time through the 1980s and into the 1990s and so we were asked to go into the Vaal and see what we could do to help those who hadn't gone to the Commission at least to start talking. Three of us went… and what amazed me was that people would come to our group – this was in the 1990s and we worked for about ten years there – and people would come with a memory that went back forty years. And that traumatic memory had really imprisoned them, if you can understand. What would happen is that the person would come and speak. Let me give you an illustration of a woman who came. She was an old woman – and she said, 'It was the 21st March in the early '60s. We had had trouble brewing in Sharpeville. I said goodbye to my husband on his way to work and I can remember being scared for his life. What was going to happen on this day?' That was all she said. She sang her hymn. And she started to weep – as if she was going to get sick. And the group heard her. And we reflected on what she had said so she knew we could hear her. She had never spoken about that day. And eventually she found her husband in the police mortuary. But she only had the strength to tell us that after three or four weeks. Now the reason I tell you that story today is because… she was paralysed by her pain. She was paralysed by the evil that had come into her life. She couldn't move without this pain being there and she came to breathe again, to let it go."

After the screening of *The Axe and the Tree*, there was a panel discussion about the situation in Zimbabwe. The discussion was about the recurring violence in Zimbabwe and how it was not acceptable that violence recurred year after year and how SADC had not taken any action. SADC should not tolerate a repeat of 2008 was the consensus. Gabriel Shumba from the Zimbabwe Exiles Forum was on the panel. He said, "I see people in this audience who have suffered."

SADC had held a summit in Livingstone, Zambia in March 2011. President Zuma from South Africa was there, as were Robert Mugabe and Morgan Tsvangirai. The summit noted with grave concern that there had been a resurgence of violence, arrests and intimidation in Zimbabwe, which was a violation of the Global Political Agreement of September 2008. It resolved that there must be an end to the violence, hate speech, and harassment. It also insisted on the need for guidelines for a future election that would be "peaceful, free and fair". Another SADC meeting was held in Johannesburg on 11 June. Many people expressed concern that SADC did not take the resolutions further. The communiqué did not convert to action, despite the ongoing violence.

In late June, Thomas walked into Central Methodist wearing a white cricket hat and a green football blazer. He looked concerned. "My back is itching," he said. He told me that he had gone with the MDC to speak to some journalists and to the SABC and that he was not sure that he'd done the right thing. "It's like when a child is hungry. You can take a bun off the floor and the child won't turn it away because he's hungry. Do you understand? They offered me help."

Thomas needed healing, physically and psychologically. He needed work so that he could reunite with his family. Theresa Chiripiti in *The Axe and the Tree* needed healing and medical care. As the film eloquently portrayed, the axe and the tree would both have to engage in charting the course for Zimbabwe's future.

Thirty

Some Healing and Some Nuptials

THE WEDNESDAY EVENING SERVICE at Central Methodist was a special one, a healing service. Cleo Buthelezi had been preparing communion for this service since 2007. On 8 June 2011, I joined her. My job was to pour Ama-Zing red grape nectar into small shot glasses. There were three trays of these, with a set of 50 communion cups on each tray. While I did that, Cleo cut pieces of white bread into small squares. "I usually use wafers from the Methodist bookstore but the Bishop owes them money so they won't give me a new supply," she said.

At 6:45pm, there were already about 50 people in the sanctuary waiting for the service to start. Cleo had a quick conversation with a group of ten guys wanting work with a farmer in Cape Town. I found a seat and greeted Priscilla Manyere, Reymond Mapakata and Thomas Kanuwera. As usual, small children played on the steps to the dais and the prayer rail. One little girl who was climbing the stairs was about three years old. It was a cool evening so she was wearing brown track suit pants, a striped jersey and a beanie. Over all of this, she also had on a pink frilly dress. Not far from her, a four year old was carrying a ten-month-old baby around the pews, putting the baby in one person's lap, then another's.

Singing started at 6:55pm. The Bishop walked in just after seven o'clock.

He called people to come forward for a healing prayer, "either for yourself or for someone else who is ill." Scores of people walked up front and knelt at the prayer rail with their heads bowed. The Bishop put his hands on each one's head, one by one, and said. "May you be blessed by healing and peace." Two people close to me were battling with cancer at the time so I went up to the prayer rail as well.

By 7:30pm, the sanctuary was packed. There were more people there than I had ever seen at a Friday night refugee meeting. It seemed that prayer brought in more people than discussion and announcements.

Two months later, some members of the congregation who attended the Sunday 10am service at Central Methodist paid a visit to a Friday night refugee meeting. One of them, a woman sporting a green Springbok jersey, addressed the residents. "Please join us at our service on Sunday," she invited them. "Some of your faces are familiar but some of you we don't know. Our only agenda item tonight is the state of the church building. All of us, regardless of race or colour or social standing, we want to be a common community. Our main goal is the cleanliness of the building. One day in April, as I'm sure you all know, we all came to scrub the church. Cleanliness is next to godliness. But since then, we don't know how to find each other. If we fix something, it breaks. Most of the good work here has gone down the drain."

Loyce Chitongo, a resident of the building, stood up and responded. "Thank you for your presence here tonight. We call this place our home. Some people bring in litter and then don't clean up after themselves. It is a problem." Blessing Derera stood up next. "We know that in every family there is a stubborn child," she said. "In this house, there are stubborn people. I cannot stay in a dirty place because of a stubborn person next to me. We need resources for cleaning in this place."

Verryn broke in. "We have a collection every weekend to try to assist to pay cleaners and security," he said, "but it's woefully inadequate."

The woman in the green Springbok jersey from the 10am service said, "From now on we are not blaming each other. There are no more Zimbabweans. No more South Africans. We must help the Bishop. Let's bring together a committee that will work together. The 10 o'clock service is not against the people from Zimbabwe." She paused and then said, "We don't want to keep you. We have come far from our homes. Thank you. Good night." As the group left, the residents clapped.

The meeting continued. Tonight it was the turn of the vendors who sold food at the church to be chastised by Verryn. "You didn't clean this morning," he said crossly. "I came in and the foyer was filthy."

I watched a little boy with a small pink back-pack pull himself up the railing along the three steps up to the dais at the front, then sit down and slide back down the three steps, bump, bump, bump, on his bottom. Then he pulled himself back up along the railing. Then he slid back down.

Austin Moyo, a resident who was an electrician by trade, was talking and I turned my attention back to the meeting. Austin had been asked to investigate what was needed to make sure that the wiring in the building was in order. He didn't have good news. "At the end of the day, you are going to die," he said frankly. "You are going to burn. There are too many illegal connections. In the vestry, there are nineteen families relying on nine plugs. There's a problem of circuit breakers. People on the first floor and the second floor won't get to the exit if this building is being gutted by fire. People will jump out the windows onto Pritchard Street. The illegal connections won't be solved unless there is a new board in the vestry."

"Austin is right," said Verryn. "Thank you, Austin. We must do that."

Just over a week later, on 28 August 2011, a special event took place at the 10am Sunday service. Reverend Verryn asked the congregants to stay on after the sermon. "We will have a wedding this morning," said Verryn from the pulpit. "It's the first time we've ever had a wedding during this service – certainly since I've been here. I ask you as we move into the wedding ceremony, please don't go. It shouldn't take long. Please celebrate for the bride and groom." There was ululating from outside the doors of the sanctuary. Festive Burundian music started up. The doors opened and in walked four couples dressed for a party. The men wore black suits with red ties and the women wore red dresses and silver shoes. They were taking their roles very seriously. Their expressions of concentration and their ponderous progress up the aisle contrasted with the festive music and the excitement in the room. Everyone's eyes were on them as they moved forward to the front of the sanctuary.

Then the doors opened again and in walked the bride and groom, none other than Leothere Nininahazwe and Monica Chiwetu. Dressed in a cream-white, three-piece suit, Leothere looked like the cat that had swallowed the canary. This was the day he had been waiting for. Monica's eyes stayed on the floor all the way, a typical blushing bride. They held hands tightly and walked up to the pulpit as the crowd clapped and cheered.

After the formal ceremony, the couple held a reception at the old

Devonshire Hotel in Braamfontein, now called the Orion. Cleo Buthelezi and Brian Muziringa were sitting at the table next to the one where my husband and I were seated, and at our own table were Peliwe Lolwana and her daughter Kungeka from the 10am Sunday service.

The master of ceremonies, one of the leaders of the French service, said, "This couple – both of them have lost their parents. He arrived at the French service on the corner of Pritchard and Smal streets. She came from Harare to the same address. She was speaking Shona. He was speaking French. But we celebrate."

Congolese music began playing and then five young women, each wearing very tight white pants, started to dance. Each one of them had a pelvis that could swivel like an oiled ball bearing. They pounded their bare feet on the floor and shook their hips. Everyone in the room was smiling, completely riveted, watching every move with fascination and delight. The drum beat of the music kept them dancing without stopping for half an hour.

Behind the dancers was the head table, decorated with a white tablecloth and red serviettes. The bride and groom sat there, straight and regal. Reverend Verryn was seated at the end, watching the dancers with a wry smile. When the MC asked him to come to the front, Verryn took the microphone and said, "Good afternoon, ladies and gentlemen. Today is really a wonderful and spectacular day because it brings together the north and the south of Africa. It actually shows that it can work. The celebration of Burundi and Zimbabwe. For me, that's a wonderful miracle because it goes through all the boundaries that we can put up in our brains. It shows that love is far more powerful than you really think." Pushing his right fist forward with emphasis on the last word of each sentence, Verryn said, "More powerful than a government. More powerful than a boundary. More powerful than a culture. So we want to congratulate you because in some way, a little bit of the dream of what the future of Africa could be, is present today."

There was ululating from the guests and we all clapped. Everyone beamed, and looked over at the bride and groom, who sat together proudly, smiling around the room.

"The last thing I want to say is that there's a beautiful thing that has happened here today," said Verryn. "There's a way in which all the preaching and all the negotiations that one can do has been achieved because communities have cared for one another. It is an amazing thing how the whole community at Central is in some way present here today. I really hope and pray that in some way your marriage enables people to unlock the doors of care so that we recognise that our ability to love one another is far more powerful than war, far more powerful than mistrust, far more powerful than xenophobia. You've really given us a great gift today. May God bless you richly."

Thirty-one

Friday Night Refugee Meetings

On a warm March evening in 2012, the entrance to the five-storey Central Methodist Church building was crowded with people buying supper. Women sat behind low tables – selling chicken and spinach, *pap* and gravy, sweets, oranges, snacks and coffee. I had attended close to 30 Friday night meetings over the past two years, and the foyer on a Friday night still felt to me like a busy train station. The number of people sleeping at the church at night had fallen to about 800, which was a big change from its peak at 3 000 in 2009. The neighbours still weren't thrilled but at least no one was sleeping outside anymore. During the day the place blended in with the rest of the Smal Street Mall. As music blared from a nearby clothing shop, entrepreneurs sold their wares on the corner, and people sat having their hair braided along the palisade fence that still cut off the entrance to the church.

Inside, Cleo Buthelezi unlocked the doors to the sanctuary and handed out the minutes as people walked in. I saw Esther Thomas, the woman who sold small items on Von Brandis Street, at the front so I went and sat next to her. She showed me her work permit. With the help of Lawyers for Human Rights, after she had applied in early 2011, she had finally received the permit in January 2012. It would be valid through 2015. "Now that I have my permit, I want to go home," said Esther. "I haven't been home for three years, since 2009. It's a long time to be away. My children tell me, 'Come home. Don't worry about the money. We'll work something out.'"

Reverend Verryn walked into the sanctuary. By this time, he had attended over 250 Friday night meetings since they had officially begun six years earlier in March 2006. He opened the meeting and then, as usual, people took turns to go down to the front and give their individual reports: the Albert Street School, adult basic education, FLOC, hotel and catering training, and Home Based Care.

Alois Mutenanhene, the man who had fled from the George Goch hostel during the xenophobia attacks, and still taught sewing at Central Methodist, reported on the classes. "We have twenty-three people who are learning to sew," he said. "People who are not working, come to us and equip yourselves with skills." Reverend Verryn motioned to Alois that he had something to say. "The Roberts Room burglar gates have been fixed," he told the meeting, "so the sewing will move down there from the fourth floor. It will be more secure." He wasn't finished. "Alois is right," he added. "I'm not prepared to tolerate people who don't work to build their skills. Dependency is worse than a prison. There are no bars, no chains, but it completely disempowers you."

I sat there thinking about how controversial Central Methodist had become at the peak of the crisis, and how things might have been different if there had been different leadership at the helm. Central Methodist became a visible reminder of so many of the challenges facing Johannesburg and South Africa – poverty, migration, xenophobia, policing, inner-city housing and shelter, the vulnerable position of women and children, and the gap between rich and poor.

Central Methodist made visible the crisis in Zimbabwe. It made visible the fact that Johannesburg is a city of migrants, many of whom live in shocking conditions. Central Methodist and the entire High Court district made visible the clash between the vision of a World Class City and the reality of many people's lives. There was a conflict between the desire for a World Class precinct and the church as a refuge for people with no resources. South Africa's high Gini coefficient was on display right there on the corner of Pritchard and Smal streets.

Back at the Friday night refugee meeting, Verryn was making an announcement. "Takudzwa has moved out of the building. Is there anyone who can take over for dance and drama, and chess and darts?" There were no volunteers tonight. The energetic Takudzwa, I thought, would be missed.

Reymond Mapakata stood up next to give feedback from a workshop that fourteen residents of the church had attended that week about conflict resolution. The day before, I had met Reymond's younger brother Phillip, who had recently arrived in Johannesburg. Their village in Zimbabwe had had no rain, he told me, and he was hoping to find work. Phillip Mapakata had been deported once already and this was his second attempt to come back in to South Africa. Although I hadn't seen anything about it in the papers, it turned out that he was one of thousands who had been deported in recent months.

A little over a week after Reymond's last arrest in September 2011, the Department of Home Affairs had quietly lifted their moratorium on deportations of undocumented Zimbabweans. Chief Director of Home Affairs Jack Monedi had assured the ZDP stakeholders that deportations would not resume until the Home Affairs Minister, Nkosazana Dlamini-Zuma, had pronounced the end of the special dispensation. In early October indications were that deportations were about to begin again.

The senior immigration official based at the border town of Beitbridge in Zimbabwe said that South Africa's Home Affairs Department had notified him of plans to resume deportations "with immediate effect". The Chief of Mission for the International Organisation for Migration (IOM) in Zimbabwe said that he had received a similar notice. "All we know for now is that immigration authorities from both countries (South Africa and Zimbabwe) have met to discuss the modalities under which forced removals may resume." A third indication was that the police received an internal directive from the Home Affairs Director General on 27 September instructing the SAPS, the SA Defence Force and Home Affairs to start deporting undocumented Zimbabwean nationals. The directive stated that deportations should only be done after verifying that the person about to be deported had not applied for asylum or any other permit. Unfortunately, it appeared that many officials weren't bothering to verify.

Other than the internal directive, there was no official, public announcement that deportations were about to begin again.

"We've worked very hard to get Zimbabweans to trust the NGOs and work with Home Affairs," said Selvan Chetty of the Solidarity Peace Trust. "If they're not being open and transparent with us then how do they expect us to engage in an open and transparent way?"

According to the *Limpopo Mirror*, the first batch of 261 deportees, mostly men, arrived at Beitbridge in four buses on Wednesday, 19 October and the second group of 370 arrived the next day, escorted by South African Home Affairs officials.

Between October 2011 and March 2012, nearly 15 000 Zimbabweans were deported from South Africa through the Beitbridge border post. On arrival in Zimbabwe, the returnees were received by the authorities at the International Organisation for Migration (IOM) who checked to determine that they were *bona fide* Zimbabweans. The *Limpopo Mirror* reported that the IOM offered the deportees overnight accommodation, medication, food and transport. The IOM said that they had assisted close to 13 000 returnees, about 11 000 of whom were males and 2 000 females. IOM officials said that a large number of the deportees had already returned to South Africa, however, using illegal entry points along the border or bribing their way through immigration controls.

In February 2012 Lawyers for Human Rights put out a statement expressing concern about unlawful arrests and hasty deportations in which neither the police nor immigration officials were verifying the person's legal status before deporting them. Some of the deportees were people who had been living in South Africa for quite some time. Clemence Uzizo was one example and he had a story. He was a 21-year-old welder who lived in Soweto. Clemence had come to South Africa from Zimbabwe with his father in 1992 when he was a year old. He was arrested in November 2011 at a local shop. He didn't have his asylum seeker permit with him and wasn't allowed to go home to get it, so he was deported to a country in which he knew no one. It is likely, however, that many of the deportees were first-time arrivals in South Africa, like Phillip Mapakata. Regardless, it is important to ask why so many people, estimated at 15 000, were still coming over the border in late 2011 and early 2012 if all was well in Zimbabwe. The answer was clear: all was not well in Zimbabwe.

Plans for the next elections in Zimbabwe were still contentious. Robert Mugabe was demanding that elections be held in 2012, but in March that year Morgan Tsvangirai, the leader of the MDC, made a speech stating that conditions were not yet ready for elections. He stated that the GPA had agreed to the necessary conditions, including a new constitution, as well as many other electoral and media reforms. Tsvangirai called on the SADC facilitation team to unlock some of the logjams and ensure that the GPA abided by its agreements. He said, "Zimbabweans want a peaceful election and not a war… The lesson of 2008 is that Zimbabwe cannot afford anything other than a credible poll."

Reverend Paul Verryn agreed that conditions for elections in 2012 were not yet in place. "I find it inconceivable," he said, "that an election is being planned. If we are looking at elections, we should strive for all opposition parties to voice their point of view. Otherwise, let's avoid elections and let dictatorship stay in place."

Mugabe did not appear to show any concern about holding onto power in the 32nd year of his presidency. When he celebrated his 88th birthday on 21 February 2012, he compared himself to Christ. "I have died many times. That's where I have beaten Christ. Christ died once and (was) resurrected once. I have died and resurrected and I don't know how many times I will die and resurrect."

Back at the Friday night refugee meeting on 23 March 2012, Verryn was thinking about the trauma from the 2008 elections. He looked out at the audience of 250 people and said, "Last night we had another meeting of the Site of Memory. It's an opportunity to talk through past pain… to sit and talk and heal." He encouraged people to attend the next Site of Memory meeting, which would be held in the Roberts Room.

Then he told the residents that Lawyers for Human Rights were working on making a case for people who had suffered human rights violations since 2008, around the elections in Zimbabwe. If anyone staying at the church felt that this applied to them and wanted to be part of the process, they should go and see him. "Gabriel Shumba, from the Zimbabwe Exiles Forum, is appearing before the High Court in Pretoria," Verryn said. "The South African Police Service and the South African government are refusing to litigate against those in Zimbabwe who have been responsible for the violence. LHR is going to argue that they must."

Verryn was referring to the long-standing case that had been submitted to the National Prosecuting Authority in March 2008 by the Zimbabwe Exiles Forum and the Southern Africa Litigation Centre (SALC). At the time, their submission described state-sanctioned abuse and torture in Zimbabwe in the wake of the police raid conducted on the MDC headquarters in March 2007 during which over 100 people had been arrested. The motivation for submitting the docket came from the fact that, since 2002, South Africa had been a signatory to the Rome Statute of the International Criminal Court, which obliges South Africa to bring perpetrators of crimes against humanity to justice, especially if "that person, after the commission of the crime, is present in the territory of the Republic [of South Africa]". Several of the perpetrators in this case travelled to South Africa on official and personal business on a regular basis.

Fourteen months after the submission, in June 2009, the NPA told SALC that they, along with the South African Police Service, would not initiate an investigation of high level Zimbawean officials accused of crimes against humanity. The SALC and the Zimbabwe Exiles Forum then instituted legal proceedings, calling for a judicial review of the NPA and SAPS's decision not to investigate. Twenty-six months later, the case was set to come before the North Gauteng High Court in Pretoria on Monday, 26 March 2012.

In an extraordinary twist, Anton Ackermann, the head of the Priority Crimes Litigation Unit (PCLU), the division of the NPA that was dealing with this case, submitted an affidavit to the court stating that as early as July 2008 he had recommended an investigation but that his recommendation had been overruled by the police and others within the NPA.

In effect, in the wake of Zimbabwe's failed elections in 2008, the National Prosecuting Authority and the South African Police Service were providing refuge to high level criminals from Zimbabwe. South African negotiators within SADC had not put enough pressure on Mugabe to cease state-sponsored violence and create conditions for a free and fair election. At the same time, South African Home Affairs and SAPS were deporting thousands of people back to Zimbabwe, the same people who had tried to flee the deplorable political and economic situation in their country. Provincial and municipal government had not stepped forward to provide a solution to the challenge of finding accommodation for the several thousand Zimbabweans who had taken refuge at Central Methodist in 2008 and 2009. Instead, these people had been continually arrested by the same police service that was protecting the criminal officials.

As if this was not enough, the United Nations was added to the list of institutions that had not taken action on Zimbabwe. In the first week of March 2012, Stephen Lewis, the co-director for the international advocacy group AIDS-Free World, spoke before the UN Human Rights Council and questioned what hold Mugabe had over the UN because Zimbabwe had been left off a list of countries that had committed serious offences of sexual violence during elections. Lewis said, "I really can't understand why this is. But mostly I think it is because of South Africa and because of Thabo Mbeki and Jacob Zuma and their refusal to move in and stop Mugabe." Lewis warned that unless the international community intervened, it was undoubtedly going to happen again.

One has to wonder why the South African government appeared to take actions that made life so difficult for itself. As Gabriel Shumba of the Zimbabwe Exiles Forum said, "Once a free and democratic Zimbawe has been realised, millions will be keen to go back to their motherland. Wouldn't it be easier for the South African government to urge Mugabe to create the conditions necessary for free and fair elections? If these conditions were in place, they wouldn't have to fend off court cases about crimes against humanity, deport thousands of Zimbaweans, handle concerns regarding housing foreign nationals in unsuitable buildings in the city of Johannesburg, and be on high alert for acts of xenophobic violence."

What was striking about the situation at Central Methodist in 2012 was that after so much time, nothing had been resolved. Mugabe was still in power. Even if he were to step down, the political and economic conditions would continue to be dire. There were still no clear policy guidelines in South Africa regarding migration, and no clarity on a temporary housing policy for migrants into Johannesburg. Xenobhobia continued to percolate in villages, towns and cities across the country, and growing poverty and inequality continued to be significant factors in building that resentment. The police and Home Affairs continued to stoke resentment by carrying on arrests and deportations. Central Methodist was still housing hundreds of people.

I thought back to when I had first attended a Friday night refugee meeting in April 2010. I had learned a lot about Central Methodist and its history since then. Despite the fact that it hadn't always been easy, it had been a privilege to get to know many of the people who were associated with this place and many of the residents.

Paul Verryn estimates that about 30 000 people have passed through Central Methodist over the past decade. I knew that many of them had moved on, getting jobs as teachers, plumbers, construction workers, welders, journalists, archivists, computer technicians, lecturers, counsellors and medical practitioners. Although there had not been a complete resolution, one thing at least was for sure – this place had served as a springboard for many people to begin to rebuild their lives, even though the church had taken terrible strain and the building had deteriorated badly over the years.

When I met with Reverend Mvume Dandala at Central Methodist in late 2011, he hadn't been back there in a long time. We met in the foyer and he said, "I suppose we should take the stairs," suggesting that he assumed the lift was no longer working. As we walked towards his old office on the third floor where he'd worked in the 1990s, he looked out of the window onto the corner of Pritchard and Smal streets and said, "Ah, that's where I used to look out and watch people being mugged."

On another occasion Dandala told me that there were unique features to an inner-city church. In addition to the constant flow of people, he said that most people come there for assistance of some kind, not only counselling, but practical assistance as well. "In my time people wanted intervention and protection from conflict in the city. In Paul Verryn's time, they were looking for shelter." He wondered whether the larger Methodist Church shared a commitment to the inner city and suggested that if Verryn had had the resources, he would probably have bought a block of flats to house the refugees. Only the broader Methodist Church would have had such resources, however. Central Methodist Mission itself wouldn't have had the money. "To minister to the Zimbabweans the way that he has," said Dandala, "is in the tradition of Central Methodist Mission. If he hadn't, he would have betrayed the legacy of that church."

Speculation about the future for Central Methodist, while it might not have been constantly in the news anymore, continued all the same, and a lot of it had to do with Paul Verryn and his future in the church. As long as he stayed there, it was unlikely that he would ask the residents to leave. The term as Superindent Minister at Central Methodist, which began for Verryn in January 2010 after he stepped down as Bishop, is set to run for five years, through to the end of 2014. If he continues at the church until that time, he will have served at Central Methodist for eighteen years.

Pastoral care and counselling were at the core of Reverend Paul Verryn's ministry since it began. Ruby Mathang, who grew up in Soweto, told me, "I've known Paul since I was a boy. He always housed people who were vulnerable. That's Paul. If he leaves Central Methodist, wherever he goes he will house those who are vulnerable. That's the way he is."

I asked Reverend Kim Alexander, who had worked at Central for three years from 2007 to 2009 and had experienced a great deal of the turmoil there first hand, what she thought might happen to the church. "Who knows?" she said. "It might have to be demolished. But the story will always be told. The story will always be told of how people came to Central Methodist and there was a place for them."

Interviews, References and Notes

PART ONE

Prologue

I first heard the story of the church residents gathering to ready themselves for a violent attack from Eric Goemare of Médecins Sans Frontières during a phone interview on 11 June 2012. Goemare confirmed from his diary that it took place on 14 May 2008. I was able to confirm events of that night in an interview with Penny Foley on 12 June 2012. Freedom Chivima and Ambrose Mapiravana remembered the event but were not present that night.

1. Friday Night Refugee Meeting

I attended my first Friday night refugee meeting on 9 April 2010. It was that night that I first met Bishop Paul Verryn. My second refugee meeting was on 16 April 2010. I continued to attend these meetings periodically throughout 2010, 2011 and early 2012.

I held my first full interview with Paul Verryn on 14 April 2010. It was that same day that I had my guided tour of the building with Ambrose Mapiravana.

2. A Clear Voice to Take on the Powers

Interviews relating to Paul Verryn's history:

Irvine, George. Email exchange, 30 January 2012
Pieterse, Edgar. Cape Town, 7 September 2011
Sempel, Fiona. Telephone interview from Grahamstown, 18 May 2012
Storey, Peter. Simonstown, Cape Town, 21 and 22 July 2011
Verryn, Paul. Johannesburg, 19 September 2011 and Rosebank, Johannesburg, 28 September 2011

References:

Moeng, Katlego. Blog entry entitled "Paul Verryn: man of the people", 7 February 2010. Accessed online, 3 September 2011 at: http://uitenhage.org.za/paul-verryn-man-of-the-people
Zucchino, David. "A Small Persecuted Class: Anti-apartheid Whites in South Africa", *Philadelphia Inquirer,* 1 December 1986. Accessed online, 29 September 2011 at: http://articles.philly.com/1986-12-01/news/26068273

The content of this chapter relating to the 30 January 2008 police raid at Central Methodist Mission was based on interviews with those present that night, as well as the press coverage that followed.

Interviews relating to the 30 January 2008 police raid:

Alexander, Kim. Killarney, Johannesburg, 8 October 2010
Buthelezi, Cleo. Johannesburg, 1 July 2010 and 6 October 2011
Cachalia, Firoz. Braamfontein, Johannesburg, 3 August 2012
Chivima, Freedom. Johannesburg, 13 May 2010
Chiwetu, Monica. Johannesburg, 24 September 2011
Kandowe, William. Johannesburg, 14 June 2011
Metcalfe, Mary. Parkview, Johannesburg, 4 June 2010
Mpembe, General Simon. Telephone interview from Limpopo province, 7 September 2012
Verryn, Paul. Johannesburg, 2 June 2010

References:

Alexander, Kim. Notes from the night of 30 January 2008, given to the author in October 2010

Bantjes, Megan and Langa, Malose, Centre for the Study of Violence and Reconciliation (CSVR). "Raid on Church Despicable", *The Sowetan*, 8 February 2008. Accessed online in May 2010 at: http://www.sowetan.co.za/Feedback/Article.aspx?id=701301

Berger, Sebastien. "Police Raid Shelter for Zimbabwean Refugees", *The Telegraph*, 1 February 2008. Accessed online in May 2010 and 1 November 2011 at: http://www.telegraph.co.uk/news/worldnews/1577293/Police-raid-shelter-for-Zimbabwean-refugees.html

Daily Mail. "South African Police Raid Church Full of Zimbabwean Refugees Seeking Sanctuary", 31 January 2008. Accessed online in May 2010 and on 1 November 2011 at: http://www.dailymail.co.uk/news/article-511503/South-African-police-raid-church-Zimbawean-refugees-seeking-sanctuary.html

Gerardy, Justine. "Judge Says Sorry to Zim Refugees", *The Star*, 16 February 2008. Accessed online in May 2010 and on 1 November 2011 at: http://www.iol.co.za/index.php?set_id=1&click_id=13&art_id=vn20080216083002352C288888

Gordin, Jeremy. "Magistrate 'wishing to go home' Refuses Bail". *Sunday Argus*, 3 February 2008

Gordin, Jeremy and Ngqiyaza, Bonile. "Cops Free all but Fifteen After Church Raid", *Sunday Independent*, 10 February 2008. Accessed online in May 2010 and on 1 November 2011 at: http://www.iol.co.za/index.php?set_id=1&click_id=13&art_id=vn20080210084528482C888874

Independent Online. "Hundreds of Zimbabweans Arrested in Church", 31 January 2008. Accessed online in May 2010 and on 1 November 2011 at: http://www.iol.co.za/index.php?set_id=1&click_id=13&art_id=nw20080131183411912C611966

Independent Online. "Police Raid on Church 'Xenophobic' – TAC", 1 February 2008. Accessed online in May 2010 and on 1 November 2011 at: http://www.iol.co.za/index.php?set_id=1&click_id=13&art_id=nw20080201104432303C933274

Independent Online. "Police Raid Shocks Church Leaders", 1 February 2008. Accessed online in May 2010 and on 1 November 2011 at: http://www.iol.co.za/index.php?set_id=1&click_id=13&art_id=nw20080201114419998C242871

Independent Online and *The Cape Times*. "Church Raid: 'Detainees Mistreated by Cops'", 4 February 2008. Accessed online in May 2010 and on 1 November 2011 at: http://www.iol.co.za/index.php?set_id=1&click_id=13&art_id=vn20080204061116274C847121

Johwa, Wilson. "Apartheid Style Migration Policy 'Alive and Well'", *Business Day*, 4 February 2008. Accessed online in May 2010 at: http://allafrica.com/stories/printable/200802040646.html

Kharsany, Zahira. "Refugees Return to Raided Church Amid Legal Wrangles", *Mail & Guardian Online,* 6 February 2008. Accessed online in May 2010 and 1 November 2011 at: http://www.mg.co.za/article/2008-02-06-refugees-return-to-raided-church-amid-legal-wrangles

Landau, Loren and Vigneswaran, Darshan. "Here Comes the Raids Again", *Mail & Guardian Online*, 11 February 2008. Accessed online in May 2010 and on 1 November 2011 at: http://www.mg.co.za/article/2008-02-11-here-come-the-raids-again

Médecins Sans Frontières. "Health of Zimbabwean Migrants at Risk After Raid at Johannesburg Methodist Church", press statement, 5 February 2008

Seale, Lebogang. "Church Refugees Speak out on Police Abuse", *The Star*, 6 February 2008. Accessed online in May 2010 and on 1 November 2011 at: http://www.iol.co.za/index.php?set_id=1&click_id=13&art_id=vn20080206061447587C240931&singlepage=1

South African Church Leaders' Forum, press statement Bonaero Park, Johannesburg, 1 February 2008

Note:

I sent an email to the Independent Complaints Directorate on 11 July 2012 asking about the investigation into the police raid. I received a phone call in response on 20 July 2012 saying that Advocate Moleshe had sent someone to the church in February 2008 but there was no co-operation so they "closed the file". Judge Sutherland's request that the Magistrate's Commission investigate Judge du Pisani took months to proceed. On 6 March 2008, Achmet Mayet from the Legal Resources Centre sent a letter to the senior stenographer at the Johannesburg Magistrate's Court because the LRC had struggled extensively to secure a full copy of the court transcripts. The letter stated that despite repeated attempts, the recordings and the transcripts were not available. On 11

September 2008, Mayet sent a letter to the Secretary of the Magistrate's Commission in Pretoria and attached Judge Sutherland's order, the founding affidavit, the transcript of the proceedings of Judge Sutherland, the partial transcript of the proceedings before Magistrate du Pisani, and the letter to the stenographer. Mayet said in the letter that while they had not been able to obtain a full set of transcripts, these would be essential for the Commission and hoped that the Commission would have "better success" in obtaining the full transcripts. The Secretary of the Magistrate's Commission responded with a letter dated 30 September 2008 stating that "The Magistrate's Commission is not empowered to interfere with judicial decisions made by judicial officers. An investigation was therefore instituted only with regard to the alleged conduct of the Magistrate. Having considered the matter, the Commission is satisfied that no evidence could be found that indicates that the Magistrate acted beyond the scope of her judicial functions. As a result thereof, the Commission has decided to close its file in this matter." This information was gathered from documents shared with me by Advocate Richard Moultrie during an interview at his offices in Sandton on 14 March 2012.

3. "An Unexpected Thunderstorm"

Interviews:

Chivima, Freedom. Johannesburg, 13 May 2010
Foley, Penny. Email to the author regarding 2008 donations, dated 29 February 2012
Foley, Penny. Parkwood, Johannesburg, 7 August 2012
Kandowe, William. Johannesburg, 14 June 2011
Mahlangu, Dorothy Qedani. Johannesburg, 15 September 2010
Mutenanhene, Alois. Johannesburg, 8 November 2011
Verryn, Paul. Johannesburg, 28 July 2012

References:

Abrahams, Ivan and Pato, Luke. "Church Leaders Call for Tougher Mediation Measures on Zimbabwe", press statement, April 2008
Amnesty International. "South Africa 'Talk for us Please': Limited Options Facing Individuals Displaced by Xenophobic Violence", 12 September 2008

Constitutional Court of South Africa, Case No CCT 65/08, Order dated 21 August 2008

Daily Sun and *The Star* headlines quoted in Harber, Anton. "Two Newspapers, Two Nations?: The Media and the Xenophobic Violence", in Hassim, Shireen, Kupe, Tawana and Worby, Eric (eds), *Go Home or Die Here*, 2008, Johannesburg, Wits University Press

Everatt, David. *South African Civil Society and Xenophobia*, produced by Strategy and Tactics and The Atlantic Philanthropies, 2010

Gordin, Jeremy. "Hopes of Returning Home Dashed", *Sunday Independent*, 13 April 2008. Accessed online on 2 March 2012 at: http://www.iol.co.za/index.php?set_id=13&art_id=vn20080413081717441C242757&singlepage=1

Hlala, Patrick and Hosken, Graeme. "Foreigners Killed in Xenophobic Rage", *Pretoria News*, 19 March 2008

Hosken, Graeme. "Attacks on foreigners 'organised'", *Cape Times*, 22 February 2008

Independent Online. "Summit Delivers no Quick Fix to Zim Deadlock", 13 April 2008. Accessed online on 2 March 2012 at: http://www.iol.co.za/news/africa/sumit-delivers-no-quick-fix-to-zim-deadlock-1.396335

Independent Online. "Boksburg hit by xenophobic violence", 19 May 2008. Accessed online in June 2010 and on 9 November 2011 at: http://www.iol.co.za/index.php?set_id=1&click_id=13&art_id=nw20080519132417370C743080&singlepage=1

Independent Online. "Donations Pour in for Victims", 27 May 2008. Accessed online in June 2010 and on 9 November 2011 at: http://www.iol.co.za/index.php?set_id=1&click_id=13&art_id=nw20080527150923186C903157

Independent Online. "Victims will stay put", 2 June 2008. Accessed online in June 2010 and on 9 November 2011 at: http://www.iol.co.za/index.php?set_id=1&click_id=13&art_id=nw20080602191612871C921143

Independent Online. "Aid Groups Apply for Interdict", 2 June 2008. Accessed online in June 2010 at: http://www.iol.co.za/index.php?set_id=1&click_id=13&art_id=nw20080602170653685C907326

Johnston, Nicole, and Foster, Warren. "The Power of Positive People", *Mail & Guardian*, 22 May 2008. Accessed online in June 2010 at: http://www.mg.co.za/article/2008-05-22-the-power-of-positive-people

Johwa, Wilson. "Apartheid-Style Migration Policy 'Alive and Well'", *Business Day*, 4 February 2008

Mbanjwa, Xolani. "Two Killed in informal Settlement", *Pretoria News*, 17 March 2008

Mbeki, Thabo. "Radio and Television Address to the Nation by the President of South Africa, Thabo Mbeki, on the Occasion of Africa Day", 25 May 2008. Accessed online on 25 March 2012 at: http://www.dfa.gov.za/docs/speeches/2008/mbek0525.html

McGreal, Chris. "Thousands Seek Santuary as South Africans Turn on Refugees", *The Guardian*, 20 May 2008. Accessed online in June 2010 and on 9 November 2011 at: http://www.guardian.co.uk/world/2008/may/20/zimbabwe.southafrica

Mkhwanazi, Siyabonga. "MPs Blast Bishop", *The Star*, 27 March 2008

Pretoria News. "Minister Calls for Indaba on Xenophobia", 26 March 2008

Proceedings of the National Council of Provinces, 26 March 2008, p 1. Available online at: www.parliament.gov.za

Rondganger, Lee, Radler, Matt and Ngqiyaza, Bonile. "Refugee Crisis Grows", *The Star*, 22 May 2008. Accessed online in June 2010 and on 9 November 2011 at: http://www.iol.co.za/index.php?set_id=1&click_id=13&art_id=vn20080522060210441C334686&singlepage=1

Sack, Adam. "Habonim Visits Central Methodist Church", statement dated 19 May 2008

South African Human Rights Commission. "Record of Way Forward From Meeting to Discuss Reintegration and Site Closure Issues", 27 August and 10 September 2008

South African Human Rights Commission. "Record of Agreements and Way Forward, Meeting Regarding Akasia Camp", 5 December 2008

South African Police Service. "Figures from Police Stations", dated 21 May 2008. Numbers of displaced people in each police station in Gauteng, given to the author by Mary Metcalfe

Tromp, Beauregard, Gifford, Gill, Ndaba, Baldwin, Eliseev, Alex, Smillie, Shaun and Molosankwe, Botho. "Cops try to Control Xenophobic Mayhem", *The Star*, 19 May 2008. Accessed online in June 2010 and on 9 November 2011 at: http://www.iol.co.za/news/south-africa/cops-try-control-xenophobic-mayhem-1.400927

Tsele, Lebogang. "US Embassy Warns Xenophobia Victims, and Delivers Big Bucks to Project-Based Aid for South Africans", *The Sowetan*,

9 June 2008. Accessed online in June 2010 at: http://www.sowetan.co.za/news/article.aspx?id=781736

Van Hoorn, Imke. "These People Get Killed for Nothing", *Mail & Guardian*, 19 May 2008. Accessed online in June 2010 and on 9 November 2011 at: http://www.mg.co.za/article/2008-05-19-these-people-get-killed-for-nothing

Verryn, Paul. Foreword in Hassim, Shireen, Kupe, Tawana and Worby, Eric (eds), *Go Home or Die Here*, Johannesburg, Wits University Press, 2008

Verryn, Paul. Founding Affidavit in the High Court of South Africa, 2 June 2008

Note:

The information about the Synod that took place in May 2008 came from Penny Foley in an email dated 19 July 2012 and a follow-up interview on 7 August 2012. I discussed it with Paul Verryn in an interview on 28 July 2012 as well.

4. The Rise and Fall of Central Hall

Interviews:

Dandala, Mvume. Midrand, Gauteng, 1 September 2011

Storey, Peter. Simonstown, Cape Town, 22 July 2011

References:

Beavon, Keith. *Johannesburg: The Making and Shaping of the City*, 2004 Pretoria, University of South Africa Press

Dandala, Mvume. Special Hearings on Faith Communities, Submission about the Methodist Church, TRC transcript, 17 November 1997. Accessed online on 14 September 2011 at: http://www.justice.gov.za/trc/special/faith/faith_a.htm

The Challenge of the City, Wesleyan Methodist Church Central Hall and Circuit, Johannesburg, 1926

Venter, David. *Inverting the Norm: Racially-Mixed Congregations in a Segregationist State*, 2007, Galjoen Academic Press

www.methodist-central-hall.org.uk. Accessed online on 19 November 2012

Meetings at Central Methodist – 2010

Interviews:
Chivima, Freedom. Johannesburg, 21 July 2010
Love, Divine. Johannesburg, 18 June 2010
Thomas, Esther. Johannesburg, 18 June 2010

Notes:
I quote from the Friday night refugee meeting on 18 June 2010.
I attended the karate class on 21 July 2010.

5. Reverend Peter Storey and the Apartheid City

Interviews:
Myeza, Lindi. Soweto, Johannesburg, 18 October 2011
Storey, Peter. Simonstown, Cape Town, 21 and 22 July 2011

References:
Beavon, Keith. *Johannesburg: The Making and Shaping of the City*, 2004, Pretoria, University of South Africa Press

Chapman, Audrey and Spong, Bernard (eds). *Religion and Reconciliation in South Africa: Voices of Religious Leaders*, 2003, Philadelphia and London, Templeton Foundation Press, pp52–56

Gilbey, Emma. *The Lady: the Life and Times of Winnie Mandela*, 1993, Random House

Storey, Peter. Superintendent's Annual Report, Johannesburg Central Circuit, 1981

Storey, Peter. *With God in the Crucible: Preaching Costly Discipleship*, 2002, Nashville, Abingdon Press

The Star. "Our Unsung Heroine – Lindy [sic] Myeza is maintaining vital links in her community during troubled times", 1 December 1976

6. Offering Political Refuge at Central

Interviews:
Bassingthwaite, Judy. Rosebank, Johannesburg, 8 July 2011

Brodrick, Janet. Norwood, Johannesburg, 14 February 2011
Dangor, Ambassador Mohammed. Email correspondence, 28 November 2012
Morobe, Murphy. Wierda Valley, Johannesburg, 4 July 2012
Myeza, Lindi. Soweto, Johannesburg, 18 October 2011
Newby, David. Telephone interview from Cape Town, 15 March 2012
Storey, Peter. Simonstown, Cape Town, 21 and 22 July 2011
Verryn, Paul. Johannesburg, 19 September 2011

References:

Beavon, Keith. *Johannesburg: The Making and Shaping of the City*, 2004, Pretoria, University of South Africa Press

Bailie, John. *The Impact of Liberation Theology on Methodism in South Africa with Regard to the Doctrine of Christian Perfection*, submitted to UNISA, January 2009. Accessed online on 21 November 2012 at: http://uir.unisa.ac.za/bitstream/handle/10500/2600/thesis_bailie_j.pdf?sequence=1

Chapman, Audrey and Spong, Bernard (eds). *Religion and Reconciliation in South Africa: Voices of Religious Leaders*, 2003, Philadelphia and London, Templeton Foundation Press, pp47–56

De Kock, Eugene. Truth and Reconciliation Commission Amnesty Hearings, held in Pretoria, 29 July 1998, pp 22–70. Accessed online on 4 October 2011 at: http://www.justice.gov.za/trc/amntrans/1998/98072031_pre_cosatu8.htm

Hochschild, Adam. *The Mirror at Midnight: A South African Journey*, 1990,New York, New York, Viking Penguin Books

South African History Archive. UDF Archive AL2341, Box G3 Actstop, "Profile of Actstop", author unknown, date circa 1990

South African History Archive. UDF Archive AL2341, Box G3 Actstop, "Information on 'Inner-City' Area of Johannesburg", author unknown, date circa 1990

Storey, Peter. Letter to Delegates to the World Methodist Peace Conference, Nairobi, October 1986

Storey, Peter. "Notes on Sanctuary", 1986

Storey, Peter. "Storey Preaches on Desecration", in *What a Family!* Number 28, July 1988

Storey, Peter. Superintendent's Annual Report, Johannesburg Central Circuit, 1976

Storey, Peter. Superintendent's Annual Report, Johannesburg Central Circuit, 1981

Storey, Peter. Superintendent's Annual Report, Johannesburg Central Mission, 1985

Storey, Peter. Superintendent's Annual Report, Johannesburg Central Methodist Mission (Circuit 901), Circuit Report to Synod of 1987, 1987

Storey, Peter. *With God in the Crucible: Preaching Costly Discipleship*, 2002, Nashville, Abingdon Press

Venter, David. *Inverting the Norm: Racially-Mixed Congregations in a Segregationist State*, 2007, Galjoen Academic Press

What a Family! "Celebrate with Us!" Newsletter of the Johannesburg Central Circuit, 1988

What a Family! Newsletter of the Johannesburg Central Circuit, April 1978

What a Family! "Refugees at Central", News from the Central Methodist Mission, Number 31, October 1988

7. The Tragedy of Stompie Seipei

Interviews:

Morobe, Murphy. Wierda Valley, Johannesburg, 4 July 2012

Storey, Peter. Simonstown, Cape Town, 21 and 22 July 2011

Verryn, Paul. Rosebank, Johannesburg, 28 September 2011

References:

Barkhuizen, Dawn. "Minister Abused Us, Say Youths", *Sunday Times*, 28 April, 1991

Barkhuizen, Dawn. "Minister Whose Morals Were Ripped Apart", *Sunday Times*, 12 May 1991

Blow, Desmond. "Winnie in Talks About Rev Verryn", *City Press*, 5 February 1989

Blow, Desmond, and Molusi, Connie. "Winnie XL, SACC in Sex Row", *City Press*, 29 January 1989

Blow, Desmond, and Molusi, Connie. "Youth Speaks out on Sex Assault Claim", *City Press*, 29 January 1989

Bothma, Stephane. "Stompie Trial: Verryn Denies Homosexual Acts", *The Citizen*, 11 May 1989

Bothma, Stephane. "Verryn: No Evidence of Sexual Misconduct", *The Citizen*, 26 May 1990

Bridgland, Fred. *Katiza's Journey*, 1997, London, Sidgwick & Jackson, Macmillan Publishers

Cebekhulu, Katiza. Submission to the Truth and Reconciliation Commission, 25 November 1997. Accessed online on 7 October 2011 at: http://www.justice.gov.za/trc/special/mandela/mufc2b.htm.

Chikane, Frank. Submission to the Truth and Reconciliation Commission, 27 November 1997. Accessed online on 10 December 2011 at: http://www.justice.gov.za/trc/special/mandela/mufc4a.htm

City Press. "Tambo's Help Needed in 'Ghastly Situation': Crisis Committee Sends Document to Exiled Leader", 19 February 1989

Eddings, Jerelyn. "Winnie Mandela Guilty of Kidnapping Wife of ANC Leader Blamed in '88 Event", *Baltimore Sun*, 14 May 1991

Editorial. "Why Pick on Dr. Asvat", *The Sowetan,* 30 January 1989

Falati, Xoliswa. Submission to the Truth and Reconciliation Commission, 25 November 1997

Gilbey, Emma. *The Lady: the Life and Times of Winnie Mandela*, 1993, Random House

Gqubule, Thandeka. "Soweto Anger at Winnie 'Team': Claims that Four Youths Kidnapped; One Still Missing", *Weekly Mail*, 27 January 1989

Johnson, Shaun. "Two Small Coffins Check the Spiral of Bloody Revenge", *Weekly Mail*, 3 March 1989

Mangena, Mosibudi. "A People's Hero Before his Time", *Sunday Independent*, 26 February 2012

Mantini, Ezra. "Winnie: I know Why Asvat Was Shot", *Sunday Times*, 29 January 1989

Mass Democratic Movement. Statement by Mass Democratic Movement on Winnie Mandela, 16 February 1989

Mathiane, Nomavenda. "Watching Winnie", *Frontline*, April 1987

Mathiane, Nomavenda. "Living a Lie, Reaping a Whirlwind", *Frontline*, March 1989

Mokoena, Aubrey. Submission to the Truth and Reconciliation Commission, 27 November 1997. Accessed online on 10 December 2011 at: http://www.justice.gov.za/trc/special/mandela/mufc4a.htm

Motlana, Dr Nthato. Submission to the Truth and Reconciliation Commission, 27 November 1997. Accessed online on 10 December 2011 at: http://www.justice.gov.za.trc/special/mandela/mufc4a.htm

Mufamadi, Sydney. Submission to the Truth and Reconciliation Commission, 27 November 1997. Accessed online on 12 October 2011 at http://www.justice.gov.za/trc/special/mandela/mufc4b.htm

Sisulu, Elinor. *Walter and Albertina Sisulu: In Our Lifetime*, 2002, Cape Town, David Philip Publishers

Soske, Dr Jon. "The Life and Death of Dr. Abu Baker 'Hurley' Asvat, February 23, 1943 – January 27, 1989", unpublished paper, Wits Institute for Social and Economic Research, delivered at Wits University, 8 June 2011

Storey, Peter. Address to the 1991 Synod of the Central District of the Methodist Church, Rosettenville or Turffontein, 1991

Storey, Peter. "I am so sorry, Mama: Funeral of Stompie Seipei at Tumahole Township", 25 February 1989, In *With God in the Crucible: Preaching Costly Discipleship*, 2002, Nashville, Abingdon Press

Storey, Peter. Submission to the Truth and Reconciliation Commission, 26 November 1997. Accessed online on 8 March 2011 and 7 October 2011 at: http://www.justice.gov.za/trc/special/mandela/mufc3b.htm and mufc3a.htm on 10 July 2011

Verryn, Paul. Submission to the Truth and Reconciliation Commission, 26 November 1997. Accessed online on 1 June 2011 at: http://www.justice.gov.za/trc/special/mandela/mufc3a.htm

Meetings at Central Methodist – 2010

Interview:

Cheza, Elizabeth. Johannesburg, 22 July 2010.

Note:

The visit to Bishop Verryn's waiting room took place on 22 July 2010.

8. Son of Soweto

Interview:

Verryn, Paul. Rosebank, Johannesburg, 28 September 2011

References:

Dixon, Robyn. "No Neighborly Love for Soweto Minister", *Los Angeles Times*, 13 February 2010

Grange, Helen. "Verryn – Veritably a 'Son of Soweto'", *The Star*, 10 June 1997

Lawson, Lesley. "A Samaritan in Soweto", *Millennium*, 1992

O'Malley, Padraig. Interview with Paul Verryn, 2 December 1993. Accessed by Ruth Muller on 1 March 2012 at: http://www.nelsonmandela.org/omalley/index.php/site/q/03lv00017/04lv00344/05lv00730/06lv00820

Stopforth, Crispin (director). *One and Undivided: The Paul Verryn Story*. Documentary produced by Cut to Black for SABC2 and aired in 2008. Accessed online on 26 June 2012 at: http://www.spirituality.org.za/files/one%20and%20undivided%20Paul%20Verryn.mp4

Note:

The scene in the opening paragraph and many of the circumstances facing Verryn in Soweto in the early 1990s were gathered from Lesley Lawson's 1992 article in *Millennium* magazine. The closing scene of attempted robbery was taken from both Grange's 1997 article in *The Star* and Dixon's 2010 article in the *Los Angeles Times.*

9. Reverend Mvume Dandala and the Quest for Peace

Interviews:

Ally, Russell. Telephone interview, 17 November 2012

Dandala, Mvume. Midrand, Gauteng, 1 September and Johannesburg, 27 November 2011

Lolwana, Peliwe. Parktown, Johannesburg, 1 April 2011

Myeza, Lindi. Soweto, Johannesburg, 27 November 2012

Randera, Fazel. Milpark, Johannesburg, 24 September 2012

References:

Arnold, Kent. *A Dispute Systems Design Analysis of Taxi and Hostel Conflict in South Africa's Transition to Majority Rule*, Conflict Resolution Consortium, working paper, #94-69, University of Colorado, 1994. Accessed online on 21 September 2011 at: http://www.colorado.edu/conflict/full_text_search/AllCRCDocs/94-69.htm

Central Methodist Mission, Johannesburg. "The Future of the Mission's Activities", undated, circa 1993

Dandala, Mvume. "The Role of the Church in the Birth and Nurture of a New Nation ". Inaugural lecture as Honorary Professor at the Faculty of Theology, University of Pretoria, published in *Verbum et Ecclesia*, Jrg 22 (1) 2001. Accessed online on 21 September 2011 at: www.ve.org.za/index/php/VE/article/download/620/715

Hostel Peace Initiative: A Ministry Initiated by Hostel Residents and Facilitated by the Central Methodist Mission, Johannesburg, Annual Report. Booklet dated October 1992–September 1993

Human Rights Violations Hearings and Submissions, Central Methodist Church, Johannesburg, 29 April – 3 May 1996. Submissions listed by name. See Elizabeth Floyd, Maggie Friedman, Catherine and Sepati Mlangeni, and Hawa Timol. Accessed online on 17 November 2012 at: http://www.justice.gov.za/trc/hrvtrans/jb_victim.htm

Madise, Mokhele and Lebeloane, Lazarus. "The Manyano Movements within the Methodist Church of Southern Africa: and Expression of Freedom of Worship (1844-1944)", *Studia Historiae Ecclesiasticae*, December 2008. Accessed online in November 2012 at: http://uir.unisa.ac.za/bitstream/handle/10500/4500/Madise-Lebeboane-SHEXXXIV_2_-December2008.pdf?sequence=1

Saki, Eric. "Dandala Promises to Return 1994 Dream", in *Growth*, February 2009. Accessed online on 22 September 2011 at: http://www.growth.co.za/index.php?option=com_content&view=article&id=103:dandala

Venter, David. *Inverting the Norm: Racially-Mixed Congregations in a Segregationist State*, 2007, Galjoen Academic Press

What a Family! Central Methodist Mission, Number 74, December 1994

10. Bishop Paul Verryn Appears before the Truth Commission

Interviews:

Storey, Peter. Simonstown, Cape Town, 21 and 22 July 2011

Verryn, Paul. Johannesburg, 19 September 2011 and Rosebank, Johannesburg, 28 September 2011

References:

Business Day. "Gauteng Methodist Bishop Inducted", 7 July 1997

Grange, Helen. "Verryn – Veritably a 'Son of Soweto'", *The Star*, 18 June 1997

Johnson, Angella. "Priest Survives Public Trial of Faith", *Weekly Mail*, June 1997

Maykuth, Andrew. "Bishop Forgives Winnie Mandela: The Rev. Paul Verryn said he Regretted the Slander by her. He also Accepted Blame for Boy's Death", *Philadelphia Inquirer*, 27 November 1997

Staff reporters. "Key Methodist Post Handed to Verryn", *The Star*, 23 May 1997

Unsworth, Andrew. "A Bishop for the People", *Sunday Times Metro*, 6 July 1997

References relating to the Truth and Reconciliation Commission:

Cebekhulu, Katiza. Submission to the TRC, 25 November 1997. Accessed online on 7 October 2011 at: http://www.justice.gov.za/trc/special/mandela/mufc2b.htm

Chikane, Frank. Submission to the TRC, 27 November 1997. Accessed online on 10 December 2011 at: http://www.justice.gov.za/trc/special/mandela/mufc4a.htm

Daley, Suzanne. "An Uncomfortable Winnie Mandela Faces Cleric She Accused", *New York Times*, 27 November 1997

Falati, Xoliswa. Submission to the TRC, 25 November 1997. Accessed online on and around 8 March 2011 and on and around 7 October 2011 at: http://www.justice.gov.za/trc/special/mandela/mufc2a.htm

Krog, Antjie. *Country of my Skull*, 1999, London, Vintage, Random House

Mokoena, Aubrey. Submission to the TRC, 27 November 1997. Accessed online on 10 December 2011 at: http://www.justice.gov.za/trc/special/mandela/mufc4a.htm

Mufamadi, Sydney. Submission to the TRC, 27 November 1997. Accessed online on 12 October 2011 at: http://www.justice.gov.za/trc/special/mandela/mufc4b.htm

Storey, Peter. Submission to the TRC, 26 November 1997. Accessed online on 8 March and 7 October 2011 at: http://www.justice.gov.za/trc/special/mandela/mufc3b.htm

Verryn, Paul. Submission to the TRC, 26 November 1997. Accessed online on 8 March and 7 October 2011 at: http://www.justice.gov.za/trc/special/mandela/mufc3b.htm

Meetings at Central Methodist – 2010

I went to the 10am service at Central Methodist on 1 August 2010 and quoted from Paul Verryn's sermon. The discussion with Verryn about theology took place in his office on 12 July 2011. Also referenced is Verryn's sermon at the 2pm Covenant Service, Albert Street Church, 30 January 2011. Osmond is Osmond Mngomezulu from the Socio-Economic Rights Institute (SERI).

11. Changing City, Changing Congregation

Interviews:

Foley, Penny. Parkwood, Johannesburg, 23 June 2010

Lolwana, Peliwe. Parktown, Johannesburg, 1 April 2011

Mkhabela, Ishmael. Killarney, Johannesburg, 9 July 2010

Mutombu, Bibiche, Paul and Wivine. Bez Valley, Johannesburg, 5 November 2011

Verryn, Paul. Rosebank, Johannesburg, 28 September 2011

References:

BBC News Africa. "South African Aids Icon Dies", 1 June 2001. Accessed online on 15 October 2011 at: http://news.bbc.co.uk./2/hi/africa/1363681.stm

BBC News Africa. "Funeral for Child Aids Icon", 9 June 2001. Accessed online on 18 May 2011 at: http://news.bbc.co.uk/2/hi/africa/1379152.stm

HIV/Aids deaths statistics accessed online at: http://www.avert.org/

safricastats.htm

Jenkins, Trefor. Interview, 12 May 2000 in Chapman, Audrey R and Spong, Bernard (eds). *Religion and Reconciliation in South Africa: Voices of Religious Leaders*, 2003, Templeton Foundation Press

Myeza, Lindi. Interview, 23 May 2000 in Chapman, Audrey R and Spong, Bernard (eds). *Religion and Reconciliation in South Africa: Voices of Religious Leaders*, 2003, Templeton Foundation Press

12. The First Residents

Interviews:

Abrahams, Ivan. Norwood, Johannesburg, 5 December 2011

Buthelezi, Cleo. Johannesburg, 1 July 2010 and 6 October 2011

Muziringa, Brian. Johannesburg, 31 May 2011

Myeza, Lindi. Johannesburg, 18 October 2011

Nininahazwe, Leothere. Johannesburg, 23 March 2011

References:

Amnesty International Report. "Zimbabwe: Rights Under Siege", 1 May 2003. Accessed online on 3 June 2012 at: http://www.amnesty.org/en/library/info/AFR46/012/2003/en

Chibba, Reesha. "Zim's New Homeless Live 'Worse than Animals'", *Mail & Guardian*, 18 July 2005 Accessed online, 11 November 2010 at: http://www.mg.co.za/printformat/single/2005-07-18-zims-new-homess-live-worse-than-animals

Dyantyi, Aurelia. "Courageous Man Honoured by Friends and Family", *The Star*, 12 January 2005

Eliseev, Alex. "Church Leaders Say Housing Blitz Must Stop", *Independent Online*, 13 July 2005. Accessed online in June 2010 and on 24 October 2011 at: http://www.iol.co.za/index.php?set_id=1&click_id=68&art_id=qw1121263201623B262&singlepage=1

Gevisser, Mark. *The Dream Deferred: Thabo Mbeki*, 2007, Johannesburg, Jonathan Ball Publishers

Human Rights Watch. "You will be Thoroughly Beaten: The Brutal Suppression of Dissent in Zimbabwe", Volume 18, No 10a, November 2006. Accessed online on 3 June 2012 at: http://www.hrw.org/reports/2006/10/31/you-will-be-thoroughly-beaten-0

Madulammoho Housing Association website. Description of Cornelius House. Accessed online on 23 October 2011 at: http://www.mh.org.za/projects/cornelius-house

Poulsen, Lone. "The Transitional Housing Programme for the Inner City Homeless Community of Johannesburg". Paper presented at the Urban Futures 2000 conference, Johannesburg, July 2000. Accessed online on 23 October 2011 at: http://architectafrica.com/bin0/papers/transhousing2.html

South African Press Association. "Mbeki 'ignored' Zim Report", *News24*, 12 May 2008. Accessed online on 3 June 2012 at: http://www.news24.com/SouthAfrica/Politics/Mbeki-ignored-Zim-report-20080512

13. A Murder in the Church

Interviews:

Buthelezi, Cleo. Johannesburg, 6 October 2011

Foley, Penny. Parkwood, Johannesburg, 11 October 2011 and email correspondence, 26 November 2012

Ncatsha, Vuyani, Ntsepe, Buntu and Tokwana, Johannes. Johannesburg, 27 October 2012

Verryn, Paul. Rosebank, Johannesburg, 28 September 2011

References:

Claasen, Larry. "A Different Method Book", *Financial Mail*, 21 December 2007. Accessed online on 28 September 2011 at: http://free.financialmail.co.za/07/1221/cover/coverstoryf.htm

Independent Online. "Hymns Highlight Violence Against Women", 6 March 2006. Accessed online in June 2010 and on 27 October 2011 at: http://www.iol.co.za/index.php?set_id=1&click_id=13&art_id=qw1141626061484B263

Landau, Loren. "SA Respects Rights for all, Except Refugees", *The Weekender*, 17-18 June 2006

Maphumula, Solly. "Fight over Clothes ends in Stabbing at Church", *The Star*, 13 March 2006

Maphumula, Solly. "Place of Worship now a Den of Iniquity", *The Star*, 8 June 2006

Mdluli, Patrick, manager, Environmental Health, Region F, City of Johannesburg. Letter to Bishop Paul Verryn headed "Insanitary Conditions – Central Methodist Church", dated 3 October 2007

Seale, Lebogang. "Tears Flow as Mourners Remember Makgabo", *The Star*, 15 March 2006

Stewart, Tamlyn. "Crowded House of Hope", *The Weekender*, 17-18 June 2006

Notes:

As of August 2012, to my knowledge, there had been three murders inside the church building. In addition to the murder of Andrew Khumalo in March 2006, a second man was murdered in 2007. I have not been able to establish his name, nor the month in which the murder occurred. Penny Foley told me in an email dated 19 July 2012 that a disabled man was killed by someone who was drunk. She wasn't sure why or how it happened. She said that another circuit steward, Sipho Arosi, was a policeman and he worked hard to get the police to the church. They took a long time to get there because the man was already dead. Foley remembers that the building security asked everyone in the building to go into the sanctuary to wait for Bishop Verryn to get there to speak to all the residents. The third murder took place in December 2011. Again, alcohol played a role as the murder was committed by someone who had been drinking. The victim was a resident of the building who was deaf and dumb. He wore his hair in short dreadlocks. Although I never knew this man's name, every time I saw him in the building, he had a broad smile and would motion to me with thumbs up.

As of October 2012, the outstanding water debt to the City was R1.08 million. The total municipal debt was R2.65 million.

Meetings at Central Methodist – 2010

Interviews:

Foley, Penny. Telephone conversation, 11 March 2011

Mapakata, Reymond. Johannesburg, 11 July 2011

References:

Gossmann, Christina. "Taking the Rough Road to the African Dream – and Back", *Mail & Guardian,* November 4–10, 2011 for more information about Reymond Mapakata. Also see short film about Reymond Mapakata's life in Bikita, Zimbabwe at: http://www.mg.co.za/zimrefugee

Geronimo, Isy India (director). *On the Edge*. Documentary film about homelessness in inner-city Johannesburg. Premiered at Encounters Film Festival, South Africa, June 2012

Mapakata, Reymond. Text message correspondence with the author, 2010 and 2011

Mapakata, Reymond. Affidavit about his first arrest in 2008, dated 29 July 2010

Notes:

The planning meeting for Peace Action where I introduced myself to Evans Kuntonda was held on 20 June 2010.

My visit to the "bad building" in Doornfontein with Evans Kuntonda took place on 21 October 2010. For more information about the building, see Alon Skuy's photo essay at: http://multimedia.timeslive.co.za/photos/2010/12/hidden-nightmare

I went with Reymond Mapakata onto the roof of Central Methodist on 11 July 2011.

14. A Ray of Hope

Interviews:

Buthelezi, Cleo. Johannesburg, 6 October 2011

Foley, Penny. Parkwood, Johannesburg, 14 February 2011 and Parkmore, Johannesburg, 28 February 2012

Lolwana, Peliwe. Parktown, Johannesburg, 1 April 2011

Goemaere, Eric. Telephone interview, 11 June 2012

McAllister, Roy. Bryanston, Johannesburg, 27 September 2012

Zwane, Wandile, Community Development, City of Johannesburg, 6 July 2010

References:

Claasen, Larry. "A Different Method Book", Financial Mail, 21 December 2007. Accessed online on 28 September 2011 at: http://free.financialmail.co.za/07/1221/cover/coverstoryf.htm

Foley, Penny. Fundraising Proposal for Central Methodist Mission, 2006 (unpublished)

McAllister, Roy and Mayer, Kerry. Email communication, including UMCOR proposals and reports, 20 November 2012

Médecins Sans Frontières. "No Refuge, Access Denied: Medical and Humanitarian Needs of Zimbabweans in South Africa", June 2009. Accessed online in June 2010 at: http://www.msf.org.za

Mdluli, Patrick, manager, Environmental Health, Region F, City of Johannesburg. Letter to Bishop Verryn headed "Insanitary Conditions – Central Methodist Church", dated 3 October 2007

Ray of Hope website. About Us and Superintendent's Office, September 2006. Accessed online on 23 October 2011 at: http://www.rayofhope.org.za

Semenya, Ishmael. Letter to Bishop Verryn headed "Utilization of the Pritchard Street Methodist Church to House More than 800 'Refugees'", dated 27 July 2006

Solidarity Peace Trust and PASSOP. *Perils and Pitfalls – Migrants and Deportation in South Africa*, 5 June 2012. This source provided the figures regarding deportations in 2007 and 2008.

Note:

UMCOR continued to support Ray of Hope via the Deaconess Society in 2007, 2008 and 2009. At some point Presiding Bishop Ivan Abrahams and the Methodist Connexional Office advised UMCOR that their money intended for the Albert Street School had to be routed through the MCO and could no longer go directly to Central Methodist. At the beginning of 2010 UMCOR stopped funding both Ray of Hope and the Albert Street School, and there were some months during 2011 when teachers at the Albert Street School were not paid. The funding began again in early 2011, but only for the Albert Street School.

15. The Thunderstorm Left Behind More than a Flood

Interviews:

Alexander, Kim. Roodepoort, 23 November 2011

Andrews, Sara. Telephone interview from New York City, USA, 1 February 2012

Buthelezi, Cleo. Johannesburg, 1 July 2010

Brickhill, Jason. Legal Resources Centre, Sandton, 21 May 2010

Chikoro, Takudzwanashe. Johannesburg, 25 May and 9 June 2011, and 7 June 2012

Chiwetu, Monica. Johannesburg, 24 September 2011

Foley, Penny. Parkmore, Johannesburg, 28 February 2012

Gundu, Joyce. Johannesburg, 28 June 2011

Kandowe, William. Johannesburg 14 and 23 June 2011

McAllister, Roy. Bryanston, Johannesburg, 27 September 2012

Ngwane, Collet, Centre for the Study of Violence and Reconciliation, Braamfontein, Johannesburg, 13 June 2011

References:

AIDS-Free World. *Electing to Rape: Sexual Terror in Mugabe's Zimbabwe*, December 2009

Alexander, Kim. Notes given to the author, October 2010

Gibson, Erika. "Mbeki Sends Generals to Zim", *News24*, 12 May 2008. Accessed online on 2 June 2012 at:http://www.news24.com/SouthAfrica/Politics/Mbeki-sends-generals-to-Zim-20080512

Karimakwenda, Tererai. "Mbeki's Generals Investigating Violence", SWRadio Africa, 13 May 2008. Accessed online on 3 June 2012 at: http://allafrica.com/stories/200805130957.html

Human Rights Watch. "Bullets for Each of You: State Sponsored Violence Since Zimbawe's March 29 Elections", June 2008. Accessed online on 3 June 2012 at:http://www.hrw.org/sites/default/files/reports/zimbabwe0608.pdf

Human Rights Watch. "They Beat Me Like a Dog: Political Persecution at Opposition Activists and Supporters in Zimbabwe", 13 August 2008. Accessed online on 3 June 2012 at: http://hrw.org/reports/2008/08/11/they-beat-me-dog-0

Independent Online. "We are Very Vulnerable Here", 24 November 2008. Accessed online on 21 May 2012 at: http://www.iol.co.za/index.

php?set_id=1&click_id=68&art_id=nw20081124090122707C212499&singlepage=1

Lapper, Richard. "South Africans' Anger Grows Over Zimbabwe", *Financial Times*, 5 January 2009. Accessed online on 21 May 2012 at: http://www.ft.com/cmc/s/0/3edb49a8-db57-11dd-be53-000077b07658.html

McAuliffe, Louise. "SADC – 'Save Zimbabwe Now' is Watching You", *The Sowetan*, 28 January 2009. Accessed online on 21 May 2012 at: http://www.sowetan.co.za/News/Article.asp?id=926608

Moeng, Katlego. "Leaders Fast in Bid to End Zim Crisis", *The Sowetan*, 22 January 2009. Accessed online on 21 May 2012 at: http://www.sowetan.co.za/News/Article.aspx?id=923017

South African Press Association. "Mbeki Considering Zim Action", *News24*, 14 May 2008. Accessed online on 2 June 2012 at: http://www.news24.com/SouthAfrica/Politics/Mbeki-considering-Zim-action-20080514

South African Press Association. "Release R650,000 Report, Zuma Told", *News24*, 19 June 2009. Accessed online on 2 June 2012 at: http://www.news24.com/Africa/News/Release-R650-000-report-Zuma-told-20090619

Zimbawe Human Rights NGO Forum and the Research and Advocacy Unit. "Damn Lies? Gross Human Rights Violation During April 2008", 9 August 2008

Note:

With regard to the report from Mbeki's generals, a group of NGOs – the South African History Archive (SAHA), The SA Litigation Centre, and the Southern African Centre for Survivors of Torture – took steps in June 2009 to force the release of the report in terms of the Promotion of Access to Information Act. President Zuma's office denied that a written report ever existed. Both Frank Chikane and Trevor Fowler in the President's office submitted signed affidavits saying that there was no written report and no supporting documentation on the generals' trip. Parliament had on record that R650 000 was spent on the trip so the NGOs said that it was unlikely that the generals were not asked to document their trip.

PART TWO

16. "A Hostile, Complex Situation"

Interviews:

Alexander, Kim. Roodepoort, 23 November 2011

Bond, Rose. Johannesburg, 22 June 2010

Brickhill, Jason. Johannesburg, 15 November 2011

Chivima, Freedom. Johannesbug, 31 July 2010

Geere, Sandy. Telephone interview, 22 May 2012. A phone call to Advocate Stephan du Toit's new offices in Sandton on 22 May 2012 confirmed that he had moved out of Pitje Chambers. His PA, Sandy Geere, said that he moved because "his clients weren't too keen to go into town" and that the travelling was easier because many other advocates were based in Sandton.

Gotz, Graeme. Johannesburg, 10 May 2010

Harrison, Philip. Braamfontein, Johannesburg, 24 May and 2 August 2010

Mahlangu, Dorothy Qedani. Johannesburg, 14 September 2010

Mathang, Ruby. Johannesburg, 26 August 2011

Mthethwa, Nathi. Johannesburg, 5 August 2011

Patel, Yusuf. Killarney, Johannesburg, 29 June 2011

References:

AFP TV. "Zimbabweans Flood to SA Church for Refuge", 25 March 2009. Accessed online in March 2012 at: www.youtube.com/watch?v=lxAMKQD_1zM

Attendance list and minutes. "Central Methodist Church Humanitarian Intervention Project", City of Johannesburg, Parktonian Hotel, 13 February 2009

Bega, Sheree. "We Condemn What Verryn is Doing – Mahlangu", *Saturday Star*, 14 March 2009 Accessed online in June 2010 and on 16 November 2011 at: http://www.iol.co.za/index.php?set_id=1&click_id=13&art_id=vn20090314065325628C773137

Bezuidenhout, Andre. "Pitje Advocates Transformation Initiative", *Advocate*, August 2007

Bond, Rose. Letter to Bishop Paul Verryn on Pitje Chambers letterhead, dated 15 August 2008

Bond, Rose. Founding affidavit, South Gauteng High Court, Johannesburg, 4 March 2009

Department of Home Affairs. "Home Affairs Still Processing Applications for Asylum in Musina", media statement, 10 March 2009. Accessed online on 14 July 2010 and 13 November 2011 at: http://www.home-affairs.gov.za/media_releases.asp?id=516

Independent Online. "Central JHB 'a haven for refugees'", 7 March 2009. Accessed online in June 2010 and on 13 November 2011 at: http://www.iol.co.za/index.php?set_id=1&click_id=13&art_id=nw20090307132615406C346074

Independent Online. "MDC 'Shell-shocked' at Mahlangu's Comments", 14 March 2009. Accessed online in June 2010 and on 16 November 2011 at: http://www.iol.co.za/index.php?set_id=1&click_id=13&art_id=nw20090314140020498C929062

Mabusa, Ernest. "Squalid Conditions Unpleasant for Lawyers at Pitje Chambers", *Business Day*, 12 March 2009. Accessed online on 14 July 2010 and 16 November 2011 at: http://www.lrc.org.za/lrc-in-the-news/871-2009-03-12-squalid-conditions-unpleasant-for-lawyers-at-Pitje-chambers

Mabusa, Ernest. "Refugees in the CBD get Indefinite Reprieve from Court", *Weekender Business,* 21 March 2009. Accessed online on 14 July 2010 and 16 November 2011 at: http://lrc.org.za/lrc-in-the-news/893-2009-03-21-refugees-in-the-cbd-get-indefinite-reprieve-from-court

Mail & Guardian. "Zim Refugees Wait for Asylum on Jo'burg Streets", 7 March 2009. Accessed online on 14 July 2010 at: http://www.mg.co.za/article/2009-03-07-zim-refugees-wait-for-asylum-on-joburg-streets

Mail & Guardian. "Special Deal on Cards for Zim Refugees in SA", 10 March 2009. Accessed online in June 2010 and on 13 November 2011 at:http://www.mg.co.za/article/2009-03-10-special-deal-on-cards-for-zim-refugees-in-sa

Mail & Guardian Online. "Jo'burg Church No Place for Zim Refugees", 13 March 2009. Accessed online in June 2010 and on 16 November 2011 at: http://www.mg.co.za/article/2009-03-13-joburg-church-no-place-for-zim-refugees

Mail & Guardian Online. "Relocation Imminent for Zim Refugees", 25 March 2009. Accessed online in June 2010 and on 16 November 2011 at:

http://www.mg.co.za/article/2009-03-25-relocation-imminent-for-zim-refugees

Mail & Guardian Online. "Zimbabwe Refugees Prepare to Move From Church", 27 March 2009. Accessed online in June 2010 and on 16 November 2011 at: http://www.mg.co.za/article/2009-03-27-zimbabwe-refugees-prepare-to-move-from-church

Mail Foreign Service. "Mugabe Finally Forced to Share Power as Zimbabwe Opposition Leader is Sworn in as Prime Minister", *Daily Mail,* 13 February 2009. Accessed online at: http://www.dailymail.co.uk/news/worldnews/article-1141557/Mugabe-FINALLY-forced-shar-power-Zimbabwe-opposition-leader-sworn-prime-minister.html

Maphumulo, Solly. "Church Refugees to be Housed, MEC Promises", *The Star*, 23 March 2009

Mthethwa, Nathi. "Methodist Church Humanitarian Crisis – Action Plan". Internal email correspondence to Ruby Mathang, Philip Harrison and Refik Bismilla, 26 January 2009

National Church Leaders' Consultation. Press statement, Stellenbosch, 20 January 2009

Ndlangisa, Sabelo. "Methodist Church Accused",*City Press* 8 March 2009. Accessed online on 14 July 2010 and 16 November 2011 at: http://lrc.org.za/lrc-in-the-news/862-2009-08-08-methodist-church-accused-city-press

Sindane, Lucky. "Mbeki Opens Transformation Law Chambers", City of Johannesburg website, 8 May 2007. Accessed online on 14 July 2010 and 12 November 2011 at: http://www.joburgnews.co.za/2007/may/may8_pitjechambers.stm

South African Press Association (SAPA). "Chaos as Zim Refugees Queue", *News24*, 23 March 2009. Accessed online on 9 December 2009 at: http://www.news24.com/printArticle.aspx?iframe&aid=acdee792

South African Press Association (SAPA). "Many Refugees Opt not to Move", *News 24*, 26 March 2009. Accessed online on 9 December 2009 at: http://www.news24.com/printArticle.aspx?iframe&aid=77d2a681

Verryn, Paul. Preliminary Affidavit, South Gauteng High Court, Johannesburg, Case No: 09/9411, 17 March 2009

Visser, Emily. "City Plans to Deal with Refugees". City of Johannesburg website, 10 March 2009. Accessed online on 17 June 2010 at: http://www.joburg.org.za/content/view/3591/254/

Note:

Jason Brickhill came from an activist Zimbabwean family. His father, Jeremy Brickhill, had served as an officer in the military wing of Joshua Nkomo's ZAPU in the 1960s and '70s, and was almost killed in 1987 for being an ANC sympathiser when a bomb went off in a vehicle next to his car. The bomb had been planted by agents of the South African apartheid regime.

Meetings at Central Methodist – 2011

I attended the UNHCR/LRC meeting in the chapel at Central Methodist on 24 February 2011.

The articles that I found online about Booker Maseti include:

"Criteria for Those in Need Expanded", City of Johannesburg website, 2 February 2009. Accessed online on 25 November 2012 at: http://www.joburg.org.za/index.php?option=com_content&task=view&id=3434<emid=241

Maseti, Booker. "Hub Johannesburg Dazzles Mrs Mbeki", 18 November 2011. Accessed online on 25 November 2012 at: http://www.the-hub.net/community/hub-Johannesburg-dazzles-mrs-mbeki

Maseti, Booker. "Bikers bonded by burning rubber of freedom", Independent Online, 3 February 2001. Accessed online on 25 November 2012 at: http://www.iol.co.za/news/south-africa/bikers-bonded-by-burning-rubber-of-freedom-1.60118

The day I met with Esther Thomas was 17 March 2011.

17. Death Threat Comes for the Bishop

Interviews:

Mapiravana, Ambrose. Johannesburg, 6 September 2012

Steffny, Ann, independent urban consultant. Parktown, Johannesburg, 9 May 2011

Thomas, Russell, and Maluleke, Norman,Central Johannesburg Partnership. Johannesburg, 28 June 2011

Zack, Tanya, independent urban consultant. Killarney, Johannesburg, 21 June 2010

References:

Jooste, Hans, Central Johannesburg Partnership. Email correspondence headed "Meeting Held with Landlord of Schreiner Chambers – 28 April 2009 at office (Methodist Church refugees, High Court Precinct, Pritchard Street)", 29 April 2009

Maluleke, Norman, Central Johannesburg Partnership." Email correspondence headed "Methodist Church", 6 April 2009

Maughan, Karyn. "R200m to fix NPA Blunder", *The Star*, 8 June 2009 (I was given a hard copy)

McGregor, Russell, Gauteng Department of Local Governmen. "Proposal for Temporary Transitional Shelter and Integration Support for Vulnerable New Arrivals to the City", draft, 13 May 2009

Médecins Sans Frontières. "No Refuge, Access Denied: Medical and Humanitarian Needs of Zimbabweans in South Africa", June 2009. Accessed online at: www.msf.org.za

Moeng, Katlego. "Crime Scare at Refugees Haven", *The Sowetan*, 21 August 2009. Accessed online in June 2010 at: http://www.soweto.co.za/News/Article.aspx?id=1053088

Mthembu, Zandile, Central Johannesburg Partnership. Email correspondence headed "Meeting Held with Landlord of Schreiner Chambers – 28 April 2009 at office (Methodist Church refugees, High Court Precinct, Pritchard Street)", 28 April 2009

News24. "'Hitman' Threatens Bishop", 8 April 2009. (I was given a hard copy.) Accessed online on 9 December 2009 at: http://www.news24.com/printArticle.aspx?iframe&aid=02318bfc

News24. "Two Held for Bishop Death Threats", 9 April 2009. (I was given a hard copy.) Accessed online on 9 December 2009 at: http://www.news24.com/printArticle.aspx?iframe&aid=9ceb7153

Pretoria News. "Bishop Blackmailed by Alleged Hitmen", 9 April 2009. Accessed online in June 2010 at:http://www.iol.co.za/index.php?set_id=1&click_id=13&art_id=vn20090409132755490C571446

Seale, Legogang. "First Batch of Immigrants to be moved from Church", *The Star*, 17 April 2009. Accessed online on Legal Resources Centre website on 14 July 2010 at: http://lrc.org.za/lrc-in-the-news/931-2009-04-17-first-batch-of-immigrants-to-be-moved-from-church

Visser, Emily, "Way Forward Found for Migrants," Official website of the City of Johannesburg, 10 June 2009. Accessed online on 17 May 2010 at: http://www.joburg.org.za/content/view/3923/245/

Notes:
In relation to the National Prosecuting Agency (NPA) buying Innes Chambers in 2004, there were ongoing delays in terms of the proposed move of prosecutors into the building. Consultants were appointed by the Department of Public Works to assist with drafting a tender for refurbishment of the building. However, disputes over the lease agreements of some of the tenants caused delays. As the refurbishment was delayed, so the terms of the appointed consultants expired. The reappointment of the consultants was approved at the end of 2007 but further technical problems arose with the quantity surveyors. It seems that there were also political tensions between the NPA and the Department of Justice about who had been responsible for the purchase of the building.

Additional quotes from MSF from "No Refuge, Access Denied: Medical and Humanitarian Needs of Zimbabweans in South Africa", June 2009:

One MSF doctor in Johannesburg said, "I had a patient who was pregnant, and we sent her to the hospital. When she got there, the water had already broken. They took her to the nurse. When they looked at the patient and where she had come from – she produced her papers – they said, 'A foreigner?' and they just walked away. They left her on the gurney."

Bianca Tolboom, nurse and project co-ordinator of the MSF clinic at Central Methodist, said, "A Zimbabwean mother brought her six-year-old child to our clinic. The child had been raped. She was examined by our medical doctor and prophylactic treatment was given. Our counsellor did an initial counselling session with the mother and referred them to Child Welfare. From there they were referred to the hospital for further medical follow-up. The child was turned away from the hospital because she and the mother did not have legal documentation. It is unacceptable and inhuman to refuse treatment for a six-year-old child who needs essential medical care after she has been raped. Not having legal documents cannot be a reason to deny access to health care."

18. Arrested for Loitering

All of the documents relating to the "loitering case" of Central Methodist Church (and Lawyers for Human Rights) versus the City of Johannesburg (and the Johannesburg Metropolitan Police Department, the South African Police Service etc) can be found on the website of the human rights organisation, Section 27 at http://www.section27.org.za/2009/10/28/central-methodist-church-vs-city-of-johannesburg-loitering-case/ Accessed in July 2010 and 26 November 2011. These documents, with reference numbers for the website, include:

Direko, Redi. "What Constitutes Loitering and is it Illegal?" *Radio 702,* 23 July 2009, reference PV33

D.S. (initials used only). Affidavit, 2 October 2009, reference PV4

Eliseev, Alex. "Joburg Cops Vow to Keep Vagrants Away", and "Man Detained While Rushing Pregnant Woman to Hospital", *The Star*, 6 July 2009, reference PV27

Flanagan, Louise. "No Solution in Sight for Destitute Zimbabweans as Arrests Persist", *The Star*, 6 July 2009, reference PV9

Minnaar, Wayne, Johannesburg Metro Police Department spokesperson. Point Blanc radio programme led by David Webber, 7 July 2009, reference PV30

Moeng, Katlego. "Homes for 2000 Zimbabweans", *The Sowetan*, 6 July 2009, reference PV10

Naidoo, Michael. Affidavit, 3 September 2009, reference PV21

Tolboom, Bianca. Affidavit, 29 September 2009, reference PV13

Van Garderen, Jacob. Second Applicant's Affidavit, 21 October 2009, reference PV2 Note: I am particularly grateful to Van Gerderen for his points about the disconnect between the July 2009 police raid and the policies of the national department of Home Affairs and cabinet.

Verryn, Paul. Founding Affidavit, 28 October 2009. Available on the above website.

Wlodarski-Welz, Agnieszk. Confirmatory Affidavit, 28 October 2009, reference PV26

Interview:

Chikoro, Takudzwanashe. Waverley Gardens, Johannesburg, 7 June 2012

References:

Eliseev, Alex. "Joburg Cops Vow to Keep Vagrants Away", *The Star*, 6 July 2009. Accessed online in July 2010 and on 27 November 2011 at: http://www.iol.co.za/index.php?set_id=1&click_id=13&art_id=vn20090706051225228C772620

Flanagan, Louise. "Refugees 'beaten, shocked' by metro cops", *The Star*, 13 July 2009. Accessed online in July 2010 and on 27 November 2011 at: http://www.iol.co.za/index.php?set_id=1&click_id=13&art_id=vn 20090713061331656C319061&singlepage=1

Independent Online. "SA Slams Arrest of Homeless Zim,", 4 July 2009. Accessed online in June 2010 and on 27 November 2011 at: http://www.iol.co.za/index.php?set_id=1&click_id=13&art_id=nw20090704185320106C509851

Lawyers for Human Rights. "Legal Challenge to Johannesburg 'Loitering' ByLaws", 30 October 2009. Accessed online on 6 August 2010 and 27 November 2011 at: http://www.lhr.org.za/news/2009/legal-challenge-johannesburgs-loitering-bylaws

Moeng, Katlego. "Sigh of Relief as JMPD Cleans up Jozi", *The Sowetan*, 10 July 2009. Accessed online on 28 November 2010 and 27 November 2011 at: http://www.sowetanlive.co.za/sowetan/archive/2009/07/10/sign-of-relief-as-jmpd-cleans-up-jozi

Moeng, Katlego. "Church Now Haven for Thugs", *The Sowetan*, 16 July 2009

South African Press Association. "Release of Refugees Welcomed", *News24*, 7 July 2009. Accessed online (and printed hard copy) on 9 July 2009 at: http://www.news24.com/Content/SouthAfrica/News/1059/6f1186e

Thakali, Thabiso. "Out in the cold", *Independent Online*, 4 July 2009. Accessed online in June 2010 at: http://www.iol.co.za/index.php

Tolboom, Bianca. Email correspondence to Jason Brickhill of LRC, Mark Heywood of ALP, Jacob Van Garderen of LHR and Mary Metcalfe, 5 July 2009

References relating to Xoliswa Falati's death:

Smith, Janet. "Falati's 'Profound Dignity' Moved Bishop", *The Star*, 19 July 2009. Accessed online on 28 March 2011 at: http://www.iol.co.za/news/politics/falati-s-profound-dignity-moved-bishop-1.450224

South African Press Association. "Winnie's Co-Accused Dies", 9 July 2009. Accessed online on 20 February 2012 at:http://www.news24.com/Africa/News/Winnies-co-accused-dies-20090709

19. Sexual Favours for a Toothbrush

Interviews:

Abrahams, Ivan. Johannesburg, 15 November 2010

Foley, Penny. Parkmore, Johannesburg, 28 February 2012

Kistner, Johanna and Simpson, Moira, Johannesburg Child Advocacy Forum. Parktown, Johannesburg, 10 June 2010

Olivier, Ross. Telephone interview from Pietermaritzburg, 27 January 2012

Schnehage, Micel, Melrose Arch, Johannesburg, 12 July 2011

Summers, Howard, Melville, Johannesburg, 24 May 2011

References:

Gifford, Gil and Maphumulo, Solly. "Verryn Rejected Offer of Shelter for Kids, Aid Groups Say", *The Star*, 17 September 2009. Accessed online in June 2010 and on 1 December 2011 at: http://www.iol.co.za/index.php?set_id=1&click_id=13&art_id=vn20090917113413710C936207

Maphumulo, Solly. "People get Sexual Favours for a Toothbrush", *Independent Online*, 14 September 2009. Accessed online in June 2010 and on 1 December 2011 at: http://www.iol.co.za/index.php?set_id=1&click_id=13&art_id=iol1252935392225S216

McCarthy, Kerrigan (RHRU), Crabtree, Ellen (RHRU), Hjalmarson, Sara (MSF), and Goemare, Eric (MSF). "Central Methodist Church TB Screening Initiative", Reproductive Health and HIV Research Unit (RHRU) of the University of the Witwatersrand, and Médecins Sans Frontières (MSF), Final Report for Circulation, May 2010

Methodist Church of Southern Africa. Communiqué: Events Related to Central Methodist Church (CMM) in Johannesburg, Pietermaritzburg, 18 September 2009

Schnehage, Micel. "Central Methodist Church Rocked by Sexual Abuse Claims", Eyewitness News' Micel Schnehage Speaks to a Zimbabwean Girl who has Allegedly been Sexually Abused at the CMC", audio clip, 14 September 2009. Accessed online on 17 March 2012 at: http://www.eyewitnessnews.co.za/Multimedia.aspx

Smith, David. "Johannesburg's Methodist Homeless Mission", *Guardian*, 2 September 2009. Also *Mail and Guardian Online.* Accessed online on 1 December 2011 at: http://www.mg.co.za/article/2009-09-02-johannesburgs-methodist-homeless-mission

Smith, David. "South African Church Faces Child Sex Abuse Claims",

Guardian, 14 September 2009. Accessed online on 1 December 2011 at: http://www.guardian.co.uk/world/2009/sep/14/south-africa-church-sex-claims

Summers, HC. "Whole School Evaluation of the Albert Street School", PhD thesis, Kumbaya Education Consultants cc, November 2009

Meetings at Central Methodist – 2011

Interviews:

Abrahams, Ivan Norwood, Johannesburg, 5 December 2011
Bansi, Tony. Johannesburg, 14 November 2011
De Rijke, Tina. Telephone conversation, 29 November 2012
Elizabeth. Informal conversations, Johannesburg, 2011
Foley, Penny. Parkwood, Johannesburg, 11 October 2011
Khanyile, Justice. Informal conversation, 26 October 2012

20. "The Horror That We Saw"

Interviews:

Alexander, Kim. Roodepoort, 23 November 2011
Bloom, Jack. Telephone interview, 30 May 2012
Bopape, Molebatsi. Email correspondence, 30 May 2012
Brickhill, Jason, Sandton, 21 May 2010
Mapiravana, Ambrose, Johannesburg, 6 September 2012

References:

Central Methodist Mission. "Submission to the Gauteng Provincial Legislature Portfolio Committee on Health and Social Development Responding to the Visit Conducted on 30 October 2009 and the Subsequent Meeting Called by the Portfolio Committee on 6 November 2009 and 13 November 2009", 20 November 2009

Mabuza, Kingdom. "Bishop Defends Living Standards in his Church", *The Sowetan*, 23 November 2009. Accessed online in June 2010 at: http://www.sowetan.co.za/News/Article.aspx?id=1090936

Mail & Guardian Online. "Central Methodist Church Could Face Closure", 30 October 2009. Accessed online on 29 January 2010 and 28

November 2011 at: http://www.mg.c0.za/article/2009-10-30-central-methodist-church-could-face-closure

Makue, Eddie, and Maluleke, Prof Tinyiko. SACC media statement on the situation at Central Methodist Church, 2 November 2009. Accessed online on 28 November 2011. Statement is not currently available on the SACC website, but it can be viewed at: http://rwnel.blogspot.com/2009/11/sacc-media-statement-on-situation-at.html

Masondo, Amos. "Joburg Launches the Johannesburg Migration Advisory Committee", 6 October 2009. Accessed online on 3 December 2011 at: http://www.joburg.org.za/index.php?option=com_content&view=article&id=4388&catid=183&It

Methodist Church of Southern Africa. Press statement: Central Methodist Church, Johannesburg, 3 November 2009

South African Press Association. "DA: Probe Verryn Cult Claims", *Independent Online*, 13 November 2009. Accessed online in June 2010 and on 28 November 2011 at: http://www.iol.co.za/index.php?set_id=1click_id=13&art_id=nw20091113171533440C544006&singlepage=1

Thakali, Thabiso. "Central Methodist Church and its 'Monster' Come Under Attack", *The Saturday Star*, 31 October 2009

Thakali, Thabiso. "Shocking Claims as Church Row Takes New Turn", *The Star*, 7 November 2009. Accessed online in June 2010 and on 28 November 2011 at: http://www.iol.co.za/index.php?set_id=1&click_id=13&art_id=vn20091107072412913C360135

The Citizen. "End for Refugee Church?", 31 October 2009

The Sowetan. "Politicians Want to Close Central Methodist Church", 30 October 2009. Accessed online in June 2010 and on 28 November 2011 at: http://www.sowetan.co.za/news/article.aspx?id=1083339

Notes:

When I asked Jack Bloom (30 May 2012) if there had ever been a final report from the Portfolio Committee after the public hearings, he said, "No, Central Methodist fell off the priority list. It was basically insoluble and other priorities developed."

Over many months, I repeatedly asked Molebatsi Bopape via e-mails, phone calls and texting if I could see the Portfolio Committee's final report with recommendations that was developed after the public hearings. She finally wrote back saying, "This matter was handed over to the

[Gauteng] Department of Social Development for implementation of recommendations from the committee." (30 May 2012)

21. The Debate over the Children

Interviews:

Abrahams, Ivan. Bedfordview, Johannesburg, 15 November 2010

Brickhill, Jason. Sandton, 21 May 2010

Chikoro, Takudzwanashe. Waverley Gardens, Johannesburg, 7 June 2012

Cock, Lorraine, Gauteng Department of Social Development. Johannesburg, 1 March 2012

Kistner, Johanna. Email correspondence, 26 May 2010 and telephone conversation, 27 May 2010

Kistner, Johanna and Simpson, Moira, Johannesburg Child Advocacy Forum. Parktown, Johannesburg, 10 June 2010

Ramjathan-Keogh, Kaajal, Lawyers for Human Rights. Braamfontein, Johannesburg, 14 June 2010

Summers, Howard. Melville, Johannesburg, 24 May 2011

References:

Coggin, Theo. "Civil Society and the Media", in Craig, Anita and Abrahams, Nazli (eds), *Inyathelo Conversation: Our World, Our Responsibility, Re-energizing Civil Society*, 2010, proceedings from Inyathelo donor conference in 2009

Editorial. "Solve Harmful Church Crisis", *The Star*, 10 December 2009. Accessed online in June 2010 at: http://www.thestar.co.za/index.php?fArticleld=5281116

Independent Online. "Groups Back Refugees' Church", 8 December 2009. Accessed online in June 2010 and on 3 December 2011 at: http://www.iol.co.za/index.php?set_id=1&click_id=13&art_id=nw20091208151300244C162712

Lawyers for Human Rights, Legal Resources Centre and AIDS Law Project. Statement on Resolving the Refugee Crisis at the Central Methodist Church. Accessed online on 3 December 2011 at: http://www.section27.org.za/2009/12/08/statement-on-resolving-the-refugee-crisis-at-the-central-methodist-church-johannesburg/

McKaiser, Eusebius. "Wicked Irony in Politicians Painting Themselves

Saviours", *Business Day*, 8 December 2009. Accessed online on 24 July 2010 and 3 December 2011 at:
http://allafrica.com/stories/printable/200912080304.html

Moeng, Katlego. "Central Methodist Kids Flee from Officials Who Plan to Relocate Them", *The Sowetan,* 10 December 2009. Accessed online in June 2010 at: http://www.sowetan.co.za/News/Article.aspx?id=1095924

Noseweek. "Abuse or Mercy", Issue #120, October 2009. Accessed online on 11 November 2009 and 3 December 2011 at: http://www.noseweek.co.za/article/2115/abuse-or-mercy?

Reuter, Hermann. "Don't Blame Verryn", *Mail & Guardian,* 11 December 2009

Thakali, Thabiso. "Refugees Living in Awful Conditions in Central Joburg: Verryn Visits Migrants in Squalid Conditions in Old Buildings", *The Saturday Star*, 28 November 2009. Accessed online on 9 March 2011 at: http://www.highbeam.com/doc/1G1-213074941.html?key=01-42160D517E1A130D0

Tromp, Beauregard. "Street is Only Backyard They Know", *The Star*, 16 September 2009

Tromp, Beauregard. "Boys at Church 'paid to act as wives'", *The Star*, 9 December 2009

Tromp, Beauregard. "Joburg's Sanctuary of Shame", *The Star*, 9 December 2009. Accessed online in June 2010 and on 3 December 2011 at: http://www.iol.co.za/index.php?set_id=1&click_id=31&art_id=vn20091209065715214C777261&singlepage=1

22. Suspended

Interviews:

De Rijke, Tina. Benmore, Johannesburg, 10 September 2012

Landau, Wendy. Braamfontein, Johannesburg, 19 July 2010

Ncatsha, Vuyani, Ntsepe, Buntu and Tokwana, Johannes, Johannesburg, 27 October 2012

References:

Abrahams, Ivan. Foreword, *Laws and Disciplines*, The Methodist Church of Southern Africa, eleventh edition, Johannesburg, March 2007

Aids Law Project. Press release: "Aids Law Project Calls for Accuracy in Reporting on Bishop Verryn", 22 January 2010. Accessed online on 3 March 2010 at: http://alp.org.za

Legal Resources Centre. Statement on Suspension of Paul Verryn, 22 January 2010

Methodist Church of Southern Africa. Statement for immediate release, "Former Bishop Paul Verryn Suspended", 22 January 2010

Parker, Faranaaz. "Paul Verryn: What Went Wrong?" *Mail & Guardian*, 29 January 2010. Accessed online on 1 December 2011 at: http://www.mg.co.za/article/2010-01-29-paul-verryn-what-went-wrong

Parker, Faranaaz, Pillay, Verashni and Tolsi, Niren. "Old Whispers, Old Wounds", *Mail & Guardian*, 29 January 2010. Accessed online on 10 December 2011 at: http://www.mg.co.za/article/2010-01-29-paul-verryn-what-went-wrong

Schnehage, Micel. "New Leadership Planned for Paul Verryn's Church", *Eyewitness News*, 22 January 2010. Accessed online on 10 December 2011 at: http://www.eyewitnessnews.co.za/Story.aspx?Id=30818

South African Press Association. "Bishop Verryn Suspended", *Independent Online*, 21 January 2010. Accessed online in June 2010 and on 10 December 2011 at: http://www.iol.co.za/index.php?set_id=1&click_id=13&art_id=nw20100121175935610C908785&singlepage=1

South African Press Association. "Friends Rally for Verryn", *Independent Online*, 25 January 2010. Accessed online in June 2010 and on 10 December 2011 at: http://www.iol.co.za/index.php?set_id=1&click_id=13&art_id=nw20100124222151211C443432

Thakali, Thabiso. "Verryn to Fight On", *Saturday Star*, 23 January 2010. Accessed online in June 2010 and on 10 December 2011 at: http://www.iol.co.za/index.php?set_id=1&click_id=13&art_id=vn20100123073218228C985673&singlepage=1

Thakali, Thabiso. "Reprieve Could See Verryn Back in the Pulpit", *Saturday Star*, 30 January 2010. Accessed online in June 2010 and on 10 December 2011 at: http://www.iol.co.za/index.php?set_id=1&click_id=13&art_id=vn20100130085255986C285361

The Sowetan. "Supporters Rally Around Embattled Cleric", 25 January 2010. Accessed online in June 2010 at: http://www.sowetan.co.za/News/Article.aspx?id=1107754

Timse, Tabelo. "Uncertain Future for Migrants at Methodist Church", *Mail & Guardian*, 1 February 2010. Accessed online on 19 March 2012 at: http://www.mg.co.za/article/2010-02-01-uncertain-future-for-migrants-at-methodist-church

Tromp, Beauregard. "A Dark Cloud Over Verryn", *The Star*, 22 January 2010. Accessed online in June 2010 and on 10 December 2011 at: http://www.thestar.co.za/indesx.php?fArticleld=5322199

Tromp, Beauregard and SAPA. "Ghosts of the Past Come Back to Haunt Brave Bishop", *The Star*, 25 January 2010. Accessed online in June 2010 at: http://www.thestar.co.za/index.php?fArticleld=3607676

Verryn, Paul. Draft answering affidavit, written in preparation for a review application of the arbitration proceedings between Paul Verryn and the MCSA, undated, circa 2010

23. Ann Skelton to the Rescue

Interviews:

Skelton, Ann. Pretoria, 3 June 2010

References:

Skelton, Ann. Filing Notice: Curatrix Ad Litem's Report, 8 February 2010

Skelton, Ann. Addendum to the Report of the Curatrix Ad Litem, 1 March 2010

Meetings at Central Methodist – 2011

The day of Cleo Buthelezi's workshop and my running into the police road block was 18 August 2011.

24. "Is this Boat Going to Sink?"

Interviews:

Buthelezi, Cleo. Informal conversation with the author, Johannesburg, 19 November 2010

Chivima, Freedom. Johannesburg, 13 May 2010

Harrison, Philip. Braamfontein, Johannesburg, 2 August 2010

Mapiravana, Ambrose. Informal conversation with the author, Johannesburg, 1 September 2010

Mapiravana, Ambrose. Johannesburg, 16 September 2010
Nyamarebvu, Father Michael, Solidarity Peace Trust. Johannesburg, 6 June 2011
Olivier, Ross. Telephone interview from Pietermaritzburg, 27 January 2012

References:

Friends of Paul Verryn Facebook page
Legal Award Statement in the matter between Reverend Verryn and the Presiding Bishop and the District Discipline Registrar: Highveld and Swaziland District, Signed by Arbitrators Peter Le Mottee and Leon De Bruyn, 27 April 2010
Médecins Sans Frontières. "Survival Migrants in South Africa Slums", briefing paper, December 2010

25. The Tip of the Iceberg

Interviews:

Bethlehem, Lael. Parkview, Johannesburg, 4 June 2010
Courtenay, Morgan, Centre for Applied Legal Studies. Telephone conversation, 20 April 2011
De Costa, Walter. Telephone interview, 11 August 2010
De Klerk, Pieter, Legal Department, City of Johannesburg. Telephone interview, 30 May 2012
Harrison, Phillip. Braamfontein, Johannesburg, 24 May 2010 and 2 August 2010
Harrison, Phillip. Email communication, 14 November 2012
Mahlangu, Dorothy Qedani, Johannesburg, 14 September 2010
McGregor, Russell. Johannesburg, 8 July 2010
McGregor, Russell. Telephone interview, 24 May 2011
Médecins Sans Frontières. Presentation to Peace Action, Johannesburg 13 September 2010
Mogoro, Leslie. Johannesburg, 15 February 2012

References:

Médecins Sans Frontières. "The Lives of Survival Migrants and Refugees in South Africa", 12 May 2010. Accessed online on 13 May 2010 at: http://www.doctorswithoutborders.org/publications/article.

cfm?id=4465&cat=briefing-doc
Médecins Sans Frontières. "Nowhere Else to Go", March 2011. Accessed online in 2012 at: http://www.msf.org.za/system/files/publication/documents/MSF_NowhereElseToGo.pdf?download=1
Médecins Sans Frontières. "Urban Survivors: Humanitarian Challenges of a Rising Slum Population", November 2011. Accessed online in 2012 at: www.urbansurvivors.org
Sosibo, Kwanele. "Here it is Every Man for Himself", *Mail & Guardian*, 11–17 March 2011
Wilson, Stuart. "Planning for Inclusion in South Africa: The State's Duty to Prevent Homelessness and the Potential of 'Meaningful Engagement'", *Urban Forum*, Vol 22 (3), 2011

26. Conflict within the Methodist Church

Interviews:

Abrahams, Ivan. Bedfordview, Johannesburg, 15 November 2010 and Norwood, Johannesburg, 5 December 2011
Storey, Peter. Simonstown, Cape Town, 21 and 22 July 2011
Verryn, Paul, Rosebank, Johannesburg, 28 September 2011
Witbooi, Peter. Benmore, Sandton, 12 April 2011

Reference:

The Methodist Church of Southern Africa. *Yearbook and Directory 2011*.

Note:

I was interested to find out how the National Prosecuting Authority followed up on the cases presented to them. I tried for ten months in 2012 to contact Advocate Thoko Majokweni via email and telephone. Majokweni set up the NPA's directorate on violence against women and children. I wrote to her, letting her know that I had met with Presiding Bishop Ivan Abrahams and that I was aware that he had submitted documents to her regarding alleged sexual abuse of minors at Central Methodist and the Albert Street School. Originally, I asked for a meeting, but then I asked only to clarify whether there was still an active file about Central Methodist and the Albert Street School, or if the file had been closed. I spoke repeatedly to Lusanda

Ntwanambi in Advocate Majokweni's chambers, who told me that she would get back to me. After many months of emails and phone calls, she never did.

27. Life (and Death) Goes on Inside Central

Interviews:

Buthelezi, Cleo. Informal conversation with the author, Johannesburg, 19 January 2011

Buthelezi, Cleo. Johannesburg, 17 February 2011

Chikoro, Takudzwanashe. Johannesburg, 9 June 2011

Chivima, Freedom. Informal conversation with the author, Johannesburg, 19 January 2011

Chivima, Freedom. Johannesburg, 22 June 2011

Chiwetu, Monica. Johannesburg, 24 September 2011

Dotwana, Zandile. Johannesburg, 28 February 2012

Foley, Penny. Parkmore, Johannesburg, 14 February 2011

Foley, Penny. Text message, 28 February 2011

Foley, Penny. Telephone interview, 11 March 2011

Goemaere, Eric. Telephone interview from Cape Town, 11 June 2012

Kuntonda, Evans. Johannesburg, 21 October 2010

Manyere, Priscilla. Johannesburg, 21 June 2011 and Braamfontein, Johannesburg, 5 June 2012

Mapakata, Reymond. Text message, 28 February 2011

Verryn, Paul. Informal conversation with the author, Johannesburg, 19 January 2011

References:

Kuntonda, Evans. Comment to a blog, http://www.darkmatter101.org/site/2010/10/10/the-roads-not-taken-migrants-labor-and-antiracism-in-Italy-in-the-age-of-the-Bossi-Fini-Law. Accessed online on 2 March 2011

Mail & Guardian Online. "Refugee Church 'Unsustainable', Say Civil Society Groups", 8 December 2009. Accessed online on 9 March 2011 at: http://mg.co.za/printformat/single/2009-12-08-refugee-church-unsustainable-say-civil-society-groups

Médecins Sans Frontières. *Obituary for Evans Tendayi Kuntonda, 15 July 1980 to 4 March 2011*, 4 March 2011

Whittall, Jonathan. Internal MSF email, 16 April 2011
Whittall, Jonathan, MSF. Obituary for Evans Kuntonda written in April 2011, sent to me via email by Liz Thomson, General Director of MSF, 23 September 2011

Notes:

I attended the Friday night refugee meetings on 21 January and 4 February 2011 as well as the 10am Sunday service on 6 February 2011. I attended the 16 April 2011 meeting of the refurbishment committee.

The second part of the chapter was written from my experience with Evans Kuntonda. I visited him at the Brenthurst Clinic in Johannesburg on 1 March 2011 and attended a memorial service for him in the chapel at Central Methodist on the day he died, 4 March 2011. I also attended a Friday night refugee meeting on 11 March 2011.

Meetings at Central Methodist – 2011

Interview:

Mahlakahlaka, Adelaide. Fordsburg, Johannesburg, 15 November 2011

Reference:

Mapakata, Reymond. "My Fifth Time of Being Arrested", personal statement submitted to Peace Action, 7 October 2011

Notes:

I met with Cleo Buthelezi in her room on Monday, 13 November 2011.
Mercy's birthday celebration at the 10am Sunday service took place on Sunday, 11 November 2012.
I met with Elizabeth many times in 2011 and 2012.

28. Sjamboks at Marabastad

This chapter was based on the day that I spent at the Marabastad Home Affairs office in Marabastad, Pretoria on 29 August 2011. A modified version of this chapter was previously published as an article in *City Press* entitled "Sjambok Rule at Home Affairs", on 18 September 2011.

I also attended two meetings of the Zimbabwe Documentation Project (ZDP) hosted by the Department of Home Affairs, one in Pretoria on 4 July 2011 and another in Johannesburg on 26 September 2011. The following references cover developments with Home Affairs, the (ZDP) and the police.

References:

Department of Home Affairs. Briefing to the Media by the Head of the Zimbabwe Documentation Project, Jacob Mamabolo, 30 June 2011. Accessed online on 5 July 2011 at: http://www.dha.gov.za/Media%20 Releases%205.html

Machengere, Reason and Nyamarebvu, Father Mike. Email from SPT to Department of Home Affairs re Harassment of Zimbabweans in JHB CBD, Solidarity Peace Trust, 28 June 2011

Mulaudzi, Khathutshelo. "Concern at Move on Illegal Zimbabweans", *Business Day*, 2 August 2011. Accessed online on 14 February 2012 at: http://www.businessday.co.za/articles/content.aspx?id=149693

Parliamentary Monitoring Group. "Zimbabwean Documentation Project: Briefing by Department of Home Affairs", 19 September 2011. Accessed online on 14 February 2012 at: http://www.pmg.org.za/report/20110920-department-home-affairs-zimbabwean-documentation-project

Ramjathan-Keogh, Kaajal. "SA Should Take U.S. Lead and Fight Crime, not Chase Illegals", *Business Day*, 21 September 2011. Accessed online on 14 February 2012 at: http://www.businessday.co.za/articles/Content.aspx?id=153904

South African Press Association. "Deportation for Illegal Zimbabweans". Accessed online on 14 February 2012 at: http://www.lhr.org.za/news/2011/deportations-illegal-zimbabweans

Zimbabwe Exiles Forum. Press statement re conclusion of the ZDP, 27 September 2011. Accessed online in February 2012 at: www.zimexilesforum.org

29. The Axe and the Tree

Interviews:

Kanuwera, Thomas. Johannesburg, 26 May 2011. For more information on Thomas Kanuwera, view the film *Into the Shadows* by Pep Bonet and Line Hadsbjerg. View a short preview on http://www.emphas.is/web/guest/discoverprojects?projectID=754#2

References:

Katenza, Rumbi (director). *The Axe and the Tree: Zimbabwe's Legacy of Political Violence*, produced by Pigou, Piers, Jammy, David, Gavshon, Harriet, and Burres, Bruni. Supported by the International Center for Transitional Justice. For more information, go to www.ictj.org. You can also view a portion of the film at: http://multimedia.timeslive.co.za/videos/2011/05/zimbabwe-torture-documentary-the-axe-and-the-tree/

SADC. Communiqué: Summit of the Organ troika on Politics, Defence and Security Cooperation, Livingstone, Republic of Zambia, 31 March 2011. Accessed online on 13 February 2012 at: http://www.sadc.int/index/browse/page/858

SADC. Communiqué on Zimbabwe Following Sandton Summit, Sandton, Johannesburg, South Africa, 14 June 2011. Accessed online on 13 February 2011 at: http://www.3rdliberation.com/2011/06/14/sadc-communique-on-zimbabwe-following-sandton-summit

Verryn, Paul. Sermon at the Covenant Service, Albert Street Church, 24 February 2011. The story of the woman who, 40 years later, was still traumatised by the events of the Sharpeville massacre in 1960 was taken from this sermon and posted on Facebook by Penny Foley. Accessed online on 24 February 2011 at: http://www.facebook.com/notes/penny-foley/sermon-at-the-14h00-covenant-service-albert-street-church-30-january-2011/10150122110215209

Notes:

I viewed *The Axe and the Tree* on 26 May 2011 at Central Methodist.

30. Some Healing and Some Nuptials

I attended the healing service on Wednesday, 8 June 2011.

I attended the Friday night refugee meeting on 19 August 2011 where members of the 10am congregation attended to discuss the building.

I attended Leothere and Monica's wedding service at Central Methodist as well as their reception in Braamfontein on 28 August 2011. I had the benefit of watching the wedding reception proceedings again on a wedding DVD given to me by Leothere and Monica.

31. Friday Night Refugee Meetings

This chapter was based on events at the Friday night refugee meeting on 23 March 2012.

Interviews:

Alexander, Kim. Roodepoort, 23 November 2011

Dandala, Mvume. Midrand, 1 September 2011 and Johannesburg, 21 November 2011

Maseti, Booker. Johannesburg, 19 October 2012

References:

Information about deportations and the legal case taken up by Lawyers for Human Rights (LHR) and the Zimbabwean Exiles Forum was taken from the sources below.

IRIN, a service of the UN Office for Coordination of Humanitarian Assistance. "South Africa: Deportations of Zimbabwean migrants set to resume", 7 October 2011. Accessed online on 26 March 2012 at: http://www.irinnews.org/Report/93912/SOUTH-AFRICA-Deportations-of-Zimbawean-migrants-set-to-resume

Lawyers for Human Rights. "Migrants Face Unlawful Arrests and Hasty Deportations", press statement, 14 February 2012. Accessed online on 26 March 2012 at: http://www.lhr.org.za/news/2012/migrants-face-unlawful-arrests-and-hasty-deportation

Mabuza, Ernest. "Prosecutor 'Swaps Sides' in Harare Rights Case", *Business Day*, 27 March 2012. Accessed online on 28 March 2012 at: http://www.businessday.co.za/articles/Content.aspx?id=168264

Masondo, Sipho. "Talk of Zim Polls Premature – Coalition,",*TimesLive*, 1 February 2012. Accessed online on 2 February 2012 at: http://www.timeslive.co.za/africa/2012/02/01/talk-of-zim-polls-premature---coalition

Netsianda, Mashudu. "SA Deport 631 Zim Illiegal Immigrants", *Zoutnet*, 24 October 2011. Accessed online on 26 March 2012 at: http://www.zoutnet.co.za/details/24-10-2011/sa deport 631 zim illegal

immigrants/9706
Netsianda, Mashudu. "SA Deports Over 14,000 Zimbos", *Chronicle*, 17 March 2012. Accessed online on 26 March 2012 at: http://www.chronicle.co.zw/index.php?option=com_content&view=article&id=article&id=31277:sa-d
South African Press Association. "'Fit as a Fiddle' Mugabe will Stand in Poll", *The Star*, 22 February 2012
South African Foreign Policy Initiative. "SA Deports 15,000 Zimbaweans in 5 months", 6 March 2012. Accessed online on 26 March 2012 at: http://www.safpi.org/news/article/2012/sa-deports-15000-zimbabweans-5-months
Zimbabwe Exiles Forum. "Renditions from South Africa", press statement, 17 November 2011. Accessed online on 26 March 2012 at: http://www.zimexilesforum.org/index.php?opion=com_content&view=article&id=374:pr...

Index

D

E

T

U

V

W

X

Y

Z

www.sanctuary-book.co.za

www.twitter.com/ChristaKuljian

http://www.facebook.com/SanctuaryChristaKuljian

christa@sanctuary-book.co.za